REPRESENTING IMPERIAL RIVALRY IN THE EARLY MODERN MEDITERRANEAN

Representing Imperial Rivalry in the Early Modern Mediterranean explores representations of national, racial, and religious identities within a region dominated by the clash of empires. Bringing together studies of English, Spanish, Italian, and Ottoman literature and cultural artefacts, the volume moves from the broadest issues of representation in the Mediterranean to a case study – early modern England – where the "Mediterranean turn" has radically changed the field.

The essays in this wide-ranging literary and cultural study examine the rhetoric that surrounds imperial competition in this era, ranging from poems commemorating the battle of Lepanto to elaborately adorned maps of contested frontiers. They will be of interest to scholars in fields such as history, comparative literary studies, and religious studies.

BARBARA FUCHS is a professor in the Departments of English and Spanish and Portuguese and the director of the William Andrews Clark Memorial Library and Center for Seventeenth- and Eighteenth-Century Studies at the University of California, Los Angeles.

EMILY WEISSBOURD is a visiting assistant professor in the Department of English at Bryn Mawr College.

THE UCLA CLARK MEMORIAL LIBRARY SERIES

General Editor: Barbara Fuchs

REPRESENTING IMPERIAL RIVALRY IN THE EARLY MODERN MEDITERRANEAN

Edited by Barbara Fuchs and Emily Weissbourd

Published by the University of Toronto Press in association with the UCLA Center for Seventeenth- and Eighteenth-Century Studies and the William Andrews Clark Memorial Library

© The Regents of the University of California 2015

utorontopress.com

Reprinted in paperback 2020

ISBN 978-1-4426-4902-6 (cloth)
ISBN 978-1-4875-2920-8 (paper)

Library and Archives Canada Cataloguing in Publication

Title: Representing imperial rivalry in the early modern Mediterranean / edited by Barbara Fuchs and Emily Weissbourd.

Names: Fuchs, Barbara, 1970– editor. | Weissbourd, Emily, editor. | William Andrews Clark Memorial Library, publisher. | University of California, Los Angeles. Center for 17th- & 18th- Century Studies, publisher.

Series: UCLA Clark Memorial Library series.

Description: Series statement: The UCLA Clark Memorial Library series | Paperback reprint. Originally published 2015. | Includes bibliographical references and index.

Identifiers: Canadiana 20200356763 | ISBN 9781487529208 (softcover)

Subjects: LCSH: Mediterranean Region – In literature. | LCSH: Imperialism in literature. | LCSH: History in literature. | LCSH: Religion in literature. | LCSH: Mediterranean Region – History – 1517-1789.

Classification: LCC PN56.3.M4 R46 2020 | DDC 809/.93321822–dc23

This book has been published with the help of a grant from the UCLA Center for Seventeenth- and Eighteenth-Century Studies.

University of Toronto Press acknowledges the financial assistance to its publishing program of the Canada Council for the Arts and the Ontario Arts Council, an agency of the Government of Ontario.

  Canada Council for the Arts   Conseil des Arts du Canada

Contents

Illustrations vii

Introduction 3
BARBARA FUCHS AND EMILY WEISSBOURD

PART ONE: ENVISIONING EMPIRE IN THE OLD WORLD

1 Mediterranean Borderlands and the Global Early Modern 13
ANIA LOOMBA

2 Mapping Trans-Imperial Ottoman Space: Alterity and Attraction 33
PALMIRA BRUMMETT

3 Europe's Turkish Nemesis 58
LARRY SILVER

4 Imperial Succession and Mirrors of Tyranny in the Houses of Habsburg and Osman 80
CARINA L. JOHNSON

5 "The ruin and slaughter of ... fellow Christians": The French as Threat to Christendom in Spanish Assertions of Sovereignty in Italy, 1479–1516 101
ANDREW W. DEVEREUX

6 Memories of War at Home and Abroad: The Story of Juan Latino's *Austrias Carmen* 126
ELIZABETH R. WRIGHT

7 Imperial Anxiety, the Roman Mirror, and the Neapolitan Academy of the Duke of Medinaceli, 1696–1701   145
THOMAS DANDELET

PART TWO: IMAGINING THE MEDITERRANEAN IN EARLY MODERN ENGLAND

8 The Meta-Theatrical Mediterranean: Theatrical Contrivance and Miraculous Reunion in *The Travels of the Three English Brothers*, *The Four Prentices of London*, and *Pericles*   163
JANE HWANG DEGENHARDT

9 Copying "the Anti-Spaniard": Post-Armada Hispanophobia and English Renaissance Drama   191
ERIC GRIFFIN

10 Spain and the Rhetoric of Imperial Rivalry in Webster's *The Duchess of Malfi*   217
EMILY WEISSBOURD

11 Catholics and Cosmopolitans Writing the Nation: The Pope's Scholars and the 1579 Student Rebellion at the English Roman College   233
BRIAN C. LOCKEY

12 Viewing Spain through Darkened Eyes: Anti-Spanish Rhetoric and Charles Cornwallis's Mission to Spain, 1605–1609   255
WILLIAM S. GOLDMAN

Contributors   269

Index   271

Illustrations

2.1 Variants by Gerhard de Jode, Antwerp, ca 1578, of Matthias Zündt, *Hungariae Totius*, Nuremberg, 1567   42
2.2 Matteo Rossi, *Dimostratione de Confini delle principale Citta' dell' Austria et Ungaria (Vienna assediata dal Turco)*, Rome, 1683   44
2.3 Seyyid Lokman, *Hünername*, Istanbul, ca 1588. Submission of John Zapolya to Süleiman at Buda   45
2.4 Matrakçı Nasuh, *Tarih-i Feth- Şaklavan*. Attack on Nice in 1543   47
2.5 Nicolas Sanson / Hubert Jaillot, *Le Course du Danube Depuis sa Source Iusqu'a ses Embouchures*, cartouche, Paris, 1693   49
2.6 Map titled *Turquie en Europe*, by Pieter Van der Aa, Leiden [1729?]   50
2.7 *Turquie en Europe*, by Pieter Van der Aa, inset, cartouche   51
2.8 John Senex, *A Map of Greece with part of Anatolia*, cartouche, London, 1720   52
3.1 Willem Blaeu, *Danubius Fluvius*, from his Atlas, engraving (published Amsterdam, 1635)   59
6.1 Map of the Gulf of Lepanto by Giovanni Francesco Camocio   131
9.1 *The Coppie of the Anti-Spaniard* (1590)   194
9.2 *Emblemata: Welch das Leben*   196
9.3 *Non sufficit orbis*   200
9.4 The "lamentable fall of Queen Elenor"   206

REPRESENTING IMPERIAL RIVALRY
IN THE EARLY MODERN MEDITERRANEAN

Introduction

BARBARA FUCHS AND EMILY WEISSBOURD

The field of Mediterranean studies has grown tremendously in recent years, with rich investigations that have transformed the national disciplines and comparative studies alike. The early modern period, when the Habsburgs and the Ottoman empires vied for primacy, has long been a focus of Mediterranean studies: Fernand Braudel's classic study, one might recall, considers the Mediterranean *à l'époque de Philippe II*. Yet much of Braudel's own work, and that of some of his most celebrated followers, brackets the ideological complexities of the age and of the discourses in which Mediterranean rivalries were expressed. As Gabriel Piterberg, Teófilo Ruiz, and Geoffrey Symcox note in their *Braudel Revisited: The Mediterranean World 1600–1800*, an earlier volume in the UCLA Center / Clark series, despite his political title, Braudel largely eschewed politics and political culture (5). For the most part, *La Méditerranée* privileges instead a macro-historical, even geological, perspective, contributing to the development of the discipline of world history (10).

Representing Imperial Rivalry in the Early Modern Mediterranean focuses on a particular range of cultural, ideological, and political phenomena within the Mediterranean world. Without losing sight of the larger frameworks that Mediterranean studies and world history make available, our collection attends to the distinct rhetorics that voice imperial competition – poems commemorating the battle of Lepanto, elaborately adorned maps of contested frontiers. Even when those rhetorics rely on universalizing frameworks, such as the legacy of Rome, the crusading impulse, or the project of universal monarchy, they remain rooted in particular circumstances and traditions. Indeed, their imaginative reach is often most striking for how it contrasts with their insularity or specificity. Attending to the representational particularities of dense, multivalent texts such as Shakespeare's *The Tempest* need not narrow our perspective, but may in fact productively challenge the limitations of even such capacious models as "the Mediterranean," as Ania Loomba suggests in her chapter in this volume. Our goal, therefore, is not to choose between a global view and specific attention to cultural complexity, but rather to recognize the broad reach of highly particularized and historicized cultural phenomena.

The inspiration for our collection, as for the related year-long program held at UCLA's William Andrews Clark Memorial Library in 2011–12, lies in our conviction that the cultural history of empires must be studied relationally rather than in isolation or even comparatively. In *Mimesis and Empire*, Barbara Fuchs offered a model for this relational approach by examining the mimetic rivalries among Spain, England, and an expanding Islamicate. More recently, Laura Doyle has theorized *inter-imperiality* as the "political and historical set of conditions created by the violent histories of plural, intersecting empires and by interacting persons moving between empires."[1] Doyle challenges the self-sufficient history of empires by arguing for their imbrication and competition: only a plural history of the intersection among empires, she suggests, can provide a fuller picture. *Representing Imperial Rivalry* explores the rhetorical dimension of inter-imperiality by focusing on the overlap and entanglement of various actors in the early modern Mediterranean: Ottomans and Habsburgs, to be sure, but also France, Naples, the Holy Roman Empire, and England. Of course, this is far from a complete list of the entities vying for power in the period; a complete survey of the region's complex political geography is beyond the scope of this volume. Rather, we intend the chapters collected here to expand the archive of Mediterranean texts and problems, bringing out the engagements among some of the area's major actors.

Our goal is, first, to offer a model for studying the interconnection of empires and would-be empires, instead of simply considering them side-by-side. By focusing on where and when imperial imaginaries overlap, these chapters chart how they evolve dialectically or in close relation to one another. Second, the volume recovers the complex registers of imperial competition, emphasizing the multiplicity of positions, ideologies, and images that express imperial rivalries. How is imperial competition managed in different genres? How do literary and cultural productions render the alterity and the attraction of the cultures encountered? Such questions, we suggest, are crucial in order to assess the imaginary as an essential component of empire. As the chapters by Andrew Devereux and Thomas Dandelet show, the intellectual engagement with imperial ideologies, whether messianic globalism or nostalgia for Rome, is central to how empire is promoted, experienced, and understood. And as scholars of early modern England, in particular, have come to understand, the rhetorical projection of empire into an as yet unrealized future can have powerful material as well as ideological consequences.

Our volume is divided into two sections, which take us from the broadest problems of representation to a case study – early modern England – for which the "Mediterranean turn" has profoundly changed the field. The first section, "Envisioning Empire in the Old World," considers problems of visual, material, and textual representation of contact zones and encounters among the Mediterranean empires. Ania Loomba's chapter opens the volume with a broad consideration of the Mediterranean in the world. The large-scale focus of Braudel's work and the subsequent rise of world-systems theory, she notes, has obscured the complexities of diverse yet specific cultural productions. Through her expansive reading of *The Tempest*, Loomba demonstrates how even the seemingly capacious category of "the Mediterranean" in fact belies the region's engagements with other geographies, other circuits of both power and knowledge.

Chapters by Palmira Brummett and Larry Silver both examine visual representations of a contested Mediterranean world. Brummett demonstrates how cartographic depictions of a Mediterranean in-between negotiate the familiarity of the geography and the intense rivalry among Habsburgs, Venetians, and Ottomans. Despite their significant differences, Brummett shows, these Mediterranean actors all share the use of maps to project their own power over frontier spaces. Silver, for his part, shows how widespread and eagerly consumed pictorial representations of "the Turk" were in the Holy Roman Empire, running the gamut from monitory images of a fearsome enemy to careful, almost ethnographic depictions of Ottoman buildings and cities.

As our contributors demonstrate, the figurative underpinnings for empire include not just visual but also elaborate rhetorical justifications and rationales. Andrew Devereux shows how, in its conquest of Naples, Spain deliberately eschewed comparisons to imperial Rome, foregrounding instead a Christian rationale that made the conquest a "holy endeavour." Claiming for itself the mantle of Defender of the Faith, Spain harnessed fears of Ottoman expansion while also delegitimizing the competing claims of the French as anti-Christian. Carina Johnson, by contrast, charts how both Ottomans and Habsburgs generally asserted their imperial claims as successors to Rome in a slightly later period, after the Habsburgs became linked to the Holy Roman Empire following Charles V's accession. At the same time, Johnson notes, the cultural production of Ottoman alterity within Europe focused closely on succession, as European observers offered the often bloody transitions of the Ottomans as a prime example of their barbarity. Yet these constructions of alterity were produced against a domestic backdrop of confessional and dynastic tensions, so that elaborate anti-Ottoman denunciations often encode references to the Habsburgs' own difficulties. Thus the rhetorical othering of "the Turk" collapses into a mirroring of the self.

Across the Mediterranean, the subjects of empire grappled with its highly localized effects, producing elaborate responses to the vicissitudes of imperial rivalries and their domestic consequences. Elizabeth Wright examines *Austrias Carmen*, a poem penned soon after the famous battle of Lepanto (1571) by Juan Latino, a Granadan poet of African origin. Wright shows how Latino negotiates the complex reverberations of the naval battle against the Ottomans in the eastern Mediterranean with Spanish campaigns against the Moriscos at home, finding unexpected touchstones of sympathy for the purported enemy. Thomas Dandelet reconstructs the learned debates on empire that animated the duke of Medinaceli's Palatine Academy in Naples, charting the intense engagement with Roman and Renaissance traditions among the Neapolitan subjects of a declining Habsburg power in the late eighteenth century, almost three centuries after the conquest that Devereux analyses. Unlike the contemporary *philosophes* of northern Europe, Dandelet argues, the Neapolitan notables saw themselves as heirs to a long tradition of intellectual engagement with empire that stretched from Rome to the Italian Renaissance, and thus naturally turned to those models when their own polity entered into crisis.

The second section of our volume turns to a case study: "Imagining the Mediterranean in Early Modern England." Although England is obviously not a Mediterranean nation, its development as an empire was intimately bound up with the Mediterranean and its ongoing rivalries. Moreover, the study of early modernity in England, while a touchstone in many fields (history of the book, theatre history, materialism, transatlantic studies), has been hampered by a certain isolationism, a linguistic and national self-sufficiency. Our volume counters such isolation, charting how a "Mediterranean turn" in English studies allows us to tell more fully the early history of English empire and locate England in relation to the central imperial and ideological conflicts of the period. This re-centring, we suggest, offers a richer and more complex vision of England's cultural production.

Indeed, in recent years a number of critics have shown how engagements with Mediterranean empires profoundly shaped constructions of English national identity. Jonathan Burton, Nabil Matar, and Daniel Vitkus, among others, have demonstrated England's reliance on an Ottoman "other" in representations of English national identity, while Fuchs and Eric Griffin have charted a similar dynamic in English engagements with Spain. More specifically, scholarship has demonstrated how representations of Mediterranean imperial struggles shaped

England's self-fashioning as an imperial power. As Fuchs has shown, this rhetorical presentation of England as an empire predates the country's possession of substantial imperial holdings. Thus England provides a particularly rich example of how discursive formations participate in the building of empire. The "Mediterranean turn" in English studies demonstrates how the rhetoric and the material holdings of empires develop relationally, as a nation outside of the Mediterranean region both seeks a place in its imperial struggles and turns obsessively to its history.

The chapters included here explore how England engages the Mediterranean as a conceptual space, examining the role that representations of Mediterranean empire play in thinking through England's own expansion. The early modern theatre is a particularly important site for analysing such English engagements with the Mediterranean, as both English and foreign identities are staged for a mass audience. Theatrical depictions of the English abroad stake a claim to England's place in imperial ventures, projecting a rhetorical construction of English empire that did not yet exist in practice.

Representations of the Mediterranean on the early modern English stage could also draw attention to the meta-theatrical contrivances of the stage itself, as Jane Degenhardt's chapter demonstrates. The distant eastern Mediterranean, with its rich religious history, becomes a nexus for representation on the English stage. Plays such as *Pericles* and *The Four Prentices of London* draw on both the history of Christian miracles in places like Jerusalem and Ephesus and meta-theatrical contrivances to foster what Degenhardt calls a "theatrical faith ... in the stage's own interventions." By focusing on these meta-theatrical moments, Degenhardt brings out the extent to which the English engagements with a notional Mediterranean often had as much to do with domestic concerns as with actual events beyond England.

While English plays stage a number of encounters between the English and foreigners, representations of the Spanish Empire on the English stage are prominent and particularly fraught. As Eric Griffin shows, the Elizabethan government's propaganda machine in the years leading up to and directly following the Armada of 1588 branded Spaniards both rapacious imperialists obsessed with their own purity of descent and themselves debased in "blood," the mongrelized descendants of Moors and Jews. Such representations grew more powerful still onstage, and Griffin traces their effect through both the plays of the 1590s and in a revival of anti-Spanish sentiment around the proposed Spanish Match in 1623–4. This staging of an "ethnicized" Spaniard as absolutely other, Griffin shows, "overwrites" a shared history of Anglo-Spanish alliances in order to define English national identity as distinct from racialized Spanishness.

We can better understand the stakes of such English representations of Spain by comparing them to Spanish texts, as Emily Weissbourd argues in her chapter on John Webster's *The Duchess of Malfi*. Weissbourd shows that historical references within the English play repeatedly evoke Spain's occupation of Naples in the period and reads the play's rhetoric of "corrupted" blood as a critique of Spanish vices. Placing Webster in dialogue with a Spanish play based on the same source text, Lope de Vega's *El mayordomo de la duquesa de Amalfi* (the duchess of Malfi's steward), Weissbourd argues that the English text does not reflect actual Spanish cultural practices but rather its own biased version of a presumed Spanish obsession with purity of blood.

While the chapters discussed above focus on essentializing visions of Mediterranean difference (and particularly of Spain and its empire), Brian Lockey's contribution, "Catholics and Cosmopolitans Writing the Nation: The Pope's Scholars and the 1579 Student Rebellion at the English Roman College," gestures in a different direction. Drawing on Catholic and Protestant scholars alike, Lockey proposes an alternative framework for reading early modern constructions of English identity; rather than defining constructions of nationhood as either Catholic or Protestant, Lockey foregrounds conceptions of the English nation as fundamentally cosmopolitan (viewing England as a part of a larger Continental Christendom), or, conversely, focused on a myth of English national purity. Attending to this distinction complicates our understanding of confessional divides, since adherents to each of these views of England and Englishness can be found among Catholics and Protestants alike.

Observing the specifics of historical Anglo-Iberian encounters can also expand our understanding of how rhetorical constructions of the Mediterranean influence both personal relationships and public policy. Charles Cornwallis, an English ambassador to Spain from 1605 to 1609, documented his experience in a number of letters to secretary of state Robert Cecil, Lord Salisbury. As William Goldman's chapter shows, Cornwallis's early letters echo a number of stereotypes found in anti-Spanish propaganda, but his years in Spain gradually transform his point of view, and he begins to represent his Spanish hosts in a more nuanced – and more complimentary – light.

From the letters home of an English ambassador in Madrid to portraits, pamphlets, and poems on rival empires; from scholars' debates in the academies to English plays that rehearse national and imperial identities for a wide audience, the chapters collected in this volume embrace a wide array of topics, methodologies, and objects of study, foregrounding throughout the recent critical engagement with the early modern Mediterranean as a conceptual space and a unit of analysis. This range of approaches, we propose, best illustrates the complexity of imperial rivalries and their cultural projections. By bringing together these varied perspectives, *Representing Imperial Rivalry* foregrounds the multiple, layered connections among early modern empires.

NOTE

1 Laura Doyle, "Inter-Imperiality: Dialectics in Postcolonial World History," *Interventions: International Journal of Postcolonial Studies* 16 (2013): 160.

PART ONE

ENVISIONING EMPIRE IN THE OLD WORLD

chapter one

Mediterranean Borderlands and the Global Early Modern

ANIA LOOMBA

For where are the boundaries in space and time of any given culture?
Samir Amin, *Eurocentrism*

The cloud-capped towers, the gorgeous palaces,
The solemn temples, the great globe itself ...
The Tempest, 4.1.152–3

Thanks to Fernand Braudel's *Mediterranean and the Mediterranean World in the Age of Philip II*, the Mediterranean was the first region in the world to be used to model transnational analysis. Braudel used it to introduce a new unit of socio-geographic analysis – a maritime basin and the lands that border it – that was subsequently used to create analogous units such as "the worlds of the Indian Ocean," "the Black Atlantic," and the "trans-Atlantic"; such conceptual spaces have been crucial in allowing historians and cultural critics to question what Braudel called the "walled gardens" of a national – and usually nationalist – focus. But Braudel's Mediterranean also offered a new unit of temporal analysis. Although particular events and historical epochs are significant, he argued, only the *longue durée* – time that moves so slowly as to approximate ecological time – can indicate the organic unity of this region. Accordingly, Braudel acknowledged that the complicated relationship between Islam and Christianity was important to the culture of the Mediterranean, but only as part of those short-lived histories that did not fundamentally affect its dynamics. Thus the dynamic cultural contact and conflicts between the Ottomans and the Habsburgs, Muslims and Christians, Spanish and English, the histories of piracy, trade and rivalry that have recently become central to early modern literary studies are peripheral to a Braudelian understanding of the region. Peregrine Horden and Nicholas

Purcell in their magnum opus, *The Corrupting Sea: A History of the Mediterranean*, offer a distinction between "history *in* the Mediterranean – contingently so, not Mediterranean-wide, perhaps better seen as part of the larger history of Christendom or Islam – and the history *of* the Mediterranean, for the understanding of which a firm sense of place and a search for Mediterranean-wide comparisons are vital."[1]

Most of what we, as early modern literary and cultural critics, engage with –literature, cross-cultural interactions, trade routes, religious identities, even the histories of slavery in the region – would be relegated to history "in" rather than the history "of" the Mediterranean. In this chapter, I want to trouble this too-neat distinction. I want to explore how the particular, the local, the textured details of expressive culture can help us grasp the larger dynamics of a particular region such as the Mediterranean, and indeed complicate our understanding of its place in the larger world. It can also help us question the idea of the organic unity of the Mediterranean and thereby understand that such units of analysis, wonderfully useful as they are in taking us beyond narrow nationalist frames, can, if deployed too literally, also become too rigid and thus exclude other kinds of transnational relations in the early modern period. I will first discuss some of the conceptual issues at stake and then address them via a single literary text – Shakespeare's *Tempest*.

Gary Tomlinson points out that there *are* some models for cultural critique on a Braudelian scale, such as Michel Foucault's *Order of Things* and *Madness and Civilization*, Gilles Deleuze and Felix Guattari's *Thousand Plateaus: Capitalism and Schizophrenia* and Jacques Derrida's *Of Grammatology*.[2] But recent literary critics interested in thinking about the literature on a large temporal and spatial scale have not followed their methods, turning instead to world-system analysis, a method also indebted to Braudel. In charting the global reach of the novel, for example, Franco Moretti, probably the most influential of such critics, eschews close textual and cultural analysis in favour of "distant reading" or a mapping of the translation and publishing histories of novels on a global scale. This method replicates world systems analysis in reaching for the big picture by privileging economic analysis and downplaying ideological and cultural critique, as well as micro-analysis. While the method itself has been the subject of both admiration and critique, what is less remarked upon, but is also significant, is that Moretti's literary map faithfully reiterates the global asymmetries indicated by world systems theory. The novel as a form, Moretti contends, spreads from the global North (or West) to the global South (or the East); the cultural centres of his literary world are thus identical to the "core" areas identified by world systems theory, areas that became richer and more powerful than those it exploited and colonized. As Fernando Cabo Aseguinolaza points out, the particular texts and time periods and trajectories chosen by Moretti dovetail in many ways with the older, Eurocentric design of "world literature." In Moretti's model, it is also the Western critic who becomes the master-synthesizer of information sent to him by "local" researchers all over the world. As in the model of Mediterranean history outlined above, details of expressive culture and ideology are understood to be fairly immaterial in grasping, let alone in establishing, this larger globality. Finally, like the world systems theorists, Moretti conceptualizes a literary globality established only after the establishment of the European capitalist-colonial modernity.

Pre-modern scholars working in disparate disciplines have shown that there were older global circuits of exchange; if we pay attention to them, then the circuits of literary transmission, and indeed of material flows of goods, appear quite different. For example, Walter Cohen argues that the history of the novel as a form in fact reveals a movement from East to West rather than the other way around: "There are precedents for the novella in Italian and for both the novella and the frame-tale collection in medieval Latin. But behind all of these lie earlier sources and analogues in Arabic, of which the best-known today is the *Thousand-and-One Nights*. These enter European literature via Latin or vernacular – especially Spanish – translation. The Arabic materials in turn draw on Persian and ultimately Indian models. In short, the origins of what is arguably the quintessential European form lie in north Africa and southwestern and south Asia."[3]

But in order to arrive at this understanding one cannot just perform a distant reading; the expressive details of a text are important in understanding such movements, as I shall detail later in this chapter. In terms of economic and environmental histories too, Janet Abu-Lughod, Andre Gunder-Frank, L. Bin Wong, and Kenneth Pomeranz, among others, have shown, in very different and detailed ways, why the dynamics evident at the end of the consolidation of a capitalist-colonialist world system cannot simply be projected backwards in time.[4] They have suggested that Europe was not the "core" of an emerging global economy until at least the eighteenth century; at the end of the seventeenth century, it appeared, as Charles Davenant put it, that whoever controlled Asian trade would be in a position to "give law to all the commercial world."[5] They have also questioned Marxist assumptions about the pre-eminent position of Europe, and especially England, in terms of their *unique* development of structures necessary for capital accumulation.

This was actually Braudel's own point of departure, in *Civilization and Capitalism*, from a Marxist understanding of the birth of capitalism. Whereas Marx had suggested that Europe, and especially England, was uniquely avant-garde in developing structures necessary for capital accumulation, Braudel suggested, "Everywhere, from Egypt to Japan, we shall find genuine capitalists, wholesalers, the rentiers of trade, and their thousands of auxiliaries – the commission agents, brokers, money-changers, and bankers. As for the techniques, possibilities or guarantees of exchange, any of these groups of merchants would stand comparison with its western equivalents."[6]

Braudel also suggested a different temporal schema for understanding the genesis of capital: "world-economies" were evident from the Middle Ages onwards, as was capitalism in an embryonic form. Here, he also accorded a greater importance to social interactions and politics than he had done in his work on the Mediterranean, suggesting that these are not just an offshoot of economic systems but shape them as well.

For Braudel, as well as for world systems theorists and Marxists working on the early modern period, the key, and difficult question that remained was this: what then made Europe metamorphose into what Braudel calls "the monstrous shaper of world history"?[7] Why did Europe manage to seize control and Asia fall behind? Questions such as these return us to the issue of methodology that I have outlined above: can such a huge change be grasped only in terms of economic developments? What role do politics and ideology have to play? And what about literature? Does it reflect only existing global relations, or can it help us understand the dynamics of such changes in ways that would both complement and complicate economic and political analysis?

The question of ideology can be illustrated quickly through the seven voyages of Zheng He, undertaken between 1405 and 1433. Zheng He, a Muslim eunuch who commanded the Ming fleet, reached as far as the Somali coast, and some argue, as far as the Cape of Good Hope, establishing Chinese supremacy over as many as thirty countries before his emperors ordered a halt to such voyages, instead of taking the final steps to become truly hegemonic in the Eurasian world system. Europe, lagging far behind technologically and in bullion accumulation, poised itself to fill the vacuum – the Portuguese journeys around the Cape of Good Hope followed shortly afterwards and have been described as an "analogue" to Zheng He's voyages.[8] Why did the Chinese abruptly pull back, creating the space for Portugal to forge ahead? Giovanni Arrighi offers an economistic argument: the "structural imbalance of European trade with the East created strong incentives for European governments and businesses to seek ways and means, through trade or conquest, to retrieve the purchasing power that relentlessly drained from West to East," whereas there was no such incentive for Zheng He "because there was no treasure to retrieve in the West." But then Arrighi suggests an ideological difference between "territorialist rulers [like the Ming emperors who] identify power with the extent and populousness of their domains, and conceive of wealth/capital as a means or a by-product of the pursuit of territorial expansion" and "capitalist rulers ... [who] identify power with the extent of their command over scarce resources and consider territorial acquisitions as a means and a by-product of the accumulation of capital."[9] Here the suggestion is that the West *already* possessed capitalist ideologies as opposed to China, ideologies that facilitated the process of expansion, rather than being their result.

Immanuel Wallerstein discusses Zheng He in order to move in the opposite direction, first taking an ideological explanation seriously and then suddenly dismissing it. The differences between Portuguese and Chinese ideologies, in his view, stemmed from the fact that China was an "empire," whereas Portugal was part of a European "world-economy composed of many smaller states." An empire, he writes, "conceives of itself as a whole, unlike a state in a 'world-economy' ... For an empire pretends to be the whole. It cannot enrich its economy by draining from other economies, since it is the only economy. (This was surely the Chinese ideology, and probably their belief)."[10] It is unclear whether Wallerstein is suggesting that such empire-thinking is produced by an actual economic-political self-sufficiency, or whether it creates an *erroneous* belief in self-sufficiency, but in either case, it seems that for him Chinese ideology is crucial here. But he then abruptly considers the argument that "there emerged in China at this time an ideology of individualism, that of the Wang Yang-ming school ... comparable to the humanist doctrines in the West." He argues that whereas such an ideology in Portugal helped knit together the commercial and royal elites, in China it pushed a wedge between the Ming rulers and the eunuch-entrepreneurs. Such a difference, he concludes, warns us against "the too simple correlation between the ideology of individualism and the rise of capitalism" but also disproves "any causal statement that would make the emergence of such an ideology primary."[11]

Wallerstein's understanding of a "materialist" approach is reductive, as Cedric Robinson also notes.[12] Wallerstein offers simplified accounts of humanism and individualism, and of their relationship to class formation, as if such ideologies were undifferentiated in their Chinese and European versions, and as if they were not shaped by other ideologies of community, or religion, or gender.[13] Other historians have offered a more nuanced account of how Chinese world views, including Confucianism, intersected with practical considerations, such as the fact that the Ming rulers were battling other enemies on their western borders, crucial in halting Zheng He's voyages.[14] As William Appleman Williams, notes, "The point is not to present the Chinese as immaculately disinterested, or whiter than white. It is simply to note that we now know that the capacity for empire does not lead irresistibly or inevitably to the reality of empire."[15] But Williams then concludes that Western culture has *always* been imperialistic in its attitudes towards the rest of the world. Instead, we need to historicize such attitudes, and this can be done only if we correlate the economic and ideological. One way of doing this is to pay serious attention to the question of race. Racial ideologies, with their deep roots in religious thought, class ideologies, as well as real and imagined cross-cultural encounters, do not simply follow upon already formed economic and social relationships, but indeed shape them. For example, there is a dialogic rather than linear relationship between the practices of sub-Saharan slavery and European attitudes to both labour and blackness. Racial ideologies, neglected in world-system analysis, can often illuminate the gap between imperial "capacity" and "desire."

Precisely because early seventeenth-century England had imperial aspirations and overseas trade interests beyond its actual capacities, it has been a fruitful site for understanding these dynamics. *The Tempest* is particularly important to these discussions because it stages, in what seems an uncannily prescient way, various aspects of colonial encounters as they were to unfold in the coming centuries. It does so by using materials from the classical past, from medieval travelogues and literature, from contemporary travel writing, and also by projecting an unusually plastic imaginative geography. Critics have recognized *The Tempest*'s uncanny prescience, and indeed the play's colonial commentary and its geographies have been a subject of continual debates. Because these debates have been so central to discussions of colonialism and empire in early modern English studies, revisiting some key arguments can help us think further about the space and time of the Braudelian Mediterranean and the formation of colonial modernity.

II

Those critics who opened up *The Tempest*'s colonial dimensions argued that, to use Peter Hulme's evocative words, Prospero's magic in the play illuminates "the space really inhabited in colonial history by gunpowder."[16] In other words, Prospero's magic, so often read by generations of critics as emblematic of Shakespeare's own art, was now interpreted as neither simply superior knowledge nor superior morality, but as part of Prospero's coercive power on the island. This power, Hulme and others suggested, needed to be understood in the context of European activity in the Caribbean and elsewhere, where authority over the natives was enforced and maintained by guns and arms.

But others, such as David Scott Kastan, disagreed, contending that the play's "relationship to colonial activity ... is not written deep into its structure ... The play is much more obviously a play about European dynastic concerns."[17] Kastan's key point was that "the Italians' journey was not to explore or settle a new world but was intended as a return home, a return from a royal wedding from Alonzo's daughter Claribel to the King of Tunis." When *The Tempest* was performed at the wedding of Princess Elizabeth to Elector Palatine, its "events were more likely to resonate with political issues in Europe than in the Americas."[18] As Kastan attempts to reinforce the conventional borders of Europe, and of Shakespearean studies, he accuses U.S.-based critics of a kind of cultural imperialism in narrowing the focus of the play to a New World context. But the problem is that "colonial" cannot be reduced to "America" or even only to the question of immediate and direct colonization. Even if we purge America from the play, we do not get a Europe that is sealed from the rest of the world and from the colonial question. The marriages between European royalty during the period, as well as the fantasies of such marriages on English stages, were shaped by rivalries for trade and for colonial possessions on a global scale.

Just before Kastan's critique was published, at least three essays focused on the very journey to which Kastan refers – that of the courtiers from Tunis to Naples – to examine how *The Tempest* speaks to Mediterranean, North African, and Irish histories.[19] Instead of counter-posing these to the play's Atlantic concerns, they showed that the interplay between these contexts reveals *both* the domestic and the colonial investments of this play. Most significant were Barbara Fuchs's and Jerry Brotton's essays that reoriented the play eastwards: if the courtiers were indeed shipwrecked while returning to Naples from "Afric," where Claribel was married to the king of Tunis, then they were traversing what Brotton calls "one of the most contested stretches of water within the Mediterranean world."[20] Here the Ottomans and the Habsburgs were locked in battle, and the English unable to enter an area that was immensely useful for controlling the lucrative trade with the East. These contests explain why Alonzo is portrayed as entering into a marriage alliance with a king of Tunis, a city where, Leo Africanus's *Geographical History of Africa* tells us, "Genoues, Venetians and other Christian merchants resort and ... repose themselves out of the tumult and concourse of the Moors."[21] But Tunis was also the site of prolonged battles between Christians and Moors, the Ottomans and the Habsburgs; as a key site for trade, diplomacy, and war, it was a fulcrum for the balance of power in the Mediterranean.

Sebastian's comparison of Claribel to "widow Dido," several critics argue, evokes not Virgil's version of the story of Dido, queen of Carthage, in which Dido is abandoned by the Roman Aeneas, but an older tradition wherein *she* is a virtuous widow who refuses the advances of an African.[22] Jerry Brotton argues that the evocation of this older mythology of the region in the play works to erase the contemporary tensions between the English and the Ottomans; thus *The Tempest* offers "a conveniently imprecise but sanitized version of the Mediterranean which could allow Englishmen to gloss over their marginalization in this region and look forward to a different enterprise in the Americas."[23] But, as Brotton himself notes, by 1574, well before *The Tempest* was written, Tunis had been decisively taken over by the Ottomans, "a final development in the struggle over North Africa and the eastern Mediterranean which saw the Habsburg authorities disengage to pursue more fruitful expansion in the Americas, while the Ottomans concentrated on their eastern frontier in Asia."[24] This allowed the English to finally enter the region, a dynamic to which Braudel's final pages attend. As Barbara Fuchs reminds us, Claribel's story evokes *contemporary* encounters between white European women and Moors in the Mediterranean, which reverberated through early modern culture.[25] Turkish emperors always sired their heirs upon women of European descent, and these alliances were widely evoked in English writings as the inappropriate possession of Christian maidens by Moorish men. Indeed in other plays such as *The Renegado*, Tunis is an Ottoman possession and the site of abduction and possible rape of Christian women, rather than arranged alliances.

In the early seventeenth century, it was in fact unimaginable for a Christian and European princess to be given in marriage to a Muslim or African king. But the alliance evokes a long literary history of such marriages, one of the most famous being that between Princess Custance of Rome and the king of Syria in Chaucer's *Man of Law's Tale*.[26] Medieval and early modern literature is also full of counter-narratives, depicting the assimilation of beautiful and fair Muslim women into Christian families. English stages featured several such alliances, what I have elsewhere called a "delicious traffick"[27] that accompanies commercial exchanges between England and North Africa, the Ottoman world and the East. Because the English did not yet have colonial mastery over the East, such narratives can be understood as imagining social relations that did not as yet exist. But it is important to remember that there were already several places in the East where European colonization had begun, such as Portuguese Goa, or where brutal force and plantation accompanied trade, such as with the Dutch presence in the Molucca Islands. Accounts of such places percolated into English, and into at least a few English plays. Although these Eastern encounters were quite different from those in the West, they often intersected on the stage, as well as in countless other representations, pictorial and narrative. Such intersections are crucial to *The Tempest*'s global imaginary, a point to which I shall return shortly.

If the play celebrates a European dynastic alliance, then, as Kastan argues, it does so by contrasting the marriage of Ferdinand and Miranda to the misalliance of Claribel and the king of Tunis, thereby placing England in a European context and Europe in a Mediterranean one. But it also evokes the threat of another misalliance, the threatened rape of Miranda by Caliban, whose mother Sycorax is only evoked in the play, like Miranda's own mother. The two women are foils for one another; whereas Prospero tells us that his wife was a "piece of virtue," Sycorax is a "hag" who has consorted with the devil. Fuchs interprets Sycorax as part of the play's "metonymic reduction of Islam to the figure of the witch,"[28] but I suggest that as an ugly and loathsome witch, she stands in stark *contrast* to the dominant representations of Muslim women at the time. Islamic lands and peoples inspired both fear and reluctant respect, abhorrence but also desire. This dynamic is made clear in the narratives I have alluded to above, where beautiful Muslim women are won over by Christian men not by force, but by consent, and detached from their own communities and men. But unlike these women, and like a series of black women in the literature of the time, Sycorax cannot be assimilated into Prospero's world.[29] She must be eliminated by Prospero and detached from her child, the "deformed slave" Caliban.

There is a tendency in the recent critical turn to "the Mediterranean" to forget that in the eyes of English people, the region not only contained the threat posed by piracy, white captivity, and Islam, but was also the last frontier bordering on even more alien zones of barbarity and bestiality – the eastern and southern parts of Africa. In 1978, Andrew Hess argued that the border between the Iberia and North Africa had become the "forgotten frontier."[30] Since then historians and literary critics have charted interactions across these regions, illuminating a "multicultural Mediterranean," often evoking it as salutary for our own contemporary world with its newly deepened fault lines between Christianity and Islam. Now, within early modern English studies, it would be more apt to say that the neglected frontier – understood as simultaneously a border and a contact zone – has shifted to the border between the Mediterranean and lands to the south and east of that region.

Leo Africanus famously indicates a cultural and indeed proto-racial distinction between Islamic and non-Islamic Africa, lighter-skinned and dark-skinned Africans, divisions that are still central to African politics today. The former Africa, he suggests, is learned, civilized, religious, and misunderstood by Europeans, whereas the latter is bestial, with no regard for religion or the norms of civil society, especially marriage, and is regarded with contempt by North Africans. He shows how such divisions are also visible within Barbary, where early modern Algiers was located. Although Barbary has people of devotion, learning and civility, he writes, it also has those "who by nature ... are a vile and base people, being no better accounted of by their governors than if they were dogs ... No people under heaven are more addicted unto covetise than this nation ... They have no churches at all, nor any kind of prayers, but being utterly estranged from all godly devotion, they lead a savage and beastly life ... Yea they so behave themselves, as if they had continually lived in a forest among wild beasts."[31]

Sycorax, recall, has been banished "for mischiefs manifold and sorceries terrible" from Algiers, and according to Prospero, has begotten Caliban by consorting with the devil. Africanus describes women in Fez who are

> witches, which are affirmed to have familiarity with devils ... and when they will tell any man's fortune, they perfume themselves with certain odours, saying, that then they possess themselves with that devil which they called for: afterward changing their voice, they faine the devil to speak within them: then they which come to enquire, ought with great fear and trembling aske these vile and abominable witches such questions as they meane to propound, and lastly offering some fee unto the devil, they depart. But the wiser and honester sort of people call these women Sahaoat, which in Latin signifieth Fricatrices, because they have a damnable custome to commit unlawful venery among themselves, which I cannot express in any modester termes.[32]

Of course we find analogous descriptions of lewd femininity and monstrosity in early modern writings set elsewhere, including the New World. Here, for example, is a passage from Girolamo Benzoni's *History of the New World* describing Venezuelan women: "She was quite naked, except where modesty forbids, such being the custom throughout all this country; she was old, and painted black, with long hair down to her waist; and her earrings had so weighed her ears down, as to make them reach her shoulders, a thing wonderful to see; she had them split down the middle and filled with rings of a certain carved wood, very light ... Her nails were immoderately long, her teeth were black, her mouth large, and she had a ring in her nostrils, called by them caricori; so she appeared like a monster to us, rather than a human being."[33]

Indeed such overlaps indicate interconnections between European encounters with non-Europeans in different parts of the world. They remind us of the fact, often forgotten by us but everywhere visible in early modern texts, that as far as Europeans were concerned, they were heading to the "Old World" when they found the "New." Jonathan Gil Harris rightly points out that Columbus's mistake, thinking he had landed in the Old World when he stumbled on the New World, may have been easily rectified, but the fantasies that accompanied it continued to shape colonial ventures in the West.[34]

But my point here is that *The Tempest* registers the ways in which different non-Europeans were being sorted and categorized anew. The king of Tunis and Sycorax are, after all, both African, but they indicate very different histories and trajectories of contact. Whereas a European monarch to seeks an alliance, however distasteful, with Tunis, Sycorax's child is eventually enslaved. The Mediterranean contains these divergent histories: to its east and south lay lands that had been central to Eurasian and Indian Ocean trade routes so coveted by Europeans. To its south lay areas that supplied most of the slaves to Europe, and eventually to the New World. The connections between them formed the world system, or colonial modernity. *The Tempest* both evokes and crosses these frontiers, putting productive pressure on our spatial and historical vision.

III

It is not coincidental that if the most influential critical readings of *The Tempest* identified Caliban as a New World native, some of the most urgent non-scholarly appropriations drew attention to the fact that a New World slave was most likely to have been brought from Africa. Alden and Virginia Vaughan point out that readings of Caliban as an African remain remarkably sparse.[35] Perhaps this has something to do with the remarkably persistent scholarly consensus that the English were not really involved in the slave trade at the time; the fear of being factually wrong did not get in the way of anti-colonial activists making the connection between the play and the history of slavery. In 1960 George Lamming, in his *Pleasures of Exiles*, described the painful journeys of the "savage and deformed slaves" of the Middle Passage to the New World, remarking that, like Caliban, "they worked, or were rebellious and often went wild with the spirit of freedom, and were imprisoned, and yet, like Caliban, they survived."[36] Lamming asserted that "it will not help to say that I am wrong in the parallels which I have set out to interpret; for I shall replay that my mistake, lived and deeply felt by millions of men like me-proves the positive value of error."[37]

What Lamming did not know, but we now do, is that, between 1551 and 1600, 1,900 slaves were carried from Africa to the New World on *English* ships. By 1642, this number was to rise to 3,400.[38] While this may not seem like a very large number, it is significant enough to contest the dominant narrative that the English were marginal to the sixteenth- and early seventeenth-century-slave trade. Gustav Ungerer shows why the assertions "that the English had no experience as slave traders in the first half of the sixteenth century, that the English slave trade was pioneered by John Hawkins, that no blacks were bought or sold in England until the seventeenth century … no longer stand the test of historical examination."[39] He traces many English slave-owners who lived in the Iberian Peninsula by the sixteenth century. After all, as Steven Epstein points out, "there was no slavery in England, France or the Netherlands, yet their merchants needed slaves to feed the plantations of the West Indies."[40] The history of slavery cannot be excavated from within narrowly defined "national" contexts, especially in a period with such deep international connections among the aristocracy as well as merchants.

Just as all Europe had contributed to the making of Joseph Conrad's Kurtz, all Europe had contributed to the making of its slaving history, including its Portuguese roots.[41] In the very early years, the Spanish left the slave trade for "their Portuguese underlings to administer."[42] So did the English, but under Portuguese and Spanish duress.[43] Jeremy Lawrence points out that by the 1550s, up to 2,000 Africans were being imported into Spain annually through the Casa dos Escravos in Lisbon, accounting for as much as 7.4 per cent of the population of Seville in 1565.[44] The slave trade was also crucial to Italian commerce and culture, as Steven Epstein has brilliantly demonstrated. Epstein describes how Italian slavers intersected with and "distorted" the older slave trades of the Black Sea; whereas the older system was more contained, Italian slavers wanted slaves for export as well as for their own use, which led the large-scale raiding and capture of people hitherto not enslaved, such as children. This was "a dress rehearsal for the way English and Dutch traders distorted the indigenous slavery."[45] As Robert Davis shows, the histories of slavery are integral to understanding the Mediterranean and the relationships between various states and people therein.[46] These histories also underscore the porosity of Mediterranean borders, and the historic connections with Tartary, the Black and Red Seas, as well as Africa.

Of course Caliban also has several features attributed to the European poor – he is ungrateful, incapable of learning, rude, rebellious, and physically repellent, a villain/villein who aspires to unite with the princess. Miranda calls him an "Abhorrèd slave / Which any print of goodness will not take" insisting that his "vile race / had that in't which good natures / Could not abide to be with" (1.2.354–62). The word *race* here indicates lineage, or inherited nature, which in the early modern period could apply to class just as easily as to race in the modern sense. However, despite the historic and ongoing overlaps between the two kinds of difference, the colonial context pushes the meaning of *race* beyond lineage or class. We see here a reshaping of the medieval Wild Man in accordance with the newer and ever-expanding borders of Europe, and in accordance with the new relations of power in those contexts, somewhat like the continual relocation of the figure of the Amazon. As Paul Brown pointed out in a pioneering essay on the colonial resonance of *The Tempest*, the older figure of the Wild Man paid loving and eloquent homage to a courtly virgin and thereby served as "an emblem of courtly power, of the capacity to reorient masterlessness and savagism into service without the naked exercise of coercive power." Caliban's entry into language does not mark his homage or humility; not only does he use it to curse, but the play also depicts his resistance as "a desire to violate the chaste virgin" and thus legitimates Prospero's use of violence against him.[47]

Brown identified such a colonial context as Ireland, England's first colony, and many brilliant readings of *The Tempest* have amplified this connection, which also troubles the division between local and global, national and colonial. But what is interesting and important is not that the play evokes several different contexts, but that it hints at their multiple overlaps, some of which became visible only later. English and especially Irish labour was exported to the Caribbean, until the development of large plantations.[48] "White indentured servitude became the training ground on which planters obtained the skills and attitudes necessary for a rapid and unproblematic transition to large-scale black slavery in the late 1640s."[49] But after the coming of blacks, such servants became a white labour elite; and by 1657, Richard Ligon was arguing that Africans could be taught only unimaginative skills. In terms that seem to rehearse the language we hear in *The Tempest*, "Governor Dutton informed Whitehall that blacks' savage brutishness renders them wholly incapable" of learning the sophisticated skills that are needed on the plantations.[50] While it is widely argued that Ireland was a model for colonization in the Americas, the same history indicates a reverse direction of influence as well.[51] Stories of the Spanish conquistadores' use of dogs to discipline Indians widely circulated in England as part of the Black Legend. Peter Hulme drew attention, in an early and influential reading of *The Tempest*, to the striking overlap between such stories and Prospero's use of dogs to hunt down Caliban and his mates at the end of act 4.[52] Were such stories, or indeed *The Tempest*, influential in shaping the strategies in Ireland where, we are told, the peasants were "hunted down as men hunt game, and were forcibly put on board ship, and sold to the planters of Barbados"?[53]

The charge of rape levelled upon Caliban, as well as his supposed bestiality, also indicate another dimension of the development of racial discourse. Whereas the marriage of Claribel to the king of Tunis evokes the power and threat of contemporary Muslim monarchs, the rape evokes a different kind of sexual threat posed by non-Europeans whose very humanity was being brought into question. This is a different direction taken by the older figure of the Wild Man; now he is rendered not just liminal but impossibly savage. This trajectory is visible in contemporary writings that explored the border between humans and animals, and that also show us how older discourses on Asia and Africa were being rewritten during this period. Here is Edward Topsell in his *History of Four-Footed Beasts*:

> The countries where apes are found are Libya, and all that desert woods betwixt Egypt, Ethiopia and Libya, and that part of Caucasus which reacheth to the Red Sea. In India they are most abundant ... Men that have low and flat nostrils are libidinous as apes that attempt women, and having thick lips, the upper hanging over the nether, they are deemed fools, like the lips of asses and apes ... There is another kind of monkey, for stature, bigness and shape like a man, for by his knees, secret parts, and face, you would judge him a wild man, such as inhabit Numidia and the Lapones, for he is altogether overgrown with hair. No creature except a man can stand so long as he; he loveth women and children dearly, like other of his own kind, and is so venerous that he will attempt to ravish women.[54]

Topsell traces an already well-worn path from the shores of the Mediterranean to those of the Indian Ocean through the Red Sea; it was traversed imaginatively to the land of the mythical Prester John, Venetians' itineraries to Ethiopia through the fifteenth century reiterated it, and the Portuguese jealously guarded it in order to control the Eastern trade.[55] It was this route that, especially until the Cape route became a viable alternative, connected the world of the Mediterranean with that of eastern and southern Africa.

A few decades after Topsell, Edward Tyson was to write in his book *Orang-Outang, Sive Homo Sylvestris, or the Anatomy of a Pygmie Compared with That of a Monkey, an Ape, and a Man*,

> That the pygmies of the ancients were a sort of ape, and not of human race, I shall endeavor to prove in the following essay. And if the pygmies were only apes, then in all probability our ape may be a pygmie; a sort of animal so much resembling man, that both the ancients and the moderns have reputed it to be a puny race of mankind, call'd to this day, Homo Sylvestris, the Wild Man, Orang-Outang, or a Man of the Woods ... Now notwithstanding our pygmie does so much resemble a man in many of its parts, more than any of the ape-kind, nor any other animal in the world that I know of, yet by no means do I look upon it as the product of a mixt generation; 'tis a brute-animal sui generic, and a particular species of ape. For when I was dissecting it, some sea-captains and merchants who came to my house to see it assured me that they had seen a great many of them in Borneo, Sumatra, and other parts, tho' this was brought from Angola in Africa.[56]

Tyson explicitly traces the lineage of the Wild Man of the Woods to African and Asian pygmies and draws upon the overlaps between Asia and Africa that inform so many fifteenth- and sixteenth-century texts. At the same time, he develops the idea of species difference that was to become so central to colonial discourses of race.

Topsell and Tyson's geographies do not quite fit into geographic-analytic units such as the Black Atlantic, or the Mediterranean, or the Indian Ocean, but highlight their intersections. One particular effect of taking these units too literally is the division of the East and West Coast of Africa into two separate conceptual units.[57] Early modern writings, including *The Tempest*, remind us that oceans flow into one another, and they intersect with land routes to create maps that were crucial to the making of early modern circuits of commerce, empire, and slavery.

IV

In a brilliant essay on Mediterranean music that I have already referred to, Gary Tomlinson suggests that the "circum-Mediterranean culture area as a whole seems to be characterized by the meeting and merging of" practices derived from shamanistic ecstasy known in Eurasia, and possession cults that dominate African, South American, and Caribbean cultural areas. "The music of the elite European tradition," he writes, "was shaped in some measure by the convergence of these two modes of mystical experience in the geographical area where it arose. My sketch will lead us not only inward, towards the great modern avatars of European high culture, Beethoven and Wagner, but also outward to another epochal cultural shift: Europe's move from the fifteenth century on to conquer and colonize vast stretches of the rest of the world."[58]

Music allows Tomlinson to trace the long histories of the Mediterranean as an area whose *very distinctiveness* bears the imprint of many encounters, over the *longue durée*, with the world beyond. While Tomlinson does not deal with the history of capital, he reminds us that the Mediterranean was never sealed off from Africa and Asia, that the pre-modern borders between these areas were fluid, and that connections between them were rewritten alongside the European investments in the New World. Thus whereas Peregrine Horden and Nicholas Purcell argue that it is only "in the twentieth century [that] the Mediterranean has ceased to be an intelligible unity,"[59] Tomlinson shows that its supposed integrity was always shaped by the sedimented interactions of Eurasia and Africa. It may be time to stop distinguishing between history "of" and history "in" the Mediterranean.

I have suggested that the different geographies that are animated by *The Tempest*, each illuminated by critics as well as appropriations of the play, remind us also of the limitations of compartmentalizing the waters, of thinking about the Atlantic without the Mediterranean, and the Mediterranean without the Indian Ocean. The waters crossed and re-crossed by Prospero and Miranda, Ariel and Sycorax, Claribel and Ferdinand, Naples and his retinue, appear, under our critical gaze, to change their colour if we look at only one or the other of the play's contexts. But if we keep them in simultaneous sight, we remember that what we have here are the connections that are essential to the forging of the European-dominated "world system." The "colonial" investments of the play cannot be illuminated only by its Atlantic or Irish contexts, because colonialism was a global and not exclusively Atlantic story. It was African slavery that allowed Europeans to use New World riches to enter Asian markets and thus tip the balance of world trade.

An orthodox "materialism" and an equally orthodox horror of "anachronism" cannot help us understand the play between literature and the making of the world system. If *The Tempest* hints at the shape of early globalization, not only as it had already happened but also as it was to become visible in the coming years, it is not because its geographies evoke *each* of these contexts, it is because it hints at the *connections* between them, the inflows and outflows of capital, commodities, bodies, and ideas about somatic, cultural, and social differences. Hence its depiction of the fluctuating rivalries and alliances between European rulers, as well as between them and North African and Islamic states, the articulation of the Mediterranean, Atlantic, and African contexts of trade and colonization, and the striking overlaps between colonial relations and domestic class relations, with the need to subdue not only an oafish villain like Caliban, but also upstarts like Stephano and Trinculo. Such a process, the play also reminds us, was not possible without certain ideologies of power. In Prospero, the play gives us a meditation on the nature of such ideologies. His control over the colonial space of the island repositions him to gain power over his European rivals, a process that was indeed historically repeated over and over again. If on the one hand, the play reminds us that no European story can be simply detached from the colonial in the name of the national, the pre-colonial, or the literary, on the other, it is also a profound statement on the ideologies that accompany and are necessary for colonial expansion, the desires that do not simply follow upon, but shape the form of mastery and expertise.

NOTES

1 Peregrine Horden and Nicolas Purcell, *The Corrupting Sea: A Study in Mediterranean History* (Oxford: Blackwell, 2000), 1:43, 485. They are drawing upon D.D. Gilmore, "Anthropology of the Mediterranean Area," *ARA* 11 (1982): 175–205.
2 Gary Tomlinson, *"Il faut mediterraniser la musique:* After Braudel," in *Braudel Revisited, The Mediterranean World, 1600–1800*, ed. Gabriel Piterberg, Teofilo F. Ruiz, and Geoffrey Symcox, 246–70 (Toronto: University of Toronto Press and UCLA, 2010).
3 Walter Cohen, *"Don Quijote* and the Intercontinental History of the Novel," *Early Modern Culture* 4 (2004), http://emc.eserver.org/1-4/cohen.html.
4 Andre Gunder Frank, *Re-Orient: Global Economy in the Asian Age* (Berkeley: University of California Press, 1998); Kenneth Pomeranz, *The Great Divergence: China, Europe, and the Making of the Modern World Economy* (Princeton: Princeton University Press, 2000); R. Bin Wong, *China Transformed: Historical Change and the Limits of European Experience* (Ithaca: Cornell University Press, 1997).
5 Charles Davenant qtd in Giovanni Arrighi, *The Long Twentieth Century* (London: Verso, 1994), 35.
6 Fernand Braudel, *The Perspective of the World* (New York: Harper and Row, 1976), 486. Arrighi, *Long Twentieth Century*, draws attention to this passage, 35.
7 Braudel qtd in ibid., 11.
8 Cedric Robinson, *Black Marxism: The Making of the Black Radical Tradition* (Chapel Hill: University of North Carolina Press, 1993), 99.
9 Arrighi, *Long Twentieth Century*, 35.
10 Immanuel Wallerstein, *The Modern World-System* (Berkeley: University of California Press, 2011), 1:60.

11 Ibid., 1:62.
12 Robinson, *Black Marxism*, 342 n. 28.
13 Wallerstein concludes that the answer must lie in China's imperial political structure that did not allow expansion, as opposed to "a world-system based on a pre-bendal bureaucracy" that facilitated imperial expansion in Europe.
14 See, for example, Hui Chun Hing, "Hunagming Zuxun and Zheng He's Voyages to the Western Oceans," *Journal of Chinese Studies* (Institute of Chinese Studies) 51 (2010): 85; Kuei-Sheng Chang, "The Maritime Scene in China at the Dawn of Great European Discoveries," *Journal of the American Oriental Society* 94, no. 3 (1974): 347–59.
15 William Appleman Williams, "Empire as a Way of life," *Nation*, 2–9 August 1980, 104.
16 Peter Hulme, "Hurricane in the Caribbees," in *1642: Literature and Power in the Seventeenth Century*, ed. Francis Barker, Jay Bernstein, John Coombes, Peter Hulme, Jennifer Stone, and Jon Stratton (Colchester: University of Essex, 1981), 74.
17 David Scott Kastan, "'The Duke of Milan / And His Brave Son': Old Histories and New in *The Tempest*," in *The Tempest; A Case Study in Critical Controversy*, ed. Gerald Graff and James Phelan (Boston: Bedford / St Martin's, 2000), 274n275.
18 Ibid., 285.
19 Barbara Fuchs, "Conquering Islands: Contextualizing *The Tempest*," *Shakespeare Quarterly* 48, no. 1 (1997), 45–62; Jerry Brotton, "'This Tunis, sir, was Carthage,' Contesting Colonialism in *The Tempest*," in *Postcolonial Shakespeares*, ed. Ania Loomba and Martin Orkin, 23–42 (London: Routledge, 1998); and Richard Wilson, "Voyage to Tunis: New History and the Old World of *The Tempest*," *English Literary History* 64, no. 2 (1997): 333–5.
20 Brotton, "'This Tunis, sir, was Carthage,'" 34.
21 Leo Africanus, *The History and Description of Africa*, ed. Robert Brown (New York: 1906), 716.
22 See Stephen Orgel, ed., *The Tempest* (Oxford: Oxford University Press, 1987), 41.
23 Brotton, "'This Tunis, sir, was Carthage,'" 37.
24 Ibid., 35.
25 See Fuchs, "Conquering Islands," 45–62.
26 Dorothee Metlitzki, *The Matter of Araby in Medieval England* (New Haven, CT: Yale University Press, 1977); Geraldine Heng, *Empire of Magic, Medieval Romance and the Politics of Cultural Fantasy* (New York: Columbia University Press, 2003); Ania Loomba, "Periodization, Race, and Global Contact," in *After Periodization, Journal of Medieval and Early Modern Studies* 37, no. 3 (2007): 596–620.
27 Ania Loomba, "Delicious Traffick: Alterity and Exchange on Early Modern Stages," *Shakespeare Survey* 52 (1999): 201–15.
28 Fuchs, "Conquering Islands," 61.

29 I have explored this at greater length in "Delicious Traffick: Alterity and Exchange on Early Modern Stages," *Shakespeare Survey* 52 (1999): 201–15.
30 Andrew Hess, *The Forgotten Frontier: A History of the Sixteenth-Century Iberia-African Frontier* (Chicago: University of Chicago Press, 1978).
31 Joannes Leo Africanus, *A Geographical Historie of Africa* ..., trans. John Pory (London: George Bishop, 1600), 41.
32 Ibid., 130–1.
33 Girolamo Benzoni, *History of the New World*, trans. W.H. Smyth (London: Hakluyt Society, 1857), 4–8.
34 Jonathan Gil Harris, *Marvelous Repossessions* (Vancouver: Ronsdale, 2012). The dream of marvellous possessions in the New World, he writes, was really one of repossessing a lost paradise shaped by centuries of dreaming about the East.
35 Alden T. Vaughan and Virginia Mason Vaughan, *Shakespeare's Caliban: A Cultural History* (Cambridge: Cambridge University Press, 1991), 52.
36 George Lamming, *The Pleasures of Exile* (Ann Arbor: University of Michigan Press, 1992), 98.
37 Ibid., ix.
38 David Eltis and David Richardson, *Atlas of the Transatlantic Slave Trade* (New Haven, CT: Yale University Press, 2012), 25.
39 Gustav Ungerer, "Recovering a Black African's Voice in an English Lawsuit: Jacques Francis and the Salvage Operations of the *Mary Rose* and the *Sancta Maria* and *Sanctus Edwardus*, 1545–ca 1550," *Medieval & Renaissance Drama in England* 17 (2005): 255. See also his *The Mediterranean Apprenticeship of British Slavery* (Madrid: Verbum, 2005).
40 Steven A. Epstein, *Speaking of Slavery, Color, Ethnicity and Human Bondage in Italy* (Ithaca, NY: Cornell University Press, 2001), 123.
41 See Robinson, *Black Marxism*, chap. 5.
42 Ibid., 105.
43 In 1481 King Edward IV of England came to an agreement with the visiting Portuguese embassy not to enter the slave trade. In 1555, the Spanish put pressure on Queen Mary of England to forbid English involvement in Guinea.

   Recently, the relationship between England and Spain has received productive critical attention and has been seen to be crucial to the making of English ideologies of race. But Portugal has received far less attention; it tends to be subsumed under Spain or confined to either an earlier history or only in relation to Asia. In a sense the division of the world imagined by the Treaty of Torsedillas has shaped our own critical maps. As Robinson (*Black Marxism*) points out, no understanding of slavery can be complete without understanding the role of the Portuguese.
44 Jeremy Lawrence, "Black Africans in Renaissance Spanish Literature," in *Black Africans in Renaissance Europe*, ed. T.F. Earle and K.J.P. Lowe (Cambridge: Cambridge University Press, 2005), 70.

45 Ibid., 123.
46 Robert Davis, "The Geography of Slaving in the Early Modern Mediterranean," *Journal of Medieval and Early Modern Studies* 37, no. 1 (2007), 57–74.
47 Paul Brown, "'This thing of darkness I acknowledge mine': *The Tempest* and the Discourse of Colonialism," in *Political Shakespeare: New Essays in Cultural Materialism*, ed. Jonathan Dollimore and Alan Sinfield (Ithaca, NY: Cornell University Press, 1985), 54 and 62.
48 Richard Pares, *Merchants and Planters* (New York: Cambridge University Press, 1960); Hilary McD. Beckles, *White Servitude and Black Slavery in Barbados, 1627–1715* (Knoxville: University of Tennessee Press, 1989).
49 Beckles, *White Servitude*, 6.
50 Both Ligon and Dutton are quoted by Beckles, ibid., 126.
51 The point is also made by Fuchs, "Conquering Islands"; and Barbara Fuchs, "Spanish Lessons: Spenser and the Irish Moriscos," *Studies in English Literature 1500–1900* 42, no. 1 (2002): 43–62.
52 Peter Hulme, *Colonial Encounters: Europe and the Native Caribbean 1492–1797* (London: Routledge and Kegan Paul, 1987), 133.
53 Robinson, *Black Marxism*, 111, is quoting Richard B. Moore, "On Barbadians and Minding Other People's Business," *New World Quarterly* 3, nos 1 and 2 (1966/7): 69.
54 Edward Topsell, *The History of Four-Footed Beasts and Snakes* (London: William Jaggard, 1607), 2–15, 295–6.
55 See *Ethiopian Itineraries circa 1400–1524*, Hakluyt Society, second series 109 (Cambridge: Cambridge University Press, 1958).
56 Edward Tyson, *Orang-Outang, Sive Homo Sylvestris, or the Anatomy of a Pygmie Compared with that of a Monkey, an Ape, and a Man* (London: Thomas Bennet and Daniel Brown, 1699), 2.
57 See also Laura Chrisman, "Journeying to Death: Gilroy's Black Atlantic," *Race and Class* 39 (1997): 51–64; Isabel Hofmeyr, "The Black Atlantic Meets the Indian Ocean: Forging New Paradigms of Transnationalism for the Global South – Literary and Cultural Perspectives," *Social Dynamics: A Journal of African Studies* 33, no. 2 (1997): 3–32.
58 Tomlinson, *"Il faut mediterraniser la musique,"* 254.
59 Horden and Purcell, *Corrupting Sea*, 43.

chapter two

Mapping Trans-Imperial Ottoman Space: Alterity and Attraction

PALMIRA BRUMMETT

As it expanded its territories across the eastern Mediterranean and into the Graeco-Balkan peninsula, the Ottoman Empire thrust itself into an enduring trans-imperial space.[1] There it became enmeshed in a long-term rivalry with the Venetian and Habsburg Empires. That rivalry was expressed in narrative and image in a complex set of rhetorics, including those found on maps. As the statesmen, writers, and artists of the Christian kingdoms of Europe attempted to come to terms with the Ottoman presence (its opportunities as well as its threats), they looked at an unfamiliar enemy in a set of familiar places, a known and "old" world. And they tried to make sense of him using a knowledge-picture that was already in place, one that took classical and biblical histories for granted. Viewing the Ottomans as usurpers occupying space that was meant to be indelibly Christian, they persisted in claiming territories already conquered by the sultans, stamping icons of Christian identity onto their maps of Ottoman domains, and translating the Ottomans as one more iteration in a historical litany of Muslim invaders. Meanwhile the Ottomans saw themselves as inheritors of the imperial patrimony of Rome, to which they were entitled by virtue of their faith (the culmination of Abrahamic prophecy) and their military success. These imperial rivals thus approached each other across a broad land and sea frontier with a sense of familiarity that affected the ways in which they imagined empire, borders, and encounters.

I propose to begin this chapter with a set of narrative vignettes that illustrate that familiarity in the context of rivalry, followed by a set of examples from the genre of mapping that suggest the possibilities for visualizing and claiming frontier space. Maps charted Ottoman domains in terms of their histories, events, and attractions, not simply as the backdrop for an enduring struggle between "fidelity" and "infidelity." The map, a visual artefact deriving from narrative accounts, was an important vehicle by which audiences in the lands of the Christian kings were made to "see" and understand the Ottomans. Maps also served as a mode of advertising empire. They were one element of the rhetorical projection of power practised by both the Ottomans and their European Christian rivals. Possession, territory, and imperial frontiers could be "fixed" within the map frame in ways that they were not and could not be fixed in fact.

The Ottomans: The Limits of Alterity

As the Ottomans became a European and Mediterranean power, the monarchs of Christian Europe and their subjects, especially in those territories proximate to Ottoman lands, were forced to take notice. And take notice they did, in text and image. Despite the rhetorical impulse to articulate the Ottomans in terms of their alterity, as an arrogant, Oriental, infidel people, indelibly linked to the Scythians and the Central Asian steppe, the Ottomans were understandable to European Christian audiences. They acted out the behaviours of their imperial predecessors, exacting submission from enemies and showing magnanimity to those willing to compromise. They occupied the familiar terrain of Constantinople, the Balkans, the Archipelago, Egypt, and Palestine, claiming the mantle of Caesar.[2] They counted Alexander and Solomon among their heroes as well as Khosrau and Muhammad. The Ottomans ascended to precedence among the Muslim kings who had challenged Christendom since the time of the Prophet. And they were brothers in the Abrahamic faith: not pagans but heretics who had supposedly lost the way and who governed populations who either remained Christian or still had the scent of Christendom upon them.[3] Their notables behaved in ways made famous by Machiavelli. And their sultans were weak or strong, dissolute or abstemious, avaricious or generous, just like their Christian counterparts. Thus the limits of their alterity were well apparent and well recognized by various audiences among their European observers.[4] As a result, neither the communal nor the continental divide of Europe and Asia sufficed to distinguish and mark Ottoman space and identity.

Each time the Ottomans took control of one of the urban points of diffusion by which goods, news, intelligence, texts, and taste circulated throughout the Afro-Eurasian Oikumene, they became more deeply enmeshed in a culture of contact. Each time they conquered a city, they were faced with the challenge of social integration and population retention, a challenge they became quite adept at meeting, particularly in the Graeco-Balkan peninsula. Frontier zones were thus areas of compromise and conviviality (as well as hostility), and of shifting or serial identities. They were places where genres of literature and art were shared, as Walter Andrews and Mehmet Kalpaklı have so eloquently demonstrated in their work on the Ottoman-Mediterranean world.[5] And they were places that, often enough, were forced to pay allegiance (and taxes) to two masters. The borders of empire were thus not so clearly defined as they might seem in official correspondence or maps. As the map, the tax register, the broadsheet, and the travel narrative struggled to fix space concretely as Christian or Muslim, congenial or hostile, "us" or "other," and to draw borders in lines, points, or blocks of space, they did so against this very real context of coexistence, shared space, and shared knowledge.

Three Vignettes: The Familiar and the Distant

Each of the three vignettes presented here addresses the borders of space and of understanding. The first two demonstrate the ways in which the Ottoman court used translation and deployed knowledge to advance its imperial agendas in the face of competition from the Christian kings of Europe. The third illustrates the limits of rhetorics of Christian unity against the "Turk," when such unity did not serve imperial ambitions. All three suggest ways in which the limits of Ottoman space were imagined and negotiated. At the trans-imperial frontier, relationships were conditioned by a combination of fear and conversation, or, as Natalie Rothman has so neatly put it, by a set of textual and visual perspectives that were both "explicitly foreignizing" and "intensely intimate."[6] My vignettes lay out some of those "foreignizing" and "intimate" textual perspectives. The maps that follow provide a complementary set of visual perspectives. Text and image demonstrate the interplay of affinity and distaste and, more to the point, the recognition of imperial self in imperial other.

In order to illustrate some of the ways that space and encounter were imagined, I would like to begin with a vignette from Evliya Çelebi (1611–1682), the seventeenth-century Ottoman raconteur. Evliya was a *kul*, a member of the extended household of the Ottoman palace, but also an adventurer who stood somewhat apart from the routine hierarchy of appointments and promotions.[7] Like many of his contemporaries, Christian and Muslim, Evliya sought the patronage of important men. But, unusually among Ottoman authors, he was expansive in his descriptions of those men and their households. In his famous multi-volume travel book, the *Seyahatname*, he provides insight into the ways a rather flamboyant "servant" of the sultan might construct his lord in narrative and imagine the relationship of "East" and "West." He also illustrates the juxtaposition of alterity and attraction that is one of the objectives of this volume.

Evliya wrote admiringly of Sultan Murad IV (r. 1623–1640), calling him a "free and easy ruler ... majestic as Jamshid," who had a "noble character" and "an inclination towards the east." Murad, Evliya tells us, both enjoyed a good joke and had a feel for language, combining the two to imitate the unpolished dialects of his subjects in eastern Anatolia. The sultan had among his courtiers

> ... a mimic (muqallid) named Qahvecizade, who had shown his capabilities in speaking twenty languages with proficiency and eloquence. Whenever a mendacious envoy came from the kings of Poland, Chekhia, France or Moscow, this mimic would don the [national] costume of that envoy and interpret without hindrance.
>
> It is true [Evliya goes on to note] that the Muslims and monotheists, as a warning for the unmindful, had been given the instruction: "He who imitates a people becomes one of them," but Sultan Murad ... made the said Qahvecizade put on the dress of every visiting envoy, and act as an interpreter and mediate the conversation in the imperial divan.[8]

This little aside in Evliya's narrative paints a picture of the Ottoman sultan that is rather different from the portraits to which we have grown accustomed. Murad is a man who enjoys and practises wordplay, a ruler with savoir faire who uses costume to suggest familiarity and who expects diplomatic exchange to take the form of conversation rather than ritual posturing before a mute and aloof majesty. He is undeterred by the suggestion that such conversation threatened to make the Ottomans "become one" with their European Christian enemies. Indeed, this passage takes for granted that the Ottomans and the foreign envoys share modes of communication and ritual understanding.

The passage also conjures a vision of imperial space. Murad is "inclined" towards the East; he was, after all, the conqueror of Baghdad (in 1638). But he is also comfortable and familiar with the "West" of France, Poland, and the Habsburgs. Even the intermediary in this story refuses to conform to assigned roles. There is no suggestion in Evliya's story that the mimic is a Greek or a renegade Hungarian. He is called "the son of a coffee server." That is, Evliya does not presume that only a Western "foreigner" could act as a translator for the sultan. The Ottomans, I suggest, had been "becoming one" with their enemies for a long time – since the beginning of the empire. It was an imperative of enduring empire.

Once we see the sultan mocking the unsophisticated speech of his subjects in the Anatolian, Islamic hearth-lands, and the more sophisticated presentations of the envoys from the West, we can begin to see him as less a *gazi* (warrior for the faith) and more a cosmopolitan king. He ruled through a complex organization of households and dispensed patronage across a disparate set of governed territories, much like the monarchs of the Spanish Empire at the other end of the Mediterranean. The Ottomans had their own ethnographies of peoples and languages, as illustrated most eloquently in the comic genre of the shadow puppet theatre, or Karagöz, which typed its characters according to ethno-linguistic, communal, and occupational identities. And the mountain peoples of eastern Anatolia (or the Balkans, for that matter) might require as much "translation" by the Ottoman court as did the more rustic minions of the Christian courts of Europe, a point Evliya himself suggests elsewhere.[9] A monarch and his advisors who proposed successfully to govern a far-flung kingdom had to be conversant in the "languages" of both subject and rival, regardless of faith. If that knowledge extended to wordplay, satire, and material culture, so much the better.

My second vignette contains a story complementary to Evliya's, though it is situated in the eighteenth century. By that time the balance of power had shifted from the Ottomans to their European rivals, and the process of information exchange had intensified. France at this time was a powerful agent in the visual construction of Ottoman space, engaged in a process of knowledge production that brought together ideology, diplomacy, and cartography to serve the French imperial project.[10] On 27 September 1784, the French ambassador, Marie Gabriel Florent Auguste de Choiseul-Gouffier (b. 1752) arrived in Istanbul.[11] But when he reached the Ottoman capital, he found to his dismay that the Grand Vizier Halil Hamid already had a translation of "damaging passages" from the introduction to a book Choiseul-Gouffier had recently completed. This "Preliminary Discourse" to *A Picturesque Voyage to Greece (1779–1783)*, according to Virginia Aksan, contained "an exquisite blend of youthful naïveté, ecstatic philhellenism and careless political ignorance, recommending the rebirth of the Greek nation in the Morea – a phoenix that would rise from the ashes of the Ottoman empire."[12] Needless to say, this proposal for the disposition of Ottoman domains was unlikely to please the vizier or facilitate the ambassador's mission. Even though Choiseul-Gouffier quickly had a sanitized version of his work presented to the sultan, the damage was done. The ambassador's "Preliminary Discourse" had, in effect, mapped a new Greek polity onto existing Ottoman domains.[13] What is interesting here is not so much the vagaries of diplomacy, but the speed with which the Ottoman vizier was made aware of the contents of the French travelogue-cum-political-treatise, a genre of literature that routinely embodied the imperial aspirations of Christian kings. Here again, we have an image of familiarity, one that links the translation projects of the eighteenth century to those of an earlier era of trans-imperial discourse. The French, after all, had been sending envoys to Istanbul and commissioning maps of Ottoman territory since the sixteenth century. And the Ottomans in the eighteenth century had increasingly exploited direct diplomatic, literary, and commercial exchange with the French.[14] The genres vary, ranging from verbal diplomatic exchange, to cartographic representation, to travel narrative, to political rhetoric. But the net effect of the two vignettes presented so far is to normalize the Ottomans, making them appear playful and astute, and, more to the point, players in a process of trans-imperial encounter and understanding that spanned the Afro-Eurasian world. Text, word, and image, circulating at home and abroad, made the empire, and its rivals, "real" to each other.

The third vignette returns us to an earlier era, again on the eastern Ottoman frontiers, to suggest that there were relevant and not so relevant spaces: those to which the honour and strategic interest of empire were attached (Jerusalem or Dubrovnik, for example), and those for which imperial attention was muted or insubstantial. As the Ottomans expanded and conquered new territories, beleaguered Christian rulers in the east, confronted with the threat of Ottoman supremacy, looked to European imperial lords to secure their survival. Thus in 1495, the Georgian king, Konstantine II, turned westward to Isabella of Spain, to request succour against the onslaught of the "Turks." Konstantine imagined a bridge of communal affinity linking the Caucasus to Iberia. But he would find that the eastern end of Christendom did not fire the Spanish imagination as did the west of the New World.

Konstantine's appeal to the Spanish court was prompted by the news of Spain's expulsion of the "Moors." Proposing to join a Spanish campaign against the Ottomans, he commended to Isabella the "fortification of all Christians." He admired her capture of the "great cities" of the Saracen, and he asked that God strengthen her in her "domination and patronage of the whole world," so that "with God's power" she might "destroy all the infidel rulers."[15] The Georgian king thus considered himself and his territory part of a greater Christian kingdom of Europe (and of the world), a kingdom anchored by Rome and Jerusalem. This was the rhetoric of a unified Christendom, well circulated (if not well acknowledged) since at least the time of the Crusades. It appears, however, that the Georgian ruler was inclined to overestimate the reach of the Spanish Crown, just as some of the South Asian Muslim petty kings, a few short years later, were inclined to overestimate the reach of the "world conquering" Ottoman sultan, who they hoped would expel the Portuguese from the Indian Ocean. For Spain, Georgia was a remote outpost of Christendom that was not only unreachable, but could serve little in advancing Spanish ambitions. Its formal reply was disappointing. Isabella promised to pray to God "that He deliver not only you, but the entire Christian population from the infidels; guard you; and grant you victory."[16] Prayer, unfortunately, was not what Konstantine had in mind. But his story demonstrates the limits of rhetorics of Christian unity. For the imperial rivals of the Ottomans, and for the Ottomans themselves in assessing the relevance of potential allies, realpolitik was always a powerful counterpart to religious or ethnic affinities. All Spain had to offer the Georgian lord was the rhetoric of rivalry, however much Konstantine might claim a historical or ideological attachment to the Christian kings.

Rivalry, Rhetoric, and Mapping Borders

Such vexed associations across shared ideological spaces also posed a dilemma for the geographers and map-makers of the time. The entry "Christians," in Abraham Ortelius's 1578 *Thesaurus Geographicus*, is followed by the notation "see Europeans," thus firmly stamping Europe as the central confessional space, but also apparently limiting the geographic scope of Christendom.[17] Boundaries were thus caught between ideologies, rhetorics, and political realities. The mapmakers of the Christian kingdoms were forced to deal with the Ottoman Empire as the unbounded ethno-regional spaces of the Ptolemaic world-vision became the bounded nation-states of the eighteenth century. The process was neither simple nor straightforward. How did one construct nominally Christian space in which a turbaned sultan sat upon the throne? One option was to refuse to acknowledge Ottoman sovereignty within the map frame. Another was to equivocate on the location of boundaries. Otherwise possession might be indicated by stamping emblems, mascots (like the Habsburg eagle or the Venetian winged lion), or Christ figures onto the body of maps representing Ottoman territory. Such iconographic alternatives transcended the notion of the borderline. In that iconography the juxtaposition of imperial entities was just as important as that of "belief" and "infidelity."

The Ottomans and their rivals delineated borders in a variety of ways, using physical features like rivers and mountain passes, and structures such as fortress cities. The notion of a border or a frontier zone presumed competing claims and the impermanence of sovereignty as territory changed hands from one imperial power to another. The cartographer Vincenzo Coronelli, for example, narrating the Ottoman-Venetian wars of the late seventeenth century described the Croatian town of Risano in the following terms: it was "taken from the Turks by the Army of the Republic in 1538" but returned the following year by the peace treaty. In 1649, "the Turks tyrannized the surrounding countryside," so the Venetian general, Foscolo, besieged the town and, after eleven days, allowed the defenders to leave with a safe conduct. Risano was restored to the Ottomans once again "in the division of the borders [*confini*] after the war of Candia."[18] Coronelli was describing actual possession, but borders were also imagined and claimed on the basis of a sense of entitlement to a given space. As far as Coronelli was concerned, Risano belonged to Venice. Regardless of who actually controlled the fortress, it was a place "consigned to the archbishop of Ragusa";

its loyalties supposedly lay with the Signoria, and it was "finally returned to the Dominion of the Republic of Venice."[19] Early modern Christian authors also claimed Cyprus and Crete as Venetian spaces long after they were conquered by the Ottomans. And European travellers insisted on narrating Constantinople and Jerusalem as annexes of Christendom long after Muslim polities had consolidated their control over those imperial or sacred capitals. It is no wonder, then, that the cartographers of the Christian kings struggled with the limits of empire, identity, and community. A certain sleight-of-hand was required when it came to pinning down whose territory was whose.

One strategy, as noted, was simply to avoid drawing borders or stamping political identity upon the map. That mode of mapping Ottoman space was common enough in the sixteenth century, though it gave way to the marking of Ottoman identity in image and text by the turn of the seventeenth century. When sovereign identity was marked, it could acknowledge the problematic nature of borders while at the same time indicating the presence of states and monarchs. That presence might be documented in the cartouche, by naming territory as belonging to a certain political entity, or it might be demonstrated by placing figures, flags, coats of arms, mascots, or other icons of identity (e.g., cross and crescent) onto the body of the map. One such device was the placement of portraits of rulers onto territorial space. The "hanging" of such portraits on the map allowed the gaze of the monarch to extend over territory that he possessed, claimed, or only hoped to possess at some later time. Portraits could make visible the imperial ambitions detailed in the vignettes presented earlier in this essay: Murad IV's inclination towards the east; Choiseul-Gouffier's aspirations to free Greece from the Ottomans; and Konstantine II's hopes that Isabella would direct her imperial gaze all the way to Georgia.

Matthias Zündt's (d. ca 1572 or 1581) map of Hungary, for example, done originally in Nuremberg, was altered in 1578 by the addition of portraits that suggest the patrimonial gaze of both Christian and Muslim monarchs (figure 2.1).[20] The map conveys a sense of contested territory. First and most dramatically, Hungary is divided physically by the broad sweep of the Danube and its tributaries. Second, it is a territory over which the coat of arms, with cross and crown, of royal Hungary (as appears in the decorative cartouche) holds sway. That emblem, southeast of Belgrade, seems to obliterate any suggestion of Muslim sovereignty in what were clearly Ottoman domains, the lands between Belgrade and Istanbul. But in the territory north of the Danube we see two portrait medallions, one of Rudolph II (Holy Roman emperor, 1576–1612) and one of the Ottoman sultan Murad III (r. 1574–95). Neither king seems more powerful than his rival; neither seems poised to seize the contested territories he sees before him. Indeed, despite the cartouche, which decidedly suggests Hungarian possession, the lower section of the map is marked with small captions indicating the years in which certain territories fell to the "Turk." One sees, for example, a caption commemorating the "unhappy" event of the Hungarian hero Sigismund's (r. 1387–1437) defeat by the "Turks."[21] Such annotations convey the potential for further Ottoman conquests, city by city. They seem to confirm the impermanent nature of imperial borders at the same time that the portrait medallion of Murad III asserts Ottoman presence more decisively than any caption.

Other map-makers in the realms of the Christian kings used portraits to assert possession in a more dramatic fashion. Thus Matteo Rossi in Rome produced a striking map of the borders in the contested space between the Habsburg and Ottoman Empires.[22] The map, *Dimostratione de Confini delle principale Citta' dell' Austria et Ungaria*, provides three registers of information (figure 2.2). In the central space is a map of Vienna with the Danube running through it, extending east and south to Buda. The fortress-city was the marker of territory and possession par excellence in early modern maps. And Vienna, which the Ottomans assailed but failed to conquer twice, in 1529 and 1683, was the enduring, acknowledged limit-city, a decisive barricade between the realms of Christendom and the realms of the "Turk." Buda, meanwhile, was the Ottoman strategic outpost, the mission-control centre from which the campaigns of the frontier were administered. The lower register of Rossi's map contains the emblems of Habsburg rule: the implements of war, the crown, and the double-headed eagle that served as a symbol of sovereignty and militarism. The eagle's necks and wings enclose the *confini* inscribed in the legend cartouche. Finally, the upper register of the map contains three portrait medallions, posed almost like busts. These figures stare haughtily out at the viewer, their position (overlooking Vienna and the Danube) leaving no doubt regarding whose possession is being certified in this map, which was published to celebrate the Habsburg victory over the Ottomans in 1683. John III Sobieski of Poland, a champion of the battle, is shown at left, Leopold I, Holy Roman emperor, at centre, and Charles V, duke of Lorraine, a commander of the Imperial Army ("Caesar's army") at right.

This map conveys the thwarting of Ottoman ambitions to push further into Europe, and the individual responsibility of specific rulers to protect the borderlands and their people. The icons and the personnel of empire thus frame the mapping of victory. It was not uncommon for Italian map-makers to pitch their maps to foreign kings, but in this case mapping the siege of Vienna had broader implications than the seeking of patronage. The Ottoman defeat was commemorated throughout Christian Europe, a symbol of the limits of Ottoman reach and, as it was hoped, an indicator of Christian victories to

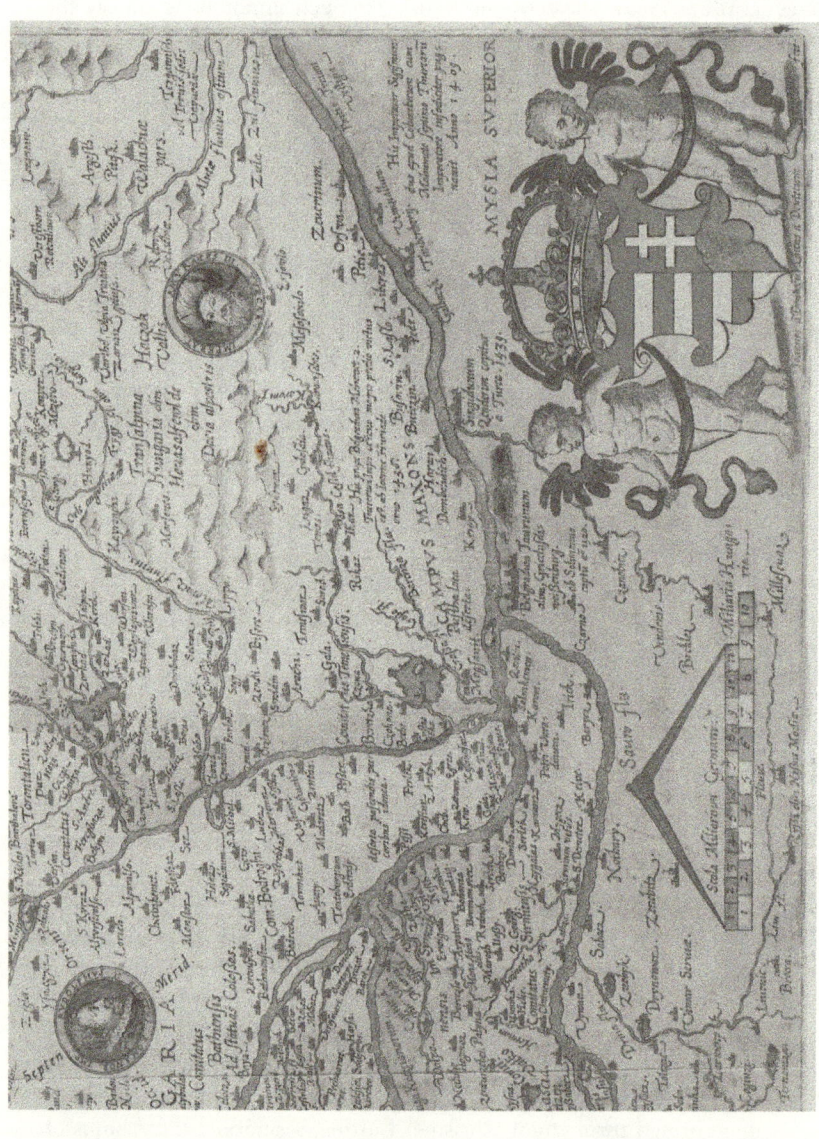

Figure 2.1 Variant by Gerhard de Jode, Antwerp, ca 1578, of Matthias Zündt, *Hungariae Totius*, Nuremberg, 1567. Harvard Map Collection.

come. Unlike Konstantine's letter to Isabella, Christian unity remains a subtext here; there are no crosses. Indeed, Christian unity never materialized amidst the rivalries of the early modern Christian monarchs, although it loomed very large in the rhetorics of the anti-Ottoman struggle. Much more directly we see an assertion of Habsburg claims and power, the notion that the Habsburg Empire, aided by its allies, might finally restore to Christian dominion the European lands lost to the Ottomans.

Ottoman cartographers also stamped the faces (and bodies) of their rulers onto contested space in order to map territory, celebrate victory, and assert imperial claims. There were no animal mascots, like the Habsburg eagle or the Venetian lion, and the sultan's artists mapped territory in the pages of illustrated campaign books in the forms dictated by the styles of Ottoman miniature painting rather than in portrait medallions.[23] Nonetheless the message in Ottoman imagery was much the same as that found in the engravings of Zündt and Rossi: "This territory is mine." It was a message of possession and entitlement. As in the maps emerging out of Christian Europe, the Ottomans mapped space in fortresses, personalities, confrontations, and acts of submission.[24] Their illustrated campaign books were a celebration of victory and power that showed the stages of the campaign, focusing on the city fortresses that were the stopping-points on the way, the places at which battles were fought, sieges undertaken, and surrender accepted.

Thus, for example, Lokman ibn Seyyid Hussein's (d. 1601–2) famed *Hünername* (Book of accomplishments) depicts the sultan, Süleiman I (r. 1520–66), seated before the fortress of Buda accepting homage from Prince John Zapolya and his regent mother (figure 2.3).[25] The fortress here is a very real symbol of the frontier, because Süleiman's army had to come to relieve the outpost city when it was attacked by the Habsburg Ferdinand I, later Holy Roman emperor (1558–64).[26] Süleiman, his men, his tents, and his cannons all mark this as Ottoman space. And although the pre-eminent message here is one of military and political power, there is also one of religious unity embodied in the two men poised on the tower at the upper right of the image, apparently issuing the call to prayer and invoking Süleiman's name, a reminder that the sovereignty being claimed was Islamic. Nonetheless, like the Christian kings of Europe, the Muslim kings of the oikumene were more interested in expanding their imperial power than in uniting as Muslim lords against the Christian foes. And in this case the message was as much Süleiman's claim to paramountcy in the Islamic world as it was a Muslim rallying cry against Christendom.

Ottoman imagery might also suggest frontiers in the seascape of the Mediterranean. The best known of these images are the numerous maps found in the *Kitab-ı Bahriye* (Book of the sea) of Piri Reis (ca 1470–1554), the famous

Figure 2.2 Matteo Rossi, *Dimostratione de Confini delle principale Città dell' Austria et Ungaria (Vienna assediata dal Turco)*, Rome, 1683. British Library Board (Maps K. Top. 90.31.2).

Mapping Trans-Imperial Ottoman Space 45

Figure 2.3 Seyyid Lokman, *Hünername*, Istanbul, ca 1588. Submission of John Zapolya to Süleiman at Buda. Topkapı Palace Museum.

Ottoman cartographer of the sixteenth century.[27] But the stages of conquest and confrontation by land and sea were also mapped by the Ottoman commander Matrakçı Nasuh, who documented Süleiman's march to Baghdad in 1535, and Hungarian campaign of 1542–3, as well as the exploits of the naval commander Hayrettin Barbarossa in the Mediterranean (1542–4).[28] Matrakçı's *Tarih-i Feth-i Şikloş* (History of the Conquest of Siklós) pictures a joint Ottoman and French fleet attacking Nice (figure 2.4).[29] This image suggests a sea frontier, one that represented the far reaches of Ottoman power along the northern coast of the Mediterranean. The attack, in August 1543, was timed to coincide with Süleiman's march into Hungary, a double-pronged assault against the Habsburgs. It was a function of Süleiman's alliance with Francis I (r. 1515–47) of France against the Holy Roman Emperor Charles V (r. 1519–56).[30] The port of Nice, like Buda, was forced to signal its submission, although unlike Buda it did not remain an Ottoman possession or a significant factor in the Ottoman-Habsburg wars. Nonetheless, here again one sees a portrait of a city facing the engines of war. And while the visual may seem tame compared with some European Christian maps of naval confrontations, its message of hegemony is straightforward. Matrakçı wanted his lord and the Ottoman court to see this image of Ottoman power projected all the way to the French countryside. While Matrakçı's maps sometimes included references to religion, their more explicit point was possession. Territory was claimed in regions (e.g., Rumelia, Anatolia, or "the two lands and the two seas") but it was also claimed one fortress and one port at a time. These (along with sacred places like Baghdad or Jerusalem) were the pre-eminent measures of imperial space, on the map and in narrative, regardless of whether the crafting of space originated in Ottoman territory or in the lands of the Christian kings.

Space as a series of contested, fortified places is also the message in the French cartographer Nicolas Sanson's (1600–67) *Le Course du Danube Depuis sa Source Iusqu'a ses Embouchures*, reworked by Hubert Jaillot in 1693.[31] The primary import of this map, as the title suggests, is the great sweep of the Danube all the way to its mouth in the Black Sea. But across the bottom of the map a set of fortress vignettes is depicted, from Varadin (Petrovaradin in Serbia) to Constantinople, all sites that had fallen to the "Turk," as their captions explain. Vienna does not appear as a significant frontier in this map (as it does in Rossi's), but there is no ignoring that much of the Danube lies in Ottoman domains. Thus the rivalry of Ottoman sultan and Christian kings holds pride of place in the large decorative cartouche found at the lower left-hand side of the map (figure 2.5). The legend box is framed by implements of war: flags, an Ottoman horsetail standard (*tugh*), and an eagle at the top. Male figures of the rivers Danube, Sava, and Drava recline at the bottom. Again we see the use of portrait medallions to indicate possession or entitlement. An image of Pope Innocent XII (r. 1691–1700) surmounts those of Joseph I, king of Hungary (r. 1687–1711); Emperor Leopold I (r. 1658–1705); John III Sobieski of Poland (r. 1674–96), champion of the relief of Vienna in 1683; and Maximilian Emanuel II of Bavaria (r. 1679–1726), who seized Belgrade from the Ottomans in 1688. The history of the Habsburg-Ottoman confrontation is thus a critical

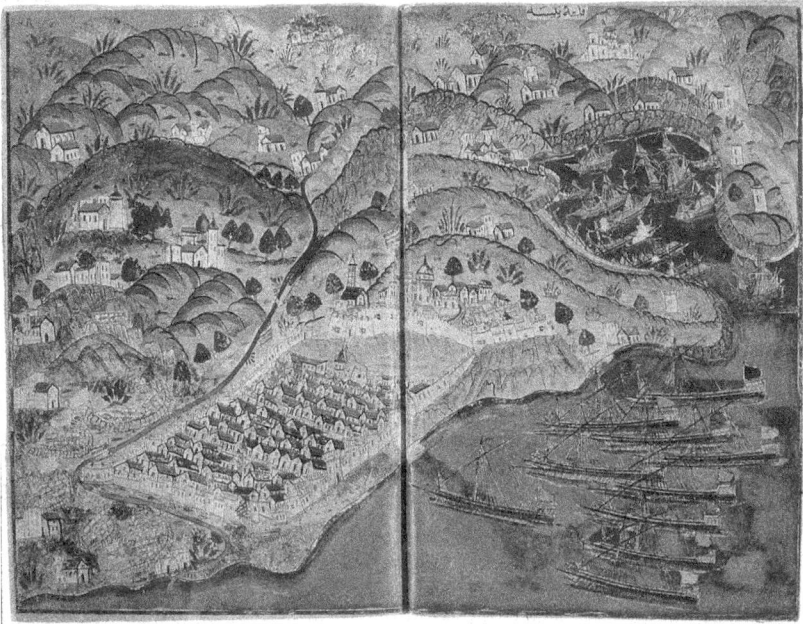

Figure 2.4 Matrakçı Nasuh, *Tarih-i Feth-Şikloş*. Attack on Nice in 1543. Topkapı Palace Museum.

frame for the representation of the Danube, whose possessors and protectors occupy the medallions.

The pope's superior position in the hierarchy of rulers signals the religious message of the map, which is made explicit in the figures that grace both sides of the cartouche. To the left, a hooded figure holding a chalice and host rests his (or possibly her) foot on a fallen man whose hand is placed on a copy of the Qur'an. The fallen man covers his eyes, perhaps an indication that he was once a Christian but had "turned Turk," reflecting the acute Christian anxieties about conversion to Islam. To the right side of the cartouche is a helmeted warrior, his sword poised over his head. He stands on another fallen man, this one grasping a broken bow, a turban on his head. These figures surround the word *Danube* on the legend cartouche, trumpeting the current and impending victories of Christendom and the men who can and presumably will affect this humiliation of the "Turk" and of Islam. They invoke a woeful past, of Ottoman victories and Christian conversions, and a glorious future, one in which the victories at Vienna and Belgrade are indicators of what is to come. Despite the crescents perched on the towers of the fortress vignettes, the map leaves no doubt concerning the true "owners" of the Danubian space. Imperium would be defined by conflict, and the "Turk" would remain indelibly the foreign foe.

But the Ottomans had become firmly ensconced in Europe, and the longer they stayed there, the more imperative it became for authors and artists to recognize that presence in text and image (as Zündt had with his portrait medallions). On the map, that recognition led to images of both conflict and coexistence. Thus I conclude with the cartouches from two early eighteenth-century maps, one presenting the "yoke" of the "Turk" on Europe, and the other suggesting the possibilities for new and enhanced commercial networks that the emergence of the expansive Ottoman Empire had created.

The first of these is another map of the Danube, although in this case the river serves as the northern border of "Turquie en Europe," a designation that was popularized in the seventeenth century. That designation by default indicated the Ottoman domains in Europe. But what concerns us here is the cartouche on this map, from the atelier of Pieter Van der Aa (1659–1733) in Leiden, dating to around 1729 (figures 2.6 and 2.7).[32] To the left one sees a quintessential embodiment of the empire, a janissary (the Ottoman gunpowder-armed, infantry soldier) distinguished by his plumed hat. But he is not a ferocious, threatening figure. Rather he appears to be smiling at his counterpart to the right of the legend box, apparently a European merchant. In the background other Europeans converse before the busy harbour of an unidentified city. The whole scene suggests productivity and prosperous trade. This is the "Turk" who has made "Turkey in Europe" a land of opportunity for some of the residents of the Christian kingdoms; he is a fraternizer, a familiar figure, his gun slung over his shoulder rather than pointed at an enemy.

A counterpart to this map, also showing Turkey in Europe, paints a rather different picture of the effects of Ottoman rule. This is the *Map of Greece* crafted in 1720 by the English cartographer John Senex (1678–1740).[33] In the cartouche, we again find a Turk figure, but he is not benign (figure 2.8). Rather he is posed over the seated figures (woman, child, and man) of Christian captives. He is holding a sword in one hand and a yoke in the other. The captives are shackled, while broken statuary lies at their feet. And the crescent emblem used in the Christian kingdoms to represent the Ottoman Empire is planted at the top of the cartouche.[34] This is an enduring representation of the notion that the Ottoman conquest of Greece brought ruin to a classical, Christian, and productive land. The idea of Greece, Christendom, and history enslaved appears in many forms in the literature and artistry of the early modern Christian kingdoms. Thus, for example, a small format book published at Oxford in 1618 had told the tale of "Christopher Angell, A Grecian, who tasted of many stripes and torments

Figure 2.5 Nicolas Sanson/Hubert Jaillot, *Le Course du Danube Depuis sa Source Iusqu'a ses Embouchures*, cartouche, Paris, 1693. Harvard Map Collection.

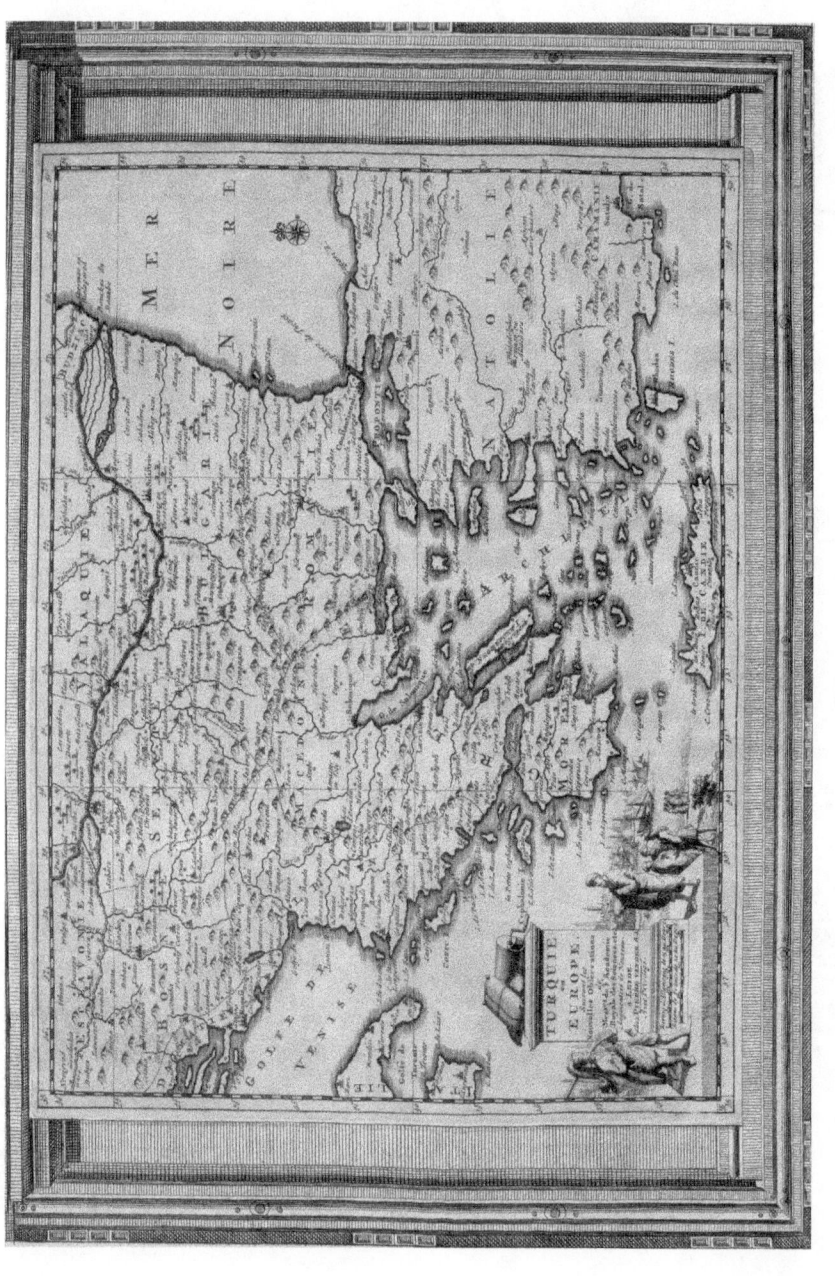

Figure 2.6 *Turquie en Europe*, by Pieter Van der Aa, Leiden [1729?]. Reproduced with permission by the Map Collection. The University of Melbourne Library.

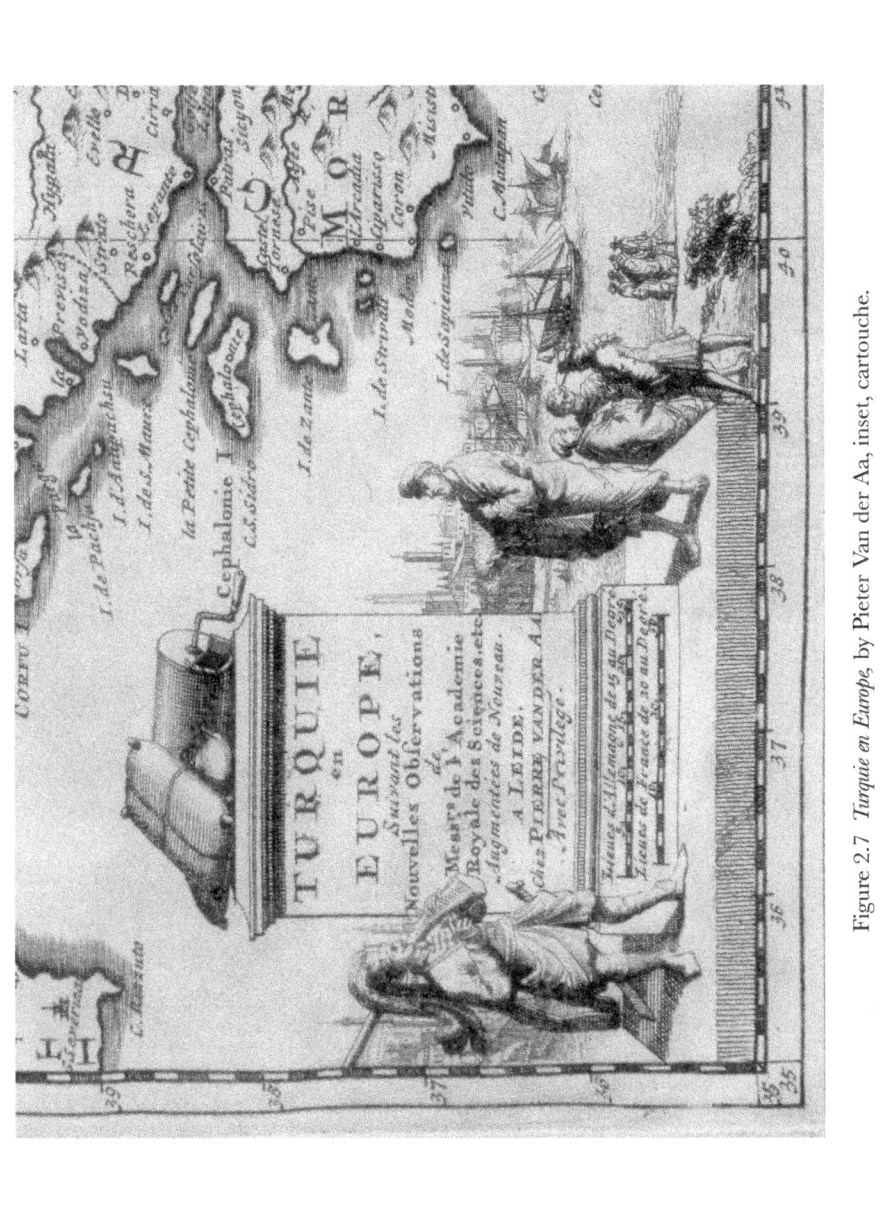

Figure 2.7 *Turquie en Europe*, by Pieter Van der Aa, inset, cartouche.

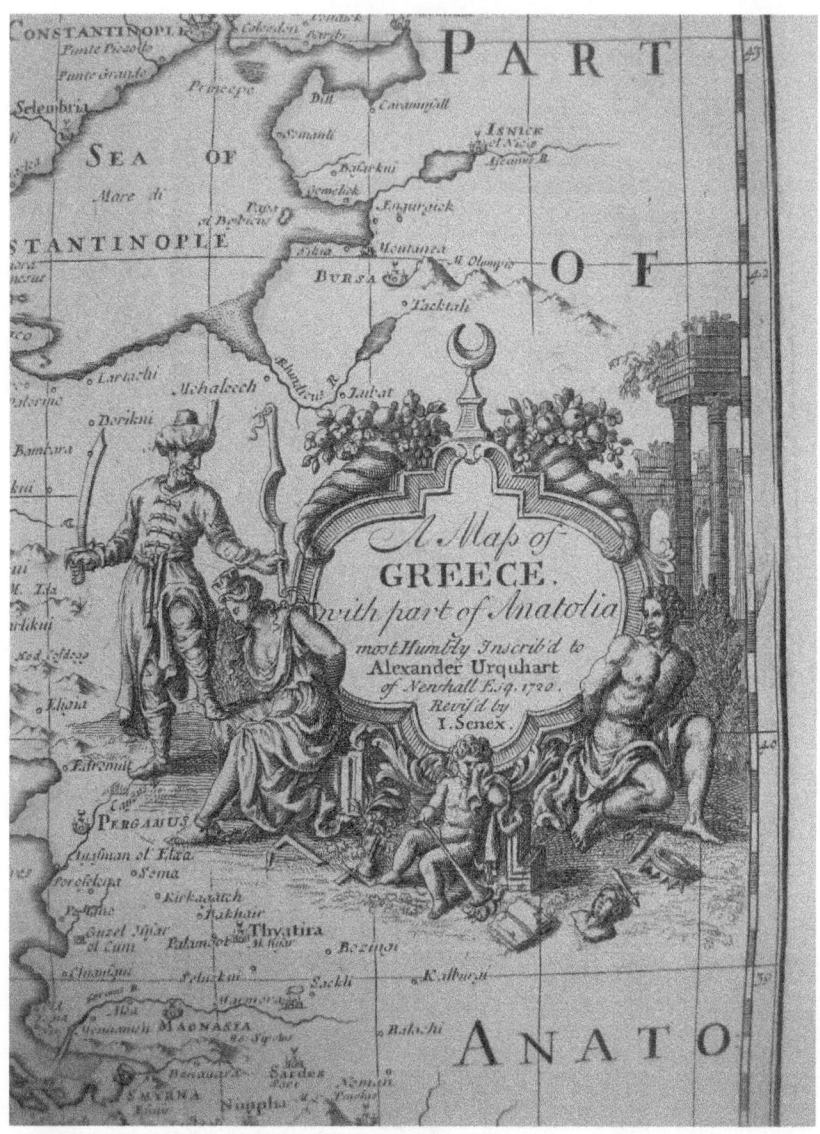

Figure 2.8 John Senex, *A Map of Greece with Part of Anatolia*, cartouche, London, 1720. Library of Congress, Washington, DC, G1015.S57.

inflicted by the Turkes," before he escaped to England.[35] The "Turk" in such imagery is an exploiter, behaving in just the ways the book's readers might expect, and his captives are both allegorical figures of historical Greek culture and stand-ins for the actual Christians either taken as captives or "turned" to the infidelity of Islam. Senex's map presents to the audience what it thinks it already "knows" about the Turk, yet at the same time it redraws the boundaries of Christian unity and asks why Greece has yet to be redeemed – the same question that Choiseul-Gouffier and later Lord Byron would ask each in his turn.

By the eighteenth century the channels of communication between the Ottomans and their rivals were elaborate and wide-reaching. These imperial powers had long experience of the struggle to grasp territory and of the rhetorics that explained and pictured that struggle. And despite the long-standing pleas of rulers like Konstantine, the Christian lords of the West had not yet managed to redeem the old centres of Christendom from the "Turk." Indeed, as suggested by the episode of Choiseul-Gouffier, the Ottomans and their antagonists were involved in an ongoing dance of rivalry and rhetoric, one facilitated by the mapping of well-known space and the verbal and pictorial translation of a well-known "other." Coats of arms, fortresses, sacred spaces, the gaze of the monarch, and rhetorics of submission were all important mechanisms for designating possession. As rulers articulated boundaries through processes of negotiation, intimidation, and representation, they employed maps to promote their claims and to celebrate their victories. On the map, possession might be something already accomplished through conquest or it might exist only in the imperial imagination.

NOTES

1 The term *space* in this chapter means more than territory. It means territory infused with its sovereign and cultural identities, and attended by rhetorics of entitlement and possession. The trans-imperial space between Ottoman, Habsburg, and Venetian empires was a place of multiple and broad (land and sea-based) frontier zones, where multiple and serial identities were prevalent, and where the imperial centres claimed but did not routinely or consistently control territory.
2 Gülru Necipoğlu, "Süleyman the Magnificent and the Representation of Power in the Context of Ottoman-Habsburg-Papal Rivalry," *Art Bulletin* 71, no. 3 (1989): 401–27, esp. 409–10.
3 See Tijana Krstić, *Contested Conversion to Islam: Narratives of Religious Change in the Early Modern Ottoman Empire* (Stanford: Stanford University Press, 2011), 1.

4 Bronwen Wilson, *The World in Venice: Print, the City, and Early Modern Identity* (Toronto: University of Toronto Press, 2005), 147, notes that in Venice, the "Turks" were "too familiar to be made exotic." That characterization may be juxtaposed to the more familiar trope, expressed by the Venetian scholar Francesco Sansovino (1521–86), that the Ottomans were distinguished by their "alterity," pomposity, and hauteur (143).

5 Walter Andrews and Mehmet Kalpaklı, *The Age of Beloveds* (Durham: Duke University Press, 2005).

6 Natalie Rothman, personal communication.

7 Robert Dankoff, *An Ottoman Mentality: The World of Evliya Çelebi* (Leiden: Brill, 2004), xii–xv, 1–6.

8 *Evliya Çelebi in Diyarbekir*, ed. and trans. Martin van Bruinessen and Hendrik Boeschoten (Leiden: Brill, 1988), 172–3.

9 Evliya Çelebi, *Evliya Çelebi in Albania and Adjacent Regions (Kosovo, Montenegro, Ohrid): The Relevant Sections of the Seyahatname*, ed. and trans. Robert Dankoff and Robert Elsie (Brill: Leiden, 2000), 85, 93, 19. See also John Covel, *Voyages en Turquie 1675–1677*, trans. Jean-Pierre Grélois (Paris: Éditions P. Lethielleux, 1998), 90–3. The narrative of Dr John Covel, a Cambridge University graduate and an exact contemporary of Evliya's, demonstrates the similarities in the ways in which a Christian, like a Muslim narrator, might tell the spaces of the Ottomans' European frontier zones. Both Evliya and Covel make a point of commenting upon the "strange" cross-communal customs and behaviours of the peoples of Ottoman Europe (Covel at Edirne and Evliya in Albania). Each one types those he meets by ethnicity, and each one manages to conjure fanciful and sexual tales of local women.

10 Faruk Bilici, *XIV Louis ve İstanbul'u Fetih Tasarısı* (Ankara: Türk Tarih Kurumu, 2004), 175–95, also 98–101 on French claims. In 1685, Louis XIV seems to have commissioned one Gravier d'Ortières to carry out a reconnaissance mission to the Ottoman Empire with a view to conquering Constantinople. D'Ortières delivered a report on the possibilities, complemented with an elaborate set of maps, sketches, and views, now housed in the Bibliothèque nationale. My thanks to John-Paul Ghobrial for this reference.

11 Virginia Aksan, "Choiseul-Gouffier at the Sublime Porte 1784–1792," in *Ottomans and Europeans: Contacts and Conflicts, Analecta Isisiana* (Istanbul: Isis, 2004), 75:61, 65.

12 Ibid., 61, 64.

13 I do not have access to the first edition of Choiseul-Gouffier's work. But the second augmented edition of his voyages, Marie Gabriel Florent Auguste de Choiseul-Gouffier, *Voyage Pittoresque dans l'empire Ottoman, en Grece ...*, 2nd ed. (Paris: Librairie de J.P. Aillaud, 1842), 2:10–17, was rich in maps and plans and included in the second volume a paean to the mappers of the Mediterranean from the Greek ancients to early modern French cartographers.

14 The Ottoman ambassador to Paris in 1720–1, Yirmisekiz Çelebi Mehmet Efendi, recorded his experiences of French nation and sovereignty. See Mehmed Efendi, *Le paradis des infidèles: Un ambassadeur ottoman en France sous la Régence*, trans. Julien-Claude Galland, ed. Gilles Veinstein (Paris: François Maspero, 1981).

15 Elguja Khintibidze, "Negotiations between the Georgian and Spanish Kings at the End of the Fifteenth Century," in *Jews, Christians, and Muslims in the Mediterranean World after 1492*, ed. Alisa Meyuhas Ginio (London: Frank Cass, 1992), 79, 80. The words, "Of Constantinople, Trebizond, and other Christian countries, we remain alone," expressed the Georgian ruler's sense of isolation.

16 Ibid., 81–2. Khintibidze sees this correspondence as an indication of "a change in the Mediterranean world's perception of geographical boundaries following the Ottoman conquest of Constantinople and the downfall of the Byzantine Empire" (82) and as evidence of "the emergence of [new] religious coalitions in the Mediterranean world" (84). I am inclined to see the correspondence rather as representative of ongoing political opportunism in conjunction with some geographic wishful thinking, rather like early sixteenth-century Christian hopes for Shah Ismail Safavi in Iran as an ally and saviour against the Ottomans.

17 Kiril Petkov, *Infidels, Turks, and Women: The South Slavs in the German Mind, ca 1400–1600* (Frankfurt: Peter Lang, 1997), 199. Petkov suggests, "The massive loss of Christian territories during the fourteenth and fifteenth century brought about this equation of the terms Christian and European."

18 Vincenzo Coronelli, *Conquiste della Serenissima Republica di Venezia Nella Dalmatia, Epiro, e Morea* (Venice: 1686), 24r. Crete was finally conquered in 1669.

19 Ibid. In his map, "Disegno Topografico del Canale di Cattaro," Venice, 1688, Coronelli depicts Risano with a small legend that reads, "Risano, a land of 150 houses loyal [*datasi alla devotione*] to the Republic." The legend, dated 1684, expresses the ambiguous position of the city, caught between empires.

20 Robert Karrow, *Mapmakers of the Sixteenth Century and Their Maps* (Chicago: Newberry Library, 1993), 618–19, notes that Gerard de Jode in Antwerp "made a reduced copy" for his *Speculum orbis terrarum* in 1578. The original by Zündt, done in Nuremberg in 1567, did not contain the portrait medallions. The Harvard Map Collection dates this particular map to 1593, which could mean that it was produced by de Jode's son, Cornelis de Jode.

21 On the Ottoman Balkan wars of the time, see Stanford Shaw, *History of the Ottoman Empire and Modern Turkey*, vol. 1, *Empire of the Gazis* (Cambridge: Cambridge University Press, 1976), 46–51; and Caroline Finkel, *Osman's Dream: The Story of the Ottoman Empire 1300–1923* (New York: Basic Books, 2005), 41–4.

22 See David Woodward, "The Italian Map Trade, 1480–1650," in *History of Cartography*, vol. 3, pt 1, *Cartography in the European Renaissance*, ed. David Woodward, 773–803 (Chicago: University of Chicago Press, 2007), on the evolution of the Italian map trade.

23 See Ayşe Orbay, *The Sultan's Portrait: Picturing the House of Osman* (Istanbul: İşbank, 2000).
24 See Palmira Brummett, "The Fortress: Defining and Mapping the Ottoman Frontier in the 16th–17th Centuries," in *Frontiers of the Ottoman World: Proceedings of the British Academy*, ed. Andrew Peacock, 31–55 (Oxford: Oxford University Press, 2009).
25 Lokman, *Hünername*, Topkapı Sarayı Müzesi, Ms. Hazine 1524, fol. 266r. Zapolya was actually an infant at the time, not a boy as shown here. On Lokman, see H. Sohrweide, "Lukman b. Sayyid Husayn," in *Encyclopedia of Islam*, CD-ROM ed., v.1.0. (Leiden: Brill, 1999). On the *Hünername*, see Metin And, *Turkish Miniature Painting: The Ottoman Period* (Istanbul: Dost, 1987), 32, 105–10, 114. See also Gábor Barta, "IV. The First Period of the Principality of Transylvania (1526–1606)," in *History of Transylvania*, gen. ed. Béla Köpecki, ed. English trans. Bennett Kovrig, trans. Péter Szaffkó, Social Science Monographs no. 581 (New York: Columbia University Press, 2001), 1:606–19; and Palmira Brummett, "A Kiss Is Just a Kiss: Rituals of Submission along the East-West Divide," in *Cultural Encounters between East and West: 1453–1699*, ed. Matthew Birchwood and Matthew Dimmock, 107–31 (Newcastle-upon-Tyne: Cambridge Scholars, 2005).
26 For different types of Ottoman mapping, see the 1565 map, or siege (*kuşatma*) plan of Mustafa Pasha for Malta, and an illustration of the siege of İnebahtı from Katib Çelebi's *Tuhfet ül-kibar*, Topkapı Sarayı Müzesi, YY. 1118, and R. 1192, vr.17a, in Idris Bostan, *Kürekli ve Yelkenli Osmanlı Gemileri* (Istanbul: Bilge, 2005), 78–9, 88–9. Gábor Ágoston, "Information, Ideology, and Limits of Imperial Policy: Ottoman Grand Strategy in the Context of Ottoman-Habsburg Rivalry," in *The Early Modern Ottoman Empire: Remapping the Empire*, ed. Virginia H. Aksan and Daniel Goffman (New York: Cambridge University Press, 2007), 89, shows that Üveys Pasha, governor of Buda from 1578 to 1580, "prepared a detailed and surprisingly accurate map of the region [around Kanizsa in Transdanubia], which indicated all the fortresses and the major river crossings, and sent it to Istanbul."
27 Svat Soucek, "Islamic Charting in the Mediterranean," in *History of Cartography*, vol. 2, bk 1, *Cartography in the Traditional Islamic and South Asian Societies*, ed. J.B. Harley and David Woodward (Chicago: University of Chicago Press, 1992), esp. 266–9.
28 See Matrakçı Nasuh, *Nasūhü's-Silāhī (Matrākçī), Beyān-ı Menāzil-i Sefer-i 'Irākeyn*, ed. and comm. H.G. Yurdaydın (Ankara: Türk Tarih Kurumu Basımevi, 1976), esp. 245–9. Matrakçı's *Menazil*, on the Baghdad campaign, highlighted Süleiman's entitlement to rule the sacred sites of Iraq, like the mosque-tomb of Imam Hussein. His image of that tomb conveyed to the viewer that Süleiman, and not the Safavid Shah in Iran, was king of kings.
29 J.M. Rogers, "Itineraries and Town Views in Ottoman Histories," in Harley and Woodward, *History of Cartography*, vol. 2, bk 1, esp. 245. There is some debate

regarding who exactly produced Matrakçı's images and when. In any case, there are significant differences between the images produced on the Baghdad campaign and those illustrating the ports of the Mediterranean. For a later Ottoman-French collaboration, see Gilles Veinstein, "Les préparatifs de la campagne navale franco-turque de 1552 à travers les ordres du Divan ottoman," *Revue de l'Occident musulman et de la Méditerranée* 39, no. 1 (1985): 35–67.

30 For a set of explorations of these imperial rivalries, see Halil İnalcık and Cemal Kafadar, eds., *Süleymân the Second and His Time* (Istanbul: Isis, 1993).
31 Nicolas Sanson and Hubert Jaillot, "Le Course du Danube Depuis da Source Iusqu'a ses Embouchures" (Paris, 1693).
32 Pieter Van der Aa, "Turquie en Europe," ca 1729, Map Collection, University of Melbourne Library. For a very similar cartouche presumably modelled on Van der Aa, see Emanuel Bowen, "A New and Accurate Map of Turky in Europe," London [ca 1752].
33 John Senex, *A New General Atlas* (London: D. Browne, 1721), 120.
34 See Nurhan Atasoy and Lale Uluç, *Impressions of Ottoman Culture in Europe: 1453–1699* (Istanbul: Turkish Cultural Foundation, 2012), 369–75, esp. 375, on the ways in which the Ottomans did and did not use the crescent.
35 Christopher Angelos, *Christopher Angell, A Grecian, who tasted of many stripes and torments inflicted by the Turkes for the faith which he had in Christ Iesus* (Oxford: John Lichfield and James Short, 1618). Interestingly the author claims that when he was seized upon by the "Hagarene" Ottoman governor in Athens, he was accused of being "a traitorous Spaniard, as we know by his beard … and his clothes" (3r).

chapter three

Europe's Turkish Nemesis

LARRY SILVER

Across the Christian-Muslim frontier during the sixteenth century, the threat of military attack, as well as the ideological war against the alien religion of Islam, preoccupied the consciousness and created a climate of fear in European Christian states. Nowhere was this anxiety concerning the rival superpower greater than within the loose German-speaking confederation known as the Holy Roman Empire, led by Habsburg emperor Maximilian I (r. 1493–1519).[1] Indeed the eventual frontier between Catholics and Muslims, established after the battle of Mohács in Hungary (1526), still coincides almost exactly with the modern, hostile frontier between Catholic Croatia and Orthodox Serbia (Catholics and Orthodox Christians who remained behind the Ottoman lines were forced to convert to Islam and became the Muslims of Bosnia-Herzegovina).

In an atlas map of the Danube watershed by Willem Blaeu, produced by his son Joan Blaeu in Amsterdam during the 1630s, we see this confrontation institutionalized around the image caption (figure 3.1). Here this heightened awareness of both a political and religious frontier, manned against a mysterious and foreign enemy at the border, is personified by the confrontation of two pairs of figures. On one side, the east, a sultan with an elaborate turban brandishes his scimitar above a round shield with the crescent moon of Islam. His female companion, surely an allegory of the Muslim faith, stands contemptuously upon a crucifix and dispenses incense smoke; but she is scantily clad in a revealingly low-cut dress and certainly is not a figure to admire. In case the viewer missed these obvious cues, a noxious toad rests on the ground between these Ottoman personifications. By contrast, on the western side of the standoff, a handsome bearded ruler figure in armour confronts this enemy with a broadsword. His shield displays the double-headed eagle of the Holy Roman Empire, and his crown resembles the official *Bügelkrone*; complementing his orb of office, he wears the pendant of the Order of the Golden Fleece, headed by the Habsburgs. His

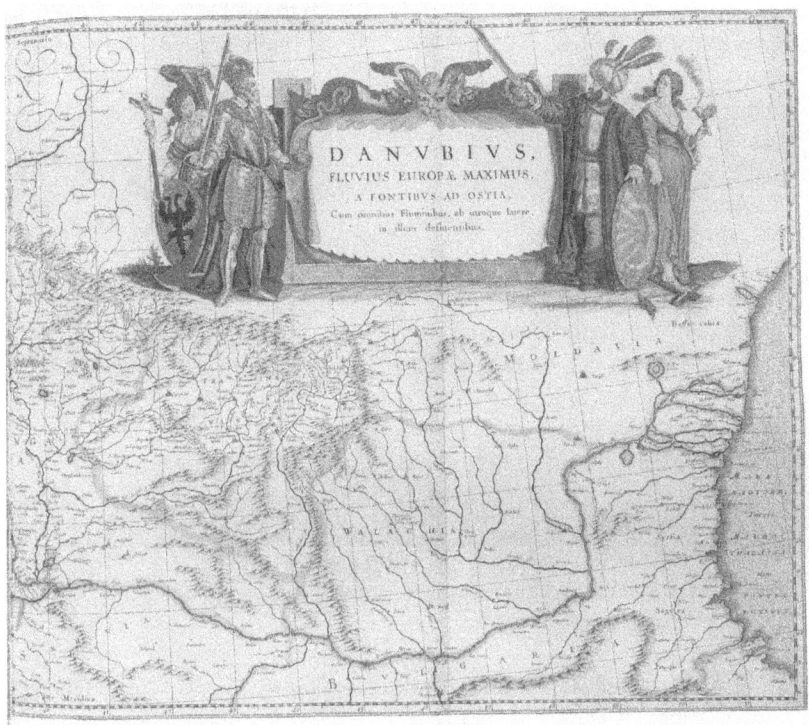

Figure 3.1 Willem Blaeu, *Danubius Fluvius*, from his Atlas, engraving (published Amsterdam, 1635).

female companion, who personifies Christianity, holds her crucifix upright and wears a modest gown.

This chapter will examine sixteenth-century imagery that represents the Turks from the perspective of the European side of that boundary. Habsburg rulers in Central Europe, but also their cousins in imperial Iberia, saw themselves as the defenders of the Christian faith against their Islamic nemesis, the powerful militaristic empire of Ottoman sultans. We shall see that their depictions range from caricatures of Turks as sadists to a more carefully observed attention to fascinating foreign costumes and customs.

Throughout the sixteenth century, leading Christian thinkers regarded Turks in apocalyptic terms as a scourge of God. This attitude began early: we can already find it prominently advanced in Sebastian Brant's 1494 *Ship of Fools*.[2] In chapter 99, "Of the Decline of the Faith," Brant intones about Christendom,

> At first the cruel heretic
> Did tear and wound it to the quick
> And then Mohammed shamefully
> Abused its noble sanctity
> With heresy and base intent ...
> So strong the Turks have grown to be
> They hold the ocean not alone
> The Danube too is now their own
> They make their inroads when they will,
> Bishoprics, churches, suffer ill.

But the poet places his trust in the young emperor-elect as the antidote:

> The noble Maximilian,
> He merits well the Roman crown.
> They'll surely come into his hand,
> The Holy Earth, the Promised Land.

Many of the woodcut illustrations in Brant's popular volume were designed by the young Albrecht Dürer (1471–1528), the same artist who produced some of the earliest German images of Ottoman Turks. In contrast to the substantial – if contested –boundaries between Germans and Turks along the Danube, Venice had fluctuating but intimate links across the Mediterranean with its Ottoman neighbours, sometimes wartime antagonists but occasionally trading and treaty partners across the sixteenth century. Thus, beginning with his first visit to Venice in 1494, Dürer could turn his omnivorous gaze to the substantial local community of Turkish visitors, documenting their exotic dress.[3] He engaged seriously with this unfamiliar nationality, and his curiosity resulted in a series of drawings that emphasize distinctive costumes.[4] Some of these coloured drawings of "Orientals" by Dürer (Winkler cat. nos 79–81) survive in copies, indicating their importance as models, used for later reference by his many followers and credited with an on-site accuracy. However, several of these drawings actually derive, not from studies of costumed models, but rather from earlier artworks by local Venetian painters, particularly Gentile Bellini, who had even visited Istanbul earlier (1479–81) on a diplomatic mission.[5] Other Dürer drawings expressly focus on the military trappings and skills of Turkish soldiers, specifically their archery (Winkler cat. nos 80–1; Ambrosiana, Milan). This other preoccupation – a focus on Turks as formidable military enemies – would strongly influence not only Dürer's own presentations but also those of many of his later German followers.

In the wake of his 1494 visit to Venice, Dürer also produced a drawing study (Winkler cat. no. 77, Washington, National Gallery) for an uncompleted engraving: an *Oriental Ruler Seated on His Throne* (ca 1496/7).[6] In this fantasy image any actual experience of Turks in Venice is overwhelmed by an intimidating suggestion of both power and majesty as well as menace. Details of exotic foreign costume still preoccupy the artist. A distinctive crowned turban (probably imaginary) marks the royal rank and status of this frontal, enthroned figure; its encrusted jewels are echoed on his robes, highlighted by an enormous necklace with pendant.[7] Exotic details of the costume speak to its "Asiatic" character: fringes added to the robe as well as the footwear of sandals beneath it. Both power and authority of this ruler are conveyed, respectively, by a huge, two-handed battle sword in his right hand and by an orb in his left. While akin to the ceremonial orb of the Holy Roman Empire, proudly guarded at Dürer's hometown of Nuremberg, the orb in the drawing significantly lacks the surmounting cross of imperial Christian regalia. The threatening authority of this bearded potentate is further enhanced by his menacing expression; despite his formal frontality, his eyes turn away to scowl out of the frame, as a kind of negative inversion of holy icons of the face of Jesus.[8] This image clearly does not record a portrait of a particular Ottoman sultan; instead, it uses a figure of authority to personify the perceived threat of Turkish Islam to Christendom. Indeed, Dürer would soon adapt this enthroned orientalist ruler as the persecuting emperor Domitian in the woodcut scene of the *Martyrdom of St John*, the first illustration of his 1498 publication of the *Apocalypse*. Here the contrast drawn distinguishes between ancient paganism and Roman emperors as the persecutors of Christian martyrs. This distinction contains irony, of course, in light of the fact that both the holy Roman emperor (dating back to Charlemagne and an era of Christian rulers who claimed connection to Rome) and the Ottoman sultan each claimed his temporal authority from the legacy of the Roman Empire (as did the Byzantine emperors of Constantinople of the Eastern Roman Empire, and through them, the Russian tsars, whose very title stems from "caesars").

At the end of his career Dürer produced a very different image of a Turkish ruler, the profile "portrait" of ruling Sultan Süleyman (monogrammed and dated 1526; Musée Bonnat, Bayonne, W. 906), in silverpoint, the artist's favoured medium for portrait drawings.[9] Its profile presentation suggests that the German artist had access to a portrait prototype, almost surely derived from a Venetian painter, in the form of a medal.[10] In fact, a specific source survives: a silver medal in which the profile faces the opposite way but with the bust truncated at the same point of the chest and shoulders. There the sultan wears the same turban as in Dürer's silverpoint, and he is identified by an inscription in the block Latin letters, "SULEYMAN.CAESAR 'TURCARUM / MELECK. ET. ARAB. TURC."[11] Both the medal of Süleyman and the Dürer profile drawing present the same distinctive long neck and prominent nose and lips. Around a decade later a Venetian painter close to Titian painted a bust of a young, moustachioed Sultan Süleyman in the same orientation as Dürer (ca 1530/40; Kunsthistorisches Museum, Vienna), presumably using the same visual source.[12] Thus for the specific likeness of a ruler, even of one's avowed enemy, for Dürer and for medallists of the sixteenth century, profile conventions in combination with individualized facial features predominated over any impulse to exaggerate or editorialize.

In 1508, in response to a commission by one of his principal courtly patrons, Frederick the Wise of Saxony, Dürer painted an image to commemorate martyrs' relics held in the prince's extensive religious collection at Wittenberg. For this image, Dürer again cast the Turks as sadistic persecutors for *The Martyrdom of the Ten Thousand* (1508, Kunsthistorisches Museum, Vienna).[13] In this early Christian subject from the Middle East, the Persian king Sapor, acting on command of Emperor Diocletian of Rome, slaughtered the Christians of Bithynia (343 CE). Dürer had depicted this same subject already a decade earlier in a woodcut (ca 1497–8; Bartsch cat. no. 117). Both compositions show Christians tortured to death, tossed from cliffs by turbaned conquerors. In the painting, however, the martyrs' imitation of Christ is emphasized by two figures on crosses and a third standing awaiting execution; two wear crowns of thorns like Christ in the Passion, a clear medieval allusion to martyrdom and sainthood as an *imitatio Christi*, but now with the oppressors represented as Turks. In this case imperial Rome again forms the antipode to Christian martyrs, but the agents of torture are more expressly linked to modern Turks by costume and geography. Opposite, in the lower right corner, both standing and mounted figures with distinctive beards, complex turbans and colourful robes clearly conflate the ancient king, through dress, to the modern Turks. His sinister commands thus become fused with those of the religious enemies of Dürer's own day.

In addition, the painting also took on more personal significance for the artist, who included his self-portrait as a darkly clad witness in the centre, inscribing himself expressly as *Alberto Dürer aleman* (Albrecht Dürer, German), to link his identity still closer to his patron, an elector of the empire and the leading lieutenant to Emperor Maximilian. He also included a friend, plausibly identified with the recently deceased poet laureate of the empire, Conrad Celtis. Thus, Dürer fuses past with present and assimilates modern Ottomans onto historic persecutions of Christians in the Levant.[14]

The year 1529 marked the climax of the conflict between the forces of Holy Roman Empire and their enemies, the Ottoman Turks, then poised in siege at the gates of Vienna after an unbroken string of victories in the Balkans and along the Danube (a series highlighted by Belgrade 1521, Mohács and Buda, 1526). Not only did the advance of the armies of Sultan Süleyman (r. 1520–66) pose an immediate threat to the Habsburg rulers in their traditional capital, but ultimately the siege undermined their own Christian claims to universal monarchy – claims implicit in the title of "holy Roman emperor." This peril was actually redoubled by the contemporary "odd couple" alliance, especially after 1530, between the Ottomans and the Habsburgs' mortal enemy in Europe, King Francis I of France, an alliance that encompassed commercial privileges and non-aggression pacts, and culminated in coordinated military campaigns (1536–7).[15] Taken together, this period of political tension heightened Germanic national self-consciousness in the empire as the ultimate bulwark against further Turkish incursion.

The Siege of Vienna in 1529, a momentous event at the Habsburg capital that turned back the tide of Turkish advances into Continental Europe, received careful documentation in the form of a large (81.2 × 85.6 cm) multi-sheet commemorative woodcut, designed by Dürer's follower Sebald Beham and printed in Nuremberg by Nicolaus Meldemann from six blocks (1530).[16] The work had an official imprimatur, a privilege granted by the Nuremberg city council. The printmaker prized reportorial accuracy of battle details; topographical accuracy was emphasized as well, with all the views based on careful studies taken from the great tower of St Stephen's cathedral in the heart of the city. To document fully the defence against the troops of the Turks, the print shows the city at the pictorial centre; the siege itself outside the city walls is seen in the round from a bird's-eye view above the central cathedral tower.[17] This composite image visualizes actual troop movements, tents, and artillery explosions characteristic of contemporary practices of warfare. In the process, Beham's woodcut celebrates victory over Turkish invaders – even as it participates in the vogue for printed images of military documentaries.

Meldemann's local rival as publisher of woodcut broadsheets in Nuremberg, Hans Guldenmundt, printed his own commemoration of the great event as a pamphlet with text by local poet Hans Sachs and prints by Sebald Beham, as *The Three Besiegers of Vienna*. His procession series of Turkish officers and soldiers included archers, armed *spahis* (roughly akin to European knights), and earnest profile equestrian portraits of Turks on horses. These Turkish besiegers were led by Sultan Süleyman himself, along with his principal counsellor Ibrahim Pasha and General Sansaco (Geisberg cat. no. 297–9).[18] The source for these images stemmed from an earlier suite of five woodcuts, produced in the

Netherlands by Jan Swart of Groningen and dated 1526, the high-water mark of Ottoman conquests along the Danube.[19] These images thus were newsworthy while also catering to the ongoing fascination with Turkish costume, particularly headwear, as well as their exotic weapons and battle instruments (trumpet, bagpipe, and shawm). The sultan himself appears in profile at the centre, riding on horseback, accompanied by a lone foot soldier and labelled "Solimanus imperator Turcharum" with the date. Other mounted triads, variously dressed, are also labelled as "Mamelukes," "Arabs," and "heathens," respectively.

A darker side of Turks at war was produced in 1530 by Hans Guldenmundt at Nuremberg as a woodcut series to shape opinion and rally imperial troops in revenge for alleged atrocities in and around Vienna. Images (G. 1239–42), attributed to Erhard Schoen but freely adapted from Swart, now show mounted Turkish warriors leading pairs of captive Christians on foot with a rope around their necks; verses by Hans Sachs describe their cruel conditions.[20] Even worse is the image detail in one woodcut, showing a baby carried by one of them on his spear. The text laments how "the evil, gruesome Turk" has killed children, stolen sheep and cattle, burned down homes, and condemned Christian captives to slavery, pulling ploughs like animals. Worse still is the 1530 Guldenmundt/Schoen broadsheet woodcut collaboration recounting the threat to civilians by Turks on the outskirts of the Vienna Woods, showing them killing babies by impaling them on stakes or slicing them with scimitars.[21] Here the Sach poem reads:

> Oh Lord God on the highest throne /
> Look at this great misery /
> The Turkish raging tyrant
> Has carried out in the Vienna Woods /
> Murdering virgins and wives /
> Cutting children in half /
> And impaling them on pikes ...
> Oh, our shepherd Jesus Christ ...
> Save us from the hand of the Turk.

No friend to either papacy or empire, Martin Luther declared in his preface to the book of Revelation (1530; published in 1546) that the Turks were a scourge sent by God to chasten Christians on the eve of the apocalypse: "Here, now the devil's final wrath gets to work: there in the East is the second woe. Mohammed and the Saracens, here in the West are papacy and empire with the third woe. To these is added for good measure the Turk, Gog and Magog ... Thus Christendom is plagued most terribly and miserably, everywhere and on all sides, with false doctrines and with wars, with scroll and with sword."[22]

But for the current emperor, also defining himself as the defender of Christendom, the ongoing contest against the Turk was conceived as a crusade, so after Vienna in 1529, Emperor Charles V looked for an opportunity to go on the offensive and reverse Turkish conquests in mainland Europe. In doing so, he could reassert his imperial status as well as his leadership of the Christian faith. Based in Spain, he got his opportunity in 1535, when he led a campaign by fleet from Barcelona against the fortified city of Goleta, near Tunis. The 1535 campaign in the Maghreb fought Berber corsair Kheir-ed-Din (known in the Christian west as "Barbarossa"), admiral of the Turks in the Mediterranean. Equipped with four hundred ships and some thirty thousand soldiers, Charles V had set out to stop Muslim raids on Christian shipping and to secure maritime dominance over the sultan's fleets. Francis I of France, Charles V's nemesis, was supplying Barbarossa with arms while treating with Sultan Süleyman (thus forging an alliance between the two principal enemies of the empire). The proximate cause of war was Barbarossa's deposing of King Mulay Hasan of Tunis, a nominal vassal of the emperor. Andrea Doria of Genoa commanded the imperial fleet; land forces served under Alfonso d'Avalos, marquess of Vastos.

Commemorating and celebrating that (short-lived) victory, the emperor was later presented with a suite of tapestries, the most costly and luxurious of all media. Using the same panoramic design as an earlier tapestry cycle, celebrating the military spectacle of the 1525 Battle of Pavia (a 1525 victory over the French in Italy), designed for Charles V at the behest of Margaret of Austria by her court artist, Bernart van Orley. This twelve-part set on the Conquest of Tunis was woven in Brussels by Willem de Pannemaker (1549–54) after designs by Dutch artist Jan Vermeyen (who had been embedded with the invading troops, like current journalists in war), probably with the help of experienced tapestry designer Pieter Coecke van Aelst (1546–50).[23]

This tapestry suite offered a mixture of careful observations, especially of costumes and settings, even as it conveyed a fully realized propaganda message. The climax of the conflict was the month-long siege of the fort of Goleta (which protected Tunis) and the subsequent sack of the capital. Particularly careful topographical renderings of the city of Tunis include mosques and city walls. Further details include ancient ruins of Carthage, especially the prominent aqueducts, seen from different angles in successive tapestries, as well as the distinctive Mediterranean oared galleys, marked by their triangular, lateen-rigged sails. Moreover, the entire series begins with an aerial map of the entire Mediterranean basin, seen from the vantage point of Barcelona, with Africa at the top. The documentary character of these tapestries is further emphasized by the inclusion of text histories in two languages; longer passages in Castilian at the top, shorter Latin verses at the bottom.[24] As if to confirm the images' documentary claims, Vermeyen even included a self-portrait while drawing in the field into the design of *The Sack of Tunis*. He also appears in the initial map panel, where a full-length self-portrait figure stands beside a tablet with the proud declaration: "The course of events is represented in this work as exactly as possible ... the action is treated in this tapestry according to nature, all that concerns cosmography leaving nothing to be desired."[25]

According to Hendrick Horn, Vermeyen distinguishes between the Maghrebi "Moors" and their Turkish allies, and he even subdivides the former group into the more urban Arabs and the nomadic Berbers. Both groups of turbaned Moors are shown more sympathetically than the Turkish warriors, janissaries, in their pointed caps, who fought for Barbarossa and are shown in several tapestries as headhunters. These varied groups are especially evident across the foreground of several works, notably the sixth tapestry, *The Quest for Fodder*. Mulay Hasan and his retinue of Moorish allies of Charles V also appear, across the foreground of the *Fall of Tunis*.

Like Vermeyen, carefully producing costume studies and landscape topographies in Tunisia, the artistically trained nobleman Melchior Lorichs of Flensberg was another northerner who exploited his privileged role in an imperial entourage to gain access to the Islamic world. Lorichs went to the Ottoman capital of Istanbul as a member of the Holy Roman Empire's entourage to the court of Süleyman under ambassador Ogier Ghiselin de Busbecq (1554–62), the same individual credited with importing the tulip into Europe from Turkey.[26] He served as the ambassador's eyes for the military capacities and resources of the Ottomans, and published several treatises (1568, 1574) on the dangers that the Turkish army posed to Christian Europe. Yet Lorichs also produced the most meticulous on-site studies of the people and buildings of Constantinople by any European visitor during the sixteenth century.

From the high ground of Galata (the part of the city opposite the Golden Horn from what is now called the Old City), Lorichs made a vast yet careful sepia and black ink panorama of Istanbul (University Library, Leiden, 45 × 1127.5 cm; now divided into twenty-one sections).[27] This panorama, obviously composed out of separate studies from various positions, records the city skyline, including not only the dominating domes and minarets of mosques but also ancient Roman memorial columns, palaces, caravanserais, gates, and city walls. Ships of all sizes and shapes, including European carracks as well as Levantine vessels with lateen-rigged sails, fill the crowded waterways. Inscriptions label the points of interest in two different colours of ink, though written in a single hand. Near the centre of the ensemble appears an idealized self-portrait; a well-dressed, youthful European, in dark costume seen from the back, prepares to write or draw on an extended scroll similar to the one today at Leiden. He dips his quill into an elaborate goblet-like inkwell that is held for him by a turbaned Turk.

Lorichs also produced a woodcut, monogrammed and dated 1570, of the great Süleymaniye mosque complex that the architect Sinan had recently built (1550–7) for Sultan Süleyman.[28] Scholars have suggested that this print lacks both the clarity and the accuracy of the skyline drawings made on-site, but such distortions may have been intended to convey the grandeur of the complex to an audience that had never actually seen it. Lorichs's print furthermore suggests a momentous historical event by placing two omens in the sky above the mosque: gathering storm clouds as well as a glowing star with a tail, like the "comets" and other celestial apparitions associated with earthly catastrophes or conflicts in contemporary German cosmology.[29] To many Europeans, the architectural splendour of this complex would have been compromised by the source of its funding, tribute amassed through conquest and colonization of Christian-ruled territories, so this may be Lorichs's way of accommodating his Western audiences.

Lorichs's careful drawings of both male and female costumes were studies for his later woodcut illustrations, composed with a clear graphic syntax of parallel and cross hatchings that indicate that he was thinking from the outset about printed reproduction. In fact, Lorichs planned a large edition of woodcut illustrations based upon his on-site drawings in Turkey. Blocks were cut from these designs in 1565, 1570, 1575, and 1576, but even though a title page was produced (1575), the planned publication was never completed.[30] A small, reduced version of this volume appeared in Antwerp in 1574 (published by Gillis Coppens van Diest, who also published the first atlas, Abraham Ortelius's *Theatrum orbis terrarum*, 1570) under the title *Soldan Soleyman Turckischen Khaysers ... Whare und eigendtliche contrafectung und bildtnuss ...* (Sultan Süleyman ... a true and real facsimile and portrait of the Turkish emperor). One drawing (Louvre, monogrammed and dated 1557) shows a richly caparisoned dromedary camel striding through a landscape with a royal drummer on his back pounding his instrument, presumably to announce the advent of the sultan behind him.[31] This image was produced as a reversed woodcut in 1576. The artist also produced other drawings of distinctive, sometimes historical, German costumes, that were probably intended for a companion volume of European costumes, akin to contemporary costume books like those by Cesare Vecellio (Venice, 1590) or Abraham de Bruyn (Antwerp 1577).[32]

Lorichs also produced portrait engravings of the Emperor Süleyman when the latter was advanced in years (1574). One, based on a drawing of 1559 and monogrammed with the artist's initials, presents the sultan at bust-length, wearing his own, distinctively high turban. Following the formula established in the late portrait engravings by Dürer, such as *Frederick the Wise* (1524; Bartsch cat. no. 104), the sitter appears before a neutral background with a ledge bearing an inscription. The print is elaborately captioned in both Arabic and Latin. The Arabic inscription declares that the sitter is "Sultan of sultans, Süleyman shah, son of Sultan Selim Khan" and concludes with the formula "May God protect his helper." The Latin inscription is even more elaborate: "Imago Suleymanni Turcorum Imp. in Oriente, Unici Filii, Qui An. Do MDXX. Patri in Imperio Successit: Quo Etiam Anno Carolus. V. Maxaemyliani Caesaris Nepos Aquisgrani in Occidente Coronatus est Christian: Imp: A Melchiore Loricis, Flensburgensi, Holsatio, Antiquitatis Studiosiss°, Constantinopoli, An. MDLIX, Men. Feb., Die XV, Verissime Express."[33] The full-bearded ruler's face is somewhat haggard and drawn, showing his age and the cumulative strain of his reign.

Lorichs's second engraved portrait of Süleyman shows the sultan standing full-length before a gate of the city, through which passes a caparisoned elephant bearing two banner-carriers, one of them displaying the crescent moon of Islam. Visible through the gate behind him is the Süleymaniye mosque complex, which Lorichs had studied on-site in preparation for his woodcut. The features of the sultan derive from the bust-length study made by Lorichs in 1559, but the engraving was produced only in 1574. In that year, inscribed as the "true and real likeness [counterfeit]" of the sultan, it accompanied Gillis Coppens van Diest's publication.[34]

Lorichs's woodcut images return us to the tradition of observant, on-site documentary treatment of the Ottoman Turks and their empire, first conveyed by the woodcut illustrations by Erhard Reuwich for the pilgrimage guide of Bernhard von Breydenbach in 1486 and maintained in Dürer's early accurate drawings of Turkish costume and custom in Venice. However, after the decisive military advances in the Balkans, especially during the 1520s, the heightened threat of Turkish armies to both the German Holy Roman Empire and to wider European Christendom made it difficult for Dürer and his followers to remain neutral observers of contemporary Islam. At around the time of the 1529 siege of Vienna, European fascination with military aspects of the Turks intensified. Both in Germany and in the Netherlands, sixteenth-century artists' designs – for printmakers and for tapestry producers alike – kept images of Turkish armies readily available to northern audiences, whether princes or general public.

After Charles V's siege of Tunis in 1535, the next signal victory over Turkish forces in the Mediterranean occurred at sea, at the Battle of Lepanto (1571). Main credit for the victory was shared between the naval forces of Venice and the armies of Charles's son, Spanish King Philip II. So appropriately two principal commemorations of Lepanto were produced for the Spanish monarch and sent to the Escorial palace by the aged Venetian painter Titian.

The first of these is an allegorical portrait, *Philip II Offering the Infante Don Ferdinand to Heaven* (1573–5), which shows a fierce naval battle behind the principals, where dark smoke silhouettes the flaming vessels.[35] Documents describe the picture as *Batalla Naval* (The naval battle). Ironically, Don Fernando, presumptive heir and first son of the king's final marriage, who was born in the very same year as the Battle of Lepanto, 1571, would die a scant three years after the image was painted. In the picture a descending angel – and/or a winged Victory – extends a laurel crown and palm of military conquest, together with a banderole with a message intended for the youth: *Maiora tibi* (Greater things for you). This same combination of classical reference with religious symbolism suffuses the main action. Philip, bareheaded, wears parade armour as he offers his son at what looks like an altar table in a christo-mimetic act, like the Presentation of Jesus in the Temple. (Panofsky has compared this gesture to imagery in late medieval manuscripts, where a priest is shown lifting up a nude child, a symbol of the soul; this scene adorns the opening of Psalm 24: "Unto thee O Lord, do I lift up my soul.") A row of columns like a temple entry recedes along the right side; the sturdy column, symbol of the virtue of Fortitude, frequently accompanies the full-length standing subjects of court portraits, such as Titian's formative 1551 image of Philip II, then a prince. This row converges perspectivally like a series of ancestors on the bright central figure of the infanta. Meanwhile, in the lower left corner crouches a shackled Turkish prisoner, identified not only by his features but also by his crescent banner and his discarded turban; the spoils of his weapons behind him were added on a strip by painter Vicente Carducho in 1625, when the painting was enlarged to match the grand dimensions of Titian's earlier great military celebration for a Spanish king in armour: his equestrian portrait, *Emperor Charles V at the Battle of Mühlberg* (1548), a conquest not of Turks but over a German Protestant alliance.

The other painting sent by Titian to Spain in celebration of King Philip's contribution to the Battle of Lepanto was an allegory, *Religion Succoured by Spain*.[36] It shows the encounter of two female personifications before a sea battle in the background. Crouching on the right side, a nude who attempts modestly to cover herself can be identified as Catholicism, from the chalice behind her and a cross leaning against a solid rock (of faith and the papacy). Above that cross, snakes on the trunk of a dead tree signify devilish threats to

Christendom, presumably by the Islamic Turks as well as by heretic Protestants in Europe. Striding boldly in from the left and facing Religion, a female warrior enters carrying a spear and a shield like the goddess Minerva in earlier mythologies by the artist. Panofsky rightly associates her with the pictorial tradition of the goddess of war, Bellona, and calls her *Ecclesia militans*. Behind her a second woman advances with upraised sword, like a figure of Fortitude; she in turn heads a troop of Amazons. Their armed force is identified with Spain through the heraldic arms of Philip II on the corner shield. Once more the spoils of war appear as weapons in the centre foreground, between Spain and Religion. At the head of the background naval battle, in place of a Neptune on his marine chariot, drawn by sea horses, we see instead the personification of a turbaned Turk, heading for shore to threaten the vulnerable figure of the Church, who turns to accept welcome reinforcement from her deliverer. Thus the allegory, deftly unpacked by Panofsky, can be described in his words as "The Christian Religion, Threatened by Internal Subversion (the snakes of Heresy) and External Enemies (the Turk), Seeking the Protection of the Church Militant and Fortitude."

One final image commemorates the Catholic unity that provided victory at Lepanto. It survives only as an ambitious vision by an artist who hoped in vain to serve the court of Philip II: El Greco, arriving in Spain in 1576, fresh from his own period of finishing school at Venice and Rome. His *Adoration of the Holy Name of Jesus* (ca 1577–9) survives in two versions, one in the Escorial, the other now in London.[37] Its subject was correctly identified in the seventeenth century by Fray Francisco de los Santos (1657), who identified it as a representation of the mouth of Hell and the bridge of Purgatory. He called it the *Gloria* by El Greco for Philip II, thus comparing it directly with Titian's *Gloria*, made earlier for the meditation of Charles V. Kneeling in adoration of the holy name, itself a Jesuit object of devotion, are three leaders of the Holy League who marshalled the forces for Lepanto: Philip II, dressed as always in black, Doge Mocenigo of Venice in a robe trimmed with ermine, and the current pope, Pius V, in clerical robes. On 9 March 1566, Pius V had issued a bull, *Cum gravissima*, exhorting all Christian powers to unite against the Turk.[38] A fourth kneeling figure at the pope's right is dressed in classical armour and holds a sword; he has been identified by Anthony Blunt as an idealized portrait of the general of the Lepanto fleet, Don Juan of Austria, half-brother of Philip II, who died in 1578 and was buried in the Escorial Royal Pantheon. Indeed, according to Francisco de los Santos, this image hung near that tomb in the mid-seventeenth century. This picture reaffirms Christian doctrine and Catholic unity while also presenting these important contemporary figures alongside resurrected souls who await redemption and admission to heaven and the company of the angels above. Even more than an allegory, this vision situates contemporary religion within a cosmos of the Last Judgment and the triumph of good over evil.

On the eastern front, the Holy Roman Empire resumed its own active Turkish Wars (1593–1606), fought during the reign of Emperor Rudolf II (r. 1576–1612). The renewed conflict began in August 1593, when Sultan Murad III broke a truce that had been in effect since 1584.[39] Although the two sides fought to a deadlock before the peace of Zsitva-Torok (11 November 1606) was ratified, this protracted activity along a Central European front held worldwide significance as another boundary contest between Christendom and Islam. It also provided the opportunity (or, indeed, the necessity) for considerable propaganda – including visual art – by the Habsburg ruler. Although Rudolf II never actually led his troops in battle, he had himself portrayed by his numerous court artists as a great military victor and preserver of the faith.

Principal propagandistic commissions went to Rudolf's court painter in Prague, Hans von Aachen, the author of a belated cycle of oil sketches on parchment, bound together in a volume under the title *Allegory of the Turkish War* (completed before 1607).[40] The latest of the military events depicted in the cycle, the Battle of Kronstadt/Brasov, dates from mid-1603. This motivation to celebrate "victories" through visual imagery echoes the heritage of the grandiose cartoons and tapestries of Charles V's earlier Tunis campaign. Like Vermeyen preparing to paint his cartoons, von Aachen made meticulous topographic studies. Yet he altered the rhetoric of the presentation by using allegorical figures, chiefly female personifications, such as winged victories or places (e.g., Hungary), along with more historically credible groupings of infantry and cavalry. In the final two images he also included banners as trophies to signify victory. Frequently the compositions display the heavens open to show divine figures overseeing the battle: classical gods appear in person or through the surrogates of their symbolic animals, and the artist does not miss the opportunity to suggest parallels between the eagle of Jupiter and the heraldic eagle of the Holy Roman Empire. The eagle clawing the crescent moon, symbol of Islam, was also a favourite *impresa* of Rudolf II.

Some of von Aachen's designs were translated into sculpted relief by Rudolf's court sculptor, Adriaen de Vries, notably the image (ca 1604–5) of the regaining (1598) of the fortress of Raab/Györ (Kunsthistorisches Museum, Vienna).[41] Both the oil sketches and the bronze relief were more personal, private items than tapestries or prints and were reserved for the notoriously withdrawn emperor himself rather than conceived for large-scale public display or broad circulation. Yet their genesis and presentation received more direct input from the ruler himself than had the tapestries, commissioned through the agency of the emperor's sister and regent, Mary of Hungary.

A characteristic von Aachen image, *The Battle of Sissek* (1593; one of the sources for de Vries's relief), inaugurates the scenes of war. It shows the emperor's eagle attacking the sultan's crescent in the sky above and places classical river gods in the corners to suggest the site. In addition, a winged Victory extends palm and laurel garlands to the seated female allegory of Croatia, who bears a crown and sceptre and heraldic blue-and-white squares on her skirt. Alongside these allegorical elements, the background clearly depicts the actual riverside setting of the city and its fortified walls. The battle is in progress: imperial forces move inexorably from left to right, sporting their banners, and vanquished Turks are cast into the river. Cavalry with lances are complemented by infantry with pikes; the modern firearm, an arquebus or musket, is visible in the left middle ground. Some Turks wear identifiable costume, especially turbans, but these are less ethnographically accurate records of dress than they are symbolic attributes to help communicate and celebrate the partisan victory over a dreaded enemy. Along with their allegorical main figures, these representations of battles by von Aachen attend more to the specific topography of the sites than they document the actual movements of armies.

Von Aachen's works survive for the most part both in the form of oil sketches (Vienna) and presentation drawings (Dresden), the latter of which were finished in 1604 and presented in 1607 to Christian II, elector of Saxony.[42] Once more both patron and audience are courtly, imperial adversaries of the Turks, and again the chosen subjects are battles – a category different from the tradition of dispassionate ethnographic study of costumes or customs, intended to satisfy curiosity and display the exotic.

By contrast, Rudolf II assembled in his castle at Prague the actual battlefield booty seized from the Turks, making it a feature within his vast collections.[43] Consisting chiefly of bows and their leather cases, as well as metal-edged weapons (daggers, swords, battleaxes), these trophies were displayed to impress visiting ambassadors. Such delegations included Safavid Persians, envoys from the empire that abutted the Ottomans on the opposite flank. This display of trophies must have helped kindle a proposed alliance between the Holy Roman Empire and the Persian Shah Abbas (1587–1629).[44]

The artist of printed portraits of Rudolf II was his court engraver, Aegidius Sadeler.[45] Sadeler, like the imperial sculptor, Adriaen de Vries, devoted his main portrait energies to depicting the majesty of Rudolf II. And his allegorical vocabulary in framing the emperor employs a new artistic vocabulary, which asserts conquest over the Turkish nemesis. After a century of visualizing Turks, this imperial program fits firmly into an ongoing Habsburg tradition, albeit with a more propagandistic purpose. Indeed the allegories, like Rubens's cycle for Queen Mother Marie de' Medici in France during the 1620s, not only offer a more learned and elite pictorial vocabulary but also serve to airbrush embarrassing setbacks and harsh realities, in this case the ultimate military stalemate with the Turkish forces by the empire. No European Christian could ever forget the clear and present danger posed to his faith and his political autonomy by the Islamic Ottoman Empire across the border. That threatening superpower, however, also held fascination and exotic allure, realized in pictorial terms all the more by artists, particularly Vermeyen and Lorichs, who had experienced Tunis and Istanbul in person instead of picturing stereotypes of Turks.

Ultimately, most images of Turks from the Holy Roman Empire necessarily blended opposing qualities: fear of and loathing for a formidable enemy that defined Christian Europe through contrast, alongside fascinated, careful observation, produced, usually in multiple print images, for the delectation in Europe of commoners as well as rulers.

NOTES

1 For a discussion of Maximilian's art patronage, including his verbal and visual campaigns for a contemporary crusade against the Ottoman Turks, see Larry Silver, *Marketing Maximilian: The Visual Ideology of a Holy Roman Emperor* (Princeton: Princeton University Press, 2008).
2 Sebastian Brant, *The Ship of Fools*, ed. and trans. Edwin Zeydel (New York: Columbia University Press, 1944), 315–22.
3 Julian Raby, *Venice, Dürer and the Oriental Mode* (London: Publisher, 1982). Jay Levenson, ed., *Circa 1492*, exhibition catalogue (Washington: National Gallery of Art, 1991), 212–13, nos 109–10.
4 Stefano Carboni, *Venice and Islam*, exhibition catalogue (New York: Metropolitan Museum of Art, 2007). See also the essay by Elizabeth Rodini in the same volume.
5 Raby, *Venice, Dürer and the Oriental Mode*, 25; Bernard Aikema and Beverly Brown, *Renaissance Venice and the North*, exhibition catalogue (Venice: Palazzo Grassi, 1999), 266–7, no. 38; Walter Koschatzky and Alice Strobl, *Dürer Drawings: The Albertina Collection* (Greenwich, CT: New York Graphic Society, 1971), 64–5, no. 15 (Winkler cat. no. 79, ca 1495); Levenson, *Circa 1492*, 213, no. 110; Giulia Bartrum, *Albrecht Dürer and His Legacy*, exhibition catalogue (London: British Museum, 2003), 108–9, no. 38 (Winkler cat. no. 78, ca 1494–5). See now Caroline Campbell, Alan Chong,

Deborah Howard, and J. Michael Rogers, *Bellini and the East*, exhibition catalogue (Boston: Isabella Stewart Gardner Museum, 2005). In the specific case of the Three Orientals (London: British Museum, Winkler cat. no. 78, ca 1494–5), Dürer explicitly replicated three small figures in the background of a large painting by Gentile Bellini, the Corpus Christi Procession in the Piazza San Marco, dated 1496; therefore, these figures must have been experienced by Dürer prior to completion of the final picture, perhaps through preliminary drawing studies.

6 Levenson, *Circa 1492*, 212–13, no. 109. Christopher White, "'An Oriental Ruler on His Throne' and 'The Entombment': Two New Drawings by Albrecht Dürer," *Master Drawings* 11 (1973): 365–74. The figure of the drawing was traced through to the other side of the sheet, to serve as the model for the engraving. That print exists in only one unfinished proof (Rijksmuseum, Amsterdam) and was unrecorded by Bartsch. See also Walter Strauss, *The Intaglio Prints of Albrecht Dürer* (New York: Abaris, 1981), 54–5; Strauss, *The Complete Drawings of Albrecht Dürer* (New York: Abaris, 1974), no. 1495/18-18a.

7 Addition of both rubies and turquoise does indeed mark a number of the sultan's personal decorative objects, including the royal mace; see Esin Atil, *The Age of Süleyman the Magnificent*, exhibition catalogue (Washington: National Gallery of Art, 1987); Atil, *Schätze aus dem Topkapi Serail*, exhibition catalogue (Berlin: Reimer, 1988).

8 Lloyd DeWitt, "Testing Tradition against Nature: Rembrandt's Radical New Image of Jesus," *Rembrandt and the Face of Jesus*, exhibition catalogue (Philadelphia: Philadelphia Museum of Art, 2011), 109–45, esp. 112–13, 121–3.

9 See Strauss, *Complete Drawings of Albrecht Dürer*, 1495/18-18a. The drawing is inscribed in German script, *Suleyman imperator, die leibfarb ist gantz lederfarb* (Emperor Süleyman, the body-colour is completely leather-coloured).

10 For the relations between portrait medals and portrait woodcuts as multiple likenesses, see Larry Silver, "The Face Is Familiar: German Renaissance Portrait Multiples in Prints and Medals," *Word and Image* 19 (2003): 6–21.

11 Dresden, Münzkabinett; *Im Lichte des Halbmonds. Das Abendland und der türkische Orient*, exhibition catalogue (Dresden: Staatliche Kunstsammlungen, 1995), 75, no. 24. This rare medal does not appear in the celebrated collections of London, Vienna, Berlin, and Munich, and its artist and origin remain unknown. It also resembles a related etching by Hieronymus Hopfer. Compare also the profile medal with turban of Sultan Mehmet II ("the Conqueror"), facing the same leftward direction as Dürer drawing, dating ca 1480 and patterned after a design by Gentile Bellini of Venice, ibid., 53, no. 5, with Gentile's celebrated near-profile painted portrait of Mehmet II (1480; London, National Gallery), ibid., 52, no. 1.

12 *Lichte des Halbmonds*, 74, no. 21; Günther Heinz and Karl Schütz, *Porträtgalerie zur*

Geschichte Österreichs von 1400 bis 1800 (Vienna: Kunsthistorisches Museum, 1976), 182–4, no. 156, fig. 101. Based on the age of the sultan, the profile model for the painting probably dates to the 1520s, like Dürer's own source.

13 Fedja Anzelewsky, *Dürer Gemälde* (Berlin: Deutscher Verlag für Kunstwissenschaft, 1971), 212–18, no. 105. A horizontal format drawing, preserved in a fastidious copy (Winkler cat. no. 438, Vienna, Albertina; Koschatzky and Strobl, *Dürer Drawings*, 168–71, no. 62), served as a preliminary composition of this complex theme. More widely on Frederick the Wise as a courtly patron of Dürer, see Larry Silver, "Civic Courtliness: Albrecht Dürer, the Duke and the Emperor," in *Artists at Court: Image-Making and Identity 1300–1500*, ed. Stephen Campbell, 149–62 (Boston: Isabella Stewart Gardner Museum, 2004).

14 Erwin Panofsky, "Conrad Celtes and Kunz von der Rosen: Two Problems in Portrait Identification," *Art Bulletin* 24 (1942): 39–54. Lewis Spitz, *Conrad Celtis* (Cambridge, MA: Harvard University Press, 1958).

15 Especially after 1530. R.J. Knecht, *Francis I* (Cambridge: Cambridge University Press, 1992), 224–5, 233–4, 294–5. For the best recent survey of the Habsburgs and the Ottomans in the sixteenth century, see Volker Press, "The Habsburg Lands: The Holy Roman Empire, 1400–1555"; and Cemal Kafadar, "The Ottomans and Europe," in *Handbook of European History*, ed. Thomas Brady, Jr, Heiko Oberman, and James Tracy (Leiden: Brill: 1994), 1:438–66 and 1:599–628, respectively.

16 *Lichte des Halbmonds*, 78–9, no. 36; David Landau and Peter Parshall, *The Renaissance Print 1470–1550* (New Haven, CT: Yale University Press, 1994), 227–8, figs 233–4; Keith Moxey, *Peasants, Warriors, and Wives: Popular Imagery in the Reformation* (Chicago: University of Chicago Press, 1989), 78–9n28 for references.

17 Charlotte Colding Smith, *Images of Islam 1453–1600: Turks in Germany and Central Europe* (London: Pickering and Chatto, 2014), 72–3; James Clifton, "Mediated War," in *Plains of Mars*, ed. James Clifton and Leslie Scattone, 41–50 (Houston: Houston Museum of Fine Arts, 2009); David Landau and Peter Parshall, *The Renaissance Print, 1470–1550* (New Haven, CT: Yale University Press, 1994), 227–8.

18 *Lichte des Halbmonds*, 79–80, no. 37. *Wien 1529. Die erste Türkenbelagerung*, exhibition catalogue (Vienna: Historisches Museum der Stadt Wien, 1979–80), 63–9, no. 151.

19 Colding Smith, *Images of Islam*. I am grateful to Dr Smith for sharing her research with me prior to publication. *Kunst voor de Beeldenstorm: Noordnederlandse kunst 1525–1580*, exhibition catalogue (Amsterdam: Rijksmuseum, 1986), 175–6, no. 59.

20 Colding Smith, *Images of Islam*, 54, with translation; Moxey, *Peasants, Warriors, and Wives*, 76–7, fig. 4.7.

21 Colding Smith, "Military Images," 1, with translation.

22 Martin Luther, *Luther's Works*, vol. 35 *Word and Sacrament I*, ed. E. Theodore

Bachman (Philadelphia: Fortress, 1960), 407.
23 Thomas Campbell, *Tapestry in the Renaissance: Art and Magnificence* (New York: Metropolitan Museum of Art, 2002), 385–91, 428–34; Lisa Jardine and Jerry Brotton, *Global Interests: Renaissance Art between East and West* (Ithaca: Cornell University Press, 2000), 82–7; also Hendrik Horn, *Jan Cornelisz Vermeyen* (Doornspijk: Davaco, 1989), 13–17, 35–7, 41–7, 111–223; Wilfried Seipel, *Der Kriegszug Kaiser Karls V gegen Tunis. Kartons und Tapisserien* (Vienna: Kunsthistorisches Museum, 2000). Scholarly debate continues about whether Vermeyen designed the tapestries alone or whether he collaborated with experienced designer Pieter Coecke van Aelst.
24 History, indeed, but not without bias. The *Sack of Tunis* uses its Latin inscription to editorialize: "The troops sent against the outskirts of the town lay siege to and take them, slaughter the enemy [*hostemque*] in armour and, taking the houses, spare the inhabitants. They use the right of conquest [*iure belli*]. More than twenty thousand captives recover their liberty and thrice salute Charles the Avenger [*Victorem Carolum*] with cries of gratitude. The conqueror re-establishes the unfortunate Hasan on the throne of his ancestors, though he hardly merited this, as he had promised so much and performed nothing." Translated by Campbell, *Tapestry in the Renaissance*, 429, no. 50. Or the Latin from the initial tapestry: "Wishing to overcome the infidel armies of the Turk and the warrior [Barbarossa] who, obeying the orders of Suleiman, raises cruel war against the realms of Spain, Caesar, Charles the Fifth of that name, gathers together with the blessings of heaven, the armies and fleets of Spain and Italy to threaten the African troops. Not brooking delay while time and the hour proceed, he energetically hastens to his ships and his loyal companions." Translated by Horn, *Jan Cornelisz Vermeyen*, 181.
25 Horn, *Jan Cornelisz Vermeyen*, 181.
26 Erik Fischer, *Melchior Lorck*, exhibition catalogue (Copenhagen: Royal Museum of Fine Arts, 1962); Fisher, *Melchior Lorck* (Copenhagen: Vandkunsten, 2009); Alexandrine St Clair, *The Image of the Turk in Europe*, exhibition catalogue (New York: Metropolitan Museum of Art, 1973), nos 6–10.
27 Nigel Westbrook, Kenneth Rainsbury Dark, and Rene van Meeuwen, "Constructing Melchior Lorichs's Panorama of Constantinople," *Journal of the Society of Architectural Historians* 69 (2010): 62–87; Helen C. Evans, ed., *Byzantium Faith and Power* (New York: Metropolitan Museum of Art, 2004), 406–8, no. 249; Cyril Mango and Stephan Ycrasimos, *Melchior Lorichs' Panorama of Istanbul 1559* (Istanbul: Ertug and Kocabiyik, 1999); S. Biadene and C. Tonini, *A volo d'uccello. Jacopo de' Barbari e le rappresentatzioni di citt nell' Europa del Rinascimento*, exhibition catalogue (Venice: Arsenale, 1999), 154–8, no. 16; S. Yerasimos, "Istanbul au XVIe siècle. Images d'une capitale," *Soliman le Magnifique*, exhibition catalogue

(Paris: Grand Palais, 1990), 184–321, esp. 294–7; Gereon Sievernach and Hendrik Budde, *Europa und der Orient* (Berlin: Martin-Gropius-Bau, 1989), 241–4; Fisher, *Melchior Lorck*, 24. For the general phenomenon, see Lucia Nuti, *Rittrata di citt* (Venice: Marsilio, 1996).

28 *Schätze aus dem Topkapi Serail*, 72, no. 6. For the building complex, see Godfrey Goodwin, *A History of Ottoman Architecture* (London: Thames and Hudson, 1971), 215–39; now see Gulru Necipoglu, *Sinan* (Princeton: Princeton University Press, 2005).

29 Larry Silver, "Nature and Nature's God: Landscape and Cosmos of Albrecht Altdorfer," *Art Bulletin* 81 (1999): 194–214, with references.

30 Fischer, *Melchior Lorck*, 38–58. After several false starts, the publication first appeared in 1626 in Hamburg with Michael Hering. Peter Ward-Jackson, "Some Rare Drawings by Melchior Lorichs," *Connoisseur* (March 1955): 83–93.

31 *Dessins de Dürer et de la Renaissance germanique dans les collections publiques parisiennes*, exhibition catalogue (Paris: Réunion des musées nationaux, 1991), 128–9, no. 120, arguing that the drawing was done at a later moment back in Germany, with the date recording the period of observation.

32 Kaufmann, 64–5, nos 14–15; Fisher, *Melchior Lorck*, 58–64, nos 64–78.

33 "The Emperor of the Turks in the East, Süleyman, only son of Selim, who ascended in the same year 1520, when in Aachen Charles V, grandson of Emperor Maximilian was made Christian Emperor of the West. Made with the greatest exactitude in Constantinople 15 February 1550 by the most studious in antiquities, the Holsteiner Melchior Lorck from Flensberg." Latin translation by Mikael Bøgh Rasmussen, "Melchior Lorck's Portrait of Sultan Süleyman the Magnificent (1562): A Double-Coded View," in Michael Andersen, Birgitte Bøggild, Hugo Johanssen, *Reframing the Danish Renaissance* (Copenhagen: National Museum of Denmark, 2011), 165–70.

34 *Soldan Soleyman Turckischen Khaysers ... Whare und eigenliche contrafectung und biltnuss*, dated 21 April 1574.

35 Peter Humfrey, *Titian: The Complete Paintings* (Ghent: Ludion, 2007), 368, no. 293; Fernando Checa, *Tiziano y la monarquía hispánica. Usos y funciones de la pintura veneciana en España (siglos XVI y XVII)* (Madrid: Nerea, 1994), 52–6; Erwin Panofsky, *Problems in Titian, Mostly Iconographic* (New York: New York University Press, 1969), 72–3.

36 Humfrey, *Titian*, 367, no. 292; Checa, *Tiziano*, 58–60; Panofsky, *Problems in Titian*, 186–90. Also Rudolf Wittkower, "Titian's Allegory of 'Religion Succoured by Spain,'" *Allegory and the Migration of Symbols* (London: Thames and Hudson, 1977), 143–6, which sees the Church Triumphant in the Minerva figure and the nude figure as the Magdalene, Sin redeemed. But see a seventeenth-century assessment of the image by Fray Francisco de los Santos, in Wittkower, "Titian's Allegory," 145n8. Humfrey rejects the notion that this picture is a reworked version of a

much earlier painting seen in the artist's studio and described in 1566 by Vasari (VII, 458) as a work begun for Alfonso d'Este, who had commissioned the Ferrara Camerino d'alabastro. However, recent technical examination does not show changes to the attributes of the main allegories, so the Vasari work is probably lost, though it is possibly identical to a work sent to Emperor Maximilian II and engraved in 1568 by Giulio Fontana. In the engraving the suppliant nude is described in Latin as "the pious image of the religion of the unvanquished Emperor of the Christians" (Panofsky, *Problems in Titian*, 187). A workshop copy of the Escorial painting is in Rome, Palazzo Doria-Pamphilij.

37 *El Greco of Toledo*, exhibition catalogue (Toledo: Toledo Museum of Art, 1982), 231–2, no. 12; Anthony Blunt, "El Greco's 'Dream of Philip II': An Allegory of the Holy League," *Journal of the Warburg and Courtauld Institutes* 3 (1939–40): 58–69.
38 Panofsky, *Problems in Titian*, 188.
39 Jutta Kappel, "Die Türkennot des Kaisers. Zu einigen Aspekten der Darstellung des Türken-krieges (1593–1606) in der Hofkunst Rudolfs II," in *Licht des Halbmonds*, 125–3; Herbert Haupt, "Der Türkenkrieg Kaiser Rudolfs II. 1593–1606," in *Prag um 1600*, exhibition catalogue (Essen-Vienna: Luca, 1988), 1:97–8. For the complex diplomatic history via an imperial perspective, see R.J.W. Evans, *Rudolf II and His World* (London: Thames and Hudson, 1997), 75–8; the Ottoman outlook, between Europe and Persia, is conveyed by Jason Goodwin, *Lords of the Horizon* (London: Chatto and Windus, 1998), 164–7.
40 Joachim Jacoby, *Hans von Aachen 1552–1615* (Berlin: Deutscher Kunstverlag, 2000), esp. 174–5, 178–80, 182–203; nos 56, 58, 60; more generally for von Aachen and the other artists at Prague, see Thomas DaCosta Kaufmann, *The School of Prague* (Chicago: University of Chicago Press, 1988), esp. 133–63, nos 1.44, 1.48–60. Ink drawing copies of the oil sketches by von Aachen's workshop show a larger original cycle.
41 Frits Scholten, *Adriaen de Vries 1556–1626*, exhibition catalogue (Amsterdam: Rijksmuseum 1998–9), 159–61, no. 18. This more composite work, derived from several of the von Aachen designs, speaks more generally to the Turkish War on the battleground of Hungary, and it features the Muslim dragon and serpent being attacked by imperial eagle and lion along with river personifications (Danube and Sava).
42 Unusually for von Aachen a pair of preliminary compositional drawings survive: one in Dusseldorf, Kunstmuseum (no. 941), the other in Moscow, Pushkin Museum (no. 7456; discussed in *Prag um 1600*, 1:333–4, no. 183).
43 Matthias Pfaffenbichler, "Die türkischen Waffen in der Kunstkammer Rudolfs II," in *Rudolf II, Prague and the World*, ed. Lubomir Konečny et al., 161–5 (Prague: Artefactum, 1998).
44 This proposed alliance was brokered by the Englishman Robert Shirley; see Evans,

Rudolf II, 77–8; see also the remarkable double portraits in Persian ambassadorial dress (1622), painted in Rome by Anthony van Dyck of Sir Robert and Teresia, Lady Shirley (Petworth House), in Christopher Brown and Hans Vlieghe, *Van Dyck 1599–1641*, exhibition catalogue (London-Antwerp: Royal Academy, 1999), 160–3, nos 29–30.

45 *Lichte des Halbmonds*, nos 132–4; *Prag um 1600*, I, nos 19, 36–7, esp. Husein Ali Beg, depicted in 1601, who also visited the elector of Saxony.

chapter four

Imperial Succession and Mirrors of Tyranny in the Houses of Habsburg and Osman

CARINA L. JOHNSON

Throughout the sixteenth century, the houses of Habsburg and Osman asserted competing claims as the true inheritors of the Roman Empire. This imperial rivalry took military, political, and rhetorical forms: wars, political manoeuvring, and representations of imperial authority were arenas in which each dynasty sought to demonstrate its ascendancy over the other. Charles V, elected emperor of the Holy Roman Empire in 1519, and Sultan Süleyman I, whose reign began in 1520, each sought to promote himself as universal monarch.[1] Military conflict between the two escalated during the first decade of their rules and was marked most sensationally in Latin Christendom by the 1529 Ottoman siege of Vienna and the 1535 Habsburg capture of Tunis. Popular awareness of this rivalry was fuelled in the Holy Roman Empire by a flood of pamphlets proclaiming the merciless Ottoman threat.[2] Depictions of the Ottomans as the hereditary enemy were bolstered by an ongoing pattern of Habsburg defeats and stalemates in the 1540s, which led to the Ottomans' formal incorporation of Hungary into their empire. Through a series of limited peace treaties in the 1540s, Charles's and Süleyman's rivalry cooled into an ongoing maintenance of borders in the Mediterranean and across Hungary while each ruler focused on other antagonists. Süleyman's attention turned to the Safavids on his eastern border, and Charles was embroiled in conflicts with France and in confessional divisions within the Holy Roman Empire. Relatively stable relations between the two houses were formalized by a new treaty in 1562, although the peace proved short-lived. The transition of rule from the generation of Habsburg Charles (and his brother Ferdinand) and Ottoman Süleyman to that of their sons heightened concerns about legitimate and illegitimate succession, and left the balance of power between the empires uncertain. The pressures of imperial rivalry encouraged evolving Latin Christian strategies of representational mirroring, in which Ottoman rule was the inversion of good governance, and the sultan was the "Turk" whose practices of succession defined him as a tyrant.

Orientalizing the Ottomans as a dynasty of despotic and sybaritic tyrants was a project fully familiar to Christian European readers by the beginning of the eighteenth century. In the more than thirty years since Edward Said defined orientalism, the early-modern-era lacunae in his study have been addressed. Scholars of Renaissance England have argued that, in the relative geographic and political distance of England from the Ottoman Empire, discursive presentations of the Turks that were beyond or prior to orientalism flourished.[3] In contrast, exoticizing and polarizing constructions dominated the cultural production of Ottoman alterity in locations closer to Ottoman lands such as Venice, where orientalizing has been identified in Venetian texts dating to the 1570s.[4] Evidence from the Germanies (the Holy Roman Empire including, nominally, the Low Countries and Italian states) highlights the relevance of Saidian orientalism, albeit in a tempered form. For Said, the production of orientalism as a melange of the "half-imagined, half-known" depends on Europe's "position of strength, not to say domination."[5] In the formative era of the mid-sixteenth century, an inversion of Said's formulation holds true. Orientalist tropes were produced not from a position of strength and political domination, but rather from a context of Habsburg imperial weakness and limitations in the face of the much more powerful Ottomans.[6]

Fear of Turkish wartime violence during the first half of the sixteenth century evolved into a more directed and condemnatory critique of Ottoman rulers as tyrants in the second half of the century. The pious and puissant Süleyman, believed by many Latin Christians to be a punishment from God in the 1520s, gradually would be perceived as the morally depraved Turk because of his familial relations. As narratives about internecine dynastic struggles filtered into the Holy Roman Empire, Süleyman's image shifted from that of a ruler who kills the children of his enemies to a ruler who kills his own children. The Habsburg court and other Holy Roman imperial elites, caught between an ascendant Ottoman empire and their own military weakness, promoted if not produced important and durable strands of this discourse as they struggled to maintain their military front with the Ottomans in Hungary. The Ottoman altern as the "tyrannical Turk," then, emerges through the interwoven elements of confession, political succession, and alterity traced in this chapter.

Family Politics and Imperial Succession

During the early 1550s, both Charles and Süleyman found themselves grappling with questions of succession within their own houses. Charles's 1530 coronation as emperor of the Holy Roman Empire had been followed, within a matter of months, by the election of his brother Ferdinand as king of the

Romans. In promoting Ferdinand as heir to the Holy Roman Empire, Charles had guaranteed and rewarded his brother's loyalty yet had passed over his own very young son Philip. Without an established default of primogeniture in the Holy Roman Empire, the designation of Ferdinand's heir, in turn, was the subject of growing tension between the two brothers. This tension became open disagreement by mid-century, with each brother seeking to secure the empire for now-adult sons. If exigency and ability were valued over primogeniture, the question of which Habsburg (or even member of another dynasty) should rule the Holy Roman Empire remained open. In 1549, Charles sent Philip to the Low Countries to garner support for Philip's candidacy. Even before Charles sent his son north, he arranged for the strongest competition, Ferdinand's eldest son Maximilian, to be absent from the German-speaking lands. Maximilian was ordered south to Valladolid, to marry Charles's daughter Maria and serve as co-regent with her in the Spanish Habsburg kingdoms. Maximilian governed in Iberia from 1548 to 1550, before bolting back to the Holy Roman Empire to promote his own candidacy among the German princes at the end of 1550. In early 1551, Charles and Ferdinand agreed to designate Philip as the next Habsburg to stand for election as king of the Romans, a decision met with open hostility by many. Continued resistance from the German princes and Maximilian led, by 1554, to the withdrawal of this stipulated succession. Ferdinand would be crowned emperor of the Holy Roman Empire in 1558, but even then, Maximilian was not assured the succession: he continued to monitor the moves of his brothers and cousin closely and was elected and crowned king of the Romans only in November 1562.[7]

Nor was primogeniture an operating principle in the Ottoman Empire: during the century after the conquest of Constantinople, the house of Osman practised open succession. Abandoning the practice of marriage, each ruler produced only one son with a particular woman. This woman's energies were then focused on raising her son and promoting his position in the family. She would follow him to his provincial appointments and work towards his continued advancement. Upon the death of the Ottoman sultan or another precipitating event, one son's display of political and military acumen would establish him as his father's rightful successor, and his mother would become a valued advisor of her son, the new sultan. The other, losing sons either died in the succession struggle or fled to the protection of other rulers. These fratricides were accepted as collateral damage; for over fifty years, open succession produced an able ruler who continued Ottoman territorial expansion.[8] At Sultan Selim I's death in 1520, Süleyman was his father's only remaining heir, and the succession was notable for its absence of violent struggle. Around 1534, Süleyman acted against one element of open succession by choosing to maintain his intimate relations with one of his concubines, Hurrem. The two married and produced multiple sons and a daughter. Süleyman soon elevated Hurrem to the position of sultana, and she was understood to serve as his, not her sons', advisor. By 1550, Süleyman had four living sons: firstborn Mustafa was the son of Mahidevran, and Bayezid, Selim, and Jihangir were the sons of his wife Hurrem. For Ottoman observers, expectations of open succession had been upset by his multiple sons with Hurrem, and the path to determining succession may have been unclear.[9] For Latin Christians, Süleyman's choice to form a monogamous marriage brought him closer to their own norms and moral expectations.

Although the parallels between the Habsburg and Ottoman modes of competitive imperial succession were not explicitly acknowledged by Latin Christian authors, Ottoman open succession as a practice was known to Latin Christian readers through Paolo Giovio's widely circulating writings. Giovio's *Commentario de le cose de' Turchi, di Paulo Iovio, Vescovo di Nocera, a' Carlo Quinto Imperadore Augusto*, printed in 1532 and appearing in Latin during September 1537 and in German the same year,[10] presented a history of the Ottoman dynasty before turning to Turkish military organization. Giovio described succession struggles between Murad I's two sons, the dispatch of Mehmed I's rival brother by a murderous uncle, and Bayezid II forcing his brother Cem to flee Ottoman lands for shelter in Latin Christendom. Giovio held up Süleyman as a virtuous contrast to his bloody-minded forefathers, a positive evaluation of Süleyman also supported in Theodoro Spandouginos's more negative discussion of the dynasty's succession practices.[11] The reception of Giovio's text was refracted through competing political claims in its translations. The initial Latin translation retained Giovio's dedication to Charles V as the leader of Christendom, and this dedication would be included in subsequent printings. The Latin edition of October 1537 was produced in Protestant Wittenberg and also invoked one of the most powerful non-Habsburg, Protestant princely houses. It contained an additional preface by reformer Philip Melanchthon to Duke Johan Ernst of Saxony, which elaborated on the threat of limitless tyranny and impiety of the "Turk."[12]

During the first half of the sixteenth century, Latin Christians both admired and dreaded the military prowess of Selim and his son Süleyman. Selim had overseen the conquest of the Mamluk Caliphate in 1517 and Süleyman the conquest of Rhodes and most of Hungary. While they were acknowledged to be instigators of military violence against multitudes, bringing death, destruction, and enslavement to Christian men, women, and children as scourges of God, the sultans and their disciplined, well-supplied armies of janissaries and sipahis were also unstoppable. When the 1529 siege of Vienna confirmed Süleyman's reputation as an aggressive military campaigner and threat, he became the subject of increasing attention in the Germanies. News pamphlets regularly reported on Ottoman troop movements and numbers.[13] Süleyman's military and political reputation led Giovio and other authors to describe him as a stern and just ruler who instituted unbiased rule for all subjects and who compared favourably with Christian princes. Reform-minded pamphleteers (however disingenuously) praised life in Ottoman lands as preferable to that in the Holy Roman Empire. Such models dominated descriptions of Süleyman before the succession events of the 1550s became known in Latin Christendom.[14]

The 1532 *Copey vnd lautter Abschrifft eins warhafftigen Sendbrieffs* ... illustrates the complex depiction of Süleyman early in his reign. The pamphlet detailed Süleyman's annual campaign departure from Constantinople, listing the many armed, ominous cohorts in the Ottoman army riding towards Hungary who were expected to besiege Vienna again. The text also includes a scene from Süleyman's intimate life that echoed late medieval romances. Before Süleyman set off to war, the pamphlet tells us, he visited his mother. She lived in a cloister with some of his "most beautiful women," including a Macedonian woman Sponiziel whom he "loved before others." The description of Süleyman's leave-taking illustrated a hero's filial and romantic affections rather than a despot's lechery or cupidity.[15]

Roger Ascham's *Report and Discourse ... of the Affaires and State of Germany and the Emperour Charles His Court* ... also positively compared Süleyman with Christian princes, in a text concerned with princely character and the impacts of character on the complicated interplay of confessional and imperial politics. The *Report* was composed while the Protestant Ascham served as a member of the English embassy to the Habsburg court from 1550 to 1553. It countered Luis de Avila y Zuñiga's adulatory account of Charles's decisive victories during the Schmalkaldic War (1546–7) against the German Protestant powers.[16] During the war, popular pamphlets had described Charles's Spanish soldiers as the bloody murderers of women and children no better than the Turkish military.[17] At the war's conclusion, Charles ordered punitive measures against his defeated enemies; in consequence, his 1549 proposal that his son Philip be elected heir to the Holy Roman Empire was extremely unpopular. In 1552, months after the succession question had tentatively been settled by the two Habsburg brothers in favour of Philip, imperial succession was destabilized again when Charles's former ally Duke Maurice of Saxony broke with him militarily.

An important goal of the *Report* was to defend the character and actions of the German Protestant princes who rebelled in the 1540s and 1550s. Ascham's highest praise was reserved for Elector John Frederick of Saxony who, along with the bigamous Landgrave Philip of Hesse, had fought against

Catholic Charles in the Schmalkaldic War after being placed under imperial ban. Once the princes had been defeated, Charles had threatened their execution and ignominiously imprisoned them, a duress that, according to Ascham, John Frederick faced with inspiring grace. John Frederick gained the love of Catholics and Protestants because he was "wise in all his doings, just in all his dealings, lowly to the meanest, princely with the biggest, and excelling gentle to all" as well as steadfast in his Protestant faith.[18] Ascham also sought to interpret Duke Maurice of Saxony's actions as virtuous, a much more difficult task. The Protestant Maurice had chosen to fight against his co-confessional Protestant cousins in the war, despite owing his inheritance to his cousin John Frederick and his filial loyalty to his father-in-law Landgrave Philip. Charles rewarded Maurice's choice by stripping the Wettin electorship from the rebellious John Frederick and assigning it to Maurice and his branch of the family. Ascham explained Maurice's neglect of family and religion as the rashness of youth, and argued that Maurice redeemed himself morally in 1552. After attempting to get his father-in-law released through peaceful means, Maurice allied with the French and attacked Charles that May, driving him into headlong flight from Innsbruck solely, Ascham argued, to free Landgrave Philip.

Ascham's history redeemed the Protestant princes' actions and character at the cost of Charles's. According to Ascham, Charles's shameful ongoing imprisonment of Landgrave Philip had forced Maurice to rebel.[19] The need to justify the actions of princes who broke their oaths drove Ascham to characterize Charles as the truly dishonourable prince. Charles was an oath breaker who, by violating his peace treaty with Süleyman, goaded the "good and merciful" sultan into retaliating against a Christian civilian population. In this history through moral biography, the importance of filial loyalty (whether son by law or blood) and keeping oaths was emphasized. Because Süleyman was a "just and liberal prince," Ascham painted Süleyman's rebellious son Mustafa as "given to all mischief, cruel, false, ... seeker of strife and war."[20] Depictions of Süleyman as virtuous and Mustafa as wicked, however, did not survive the detailed news of Mustafa's death.

Discourses of Tyranny

In 1555, the Burgundian Nicholas de Moffan introduced the most recent Ottoman family succession conflicts (1552–3) to a Latin Christian audience. Moffan had been captured by the Ottomans while fighting in Hungary in 1552, and remained imprisoned for more than two years. During his captivity, Moffan learned about Ottoman current events from a fellow-prisoner who was Turkish.

Upon returning to the Holy Roman Empire, Moffan spread the news that Süleyman's family had been riven by filicide. The accounts, appearing in Latin as *Acta Impia Soltani Seuleimani Imperatoris Turcharum in scelerato parricidio Mustaphae primogeniti eius filii anno MDLIII* ... and in German as *Ein Grausame that / des yetzigen Türckischen Kaysers Soltani Seuleimani / die er an dem schandtlichen Todtschlag seines erstgeborn Suns Mustaphe begangen hat* ...[21] proffer moral judgment even in the titles. Süleyman has murdered his eldest son Mustafa and is judged impious, depraved, and wicked. A poem on the reverse of the German-language title page defines the Turkish sultan's actions as bestial and cannibalistic: "No lion or bear is so wild that he devours his own young."[22] Süleyman had crossed the line from just to depraved rule.

Moffan began his narrative by explaining the complications of open succession and emphasizing the Ottoman dynasty's moral failure to practise honourable marriage. Because Süleyman's talented son Mustafa was admired throughout the Ottoman Empire, Hurrem (named Rosa and not accorded the status of legitimate wife in Moffan's account) is consumed by anxiety for her own sons' futures. Spurred by jealousy and ambition, Hurrem works to cause her stepson Mustafa's death by convincing Süleyman of his treachery. Hurrem enlists the aid of the vezir Rustem, who was married to her daughter Mihrimah, in this effort. Over the course of a year, the two schemers remind Süleyman of his family's capacity for unfilial betrayals; his father Selim had deposed his own father in order to become sultan. The two encourage Süleyman to interpret Mustafa's disciplined and effective troops and his orderly governance as evidence that Mustafa is preparing to seize rule from Süleyman. Hurrem also attempts to dispatch Mustafa with poison. When Hurrem and Rustem's initial efforts do not provoke his suspicions to the point of action, they fan the flames of Süleyman's mistrust further. They produce a forged document as evidence that Mustafa had arranged a marriage with the daughter of the Persian shah, Süleyman's enemy.[23]

The next year, when the ruler of Persia attacks the Syrian border and Mustafa rallies his troops to defend the empire, Süleyman finally moves against Mustafa. He brings his own forces to Aleppo to confront both his son and the Persian threat. Ministers loyal to Mustafa warn him of his father's suspicions, and then the pamphlet pauses in its narrative of events to discuss Mustafa's moral dilemma at some length; he could remain a loyal son, answer his father's summons, and ride to his likely death, or he could illegitimately and thus tyrannically seize power from his father in order to save his life and attain greater worldly glory. Mustafa consults with his political and moral advisor, a learned "doctor" who presents his dilemma in terms familiar to a Christian reader: a choice between worldly power or eternal peace for Mustafa's soul. Mustafa decides to act virtuously and obey his father's command to appear before him. He voluntarily disarms himself before entering his father's tent, in order to avoid the disloyalty of bearing arms in his father's presence. Süleyman commands his mute servants to strangle the unarmed prince, without giving him an opportunity to defend himself from accusations of wrongdoing. In ordering this murder, Süleyman vaults from the status of a feared military opponent whose troops killed the babies of enemies, to that of a tyrant, an unjust ruler misguided enough to kill his own eldest son on the basis of corrupt advisors' counsel. The enormity of Süleyman's shameful and tyrannical[24] behaviour becomes apparent at the close of Moffan's text. Upon finding his beloved brother lying strangled on the ground, Süleyman's youngest son Jihangir condemns his father as a depraved and godless tyrant. Jihangir then kills himself with the dagger Mustafa had set aside in filial obedience.[25] Moffan concludes with Süleyman's efforts to perform penance for his deed.

Moffan's dramatic account of the internecine Ottoman dynasty appeared first in Augsburg, in a printing by Philip Ulhart issued soon after Moffan's dedication was completed on 13 August 1555. The imperial diet was in session during the summer and fall (concluding in late September) to negotiate the agreements that became known as the Peace of Augsburg. The diet ensured that a wide audience was available, and Ulhart bolstered the account's accessibility and authority by printing Latin and German editions, and by securing an imperial privilege for the pamphlet. Although the imperial privilege represented an imperial endorsement of content, the pamphlets also named a Protestant prince as an intended reader. Both Latin and German editions include Moffan's preface addressed to Duke Christoph of Württemberg, a committed Lutheran and, in 1555, Maximilian's intimate peer.[26] Amidst the confessional wrangling of the Augsburg diet and the military reversals of the previous few years, the future of imperial leadership and rule were unclear. Ferdinand, rather than the absent Charles, worked to broker the Peace of Augsburg even as the succession of Ferdinand's son Maximilian, thought by many to have strong Protestant leanings, remained unconfirmed. Although no explicit parallels were drawn between Süleyman and either Habsburg brother in the Moffan texts, the story of Süleyman and his sons stood as a salutary warning about the consequences of unclarified succession. The moral lesson cautioned on two levels: open succession and personal ambition are condemned as gateways to family violence, and dynastic divisiveness might lead a ruler to turn from just, legitimate governance to tyranny.

The story was sufficiently popular that a second Latin edition appeared within a few months and a German version soon after.[27] Although it is not known if Charles or any other Habsburg read the tale of Mustafa, Charles's son Philip was not confirmed as heir to the Holy Roman Empire during the imperial diet, despite Charles's and Ferdinand's prior agreement. Having already ceded Naples to Philip prior to his marriage to Mary I of England, Charles passed to his son the rule of the Netherlands (in October 1555, after the close of the imperial diet) and his Iberian kingdoms, including Sicily and the Indies (in January 1556). Abdicating his sovereignty over the Holy Roman Empire in favour of his brother Ferdinand, without mention of Philip as heir, would be completed only at the end of Charles's life.[28]

The Ottoman internecine drama added a layer of critique to the earlier discourse about the Turk as the scourge of God; Süleyman had become a tyrant. In the Moffan text, Süleyman's act of murder, inspired by insecurity about his worldly power, is a perversion of virtue, and several aspects of his despotism are elaborated. Süleyman's intimate relations with Hurrem are not presented as honourable marriage; rather, she is a concubine. She receives assistance in her plots not only from the corrupt renegade vezir Rustem, but also from a Jewish sorceress. Hurrem's power over her husband is taken as an additional sign of his lack of self-discipline and immoderation, another failing of despots.[29] Süleyman's actions severed the bonds of paternal and filial loyalty and were defined as beyond human or natural religion and morality. Moffan notes that Süleyman offers up a sacrifice in Jerusalem, to atone for the murder he commanded. Implicitly, Süleyman's act stood in contrast with the story of Abraham, who received a dreadful divine command to obey God by sacrificing his son Isaac, a test mercifully halted at the last moment.

For Latin Christians, filicide would continue to signify tyrannical excess in subsequent decades; perceptions of Süleyman's cruelty and impiety were solidified through the news that another of Süleyman's sons, Bayezid, was killed at Süleyman's command in 1561. Bayezid had fled to the shah of Persia's court after losing his own struggle for primacy with his brother Selim. Selim became the only remaining son in the Ottoman Empire and thus his inheritance of the empire was clear. According to Latin Christian observers, this outcome was insufficient for Süleyman. He sent agents to kill Bayezid at the Persian court and Bayezid's young sons at their scattered locations. Hurrem was not held responsible for her son Bayezid's death, and by implication Süleyman's mercilessness and responsibility for eliminating Bayezid and his family were heightened. The importance of these filicides is highlighted in the one negative discussion of Ottoman rule in pre-1570 Venetian diplomatic reports. A 1562 report by Marcantonio Donini noted that Süleyman's reputation as a just and wise ruler had been destroyed by the news that Süleyman had murdered three sons and five grandsons.[30]

Diplomatic Orientalizing

Bayezid's death and Ottoman succession also figured in the symbolic gestures of diplomacy. When the news of Bayezid's death reached Constantinople, the Habsburg envoy Ogier de Busbecq was informed that, with the Ottoman succession resolved, no better treaty terms would be forthcoming. Busbecq quickly agreed to the proffered terms and took the draft treaty back to Ferdinand for his ratification. After Busbecq, the Ottoman envoy Ibrahim Bey, and their retinues reached Vienna, it was decided to send Busbecq and Ibrahim Bey on to Frankfurt on Main, where the princes of the Holy Roman Empire were gathering to elect Maximilian king of the Romans. For the Austrian Habsburgs, the ensuing spectacle should pronounce a double triumph: Maximilian's new status as official heir to the Holy Roman Empire and, after decades of negotiation, a peace treaty carried by an Ottoman ambassador to the heartlands of the Holy Roman Empire.[31]

Almost everything about Ibrahim's presence at Frankfurt in November 1562 was by Habsburg design, except the terms of the treaty itself. In the new treaty, the Habsburgs gained a small amount of symbolic ground: they were permitted to establish a recognized embassy in Constantinople, and the two empires regularized exchanges across their shared border. Overall, however, the treaty reinscribed the Habsburgs' weaker status: they were forced to continue paying an annual 30,000 gulden gift to the Ottomans in exchange for recognition of Habsburg Hungary. In subsequent decades, this treaty provision would be interpreted as a shameful tax or tribute by German observers, and its status became a precipitant of the Long War (1593–1606) between the two empires.[32]

In the public production of Maximilian's election and coronation at Frankfurt in 1562, the Habsburgs sought to obscure the ongoing reality of their military weakness by taking advantage of Ibrahim's appearance. Ibrahim observed the election and coronation processions from a viewing platform, designed so that he could see and be seen by the gathered notables of the Holy Roman Empire. The assembled princes each brought retinues of armed men, sometimes numbering in the hundreds, so that the number of witnesses was in the thousands. The events were described for an even wider audience in a spate of pamphlets printed in 1562–3. The Habsburgs and their supporters emphasized Ibrahim's foreignness, highlighting the distance and difference between Ottoman and Habsburg courts and between Muslim and Christian cultures through their presentation of Ibrahim's "Turkish" appearance, language skills, and rank in the Ottoman court. Ibrahim's past as a Polish renegade and his current status as a mid-ranking court translator with considerable linguistic abilities at the Ottoman court were elided. In contrast, pamphlets authored by Habsburg critics made Ibrahim's Christian faithlessness and Polish origin highly visible. The exoticization of Ibrahim was most evident in the description of Ibrahim's reception with Ferdinand, a few days after Maximilian's election. The diplomatic scene of translated speeches and gifted exotic material objects and animals reinforced the impression of Ibrahim's linguistic and cultural distance.[33]

Ferdinand received Ibrahim Bey at a public audience in the presence of the new king of the Romans, Maximilian, and other princes of the empire. Ibrahim Bey proffered a treaty between Habsburgs and Ottomans to Ferdinand for official recognition, and presented diplomatic gifts. The audience followed customary diplomatic practices: in a courtly speech, Ibrahim presented his credentials and the proposed treaty between the emperors of the Ottoman and Holy Roman Empires, proclaiming his sovereign Süleyman's wish for peace between their two territories. Following the formal discussion of the treaty, Ibrahim Bey moved to the ceremonies of gift-giving, which were important in diplomatic exchanges between rulers in the sixteenth century. Before the gifts were presented, several accounts noted an additional, elaborate diplomatic compliment. Ibrahim requested that Ferdinand single out his son and heir among the assembled princes in the audience room. Ferdinand responded by pointing out Maximilian, seated at his left hand, as his son. Ibrahim congratulated Maximilian on a smooth succession and bowed to him. Wishing Maximilian a happy life, Ibrahim stated that he hoped Maximilian's inheritance of the Holy Roman Empire would proceed fortuitously. He then complimented the father's rule and added that with such a great father, and the good omen of the name "Maximilian" derived from *maximus*, the son could only become a "greater and higher" ruler. After this speech, Ibrahim proceeded to give Maximilian a small selection of valuable exotic gifts.[34] Habsburg accounts publicized Ibrahim's compliment about the Habsburg peaceful succession. After years of uncertainty, the successful election of Maximilian could only seem more triumphant in comparison with the Ottoman state's violent and immoral mechanisms of succession.

After Ferdinand's death and Maximilian's succession as emperor in 1564, Habsburg desires to test the relative strength of the two empires led to open warfare on the Hungarian border. During this indecisive war of 1565–7, Maximilian's forces lost key strongholds, most notably Sziget. In the course of that siege, the aged Süleyman died from battle wounds,[35] although Ottoman generals hid the fact of his death until after Sziget's capture. With the loss of Süleyman and Ottoman attention focused internally on Selim II's accession, the Ottomans did not press their military advantage. The war fizzled out inconclusively without much shift in the boundary between Habsburg and Ottoman lands. In the Germanies, the imperial estates and other representative bodies continued to support the Turkish tax that funded border fortifications, and public awareness of the Turkish threat would continue to be fuelled by printed propaganda.[36]

The internecine violence in the house of Osman was one of the topics popularized in texts produced in the Holy Roman Empire through the end of the century. When Selim II died in 1574, a pamphlet quickly reported that his son Murad III had secured the succession with not one but five fratricides. The death toll accompanying the succession did not stop there: mothers of these boys killed themselves out of grief, and in an orgy of slaughter, Murad sacrificed seven hundred sheep to his dead father, echoing an Old Testament offering pyre. These deaths, along with Süleyman's filicides, appeared in Johannes Leunclavius's popular, often-reprinted compendium.[37] Busbecq's 1589 printed account of his ambassadorial travels not only detailed Süleyman's ruthless role in killing his grandchildren, it also drove home the contrast between Ferdinand and Süleyman as fathers. Busbecq wrote that Ferdinand's only fault as a father was his moderation in promoting his children; in his paternal care for the well-being of the Holy Roman Empire he neglected his dynastic interests.[38] Salomon Schweigger's account of his 1577 embassy to Constantinople, published in 1608, drew on German understandings about Ottoman succession to define the nature of the Turkish state explicitly as a tyranny rather than an empire or a monarchy. Schweigger based his classification on the fact that Ottoman "governance was spotted with fratricide" and that their law perversely required claimants to kill their brothers in order to secure rule. Schweigger compared the Ottomans to that classical exemplar of tyrannical excess, Roman Emperor Nero, who committed incest with his mother and unjustly executed councillors. By 1628, when the 1587 travel account of Reinhold Lubenau was published, fratricide was "at the root of Turkish Tyranny." Lubenau cited, as key evidence, Süleyman's command that his own children be garrotted before his eyes and his young grandchildren killed.[39]

Tyranny and Primogeniture

In the second half of the sixteenth century, Latin Christian and Habsburg constructions of the Ottoman dynasty focused on filicidal and fratricidal elements of succession against the backdrop of growing legal and cultural support for patriarchal authority in the Germanies.[40] For ruling princes, paternal responsibilities included the decision to divide territories relatively equally or to observe primogeniture. The issue was often settled while a father was still alive, to circumvent future conflicts among his heirs. Primogeniture as a mode of succession was increasingly popular, but its adoption was confessionally uneven; most Catholic princes adopted primogeniture by the later sixteenth century, while many Protestant princes retained practices of partible inheritance through the early seventeenth century. In this era of high mortality rates, the continuation of partible inheritance offered a dynasty significant advantages; it prepared multiple family members for rule in the eventuality of another branch dying out.[41] Dynasties might fluctuate between inheritance strategies; the Habsburgs, for example, divided their territories after experimenting with primogeniture in Charles V's reign. Other prominent dynasties such as the Braunschweig-Lüneburgs survived as a result of their continued reliance on partible inheritance during the second half of the sixteenth century. The instability of succession in the sixteenth-century Holy Roman Empire allowed for the possibility, despite patriarchal rhetoric, of irresponsible ruling fathers deposed so that sons could rule, as in the cases of the Wittelsbach Wilhelm V of Bavaria, considered financially irresponsible, and other princely rulers who were deemed unbalanced.[42]

At the end of the sixteenth century, portraits of internecine tyranny were not restricted to the example of the Ottoman dynasty; perhaps most notably, Duke Heinrich Julius of Braunschweig authored a tragedy of primogeniture in 1594. The play *Von einem ungeratenen Sohn* offers up a bloody story of patricide and fratricide. Set in an unspecified but possibly non-Christian court,[43] the main characters are the ruling family and their closest advisors. The duke Severus, his wife Patientia, their eldest son Probus, and Probus's wife Pudica are as temperate, pious, and virtuous as their names suggest. In contrast, Nero, Severus and Patientia's second son, bears the name and character flaws of the classical Roman tyrant. Second-son Nero lives in a state of licentious immoderation. He spends his days and nights feasting and drinking, and he has an illegitimate child, Infans. Severus decides that his eldest son Probus should inherit all of his lands and authority, and that Nero should be granted a pension and sent away to live beyond the bounds of the territory where his "wildness" will not trouble the realm. Stirring declarations of Severus's just and merciful rule, as well as support for the proposed succession, are offered by various councillors and family members. When Nero learns of the proposed primogeniture, however, he is not so equanimous. His response is murderous and unfilial. In a scene resonating with those of idolatrous Old Testament practices or fantasies of New World child sacrifice to the devil, Nero sacrifices his illegitimate son, cutting out his son's heart while the child still lives, drinking his blood mixed with wine, and roasting and eating his heart.[44] Having formed a compact with the devil through this depraved act, Nero is empowered to murder the rest of his family. Nero stabs his father, cuts his mother's throat, and strangles his nephew Innocens in the castle garden. Probus finds the bodies of his parents and son, mourning their deaths with appropriate sorrow and no thought of his own worldly benefit. With Severus's wishes regarding primogeniture known and accepted by the inheriting elder brother Probus, Nero continues on his murderous path. He poisons the grieving Pudica with an apple that he has tampered with and then murders his brother with a long dagger. He pins the crimes on his father's three virtuous counsellors Iustus, Verax, and Constans, who are beheaded for the murders. At the play's conclusion, Nero is confronted with the ghosts of his victims and calls on the devil to take him to hell so that he can escape being tormented by the ghosts.

Heinrich Julius's play, often considered innovative for its gory violence, reflects the tensions and concerns of the late sixteenth-century Holy Roman Empire.[45] The play vividly depicted the consequences of insatiable, ungoverned wickedness in the service of the devil and offered a commentary on succession practices. Through the vagaries of the sixteenth century, the Braunschweig-Lüneburgs had continued to practise partible inheritance, despite efforts by Heinrich Julius's grandfather Duke Heinrich V to disinherit Heinrich Julius's father Julius.[46] *Von dem ungeratenen Sohn* illustrated the dangerous stresses of an ill-advised primogeniture. In addition to his own family history, Heinrich Julius could have targeted several different dynasties with political difficulties through his critique. In the Holy Roman Empire, two Habsburg eldest sons had succeeded their fathers as emperor in turn, Maximilian II and then Maximilian's own son Rudolf II. Maximilian's brothers had inherited portions of the Habsburg lands and governed them independently, but at Rudolf's accession in 1567, his five brothers were offered annual pensions as their inheritance portions. By 1594, Rudolf was beginning to gain a reputation for ineffective rule and lack of moderation, and his younger brothers were drawn into projects and plots involving the governance of Habsburg territories. His brother Matthias, next in line for rule, would eventually force Rudolf's abdication and become emperor after first failing to gain acceptance as Philip II's replacement in the Low Countries.[47]

Also in 1594, the rivalry between the Habsburgs and the Ottomans had heated up again and the two empires were one year into the Long War. Heinrich Julius's play could also serve as propaganda about the blood-thirsty Ottoman fratricidal tyrants. During the reign of Selim II, open succession was modified into something quite closely resembling primogeniture with a murderous element. Selim II had competed with several brothers who had served as competent provincial governors, but he structured his own succession differently. He gave public recognition and responsibilities only to his eldest son, who became Murad III after Selim's death. Without any experienced adult rivals, Murad's accession was unquestioned. Murad followed the same practice of elevating his eldest son Mehmed into positions of provincial responsibility, and Mehmed also succeeded as Mehmed III in 1595 without serious competition. Each of these late sixteenth-century Ottoman successions included the fratricide of the remaining inexperienced heirs.[48]

A third critique, of the Spanish Habsburg family and its growing Black Legend, may also have been a target of the play. During the 1560s, Philip II's son Prince Carlos had become increasingly ungovernable and wild after a serious head injury. The news of his death in 1568, while being held in detention by his father, circulated widely north of the Alps. A sinister interpretation of Carlos's death was promoted by William of Orange in his 1581 *Apologia ... ad proscriptionem ab Hispaniarum rege in eum promulgatam*. The *Apologia*, particularly in its English translation, is well known as a key text in the development of the Black Legend;[49] its call for virtuous rule is based on the delegitimization of Philip II's rule. It delineated a history of murders and illegitimacy within the Spanish branch of the Habsburgs. William begins the pamphlet by defending his own succession to Orange and Nassau, confirmed by the deceased Charles V. William emphasizes his loyal service and dedication to Charles before comparing Philip II to Nero and several other tyrants from the past. William accuses Philip II of murdering his third wife Elizabeth of Valois, in order to make way for an incestuous marriage to his niece Anna, the daughter of Maximilian and Maria. The depraved Philip has also murdered his son Carlos, because Philip II's marriage to Carlos's mother was bigamous as the result of a secret prior marriage. William alleges that, with the successful filicide of his secretly illegitimate son, Philip II could engender a legitimate heir with Anna. The *Apologia* also attributes the origins of the Spanish Habsburgs' immorality to their descent from another secretly illegitimate sovereign.[50] Even if Heinrich Julius did not have these princely houses in mind, his audiences would have been able to draw connections easily between the blood-thirsty, disinherited Nero and these contemporary dynastic politics.

The *Apologia* illustrates the close links between confessionally informed political positions and the expanding possibilities for the defamatory label of tyrant in the Habsburg lands during the second half of the sixteenth century. Mid-century uncertainties about succession and a new phase of Habsburg-Ottoman diplomatic relations had fuelled new representations of the orientalist Turk. In the now multi-confessional Holy Roman Empire, the Habsburgs needed to generate new discursive strategies to unify their people, and the Turk could serve well as a menacing and common enemy to all Christians, regardless of confession. In the propaganda about the Ottoman dynasty and in Habsburg-Ottoman diplomatic exchanges, the Habsburgs promoted a cultural distancing between the Holy Roman Empire and Ottoman tyranny, between prudent Christian and violent Muslim rulers. Strategies of exoticizing the Ottoman dynasty, which emphasized the discourse of personally undisciplined, libertine, despotic sultans, would be applied with increasing frequency and strength in the seventeenth century. In the second half of the sixteenth century, the Habsburg family and German writers had few available options other than this orientalizing strategy. The lack of political and religious unity or military power in the Holy Roman Empire offered no position from which to criticize Ottoman military strength or Muslim religious unity and piety. During these decades of Habsburg family loyalty, German authors could only attack family relations between Ottoman fathers, sons, and brothers.

NOTES

1 Cornell Fleischer, "Shadows of Shadows," *International Journal of Turkish Studies* 13 (2007): 51–62; and Robert Finlay, "Prophecy and Politics in Istanbul," *Journal of Early Modern History* 2 (1998): 1–31.
2 Walter Sturminger, *Bibliographie und Ikonographie der Türkenbelagerungen Wiens 1529 und 1683*, Veröffentlichungen der Kommission für Neuere Geschichte Österreichs 41 (Graz: Böhlau, 1955); and Carl Göllner, *Turcica*, 3 vols. (Bucharest: Academy, 1961–78).
3 Edward Said, *Orientalism* (New York: Vintage, 1978). Barbara Fuchs, *Mimesis and Empire* (Cambridge: Cambridge University Press, 2001) points out the importance of cultural mimesis for Spanish and English cultural strategies in the sixteenth century; for the possibilities of Michel DeCerteau's Levinasian alterity, see Wlad Godzich's introduction to Michel DeCerteau, *Heterologies* (Minneapolis: University of Minnesota Press, 1986), xiii–xxi; and Jonathan Burton, *Traffic and Turning: Islam and English Drama: 1579–1624* (Newark: University of Delaware Press, 2005), 1–52 offers a thoughtful introduction to the English scholarship on the ambivalent engagement he names "traffic."
4 Lucette Valensi, *The Birth of the Despot: Venice and the Sublime Porte* (Ithaca: Cornell University Press, 1993); Douglas Howard also notes that internal critics of Ottoman rule linked the dynasty's decline to the end of Süleyman's reign in "Genre and Myth in the Ottoman Advice for Kings Literature," in *The Early Modern Ottomans*, ed. Virginia Aksan and Daniel Goffman, 137–66 (Cambridge: Cambridge University Press, 2007).
5 Said, *Orientalism*, 40, 62–3.
6 Medieval characterizations of Muslims were also produced in an era of significant Muslim power. See John V. Tolan, *Saracens* (New York: Columbia University Press, 2002). Similarly, Heather Ferguson places the Venetian rhetorical turn of describing the Ottoman ruler as a sybaritic, personally violent despot within the context of Ottoman strength and Venetian weakness after the 1570 Ottoman

seizure of Cyprus, in "Ideologies on the Defense: Venetians, Ottomans, and Theories of Just Rule in the Mediterranean," presented at *Connected Histories of the Middle East, Africa, and South Asia*, Pomona College, February 2012.

7 Paula Sutter Fichtner, *Emperor Maximilian II* (New Haven: Yale University Press, 2001), 17–29; Friedrich Edelmayer, "Die Vorgeschichte der Krönungen Maximilians II," in *Die Krönungen Maximilians II. zum König von Böhmen, Römischen König und König von Ungarn (1562/63) nach der Beschreibung des Hans Habersack* (Vienna: Österreichische Akademie der Wissenschaften, 1990), 21–38; and Heinrich Lutz, *Christianitas Afflicta* (Göttingen: Vanderhoeck & Ruprecht, 1964).

8 Cemal Kafadar, *Between Two Worlds: The Construction of the Ottoman State* (Berkeley: University of California Press, 2005), 95–109, 136–7; and Leslie Peirce, *The Imperial Harem* (New York: Oxford University Press, 1993). Süleyman's sons and succession are discussed in Alan Fisher, "Süleymân and His Sons," and Leslie Peirce, "The Family as Faction: Dynastic Politics in the Reign of Süleymân," in *Soliman le Magnifique et Son Temps*, ed. Gilles Veinstein, 117–24, 105–16 (Paris: Documentation Française, 1992).

9 For a summary of contemporary Ottoman views of Süleyman, see Christine Woodhead's "Perspectives on Süleyman," in *Süleyman the Magnificent and His Age*, ed. Metin Kunt and Christine Woodhead (London: Longman, 1995), 164–90, esp. 177–80 for perceptions of succession issues in the 1550s.

10 The Italian *Commentario* (Rome: Blado, 1532) was reprinted multiple times before other language versions appeared. The Latin translation was *Turcicarum Rerum Commentarius Pauli Iovii Episcopi Nucerini ad Carolum V Imperatorem Augustum* (Wendelin Ribel: Strasbourg, 1537), and the German translation by reformer Justus Jonas was titled *Ursprung des Türckischen Reichs* ... (Wittenberg, 1537). For additional printing history, see T.C. Price Zimmerman, *Paolo Giovio: The Historian and the Crisis of Sixteenth-Century Italy* (Princeton: Princeton University Press, 1995), 121, 289; for Giovio's texts and sources, see Erich Cochrane, *Historians and Historiography in the Italian Renaissance* (Chicago: University of Chicago Press, 1981); and V.J. Parry, "Renaissance Historical Literature in Relation to the Near and Middle East (with Special Reference to Paolo Giovio)," in *Historians of the Middle East*, ed. Bernard Lewis and P.M. Holt, 277–89 (London: Oxford University Press, 1962).

11 Giovio, *Turcicarum Rerum Commentarius* (Strasbourg), Biiii, B[vii], Dii–Dii^v. For Cem's subsequent fate, see Nicolas Vatin, *Sultan Jem* (Ankara: Société Turque d'Histoire, 1997). In a text finalized in 1538 and printed in 1550, Spandounes details many Ottoman succession-related murders but identifies only Mehmed II, whose conquest of Constantinople was devastating for the Spandounes family, as a cruel filicide. See *On the Origin of the Ottoman Emperors*, trans. D. Nicol (Cambridge: Cambridge University Press, 1997), xvii–xviii, xxv, 20–2, 25, 32, 53–5, 63–4, 68.

12 The dedicatory remarks from 1531 are relatively brief: *Turcicarum Rerum Commentarius* (Strasbourg, 1537), A2–A3. For Melanchthon's comments, see *Turcicarum Rerum Commentarius* (Wittenberg, 1537), Aii–Avii^v. Arguably, Melanchthon intended readers to think not only of Süleyman, but also of the other "Antichrists" who afflicted Protestants: Pope Paul III and Emperor Charles V.
13 E.g., *Haimliche Anschleg vnd fürnemumb des Turckischen Kaysers* ... (Augsburg: Steiner, 1523); *Der krieg zwischen dem groszmechtigen propheten Sophi / Turcken vnnd dem Soldan* ... (1517); and *Des Turckischen Keysers Heerzug / wie er von Constantinopel ... kummen / ...* (Nuremberg: Zell, 1530).
14 Giovio, *Turcicarum Rerum Commentarius*; Roger Ascham, *A Report and Discourse written by Roger Ascham, of the affaires and state of Germany and the Emperour Charles his court, duryng certaine yeares while the sayd Roger was there* (London: John Day) reprinted in *The Whole Works of Roger Ascham*, ed. J.A. Giles (London: John Russell Smith, 1864), 3:13; *Auß Zug eynes Briefes / wie eyner so in der Turckey wonhafft / seynem freund in dise land geschriben vnd angezeygt* ... ([Magdeburg: Ottinger], 1526), aii; and *Antwurten so ein Burger meyster / Radt / vnd der Groß Radt / die man nempt die zwey hundert der Statt Zürich ... [1524]*, c^v.
15 *Copey vnnd lautter Abschrifft ains warhafftigen sendbrieffs* ... (1532), esp. Aiii.
16 Avila y Zuñiga's *Commentario nella guerra della Germania* (1548) had been printed in Latin, Spanish, French, and German by 1551. Although likely composed by the end of 1553, Ascham's *Report* did not appear in print until ca 1570, after Ascham's death and the beginning of the reign of Protestant Elizabeth I of England. Lawrence V. Ryan, *Roger Ascham* (Stanford: Stanford University Press, 1963), 157; and Ascham, *Report*, 29–31.
17 E. Hühns, "'Nationale' Propaganda im Schmalkaldischen Krieg," *Zeitschrift für Geschichtswissenschaft* 6 (1958): 1037–40; and *Ein schönes neues Lied von Carolo den Fünfften ...* [1547], Biv.
18 Ascham, *Report*, 41–2.
19 Ibid., 40–62.
20 Ibid., 10–14.
21 *Acta Impia* ... (Augsburg: Ulhart, [1555]); and *Ein Grausame that* ... (Augsburg: Ulhart, [1555]). While general events are supported by Ottoman sources, the particulars of motivation here are Moffan's.
22 "Kain Low / kain Beer / also wild ist / Das er sein aigen jungen frist." Moffan, *Ein Grausame that* ..., Ai^v.
23 Moffan, *Ein Grausame that*, Aii–Biii^v.
24 Ibid., Cii–Diii.
25 Ibid., Diii^v–Div.
26 For the relationship between Duke Christoph and Archduke Maximilian, see Fichtner, *Maximilian*, 53–8. Lutz discusses the intersection of religious and dynastic politics at the diet.

27 Johannes Oporinus of Basel printed a second Latin edition *Soltani Solymanni Turcarum Imperatoris horrendum facinus, scelerato in proprium filium, natu maximum, Soltanum Mustapham, parricidio* ... in November 1555, and in 1556 a Wittenberg press produced *Wie die Turckisch Tyrann Solyman / der itzund regiert / seinen eltesten Son Mustapha / der ein freidiger Kriegsman gewesen ist / mit einem schmehlichem Tode hat lassen vmbbringen / der felschlich verklagt ist / durch ein unehrlich Weib / vnd durch den Wascha Rustan* ..., with the address to Duke Christoph excised.

28 Although Charles sent a letter declaring his intentions in September 1556, the abdication was not accepted by the Imperial Estates until February 1558. Karl Brandi, *The Emperor Charles V* (1939; Atlantic Highlands, NJ: Humanities, 1980), 629–36; and a detailed account is in Lutz, *Christianitas Afflicta*.

29 Moffan, *Ein Grausame that*, Bi^v, Biii^v.

30 Ogier Ghiselin de Busbecq, *Augerii Gislenii Busbequii D. Legationis Turcicae Epistolae quatuor* (1589; Frankfurt: Andrea Wechel, Claud. Marnius, Ioannis Aubrius, 1595), 275–82; and Valensi, *Birth of the Despot*, 38.

31 HHStA Turcica 16 Konv. 2, fols. 131–49^v. Busbecq repeated his arguments of fols. 147–8^v in his published account of his embassy, *Turcicae Epistolae quatuor*, 296–7.

32 Ernst Petritsch, "Tribut oder Ehrengeschenk?," *Archiv und Forschung*, ed. Elisabeth Springer and Leopold Kammerhofer, Wiener Beiträge zur Geschichte der Neuzeit, 20 (Vienna: Verlag für Geschichte und Politik, 1993), 49–58. For a more detailed analysis of Ibrahim's visit and Habsburg exoticizing strategies, see Carina L. Johnson, *Cultural Hierarchies in Sixteenth-Century Europe* (Cambridge: Cambridge University Press, 2011), chap. 5.

33 Göllner, *Turcica*, 2:91–101; Hans Habersack, *Die Krönungen Maximilians II. zum König von Böhmen, Römischen König und König von Ungarn (1562/63) nach der Beschreibung des Hans Habersack* (Vienna: Österreichische Akademie der Wissenschaften, 1990); Michael Beuther, *Ordenliche Verzeychniß / welcher gestalt / die Erwehlung unnd Krönung / des Allerdurchleuchtigsten Großmächtigsten Fürsten und Herrn / Herrn Maximilian / Römischen unnd zu Böheym Königs etc. zu Franckfurt am Main / im Wintermonat nähestverschienen 1562 jars / geschehen* (Frankfurt am Main: David Zöpffeln, 1563); *Wahrhafftige Beschreibung / welcher gestalt die königkliche wirde Maximilian* ... (Frankfurt am Main: Corvinus, Feyerabend, heirs of Gallus, 1563); *Anbringen Türkischer Legation / Ebrahimi Strotschü / gebornen Polecken* ... (Nuremberg: Berg and Newber, 1562); Laurentius Fuchs, *Kurtze Beschreibung der Königlichen Wirden und Magistrat Ampt* (1563).

34 Habersack, *Die Krönungen Maximilians II*; Beuther, *Ordenliche Verzeychniß*; *Wahrhafftige Beschreibung / welcher gestalt die königkliche wirde Maximilian*; and *Anbringen Türkischer Legation*.

35 In popular pamphlets, even Süleyman's death was suspected to be the result of foul play. *Newe Zeitungen von des Turckischen keysers / Soldan Solimanus / todlichem Abgang* ... (1567), Aii–Aiii.

36 Gunther Rosenberg, *The Austrian Military Border in Croatia, 1552–1747* (Urbana: University of Illinois Press, 1960); Winfried Schulze, *Reich und Türkengefahr im späten 16. Jahrhundert* (Munich: C.H. Beck, 1978); and Karl Vocelka, *Die Politische Propaganda Kaiser Rudolfs II. (1576–1612)* (Vienna: Österreichische Akademie der Wissenschaften, 1980).
37 *Newe zeittung vnnd gründtliche Beschreibung / Von des Turckischen Keysers absterben / vnnd des Newen ankunfft: Wie er inn das Keysertumb kommen ...* (Munich: Adam Berg, 1575). Johannes Leunclavius, *Annales Svltanorvm Othmanidarvm ...* 2nd ed. (Frankfurt am Main: Marne and Aubri, 1596), 55–7, 72; and *Neuwe Chronica Turckischer nation ...* (Frankfurt am Main: Marne und Aubri, 1595), 56–8, 89. Johannes Leunclavius's chronicle does not continue to 1595, when Mehmed III killed his nineteen brothers upon his succession. For Mehmed III's succession, see Peirce, *Imperial Harem*, 96–100.
38 Busbecq, *Augerii Gislenii Busbequii*, 301.
39 Salomon Schweigger, *Ein Newe Reyssbeschreibung auss Teutschland nach Constantinopel und Jerusalem* (Nuremberg: Johann Lantzenberger, 1608; facs. Graz: Akademische Druck u. Verlagsanstalt, 1964), sii; and Reinhold Lubenau, *Beschreibung der reisen des Reinhold Lubenau*, ed. W. Sahm (Königsburg I. Pr.: Beyer, 1912–20), 289.
40 Lyndal Roper, *Holy Household* (Oxford: Clarendon, 1991) is the seminal study.
41 Explanations for the confessional-based difference remain suggestive. See Paula Fichtner's *Protestantism and Primogeniture in Early Modern Germany* (New Haven: Yale University Press, 1989), which theorizes that the absence of bishoprics drove Protestants to maintain partible inheritance, and Karl-Heinz Spiess's careful "Lordship, Kinship, and Inheritance among the German High Nobility in the Middle Ages and Early Modern Period," in *Kinship in Europe: Approaches to Long-term Development (1300–1900)*, ed. David Sabean, Simon Teuscher, and John Mathieu, 57–75 (New York: Berghahn, 2007).
42 H.C. Erik Midelfort, *Mad Princes of Renaissance Germany* (Charlottesville: University of Virginia Press, 1996).
43 The absence of clerical characters suggests that the play may not be located in a Christian court. Heinrich Julius von Braunschweig, *Tragoedia. Hiehadbel. Von einem Vngeratenen Sohn* (Wolfenbüttel, 1594), in *Die Schauspiele des Herzogs Heinrich Julius von Braunschweig*, ed. W.L. Holland, Bibliothek des Literarischen Vereins in Stuttgart, vol. 36 (Stuttgart, 1855).
44 For these tropes of child sacrifice in the sixteenth century, see Johnson, *Cultural Hierarchies*, 41–53.
45 For an introduction to commentaries on this play, see Arnd Beise, "Verbrecherische und heilige Gewalt im deutschsprachigen Trauerspiel des 17. Jahrhunderts," in *Ein Schauplatz herber Angst*, ed. Markus Meumann and Dirk Niefanger, 106–10 (Göttingen: Wallstein, 1997); and A.H.J. Knight, "Zum Studium der Tragödien des Herzogs Heinrich Julius von Braunschweig," *Germanisch-Romanische Monatsschrift* 25 (1937): 100–19.

46 Heinrich Julius took the presence of the devil in the world seriously, as a ruler he prominently prosecuted witches for their demonic associations. For Duke Heinrich's maneouvres, see Fichtner, *Primogeniture*.
47 Luc Duerloo, *Dynasty and Piety: Archduke Albert (1598–1621) and Habsburg Political Culture in an Age of Religious Wars* (Burlington: Ashgate, 2012); and Midelfort, *Mad Princes*, 126–40.
48 In political reality, the dynasty had begun to develop alternate succession strategies and in the seventeenth century moved to confining rather than killing surplus princes. Peirce, *Imperial Harem*, 96–105.
49 William of Orange, *Apologia principis Wilhelmi Auricae, comitis Nassaviae ad proscriptionem ab Hispaniarum rege in eum promulgatam* (1581). Useful starting points for the Black Legend and the *Apologia* are J.N. Hillgarth, *The Mirror of Spain, 1500–1700* (Ann Arbor: University of Michigan Press, 2000); and Richard Kagan, *Clio and the Crown* (Baltimore, MD: Johns Hopkins University Press, 2009), 128. For the political context, Peter Arnade, *Beggars, Iconoclasts, and Civic Patriots* (Ithaca, NY: Cornell University Press, 2008), 260–303.
50 William of Orange, *Apologia*, 9, 28–32.

chapter five

"The ruin and slaughter of ... fellow Christians": The French as a Threat to Christendom in Spanish Assertions of Sovereignty in Italy, 1479–1516

ANDREW W. DEVEREUX

In the final two decades of the fifteenth century, the Kingdom of Naples, comprising the southern half of the boot of Italy, became the object of the expansionist designs of three ascendant states that sought to become hegemonic powers in the Mediterranean. Between 1480 and 1495, Naples was invaded successively by the Ottoman Empire, France, and Spain, before finally being incorporated into the Spanish Crown of Aragon in 1503. The conflicts for control of Naples and, more broadly, for hegemony in the central Mediterranean basin, constitute the opening chapter of the imperial rivalries of the early modern Mediterranean. These events have traditionally been interpreted through the lens of the Italian Wars (1494–1559), marking the struggle between France and Spain for European hegemony.[1] Yet there was simultaneously a broader, pan-Mediterranean component to the conflict. Analysing the Italian Wars in the wider context of the Mediterranean allows us to consider the role played, both directly and indirectly, by the Ottoman state, an empire that also sought to become the dominant power in the region.

Indeed, each of these three states viewed the Mediterranean Sea as a locus of strategic, geopolitical importance. Its significance, however, went beyond these practical concerns. The inner sea, as a conceptual space, carried a plethora of resonances, all of which played some part in the political thought, and resulting policies, of Spain, France, and the Ottoman Empire. For most late fifteenth-century Europeans, the Mediterranean lay at the centre of the world; it was the site where the three known terrestrial parts of the globe (Africa, Asia, and Europe) intersected. According to most geographers, the precise point of intersection between the Earth's three constituent parts was Jerusalem.[2] Not all, however, subscribed to this opinion. The Spanish courtier Cristóbal de Santesteban argued that Sicily lay at the centre of the world, and he viewed control of the island kingdom as a key to the establishment of a universal empire, concluding that "no one might call himself lord of the world, nor even think of doing so, without first ruling Sicily."³

To this geographic understanding of the centrality of the Mediterranean was melded a Christian conception of history. Many fifteenth-century Europeans held a halcyon view of early Christian history and longed for the restoration of the primitive church, in its embrace of the Mediterranean shores of Asia, Africa, and Europe.⁴ Finally, the Mediterranean carried the imperial resonances of ancient Rome. No state could embark on an expansionist venture in the *mare nostrum* without engaging in some way with the preeminent imperial model of antiquity. Thus the Ottoman Sultan Mehmet II (r. 1451–81) famously claimed the title of *Kayser-I Rum*, or Roman caesar, following his conquest of Constantinople (1453), representing himself as the legitimate successor of the Roman emperors of antiquity.⁵ In a 1506 *memorial* to King Ferdinand of Aragon (r. 1479–1516), the Spanish naval commander Pedro Navarro presented the king with a strategy for the subjugation of the Ottoman Empire by invoking the model of imperial Rome and comparing the Aragonese monarch's resources for conquest favourably with those of the ancient empire.⁶

The legacies of these intersecting and overlapping conceptual understandings were never far from the surface in the political landscape of the fifteenth- and sixteenth-century Mediterranean, and every state with aspirations of Mediterranean conquests negotiated these legacies according to the exigencies of each situation encountered. Within this Mediterranean space, the Kingdom of Naples held particular importance. The geographic position of Naples in the central Mediterranean, with a long coastline on both the Adriatic and Tyrrhenian Seas, gave it obvious strategic significance. The Italian Peninsula also evoked ancient Rome, a factor that led numerous writers to equate hegemonic control over Italy with a revival of Roman *imperium*: "To Dante Italy was the garden of the Empire; to Petrarch, a land most holy, destined to be the mistress of all the world. Even to Paolo Giovio, the contemporary historian of Charles V's reign, she was still that infallible ladder of true monarchy."⁷ For these reasons, material as well as symbolic, the struggles for control of Naples carried obvious imperial overtones.

In spite of such imperial resonances, at the outset of the Italian Wars, during the reign of Ferdinand of Aragon, the Spanish Crown made little appeal to the imperial model of ancient Rome in pressing its interests in Naples. This may be because Ferdinand possessed no claim to the imperial title, held at that time by his ally the Holy Roman Emperor Maximilian I (r. 1493–1519). In two discrete episodes of conflict, one against the Ottoman Empire and the other against France, the "Catholic monarchs" Ferdinand of Aragon and Isabella of Castile

(r. 1474–1504), along with their diplomats, instead articulated their Italian policies as a holy war undertaken in defence of the church and the body politic of Christendom. The Spanish Crown asserted its sovereignty in the Neapolitan kingdom through the use of a rhetoric that represented Spain as the guarantor of peace and stability within the Christian commonwealth. Commensurately, Spaniards attempted to invalidate the claims put forward by their French rivals, depicting the French as a threat to the security of Christendom on a magnitude equal to or greater than that posed by the Ottoman Empire.

The geopolitical particulars of the contest for Naples combined with domestic Iberian politics to allow for Spain's articulation of its Italian interests in a vocabulary of holy war. While such a rhetorical strategy comes as no surprise in the context of Spanish conflict with the Ottoman Empire, Spain's deployment of the same tactic against its French rivals represents an early phase of the early modern assertions of sovereignty as deriving from claims of religious orthodoxy and defence of the church, an approach that would only intensify through the course of the sixteenth century.

The Ottoman Threat

The circumstances that stimulated King Ferdinand of Aragon's initial representation of his Italian interests as being solely in defence of the church stemmed from an episode of Ottoman westward expansion at the outset of his reign, in which a Turkish fleet besieged the island of Rhodes and then occupied the Italian city of Otranto for thirteen months in 1480–1. These events occurred at a time when Western European fears of Ottoman advances were acute, particularly in Italy.[8] In 1473, Turkish troops had made incursions into the Venetian Terra Ferma in Friuli and threatened Venice's commerce in the eastern Mediterranean.[9] Surviving documentation from the 1470s illustrates the degree to which residents of the Italian Peninsula saw themselves as standing on the front lines of an imminent Ottoman invasion that would threaten not only Italy, but also all of Europe. In February 1474 Count Brotardi wrote from Trent, in northern Italy, that he had heard that Turkish armies were preparing to invade "Europe" and to destroy Christendom. The count concluded his letter with a plea: "May God's hand protect us, for if God does not confound the power of these dogs the ruin of Europe, of Italy, and of Christendom appears imminent."[10] Two years later, Italians circulated a manuscript purported to be an oath sworn by Mehmet II in late summer 1476, vowing to pursue with blood and fire everything related to the Christian religion.[11]

In July 1480, the Ottoman fleet surrounded Rhodes, which was at that time the headquarters of the Knights of St John of Jerusalem. The grand master of the military order wrote to Ferdinand, pleading for assistance in the face of this threat, for the sake of what he termed the well-being of Christendom.[12] Ferdinand responded by taking the military order under his custody, for the benefit of the body politic of Christian believers, the *rei publica christianorum*.[13] Ferdinand of Aragon's rhetoric on his Mediterranean military intervention thus responded to the atmosphere of fear conveyed in the letters written by anxious Italians.

Days later, on 11 August 1480, Ottoman forces invaded and occupied Otranto, on the Adriatic coast of the Kingdom of Naples. Western Europeans viewed the Ottoman occupation of Otranto as a grave threat to the stability of the Neapolitan kingdom and to the Italian Peninsula. In light of Ottoman conquests in the Balkans during the late fourteenth and early fifteenth centuries, there was a real possibility that Naples might succumb. Moreover, should Naples fall, the kingdom's immediate neighbour to the north, the Papal States, including the City of Rome, would lie exposed to the forces of Mehmet, who had earned the sobriquet of "conqueror" through his capture of Constantinople in 1453.[14] Prophecies of a Turkish advance as far as Rome circulated in both Christian and Islamic lands during the second half of the fifteenth century. Within Ottoman territories, Rome was represented as the "Red Apple," the conquest of which (in the wake of their conquest of Constantinople) would affirm the Ottomans' legitimacy as heirs to the Roman Empire of antiquity.[15] In Western Europe, of course, prophecies of an Ottoman conquest of Rome sparked dread. In 1480, when the Ottomans captured Otranto, the news quickly spread throughout Europe. Peter Schott, a canon of Strasbourg whose study of the classics no doubt influenced his views of Rome, was so concerned that the Ottoman advance would not be stemmed that he travelled to Rome to visit the Holy See, in case it should fall to the Turks and be lost to Christendom forever.[16]

Ferdinand of Aragon portrayed the Ottoman presence on Italian soil in terms that reflected this sense of an existential crisis threatening the entirety of Christendom. Ferdinand emphasized that the Turkish occupation of Otranto posed a threat well beyond Naples, warning of "the hardship that all Christendom suffers as a result of the Turkish invasion of Italy" and positing that if Christians did not resist, then the Ottomans "would easily establish dominion over Italy and Rome, to the great offense of our Lord God, and to the detriment of the Christian religion."[17] When Neapolitan forces ultimately recovered Otranto, Ferdinand celebrated the news, in a letter to the duke of Milan, as representing the liberation of Italy and "the restoration of a significant portion of the republic of Christendom."[18]

At the time of the Ottoman occupation of Otranto, the Neapolitan kingdom was already prone to instability. The realm was ruled by a cadet branch of the House of Aragon in the person of Ferdinand's cousin, King Ferrante I of Naples (r. 1458–94). Ferrante, of illegitimate birth, had struggled to gain the papal investiture to his realm, had fought off Angevin counter-claimants to the Neapolitan throne, and continually faced a restive baronial faction.[19] Adding to these sources of instability, Ferdinand of Aragon viewed Ferrante's rule as illegal (as a result of his illegitimate birth) and sought to press his own claims to the realm. Significantly, though, the Aragonese monarch did not frame his Italian interests in dynastic terms. Instead, he elected to portray his interest in Naples as stemming from a desire to ensure the kingdom's stability and to protect it from the external threat of the Turkish presence just across the Adriatic.

Indeed, for years following the Ottoman withdrawal from Otranto, Ferdinand continued to use a Christian universalist discourse to frame the external forces menacing the Italian Peninsula. In June 1482, Ferdinand expressed deep concern over the Ottoman presence in "Velona" (modern Vlorë, Albania, just eighty kilometres across the Adriatic from the Kingdom of Naples): "Being in Velona, so close to Italy, should the enemy of our faith see Italy divided and weakened by war, he will launch an attack." Such an invasion, suggested Ferdinand, would pose a threat not only to the Neapolitan kingdom and the other Italian states, but would jeopardize the very survival of Christianity by inflicting "such great universal harm to Christendom" as might follow from an Ottoman assault, should the internecine turmoil in Italy persist.[20] Emphasizing the extent to which Naples was under threat of conquest by the Turks, Ferdinand portrayed his own actions in the region as deriving not from a desire to preserve or to recoup his alienated patrimony, but from a commitment to defend and protect Christendom from the external threat posed by the Ottomans.

It comes as little surprise that Christian rulers in fifteenth-century Europe portrayed Ottoman westward advances as posing a threat to the survival of Christendom. This was a sincere fear for many, and a fear that others may have exploited for cynical ends. These concerns were significant enough that the Republic of Venice, in the wake of Ottoman incursions into Friuli, took the pragmatic course of agreeing to a treaty with the Ottoman Empire on 25 January 1479. According to the terms, Venice agreed not to intervene on behalf of other powers in the Italian Peninsula.[21] In contrast to the policy pursued by Venice, numerous European rulers chose a path of more direct confrontation, expressing their political agenda through a vocabulary that characterized the Ottomans as an existential threat, and presenting themselves as guardians of Christendom. King Charles VIII of France (r. 1483–98), like Ferdinand of Aragon, styled himself an exemplary Christian prince and champion of the Christian commonwealth. Intriguingly, King Charles soon found himself the target of precisely the same rhetoric the Spanish had recently deployed to characterize the Ottoman threat. In fact, decades before King Francis I of France (r. 1515–47) and Suleiman "the Magnificent" (r. 1520–66) signed the "Impious Alliance" of 1536, and here in the context of an intra-European dispute, Spaniards originated the practice of depicting the French as "the Turk within" that posed an internal threat to the body politic of Christendom.

The Threat from the *Roi Très Chrétien*

In September 1494, Charles VIII of France led forces across the Alps and into Italy, pressing his own dynastic claim to the Kingdom of Naples. Drawing on centuries-old crusading associations between the southern Italian lands and the Holy Land, the French king indicated that his incursion into Naples would be merely the first step in a much grander design of Mediterranean conquests. In the context of the 1490s, with the "Second Rome," Constantinople, now the seat of an Islamic empire, the crusading resonances Charles invoked took on a new sense of urgency. Looking well beyond the southern reaches of the Italian Peninsula, Charles depicted his actions as part of a strategy to subjugate the Ottoman Empire and as an important first step towards a Christian recovery of the Holy Land. At the time, prophecies circulated in France depicting him as a "second Charlemagne," linking the late fifteenth-century French king to his "crusading" forbear and namesake. Throughout the French invasion of Italy, their partisans depicted Charles VIII as a liberator working against the forces of tyranny and as a just prince who would bring order to the politically fragmented and volatile Italian Peninsula. Charles's chronicler Philippe de Commynes depicted King Ferrante of Naples and his son, the future Alfonso II (r. 1494–5), as the very embodiment of evil and despotic rule, thereby justifying the French invasion.[22] Italians, too, propagated this image: Francesco Guicciardini and Bernardino Corio both portrayed King Ferrante of Naples as a tyrant, and Charles's invasion as a remedy for Ferrante's abuses, with Corio going so far as to depict Charles as Christ-like.[23]

As the French forces marched south through Italy, Ferdinand of Aragon responded immediately in a desperate attempt to prevent his arch-rival from attaining a position of hegemony in Italy. In October 1494, Ferdinand and Isabella wrote their ambassadors in Rome, counselling them on how to represent the Spanish monarchs' protest against the French king's actions before the papal curia, and urging them to emphasize the degree to which Ferdinand and Isabella had always worked for "the peace and tranquillity of the Christian republic and the union and concord of Christian princes."[24]

This vocabulary was of a piece with Ferdinand's response to the Ottoman threat during the occupation of Otranto. In the face of the invading French forces, the Aragonese king presented himself as the guarantor of peace and stability. Such discourse tapped into established European ideals of rulership by depicting the Spanish monarchs as fulfilling the responsibilities of an idealized Christian emperor, whose duty was to forge a universal peace among Christian princes prior to leading the forces of Christendom in a grand crusade.[25] Spanish monarchs worked against the forces of tyranny, be they Muslim or Christian. Painting the French as a threat equal to that posed by the Turks, Ferdinand and Isabella lamented that the eruption of war in Italy would cause as much harm to Christians as would war against the Turks. The Spanish monarchs went on to warn that if the French did not desist, there would result "universal harm and great danger to the Christian republic."[26]

Spanish representations of their response to French aggression were, of course, but one side of a dialogue of competing claims. The French king appealed to a similar political ideology, representing himself as a crusading king and portraying his invasion as divinely sanctioned. The king's Italian partisans appealed to the same imagery. In Florence, the charismatic preacher Savonarola painted Charles as a leader sent by God to punish the institutional church for its sins and to purge it of impurities.[27] When Charles entered the city of Naples in triumph on 22 February 1495, the ceremony was designed to convey the legitimacy of the French king's conquest. In the procession, Charles rode through Naples wearing the imperial cloak and adorned with a quadruple crown, representing France, Naples, Constantinople, and Jerusalem.[28] The regalia of Constantinople was intended to convey Charles's imperial rank, affirming the French king as the long-awaited leader who would reunite the eastern and western halves of the Roman Empire. While on an embassy to England, Robert Gaguin assured the English court that Charles VIII's objective in conquering Naples was to reverse the Ottoman advances and to recover Greece for Christendom.[29]

In response to such French claims, however, the Spanish issued their own, suggesting that Charles's crusading professions amounted to naught and that his actions were, in fact, counterproductive insofar as the instability they wrought in Italy could invite a second Turkish invasion. Several months after Charles's triumphal entry into Naples, agents in the employ of the Spanish Crown issued a document for circulation outside Spain that portrayed the French invasion as anti-Christian, an act of aggression that distracted from the universal goal of crusade against the infidel that Christian princes ought to share. In stark contrast to Charles's triumphal entry into the city of Naples as a crusading king, the document depicted the French king, in his assertion of his claim to Naples, as an enemy of Christendom and of the Church:

> Their majesties [Ferdinand and Isabella] wanted nothing more than to undertake the holy and just war against the Muslim kings of Africa, and toward this end they were already making preparations in Andalucía and in the ports along the coast, and it is to be assumed that their plans would have succeeded, due to the justice of their cause and their holy intentions. But as a result of the machinations of the devil, enemy of Christianity and of the church, the king of France at that time took it upon himself to invade and conquer the Kingdom of Naples without first adjudicating his rights to the realm ... and their Highnesses [Ferdinand and Isabella] feared that the war of Naples would disrupt the peace of the church and that the pope would be grievously harmed by this, and that from this would follow an infinite number of misfortunes throughout all Christendom, as indeed was later shown to be the case.[30]

The Spaniards' rhetoric implies that Ferdinand and Isabella did not act as did Charles VIII: they were defenders of Christendom, not violators of the *Pax christiana*.

The Particularity of Naples

Ultimately, the Spanish monarchs responded to the French conquest of Naples by sending a military force led by the *Gran Capitán*, Gonzalo Fernández de Córdoba. After eight years of intermittent warfare, Ferdinand and Isabella finally incorporated the Neapolitan kingdom into the Spanish Crown in 1503. Aware of the charge that their counter-invasion could be viewed as further destabilizing the Italian Peninsula, Ferdinand and Isabella made several strategic choices concerning the portrayal of their military response. The Spanish monarchs and their councillors could have argued that they had a dynastic obligation to intervene, and that the armada was sent to assist their cousin, the Neapolitan king. Alternatively, in light of intimations that the French king was contemplating an invasion of Aragonese Sicily, Ferdinand could have cast a military response as a defensive move to protect his island kingdom. Ferdinand and Isabella and their councillors, however, chose not to employ a dynastic discourse to legitimate their policy. Instead, drawing on a similar approach to the one they had employed fifteen years earlier during the Ottoman occupation of Otranto, they opted to depict their military response to the French invasion as a defence of the church. Throughout the period of Franco-Spanish hostilities in Naples, the Spanish Crown portrayed the French as disruptive to the well-being of

Christendom and depicted its own response as motivated solely by a desire to protect the church. At a meeting of the Catalan parliament (*Corts*) in December 1495, Ferdinand addressed the assembled representatives on the matter of the French conquest of Naples in a bid to convince the Catalans to furnish troops. Ferdinand represented Charles's actions as constituting an act of war against the church and as sowing division throughout Christendom.[31] As an exemplary Christian prince, Ferdinand had avoided declaring war against France for as long as possible, but events had finally forced him to form a league with the pope, the Holy Roman emperor, Venice, and the Duke of Milan, "for the well-being and peace of Christendom."[32] Ferdinand stressed to his Catalan subjects, traditionally enemies of France, that the alliance stood not to the detriment of France but rather in defence of the church.

Several particularities in the struggle for Naples may have led the Spanish monarchs to represent their actions as undertaken solely in defence of the church. These derived from the contingencies of both Iberian and Italian politics. Throughout the 1480s Ferdinand and Isabella demonstrated a conscious effort to incorporate the War of Granada into what they styled a broader Christian conflict with Islam. In a 1485 letter to his ambassador in Rome, Francisco de Rojas, Ferdinand presented the War of Granada as an integral part of a broader crusading strategy. In doing so, he depicted it as a step that must be taken before he might carry the war against Islam beyond Iberia, "so that I should be able to go and assist those Christians in other regions who are oppressed and afflicted by the infidels."[33] Ferdinand and Isabella thus used the war against the Nasrids to bolster their image as champions of Christendom. If the Ottoman conquest of Constantinople in 1453 aroused fears of an Islamic conquest among some Europeans, Islam did not appear quite so triumphant when one looked to the Iberian Peninsula.

In addition to the role played by internal Iberian politics, Italian politics also factored into the forms of representation Ferdinand and Isabella opted for. First, the Kingdom of Naples was a fief of the papacy, meaning that an invasion of Naples could be construed as aggression against the pope. Moreover, the French armies marched through the Papal States in order to reach Naples from France. In the process, they occupied the port of Ostia, the main supply-point for Rome, commandeering supplies and infuriating Pope Alexander VI (r. 1492–1503). Spanish diplomatic correspondence stressed the harm the French did to the church and asserted that Spain's military response came only from a desire to comply with the pope's pleas for military assistance: "His Holiness then sent their Highnesses [Ferdinand and Isabella] a brief begging them and commanding them to assist him by supplying an armed force, to counter the spilling of divine blood, and out of the obligation that all Catholic princes hold to protect and defend the Roman Church, particularly at a time when it is placed in such need and distress."[34]

Thus, French manoeuvres throughout the Italian Peninsula did not accord with French royal propaganda representing Charles VIII as a liberator from the forces of tyranny. Italians who had greeted the French as liberators in 1494 and 1495 soon changed their opinion and began to view Charles VIII as lacking many of the cardinal virtues. Italians also developed a representation of French soldiers as particularly brutal and prone to violence, forging something of a precursor to the *Leyenda Negra* that was subsequently applied to Spanish conquistadors.[35] The Spanish seized upon this opportunity to portray French military engagement in Italy as destabilizing the peninsula, thus inviting another Ottoman invasion. Along these lines, Spaniards depicted the French as violators of the Christian peace and as a threat to the security of the Christian commonwealth. By contrast, the Spanish justified their own counter-invasion as a *defence of church lands* and as being done solely for the good of the Christian republic.

Italy's proximity to Ottoman-ruled lands in the Balkan Peninsula and the eastern Mediterranean served to increase the perception of an Italy (and a Christendom) under siege. Meanwhile, contemporaneous Spanish conquests of strategic *presidios* along the coast of North Africa (1497–1510) cemented the image of Ferdinand as protector and guardian of Christendom against the forces of Islam. As in the case with the Castilian conquest of Granada, Spain's African victories appeared to offset, if only marginally, the Ottoman gains in southeastern Europe. As the diplomatic correspondence examined thus far demonstrates, Ferdinand and his councillors frequently elided the safety and security of the Italian Peninsula with that of Christendom writ large. The evidence presented here suggests that the equation between the security of Italy and the security of the body politic of Christendom was an intentional strategy to depict Ferdinand's interests and actions in the Italian Peninsula as deriving from a devotion to the defence of Christendom rather than a desire to attain dominion over any part (or parts) of Italy. In this way Ferdinand could portray his military responses to events such as the Ottoman invasion of Otranto or the French invasion of Italy as originating in a desire to protect the boundaries of Christendom and the lands of the papacy, rather than in a conqueror's greed or avarice. Unlike Charles of France, Ferdinand was exemplary of the cardinal virtues.

In a treatise composed in 1503 in support of Ferdinand and Isabella's claim to Naples, the Castilian courtier Cristóbal de Santesteban dutifully painted his patrons as champions of Christendom who, in spite of ruling over the nation furthest from the Turkish threat, had done more than any other monarchs "for the benefit and succour of the Christian people, who were in such grave danger."[36] Unlike those of the French, the military engagements that the Spanish undertook in Italy were conducted solely, as Santesteban noted, "in defence of the Holy Father."[37]

Spanish poetry of the early sixteenth century equated the war in Italy with other "holy endeavours." In the *coplas* of Gracia Dei, the poet placed the "recovery" of Naples on the same plane as the other deeds of Ferdinand and Isabella's reign that demonstrated God's clemency, including the conquest of Granada and the "discovery" of the Americas:

> They punished the Canarians,
> The heretics, and the ungodly,
> They expelled the Jews.
> They triumphed over Granada,
> Reformed all of Spain,
> Baptized the two peoples,
> Discovered new nations,
> Recovered Naples.[38]

During the early years of the sixteenth century, Spanish attempts to paint the French as a threat to the well-being of Christendom gained traction, including in lands beyond Spain. In 1511, with the backing of King Louis XII of France (r. 1498–1515), a group of disaffected cardinals called a church council, to be convened at Pisa on 1 September 1511. In the months leading up to the Council of Pisa, it was known throughout Europe that a principal aim of the council was to sanction Pope Julius II and, indeed, when council proceedings finally got under way in October, they suspended the pope.[39] Thus, as Louis XII readied an army to invade Italy in late summer 1511, French support for the council about to convene was interpreted as a sign that Louis had designs of conquering the whole of the Italian Peninsula, church lands included. Peter Martyr, the Italian humanist then resident at Ferdinand's court in Spain, wrote to a friend in his native Lombardy and portrayed the Italian Wars in terms similar to those Ferdinand himself employed. Martyr discussed the French king's ambitions in Italy, positing that he aimed to make himself lord of the whole peninsula. "In contrast," he wrote, Ferdinand would "defend with determination the cause of the church."[40] This image of Ferdinand as protector and guardian of the church and of Christendom spread far and wide. Emery d'Amboise, the master of the Knights of St John of Jerusalem, wrote to Ferdinand from Rhodes in September 1510, styling Ferdinand as a de facto leader against the enemies of the Christian faith, and addressing the

Aragonese king as "protector and defender of the Christian commonwealth," or *"firmísimo amparo de la republica Christiana."*[41]

At home and abroad, then, Ferdinand was able to present himself as a champion of the church, a guardian of Christendom against all threats, be they the Nasrid rulers of Granada, the Ottoman Empire, or France's *Roi très chrétien*. At the level of royal discourse, the Italian Wars came to transcend the matter of establishing hegemony within the Italian Peninsula. Indeed, the dynastic dispute over Naples between the houses of Valois and Trastámara was transformed into a referendum on the survival of Christendom in the face of the ascendant Ottoman Empire, a fact reflected in the rhetoric that the French and Spanish sides deployed throughout the conflict. Thus, what was at root the continuation of a centuries-old dynastic struggle took on the aspect of a holy war for the defence of Christendom.

Naples as a Holy War

The contest for control of the Kingdom of Naples assumed a religious dimension that distinguished it from a mere dynastic dispute to recoup an alienated patrimony. The factors elucidated above, particularly the political instability of Naples and its exposure to Ottoman attack, raised the stakes of the Franco-Spanish struggle, imbuing it with the aura of a crusade. The papacy's actions contributed to this perception, as evidenced by Pope Alexander VI's granting of plenary indulgences in July 1496 to those who died in Naples fighting to defend the church against the French invaders.[42]

Nor was this understanding of the Italian Wars as having such a strongly religious component confined to southern Europe. Indeed, the perception of the War of Naples as a holy war extended well beyond the Iberian and Italian Peninsulas. Soldiers from Germany and other northern European lands ventured to Italy to fight, viewing their military service as merely one facet of a holy pilgrimage of sorts. This phenomenon developed from a practice that originated during the War of Granada. Soldiers from northern Europe who travelled to the Iberian Peninsula to fight for Castile in the war against Nasrid Granada from 1482 to 1492 frequently combined their military service with religious pilgrimage to Santiago de Compostela in northwestern Spain. Surviving safe conduct passes issued by Ferdinand and Isabella attest to German soldiers journeying to Santiago following their fulfilment of military obligations.[43] In light of the fact that Granada was under Islamic rule, it is not surprising that these Germans viewed their military service in southern Iberia and their pilgrimage to Santiago as two parts of a whole, a religiously "purifying" experience in the Iberian Peninsula, as the War of Granada was depicted throughout Europe as a crusade undertaken for the whole of Christendom.

The fact that precisely the same practice developed in the Italian Wars comes as a bit more of a surprise, given that the warring parties were both Christian kingdoms. Indeed, some German soldiers fought for Spain in Naples, and in certain instances King Ferdinand granted safe conduct passes so that these northern Europeans could perform a pilgrimage to Santiago following the fulfilment of their military obligations in Italy.[44] The proffer of plenary indulgences by the papacy for those who fought to repulse the French forces from Naples no doubt attracted soldiers from other parts of Europe. For some, at least, fighting in the Italian Peninsula was viewed as one component in a larger religious undertaking in southern Europe that presented possibilities for salvation in a variety of ways. The Wars of Italy between France and Spain and the War of Granada, in which Castile conquered the last Islamic polity in Iberia, were equivalent as holy endeavours that afforded opportunities for spiritual salvation through holy war and devotional pilgrimage.

German perceptions of the religious valence of warfare conducted in the Italian *Mezzogiorno* might be partially attributable to political alliances. Since May 1493, with the enactment of the Treaty of Senlis, Spain had been allied with the Holy Roman Empire through a dual marriage alliance. The treaty was one component of Ferdinand of Aragon's tactic to encircle France by forming alliances with all of France's neighbours. In light of the enmity between the Emperor Maximilian (r. 1493–1519) and the monarchs of France, it is likely that the war in Naples was also portrayed in German lands as a religious obligation.

The pilgrimage destination of Santiago, however, raises further questions. Medieval Castilians had developed an association between Santiago and wars against Muslims, an association that had led to the transformation of the apostle into a medieval crusader, Santiago Matamoros, or "Saint James the Moor-slayer." This association of Santiago with war against enemies of the faith may explain in part the decision by German soldiers to undertake the lengthy journey from southern Italy to northwest Spain. They might have understood their service in Naples as a defence of Christendom against an Islamic threat. Their choice of pilgrimage destination likely reflects the perception that southern Italy formed a frontier zone on the front lines in a struggle against the forces of Islam, as embodied by the Ottoman Empire. In some sense, the Spanish Crown's choice of rhetoric through which to represent the Italian Wars represented a transposition of the confessional frontier from southern Iberia to southern Italy. In both locales, the Spanish Crown claimed to act as a bulwark against the Islamic world.

Those who supported Spain in the Italian Wars often represented the French as every bit as much a threat to Christendom as the Turks. By 1511, the French Crown and the papacy were increasingly at odds. French support for the Council of Pisa, called in 1511, determined that the papacy too came to portray French involvement in Italy as akin to, or worse than, the Turkish threat. Following the Battle of Ravenna (1512), in which a French army defeated a joint Spanish-papal force, a papal nuncio wrote a letter to Pope Julius II detailing the carnage and describing the actions of the French victors as worse than those of the Turks when they conquered Constantinople: "They have despoiled monasteries and churches, and have made off with chalices and crucifixes, throwing the Eucharist and relics on the ground and stealing the silver. Never did the Turks commit such acts of cruelty when they conquered Constantinople and Negroponte."[45]

The religious argument that diplomats and jurists writing on behalf of the Spanish Crown crafted was that Ferdinand and Isabella acted in defence of the rights of the church in southern Italy, rights that the French monarchs threatened. Spanish actions in Naples, in other words, were intended to assist the church in recovering the lands over which it claimed tributary lordship, and to safeguard Italy and Christendom from the possibility of another Ottoman attack. This was the portrayal of the Spanish military engagements that infused Alexander VI's grant of plenary indulgences to combatants as well as his investiture of Ferdinand and Isabella with the honorific title of "Catholic monarchs," or *Reyes Católicos*, in December 1496. In the bull of investiture, Alexander specifically cited the Spanish monarchs' contributions to the church through demonstrated devotion to the apostolic see during the recent war of Naples, including an implicit critique of the French king, Charles VIII, in the wording of the bull: "You serve as examples to all Christian princes, for you have not employed your arms in the ruin and slaughter of your fellow Christians out of ambition for lands and dominion, but rather for the prosperity of Christians and for the defence of the church and the faith ... your devotion to the apostolic see was once again evident in the recent war of Naples."[46]

Conclusion

Ferdinand "the Catholic" died in 1516. Throughout the nearly four decades of his reign, the Spanish Crown persisted in its assertion of its Italian claims through a politico-religious vocabulary that represented Spain as guardian of Christendom and France as a violator of the Christian peace. At times, the actions of the French Crown contributed to the currency this Spanish rhetoric gained. For instance, Louis XII's support for the Council of Pisa (1511) in turn prompted Pope Julius II to issue bulls in 1512 and 1513 excommunicating and depriving of their goods and royal dignities any who confederated with the French king.[47]

Events that lie beyond the scope of this chapter further contributed to this tactic of portraying the early modern French monarchs as a threat to the body politic of Christendom. When King Francis I of France signed an alliance with the Ottoman Sultan Suleiman I in 1536, France's opponents immediately labelled the agreement the "Impious Alliance." Even after the formal conclusion of the Italian Wars, achieved through the treaty of Cateau-Cambrésis (1559), other European powers continued to represent the French as a threat to Christendom. As late as 1689, British pamphleteers circulated depictions of Louis XIV of France (r. 1643–1715) as "the Christian Turk," after his inducement to the Ottomans to invade the lands of his enemy, the Habsburg emperor.[48] The significance of the processes examined in this chapter lies in the initial development of this method of asserting claims of sovereignty long before Francis I signed the "Impious Alliance."

The justification for conquest according to the argument of the defence of Christendom originated in the particular circumstances of the struggle for Naples, but this means of articulating imperial claims held much broader ramifications. First, the use of these techniques of religious legitimation by Spaniards against a fellow Catholic power productively complicates our sense of how religious discourses were accessed and deployed in the early modern Mediterranean. While the grounds upon which this rhetoric was deployed were ostensibly the "external" threat posed by the expansionist Ottoman Empire, the religious discourse that permeates the documents I have drawn on was directed primarily towards an "internal" threat as embodied by the Kingdom of France.[49]

Second, these means of asserting sovereignty through the claim to act as defender of the church developed in the context of Mediterranean conflicts but were also deployed in other arenas of early modern imperial expansion, namely Spanish claims to the Americas. The Castilian jurist Juan López de Palacios Rubios, author of the infamous *Requerimiento* that Spanish conquistadors read to indigenous inhabitants of the Americas when claiming lands for Spain, wrote a tract offering a legal argument for Spanish claims to the Americas (composed sometime between 1512 and 1516). In his *De Insulis*, the Spanish Crown's claims to lands in the Old World as well as the New derive from their divine "mission" to defend and propagate the faith throughout the world. In this respect, Spain's mission in bringing Christianity to the gentiles of the Americas continued the Crown's divinely sanctioned task of recovering the lands of Africa and Asia that had constituted integral parts of early Christendom.[50]

Finally, the techniques deployed by the Spanish Crown and its supporters in the Italian Wars against France bear comparison with a conflict at the eastern end of the Mediterranean that was essentially contemporary to the events examined here. During the Ottoman-Mamluk struggle for hegemony in the eastern Mediterranean, in particular the conflict for control over Egypt and the holy cities of the Levant and Hijaz, the Ottoman ruler Selim I (r. 1512–20) employed a religious discourse of legitimation that would not have been altogether foreign to the councillors at Ferdinand of Aragon's court. As Palmira Brummet and Giancarlo Casale have both argued, during a period of rapid expansion and at times contested political legitimacy, Selim employed a form of political theology to cement his authority within the Islamic world. Following the Ottoman conquest of Jerusalem, Medina, and Mecca in 1516 and 1517, Selim participated in a triumphal entry into Cairo, the former Mamluk capital, in which he proclaimed himself "protector of the Holy Cities" and assumed the title of "caliph," thus claiming sovereignty over all Muslims everywhere in a politico-religious sense that Casale has termed "extra-territorial."[51]

While Spanish monarchs never asserted claims of sovereignty over the body politic of Christendom quite as far-reaching as Selim's proclamation, the similarities between the means of claiming political legitimacy through defence of the faithful by rulers of the two ascendant empires at opposite ends of the Mediterranean point to commonalities in the way both empires represented their mission according to a complexly negotiated engagement with the accreted legacies of the Mediterranean world, including the imperial legacy of ancient Rome as well as the universalist doctrines of both Christianity and Islam.

NOTES

1 See Michael Mallett and Christine Shaw, *The Italian Wars 1494–1559: War, State and Society in Early Modern Europe* (Upper Saddle River, NJ: Pearson, 2012); and David Abulafia, ed., *The French Descent into Renaissance Italy, 1494–1495: Antecedents and Effects* (Aldershot, UK: Variorum, 1995).

2 Seymour Phillips, "Outer World of the European Middle Ages," in *Implicit Understandings: Observing, Reporting, and Reflecting on the Encounters between Europeans and Other Peoples in the Early Modern Era*, ed. Stuart Schwartz (New York: Cambridge University Press, 1994), 34n33.

3 "Nadie llamasse sennor del mundo ni lo penso ser si a ella le faltasse," Cristóbal de Santesteban (1440?–1520), *Tratado de la successión de los reynos de Jerusalén y de Nápoles y de Cecilia y de las provincias de Pulla y Calabria* (Zaragoza: Jorge Coci, 1503). Biblioteca Nacional de España, Madrid, post-incunable: R/29905(2), chap. 6.

4 Miguel Ángel de Bunes Ibarra writes that the Earth was understood as a *corpus mysticum*, with two of the three parts (Asia and Africa) having fallen under the rule of infidels by the later Middle Ages. It was the responsibility of Christians to restore those parts, thus bringing unity to the Earth and to God's divine plan. See M.A. de Bunes Ibarra, "El marco ideológico de la expansión española por el norte de África," *Revista Aldaba* 26 (September 1995): 117.
5 Robert Finlay, "Prophecy and Politics in Istanbul: Charles V, Sultan Süleyman, and the Habsburg Embassy of 1533–1534," *Journal of Early Modern History* 2, no. 1 (1998): 2n3.
6 "Sollo Spagna secilia: puglia son los harneros del mundo a toda natura de victuaglias. Con sollo la Sicilia Los Romanos del universo tomaron la Impresa: quanto mas: y spagna y puglia: non al universo amas a solo restaurar el sangre de Xo." Pedro Navarro (1460?–1528), *Memorial para la Magestad en orden a la Conquista de Jerusalen* (1506). Biblioteca Nacional, Madrid, ms./19699, caja 60, fol. 1v.
7 John Headley, "Rhetoric and Reality: Messianic, Humanist, and Civilian Themes in the Imperial Ethos of Gattinara," in *Prophetic Rome in the High Renaissance Period*, ed. Marjorie E. Reeves (London: Warburg Institute / Clarendon, 1992), 257. Headley goes on to write, "Nor did one have to be a Ghibelline to admire Italy's centrality within Christendom. A century after Giovio, Richelieu would allow in his *Political Testament* that Italy was deemed the heart of the world and the preeminent part of the Spanish empire."
8 Kenneth M. Setton, *Western Hostility to Islam and Prophecies of Turkish Doom* (Philadelphia: American Philosophical Society, 1992), 15.
9 Mustafa Soykut, *Image of the "Turk" in Italy: A History of the "Other" in Early Modern Europe: 1453–1683* (Berlin: Klaus Schwarz Verlag, 2001), 2.
10 Real Academia de la Historia, Madrid, Colección Salazar y Castro, A-7, fol. 158 (*Otra del conde Brotardi a ... (no se expresa), avisándole de los preparativos que estaban haciendo los turcos para la invasión de Europa y que se preparaba la ruina de la Cristiandad*. Trent, 7 February 1474. Copia ms. en italiano, letra del siglo XVI): "Ma ne modo ne forza humana li assecura. Dio li metta la mano sua che vedo preparata la ruina de Europa de Italia et de Christiani se Idio non confunde la potentia di questo cane." See also A-7, fol. 158 (*Carta de Karolus Vitalis Caurell a ... [no cita destinario], remitiendo el juramento que se menciona en la ficha siguiente y el gran temor que había sobre una invasión de los turcos en Ragusa y Venecia*. Sibia, 27 October 1474, copia ms. en italiano, de la misma letra que el documento anterior).
11 Real Academia de la Historia, Colección Salazar y Castro: A-7, fol. 158 (*Juramento que hizo Mohamed Amirant, sultán de Constantinopla, de perseguir a sangre y fuego todo cuanto se relacionase con el nombre cristiano. Es Mohamed II el conquistador de Constantinopla. Constantinopla, 20 de agosto del año 25 de su imperio* [1476]. Copia ms. en italiano, de la misma letra que los documentos anteriores).

12 Real Academia de la Historia, Madrid, Colección Salazar y Castro, A-8, fol. 54: *Carta del maestre de Rodas a Fernando el Católico por la que le informaba de la necesidad de defender y sostener, para bien de la cristiandad, la plaza e isla de Rodas.*
13 Ferdinand wrote (1 August 1480), "Nichil magis animo nostro insitum est quam ea aggredi studioseque decus christiani nominis conseruacionemque rei publica christianorum concernere dignoscuntur." Antonio de la Torre, ed., *Documentos sobre relaciones internacionales de los Reyes Católicos* (Barcelona: CSIC, 1949), 1:107.
14 Franz Babinger argued that the Ottoman occupation of Otranto led to acute fear in the Papal States, and that Pope Sixtus IV actually contemplated fleeing Rome. Babinger suggested that Mehmet held the objective of conquering Rome, and that this goal was well known throughout the Italian Peninsula. See *Mehmed the Conqueror and His Time*, trans. Ralph Manheim (Princeton: Princeton University Press, 1978), 393, 494–5. Along similar lines, see Paulino Toledo, "La idea de la Hegemonía Mundial en la jerarquía político-administrativa de los imperios otomano y español durante el siglo XVI," in *España-Turquía: del enfrentamiento al análisis mutuo. Actas de las I Jornadas de Historia organizadas por el Instituto Cervantes de Estambul en la Universidad del Bósforo los días 31 de octubre y 1 y 2 de noviembre de 2002*, ed. Pablo Martín Asuero (Istanbul: Editorial Isis, 2002), 19–33. Toledo argues that the Ottomans viewed their conquest of Constantinople as auguring well for the future of their empire, representing the legitimate continuation of the eastern Roman Empire (20).
15 Kenneth M. Setton, *Western Hostility to Islam and Prophecies of Turkish Doom* (Philadelphia: American Philosophical Society, 1992). The Turks identified the "Red Apple" (from a tradition of chiliastic prophecy) with Rome and believed this prophecy foretold their successful invasion of Italy (35).
16 Ibid., 35.
17 Ferdinand, on 19 February 1481, wrote of "la necessidat que a toda la cristiandat occore por causa de la entrada del turco en la Italia, y en quanto perpleixo sta constituydo el realme de Napoles, y por consiguiente, por la vicinidat que Roma tiene con aquel, quanto peligro passa, e como el dicho turco, de la Sancta fe catholica enemigo, manaça e continuamente comina venir en Roma e ocupar aquella." The king asserted that if Christians did not resist, then "facilmente se ensenyoriria de la Italia e de Roma, en gran offensa de Nuestro Senyor Dios, e detriment grande de la religion christiana." De la Torre, *Documentos sobre relaciones internacionales de los Reyes Católicos*, 1:131.
18 Archivio di Stato, Milan, Visconteo Sforzesco, Potenze Estere, cart. 653: Ferdinand to Duke of Milan (Barcelona, 16 October 1481): "Illique enim recuperacione ut … a vobis scriptum est cum Regno Serenissimi Regis Ferdinandi fratris nostri amantissimi Italia liberata est addunque et nos magnam partem rei publice xpiane ad quam ex Italia se iam metus reciperat: Itaque duplice racione exultamque et omnipotenti deo publice gracias …: Scilicet que

religio xpiana metu et quod ei Iminebat pericolo liberata et que ergdem Regis statui et quieti optime consultum est."

19 For the details of these events, see David Abulafia, "From Ferrante I to Charles VIII," in Abulafia, *French Descent into Renaissance Italy*, 8–9; Abulafia, "The Inception of the Reign of King Ferrante," in ibid., 76; A.J. Ryder, "The Angevin Bid for Naples, 1380–1480," in ibid., 67; and Michael T. Reynolds, "René of Anjou, King of Sicily, and the Order of the Croissant," *Journal of Medieval History* 19 (1993): 157.

20 De la Torre, *Documentos sobre relaciones internacionales de los Reyes Católicos*, doc. 30 (15-VI-1482): "Mayormente stando el enemigo de nuestra fe a la Velona, vezina de Italia, con tal potencia para que, viendo Italia en armas diuisa, e port al diuision sus fuerças debilitadas, entre en ella" (1:236); "porque, siendo todos juntos, se pudiesse entender, con mayores fuerças e poder, contra los infieles, que alla e aqua siempre procuran y entienden en destruyr la religion christiana" (1:237); "se podria seguir gran danyo y detrimento a la religion Christiana, specialmente segun el poder que el turco tiene en la Velona, que es tan vezina a tierra de christianos; e por obuiar a tanto danyo uniuersal de la christiandat, que de las dichas differencias podria recebir, si aquellas se continuassen" (1:238).

21 Ibid., 1:408.

22 David Abulafia, *The Western Mediterranean Kingdoms 1200–1500: The Struggle for Dominion* (London: Longman, 1997), 224.

23 Anne Denis, *Charles VIII et les italiens: histoire et mythe* (Geneva: Droz, 1979), 36, 50.

24 José María Doussinague, *La política internacional de Fernando el Católico* (Madrid: Espasa-Calpe, SA, 1944), Appendix 3, 518–19: "Poder a Alonso de Silva," 11 October 1494; Paris, Archives Nationales: K 1638 (27–33). Ms. no. 6: "Siempre hemos deseado la paz y tranquilidad de la república cristiana y la union y concordia de los príncipes cristianos."

25 For the articulation of this ideal, see Björn Weiler, "The *Negotium Terrae Sanctae* in the Political Discourse of Latin Christendom, 1215–1311," *International History Review* 25, no. 1 (2003): 1–36. Weiler emphasizes the degree to which a universal Christian peace was viewed as a necessary attainment prior to a successful crusade: "a principle universally acknowledged to be the prerequisite for an expedition to the Holy Land: the settlement of Christendom's internal conflicts in preparation for a war against its external enemies" (2). See also Chris Jones, *Eclipse of Empire? Perceptions of the Western Empire and Its Rulers in Late-Medieval France* (Turnhout: Brepols, 2007). Jones refers to the establishment of peace as "one of the essential tasks of an imperial ruler" (336).

26 Doussinague, *La política internacional*, Appendix 3, 519: "Poder a Alonso de Silva," 11 October 1494; Paris, Archives Nationales: K 1638 (27–33). Ms. no. 6: "Por

tanto, si no se quitan de en medio estas discordias se seguirá un daño universal y lo que Dios no consienta, un peligro no pequeño para la república cristiana."
27 There is an enormous body of scholarship on the enigmatic figure of Savonarola. For the purposes of this chapter, see especially Donald Weinstein, *Savonarola and Florence: Prophecy and Patriotism in the Renaissance* (Princeton: Princeton University Press, 1970); and Lauro Martines, *Fire in the City: Savonarola and the Struggle for the Soul of Renaissance Florence* (Oxford: Oxford University Press, 2006).
28 "Cuando hizo el rey su entrada solemne en Nápoles, el 22 de febrero de 1495, iba vestido con el manto imperial y ceñía la cuádruple corona: de Francia, de Nápoles, de Constantinopla y de Jerusalén." Alain Milhou, *Colón y su mentalidad mesiánica en el ambiente franciscanista español* (Valladolid: Cuadernos Colombinos, 1983), 338. On the symbolism deployed during Charles VIII's entry into Naples, see also David Abulafia, "La politica italiana della monarchia francese da Carlo VIII a Francesco I," in *El reino de Nápoles y la monarquía de España: Entre agregación y conquista (1485–1535)*, ed. Giuseppe Galasso and Carlos José Hernando Sánchez, 518–32 (Rome: Real Academia de España en Roma, 2004).
29 Ivan Cloulas, *Charles VIII et le mirage italien* (Paris: A. Michel, 1986), 27.
30 "Sus magestades quisieran luego enprender la guerra e conquista tan santa y tan justa contra los Reyes e moros de la parte de Africa e para ello se hazian ya en las partes de Andaluçia e de los puertos de la mar e donde convenia todos las aparejos que eran menester, y es de creer que subçediera todo prosperamente segun la justicia de la cabsa e la santa yntencion con que se començaua, pero procurandolo el demonio adversario enemigo del nombre christiano e de la honrra de la yglesia fue fecho que en aquella sazon, el Rey de francia se puso en ynvadir e conquistar el Reyno de Napoles de fecho e sin primero ver el derecho que a el tenia … y que temian sus Altezas como despues paresçio por esperiençia que con la dicha guerra de napoles se turbaria la paz de la yglesia e nuestro muy santo padre e su santa fe apostolica podria ser de aquesto ofendidos e maltratados e avn que de ally podrian rresultar e rrecrearse otros ynfinitos daños e estragos e males en toda la christiandad vniversalmente." Doussinague, *La política internacional*, Appendix 5, 525–6: "Traslado de las cosas pasadas con el Rey de Francia para embiar fuera del reyno (Año 1495)"; Paris, Archives Nationales. K. 1638 (27–33).
31 "Lo que, per semblant, lo dit rei de França recusà fer; ans proseguint son propòsit e metent divisió e foc, com havem vist, en tota la cristiandat, perseverà en fer tots los dans e guerra que pogué a la sancta mare Església i en lo dit realme de Nàpols." "Addressing the *Corts* of Tortosa (14 December 1495)," *Parlaments a les Corts Catalanes, a cura de Ricard Albert i Joan Gassiot (1928)* (Barcelona: Editorial Barcino, 1988), 230.
32 "Ans lo dit rei tota via perseverava e continuava en fer la dita guerra, nos fonc forçat, per lo bé e pau de la cristiandat e per escusar majors dans, fer lliga ab

nostre sanct pare e ab lo serenissimo rei dels romans, nostre germà, e ab lo molt il•lustre duc e senyoria de Venècia, e ab lo molt il•lustre duc de Milà, sense prejuí del dit rei de França ni d'altre algú, solament per la defensió de l'Església e dels propris estats nostres e de cascú dels dits col•ligats." *Parlaments a les Corts Catalanes*, 231–2.

33 De la Torre, *Documentos sobre relaciones internacionales*, vol. 2, doc. 36 (3-VI-1485): Ferdinand to the protonotary Antonio Geraldino and the *comendador* Francisco de Rojas, informing them of the conquest of Ronda and other towns in the Kingdom of Granada: "Se faría cosas con que Dios fuesse mucho seruido y estos mis reynos quedassen desembaraçados, para poder ir a valer y ayudar los cristianos que en otras prouincias estan aquexados por los infieles" (207).

34 "Pero el dicho Rey de frança no quiso condesçender en medio ninguno de aquestos y continuo su camino, y en este tiempo sus gentes tomaron e ocuparon la cibdad e fortaleza de ostia, camara de nuestro muy santo padre de donde le quitavan todos los mantenimientos que venian a Roma y entonçes su santidad enbio a sus altezas vn breue rrogandoles y encargandoles por la aspercion e derramiento de la sangre diuina e por la obligaçion que los prinçipes catolicos tienen de anparar e defender a la yglesia rromana mayormente puesta en tanta neçesidad y congoxa que sus altezas poderosamente con mano armada le ayudasen a rreprimir las dichas fuerças notificando su santidad a sus altezas la dicha toma de ostia e neçesidades de la yglesia pidiendoles ayuda y Socorro con mucha ynstancia para todo ello." Doussinague, *La política internacional*, Appendix 5: "Traslado de las cosas pasadas con el Rey de Francia para embiar fuera del reyno (Año 1495)"; Paris, Archives Nationales. K. 1638 (27–33), 527.

35 Anne Denis, *Charles VIII et les italiens: histoire et mythe* (Geneva: Droz, 1979), 125.

36 "Cosa es cierto de loar que syendo España la nacion de toda la xpiandad q mas lexos y mas segura este del Turco: y teniendo sus altezas las guerras que han tenido: y hauiendo fecho la conquista del reyno de Granada: y escomençado a conquistar el de Fez/ se haya mouido por seruicio de dios y por remedio del pueblo xpiano que en tanto peligro estaua a enbiar tantos cauallos y otras muchas gentes: y tan gran numero de fustas como en esta armada enbiaron: y gran honrra ha sydo para ellos y para sus reynos lo que alla ha fecho." Cristóbal de Santesteban, *Tratado de la succesión de los reynos de Jerusalén y de Nápoles y de Cecilia y de las provincias de Pulla y Calabria* (Zaragoza: Jorge Coci, 1503), chap. 11.

37 Santesteban described the Spanish armada that went to Italy as having gone "en socorro del santo padre" (ibid.).

38 Gracia Dei, "*Coplas de Gracia Dei*, criado y rey de armas de los muy altos, e catholicos reyes don Fernando e doña Ysabel, etc., & Juana & Felipe." This appears in the following manuscript: B.N. Madrid, Ms./ 3449: Documentos

tocantes a Pedro de Navarro, Fernando el Católico et al., fol. 3r. These couplets appear to have been composed after Isabella's death, but before Philip of Austria's (i.e., between 26 November 1504 and 25 September 1506); they contain the following verses: "Son FERNando, E YSAbel / los dos bienauenturados. / Que hizieron. / Vencieron reyes contrarios, / Cobraron sus señorios, / Castigaron los Canarios, / Los hereges y nefarios, / alançando los Judios. / De Granada triumpharon, / toda España reformaron, / los dos pueblos baptizando, / y nueuas gentes hallando, / a Napoles recobraron."

39 R.J. Knecht, *Renaissance Warrior and Patron: The Reign of Francis I* (Cambridge: Cambridge University Press, 1994), 92.

40 Peter Martyr, "Epistolario de Pedro Mártir de Anglería," trans. J. López de Toro, in *Documentos inéditos para la historia de España* (Madrid: Imprenta Góngora, 1953–7), vol. 10, doc. 462 (368–9), Peter Martyr to Count Trivulzio, 23 August 1511 from Burgos. In this letter, Martyr discusses France's pretensions in Italy: "Ese tu Rey Cristianísimo parece querer sorberse toda Italia, buscando diferentes oportunidades para ello. Mi Rey Católico, por el contrario, conocedor de la ambición francesa, defenderá con tesón la causa de la Iglesia" (369).

41 María Isabel Hernández-González, *El Taller Historiografico: Cartas de Relación de la Conquista de Orán (1509) y Textos Afines*. Papers of the Medieval Hispanic Research Seminar, 8 (London: Queen Mary & Westfield College, 1997), 60. Emery d'Amboise writes, "Plazerá al Soberano que todos los christianos, a enxenplo de vuestra Magestad, tomen las armas contra los infieles que tanto tienpo han fatigado la naçión christiana." The Valencian Jerónimo Torrella employed nearly identical language to describe the Aragonese monarch as guardian of Christendom. In his dedication of his work on astrology to Ferdinand, Torrella addressed the Aragonese king as "defender of the Christian republic, King of Spain and of the islands of our sea." Torrella's use of *insularum maris nostri* here likely refers specifically to Ferdinand's Mediterranean islands, and not to the Canary Islands or to Caribbean islands of Hispaniola or Cuba: "christianae reipublicae tutori Hispaniae atque insularum maris nri Regi." Jerónimo Torrella, *Opus praeclarum de imaginibus astrologicis* (Valencia: Press of Alfonso de Orta, 1 December 1496).

42 The bull is held at the Archivo General de Simancas, Patronato Real, leg. 27, fol. 45. It is printed in Luis Suárez-Fernández, *La política internacional de Isabel la Católica: Estudio y Documentos*, vol. 4, doc. 166, 589–90: "Traslado de una bula de Alejandro VI concediendo indulgencia plenaria a los que muriesen en la guerra de Nápoles" (3-VII-1496): "Ut veri catholici reges, principes ac huius sanctissime Sedis devotissimi filii pro defensione Sancte Romane Ecclesie ac regni Sicilie citra Farum, quod ex speciale patrimonium beati Petri et adhuc magna ex parte per carissimum in Christo filium nostrum Carolum, Francorum regem illustrem

gentesque suas armigeras occupatum detinetur, necnon arcis nostre Ostiense recuperacione bellum adversus eundem Carolum regem qui nunquam viam justicie si quam sibi in dicto regno competere putabat per nos totiens sibi paterna caritate oblatam amplecti voluit non sine maximis impensis promptissimis animis susceperint, et propterea magnum exercitum tam mari quam terra paraverint, nec desistere intendant donec prefatus Carolus rex occupata per eum in pristinum statum restituerit ipsamque Romanam Ecclesiam plurimum lesam et offensam reintegraverit et contingere posset prout sepe numero in bellis evenire solet, quod sequentes castra Ferdinandi regis et regine predictorum qui pro tam justo bello personam, vite periculis exponere non formidant, in dicto bello decederent. Non volentes animarum eorumdem Christi fidelium sic decedentium saluti consulere de Omnipotentis Dei misericordia ac Beatorum Petri et Pauli apostolorum eius auctoritate confisi omnibus et singulis Christi fidelibus qui in castris Ferdinandi regis et regine predictorum donec prefatus Carolus rex resipiscens ab occupacione huiusmodi destiterit et ipsam romanam Ecclesiam sic lesam in suis juribus reintegraverit decesserint plenariam omnium suorum peccatorum de quibus corde contricti et ore confessi fuerint indulgentiam et remissionem auctoritate apostolica tenore presentium elargimus. Presentibus dicto bello cessante minime valituris. Nulli ergo, etc. Datum Rome apud Sanctum Petrum anno Incarnationis Dominice millesimo quadringentesimo nonagesimo sexto, quinto nona julii Pontificatus nostri anno quarto." This bull in fact represented a course reversal by Alexander VI. Less than two years earlier, he had offered indulgences to French soldiers who participated in the conquest of Naples. See Didier Le Fur, *Louis XII: Un Autre César* (Paris: Perrin, 2001), 64. This reversal may have occurred in response to the French occupation of Ostia, an event described in note 34.

43 De la Torre, *Documentos sobre relaciones internacionales de los Reyes Católicos*, vol. 3, doc. 49 (4-V-1491): Ferdinand grants commendations to a number of people of the "nacionis Sueuiorum" who had fought in the war of Granada, so that they might travel to Santiago (400–1): "Cum deuoti nostri Enricus Haxinger, Ursus Staygar, Hulis de Huelgon nacionis Sueuiorum, et frater Petrus de Dossa, ordinis Sancti Francisci, nacionis eiusdem, presencium exhibitors, moti deuocione et pro seruicio nostro, propriam patriam deserentes, pugnare contra infideles mauros regni Granate venerint, in quo bello aliquandiu manserunt, fortiter preliando; cumque in presenciarum, licencia et beneplacito nostris, preheuntibus ad limen beati Jacobi de Galicia visitare proposuerunt et, post dictam peregrinacionem, ad propriam patriam redire decreuerunt."

44 Ibid., vol. 6, doc. 26, 392: King Ferdinand grants safe conduct to Germans who had fought in the war of Naples, in order to make a pilgrimage to Santiago de Compostela (3 November 1504): "Quia deuoti nostri Peurlegu Enricus Georgius et Andreas de Vlma ac Vrbanus de Lot et Jacobus de Vezlingun, germani, qui sub

nostro exercitu in dicto Sicilie citra Farum regno expugnarunt, ad minima sancti Jacobi in Compostella reddituri, vota quibus obnoxii sunt, vt asserunt, peregrinari intendunt, et ob seruicia per eos in dicto Sicilie regno nobis pretista, volumus et intendimus eos omni quo possimus fauore prossequi, ideo vos confederatos et amicos nostros enixe rogamus, vobis vero officialibus et subditis nostris, tam terrestibus quam maritimis, dicimus, precipimus et jubemus, scienter et expresse sub ire et indignationis nostre incursu, penaque florenorum auri Aragonum mille nostris inferendorum erariis quatenus si et quociens predicti germani ad vos loca et jurisdicciones vestras accesserint, eos beniuole recipiatis, tractetis et comendatis habeatis, nullum impedimentum eis inferendo seu inferri permittendo."

45 Real Academia de la Historia, Colección Salazar y Castro, no. 736, Carta a Julio II de su nuncio en Venecia relatando la batalla de Rávena (Venice, 19 April 1512). Printed in Terrateig, Barón de, ed., *Política en Italia del Rey Católico (1507–1516). Correspondencia inédita con el embajador Vich*, 2 vols. (Madrid: Consejo Superior de Investigaciones Científicas, 1963), doc. 74: "Han saqueado a Rabena y han muerto todos los biejos y moços hasta los ninyos, las mugeres assi biejas como moças e monjas lleban todas consigo, han despojado los monesterios y las yglesias y lievan calices y cruzes echando el Corpus Christi con las reliquias por tierra tomando la plata que nunca jamas turcos hizieron tan grande crueldat quando tomaron Constantinobla con Nigroponte y de todo este estrago y crueldat ha seydo causa Federyco de Sant Seberino cardenal privado diziendo que en qualquiere lugar hara otro tanto" (193–4).

46 Miguel Ángel Ladero Quesada, *Los Reyes Católicos: La Corona y la Unidad de España* (Madrid: Asociación Francisco López de Gómara, 1989), 285-6. Ladero Quesada here includes a Castilian translation of the papal bull: "Vosotros servís de aviso y ejemplo a los príncipes cristianos, porque vuestras fuerzas y vuestras armas no las habéis empleado en la ruina y matanza de otros cristianos, por ambición de tierras y de dominio, sino en la prosperidad de los cristianos y en la defensa de la Iglesia y de la fe … Vuestra reverencia y devoción a la sede apostólica, tantas veces demostradas, de nuevo se patentiza a todas luces en la reciente guerra de Nápoles. ¿A quién, pues, cuadra mejor el título de Reyes Católicos que a vuestras majestades, que continuamente os esforzáis en defender y propagar la fe católica y la Católica Iglesia?"

47 On the political repercussions this had, including the Spanish conquest of the Kingdom of Navarre, see Juan López de Palacios Rubios, *De insulis, aka: De las Islas del Mar Océano*, intro. Silvio Zavala, trans., notes, and bib. Agustín Millares Carlo (México-Buenos Aires: Fondo de Cultura Económica, 1954), xxiii–xxiv. See also Palacios Rubios's juridical tract on the same subject: *De iusticia et iure obtentionis ac retentionis regni Nauarre, necnon et de ipsius terrae situ et antiquitate* (Burgos: Fadrique de Basilea, ca 1515–17). A copy of the first edition of this work is held at the Biblioteca Nacional, Madrid, R/31345.

48 The author of this pamphlet wrote that Louis XIV "has far out-done the Turks themselves in the severest manner of making War against his Fellow-Christians; and has done his utmost to deserve the Character given by the late Pope, viz. the Christian Turk, and as great an Enemy to Europe as the Mahumetan one." See *The Intreigues of the French King at Constantinople to emroil Christendom: discovered in several dispatches past betwixt him and the late Grand Seignior, Gran Vizier and Count Teckily: all of them found among that Count's papers seiz'd in December last: with some reflections upon them* (London: Printed for Dorman Newman ..., 1689), 23–4.

49 In something of a mirror image, at the far end of the Mediterranean the Ottomans employed a similar tactic against their Safavid enemies. See Gábor Ágoston, "Information, Ideology, and Limits of Imperial Policy: Ottoman Grand Strategy in the Context of Ottoman-Habsburg Rivalry," in *The Early Modern Ottomans: Remapping the Empire*, ed. Virginia H. Aksan and Daniel Goffman, 75–103 (Cambridge: Cambridge University Press, 2007). "Ottoman propaganda justified Selim's campaigns against the Safavids by portraying the Shi'ite enemy and its *kizilbas* allies in eastern Anatolia as 'heretics' and even 'infidels,' whose revolts hindered the Ottomans' struggle against the Christian adversaries of the Empire, the main task of the ghazi (warrior; often warrior for the faith) Sultans according to fifteenth- and sixteenth-century Ottoman chroniclers and authors of advice-for-princes literature. Since the Sunni Mamluks cooperated with the 'heretic' Safavids, the war against them was also justifiable. Before the Sultan could turn against the empire's Christian enemies, claimed Ottoman propagandists, these rebel Muslims had to be dealt with" (93).

50 "África, que antaño, en tiempos de San Agustín, Obispo de Hipona, estuvo bajo el dominio de los Reyes Cristianos de España ... Más tarde fué esa tierra ocupada, como lo está actualmente, por los infieles y debe ser subyugada por uno de estirpe regia." Juan López de Palacios Rubios, *De insulis, aka: De las islas del mar océano*, ed. S. Zavala (México-Buenos Aires: Fondo de Cultura Económica, 1954), 64–5.

51 Palmira Brummett, *Ottoman Seapower and Levantine Diplomacy in the Age of Discovery* (Albany: State University of New York Press, 1994), 6; Giancarlo Casale, *The Ottoman Age of Exploration* (New York: Oxford University Press, 2010), 7, 30.

chapter six

Memories of War at Home and Abroad: The Story of Juan Latino's *Austrias Carmen*

ELIZABETH R. WRIGHT

In the early months of 1571, Granada's most theatrical public space, the Bib-Rambla plaza, witnessed a macabre drama of human misery. Between February and May, over one hundred men, women, and children were sold into slavery. Proclamations read aloud by town criers justified the sales by labelling these native *granadinos* captives seized in a just war. Anthropologist Aurelia Martín Casares documented these auctions through path-breaking research in notarial archives, drawing attention to how they culminated the Crown's harsh collective punishment of the Moriscos in the aftermath of the uprising known as the Second Alpujarras Revolt.[1] On Christmas Eve, 1568, several thousand Moriscos had taken up arms to resist a series of royal decrees (*pragmáticas*) issued a year earlier, with the goal of eliminating cultural practices associated with Granada's Islamic heritage. Though rebels ensconced in the rugged Alpujarras mountains ultimately succumbed to the superior firepower of Crown troops, they inflicted many devastating and embarrassing defeats on the squadrons sent out against them. Commanders lamented that the Crown battalions focused more on capturing valuable war spoils – Morisco slaves foremost – than on military goals. These excesses, in turn, swelled the initially thin ranks of rebels. When the last rebel holdouts gave up in 1570, the king ordered that approximately eighty thousand Moriscos from Granada be expelled to other parts of Castile, regardless of whether or not they had rebelled. Another ten thousand Moriscos classified as rebels (*moriscos de guerra*) were sold into slavery. The Bib-Rambla auctions of early 1571 were but the final rounds of this mass retribution.[2]

The sinister sounds of ad hoc slave markets might well have echoed within earshot of a stately seminar room that looked down one story onto the plaza's northeast corner. There, Juan Latino (a.k.a. Joannes Latinus), a black African former slave, taught Latin to young *granadinos* preparing for university studies.

Latino would later claim he was born in sub-Saharan Africa and transported in infancy to Spain, though another reliable testimony reported he was the son of black African slaves, but born in Andalusia. He served as both slave and companion to the third duke of Sessa, a near contemporary who enjoyed the prestige of being the grandson and namesake of the grand captain, the mastermind of Spain's conquest of Naples. Despite this family's abiding interest in charting their own lineage, they did not keep precise records on the birth and parentage of enslaved individuals in their household. Though Juan Latino's service to the family would, in the early seventeenth century, become a point of pride, no reliable records that would allow us to determine the facts of his birth, baptism, parentage, or manumission have come to light. These gaps in the record attest to how slaves in early modern Spain suffered the systematic disruption of family ties that Frederick Douglass would later denounce in the opening passage of his autobiography. Intriguingly, the most comprehensive Sessa family chronicle, from the early seventeenth century, suggests another thread that connects Latino's life story to that of Douglass and so many other enslaved individuals in the Atlantic world: citing family oral history, Francisco Fernández de Córdoba (the abbot of Rute) reports that Latino first learned the Roman language by secretly attending his young master's private lessons. Though beyond the scope of this chapter, these two recurring patterns within the African Diaspora – family separation and clandestine education – suggest future lines of inquiry that would explore links that connect Juan Latino and other black Africans in early modern Iberia to the unfolding history of Atlantic slavery.[3]

Though he does not record Latino's manumission, the abbot of Rute's chronicle of the Sessa family does point to a life-changing event for the slave: when the duke of Sessa reached early adolescence, he left his family estate in Andalusia for court. At this point, Latino, about sixteen years old, relocated to Granada. Though we cannot pinpoint the moment he gained his freedom, we do know that he studied at the city's newly founded grammar school and university, then married and started a family. By the time of the Morisco rebellion, he had gained local prominence teaching Latin under the auspices of the same institutions where he had studied.

Notwithstanding the enviable degree of respectability Latino had attained as an educator, post-bellum Granada was a less comfortable place for a visible minority. Latino was himself a prominent *cristiano nuevo* (New Christian), albeit of black African rather than Hispano-Muslim origins. Attitudes towards blacks in Granada, as elsewhere in early modern Europe, were contradictory. On one hand, long-standing narratives of Christian piety in black Africa brought positive associations. But on the other, a medieval association of blacks in Iberia with invading Muslim armies engendered the menacing image of the black Moor or blackamoor. In sixteenth-century Granada in particular, this negative conception meshed with anxieties focused on unassimilated Christian converts of Hispano-Muslim origins. Hence, one of the infamous *pragmáticas* of 1567 prohibited Moriscos from owning black slaves, alleging that these New Christians routinely inculcated them in Islam, thus swelling the ranks of secret Muslims.[4]

In the specific case of Juan Latino, one could debate the extent to which biases directed against recently transported black Africans shaped attitudes to an assimilated freedman known for his Latin erudition. Still, the plight of Granada's Moriscos did bring one ineluctable peril for him and anyone else susceptible to identification as a New Christian. The expulsion of baptized Christians from the realm negated the efficacy of baptism and elevated affiliations of ethnicity or race over individual free will. After all, the collective accusation that Moriscos clung to Islam ignored Christianity's long embrace of converts.

The plight of Granada's Moriscos cut close to Latino in other ways. He and his family lived in the Santa Ana parish neighbourhood, which lost an estimated one-third of its residents in the 1570 expulsion. In fact, the city's population mix also changed dramatically: Aurelia Martín Casares estimates a fivefold increase in the number of slaves, to the point that they made up a staggering 14 per cent of Granada's residents.[5] Regardless of how much or little sympathy the freedman felt with the many men, women, and children sold into slavery just outside his classroom window in early 1571, he and other remaining *granadinos* contended with a vastly changed city.

Later this same year – as residents of Granada were still coming to terms with the trauma of war at home – news arrived of an epochal naval clash that had transpired across the Mediterranean, in the waters of western Greece. On Sunday, 7 October, Don Juan de Austria led an allied Catholic fleet to an unexpected and decisive victory over the Ottoman Turks in the Battle of Lepanto. Local echoes resounded. For one, Lepanto's victor, Don Juan, had taken over the campaign against the rebels in Granada after its persistence and severity had alarmed Philip II. He also oversaw the mass expulsion of Moriscos, first from the city itself and then from the entire region. The four *tercios* (infantry units) that had been charged with quelling the uprising triumphed again at Lepanto, albeit with substantially replenished ranks. Dispatches and letters from Lepanto reveal that, much as in the Granada campaign, officials and foot soldiers alike coveted enemy loot and captives as their most reliable compensation.[6]

Evidence suggests that as soon as the news of the naval victory reached Granada, Juan Latino set to work crafting an accurate and vivid narration of the battle. He turned to the classical genre that poets and schoolmasters of the early modern era revered for its imperial resonances and artistic dimensions: Vergilian epic. His *Austrias Carmen*, or *The Song of John of Austria*, is a two-book epic in Latin hexameter verse that celebrates Don Juan de Austria's victory at Lepanto, emulating Vergil's *Aeneid* in structural, thematic, and linguistic terms. As published, the poem culminated a volume of occasional poetry on the naval clash. Despite the considerable technical demands of composing densely allusive hexameter verse, Latino completed the volume in time for the battle's first anniversary.[7] This immediacy had profound consequences. On one hand, the temporal proximity to Lepanto charged the *Austrias Carmen* with relevance and made Latino a protagonist in an international news event. But it also brought more troubling echoes of the drawn-out war of attrition that had so recently sowed destruction at home. In the pages ahead, I examine this duality, considering how events and alliances in Granada haunt Latino's commemoration of Lepanto.

By striving to prepare his literary commemoration of the naval clash in such short order, Latino inserted himself into an international news event that played out with unprecedented speed. Across Europe, chroniclers, cartographers, poets, and musicians pressed the limits of print technology, manuscript production, and courier networks to circulate accounts of the victory as quickly as possible. In Spanish letters, José López de Toro describes a "volcanic eruption" of poems; on the Italian peninsula, Carlo Dionisotti finds a "poetic plebiscite" that cut across regional barriers and the elite confines of literary academies.[8] Expanding on the long-standing focus on poetry in Spanish and Italian to include the astounding number of writers who responded to Lepanto in Latin, Sarah Spence, Andrew Lemons, and I have translated and edited the work of twenty-three poets – Latino included – who completed poems of Lepanto during the months after the event.[9] Setting out two years ago to locate first-line poetic responses to the news, we were surprised at the number and variety of works, even after narrowing the scope to those writers who explicitly emulated Vergil. My discussions here on Juan Latino follow from my collaboration with Spence and Lemons.

A powerful impulse that Juan Latino shares with other poets, chroniclers, and cartographers who responded to Lepanto is the need to locate the battle, both in geographic and cultural terms. Unlike the pockmarked fortifications of Malta or Cyprus – battle sites still fresh in the memories of Catholic Europe – the Ionian sea swallowed or swept away the material evidence of Lepanto. A compelling example of the care that cartographers took to locate the battle site for book consumers is the map Giovanni Francesco Camocio published in Venice shortly after the battle (see figure 6.1). A cartouche placed just east of the Curzolari Islands pinpoints where the clash occurred, while in the lower right, a note to the *benigni lettori* (gentle readers) gives the precise geographic coordinates and dimensions of the Gulf of Lepanto, offering the book consumer a chance to compare its size to bodies of water closer to home. Considering the cultural geography, many chroniclers, cartographers, and poets underscored the close proximity of Lepanto to the site of the Battle of Actium, in which Octavian defeated Antony and Cleopatra in 31 BC, an episode widely familiar from Vergil's vivid account of this battle in *Aeneid* 8.675–728. Trained from grammar school to revere and emulate the Roman poet, Europeans who responded to news of Lepanto were keen to compare and contrast it to Actium.[10]

The intertwining goals of helping readers locate Lepanto on a map and pondering its cultural implications undergird Juan Latino's *Austrias Carmen*. In common with the Camocio map, Juan Latino's poem takes pains to locate the clash in both geographic and cultural terms. The poetic voice invokes the muses as he prepares to recount the fighting:

Pandite, Musae faciles, Helicona virentem.
Tu cantus resona divino a vertice, Apollo.
Et tu prosper ades, Maecenas Deza, cruentos
magnanimosque duces cernes, et proelia numquam
sic Martem visum pugnas accendere ponto,
queis, neque in Actiaco vicino hic litore Marcum
Augustus vicit, Cleopatram aut mille carinis,
nec gentes umquam pugnarunt puppibus aequis,
nec magis infestis animis ad bella paratae,
quam tunc Naupacto pugnatum est fluctibus, illic
saxa ubi consurgunt Acheloia flumina contra.

(Now gentle Muses, open verdant Helicon. You, Apollo, intone your songs from the holy peak. Deza, my generous Maecenas, be present with your favour; you will see courageous and blood-soaked leaders and battles, on a scale, it seems, that Mars has never kindled on the sea; which not even Augustus surpassed, when he conquered Marc Antony on the nearby shore at Actium or Cleopatra, with her thousand ships. Nations have never fought with so many ships, nor were they more fired up for battle than in the clash on the waves at Naupactus, where rocks rise up beside the Achelous river. (*Austrias Carmen*, or *Song of John of Austria*, 980–90, *princeps* fol. 20r)[11]

The allusion to Actium likens the multinational Ottoman coalition navy to Cleopatra's fleet, alleging that the new naval victory surpasses even the epochal Roman triumph. Yet the final hexameters serve more practical documentary

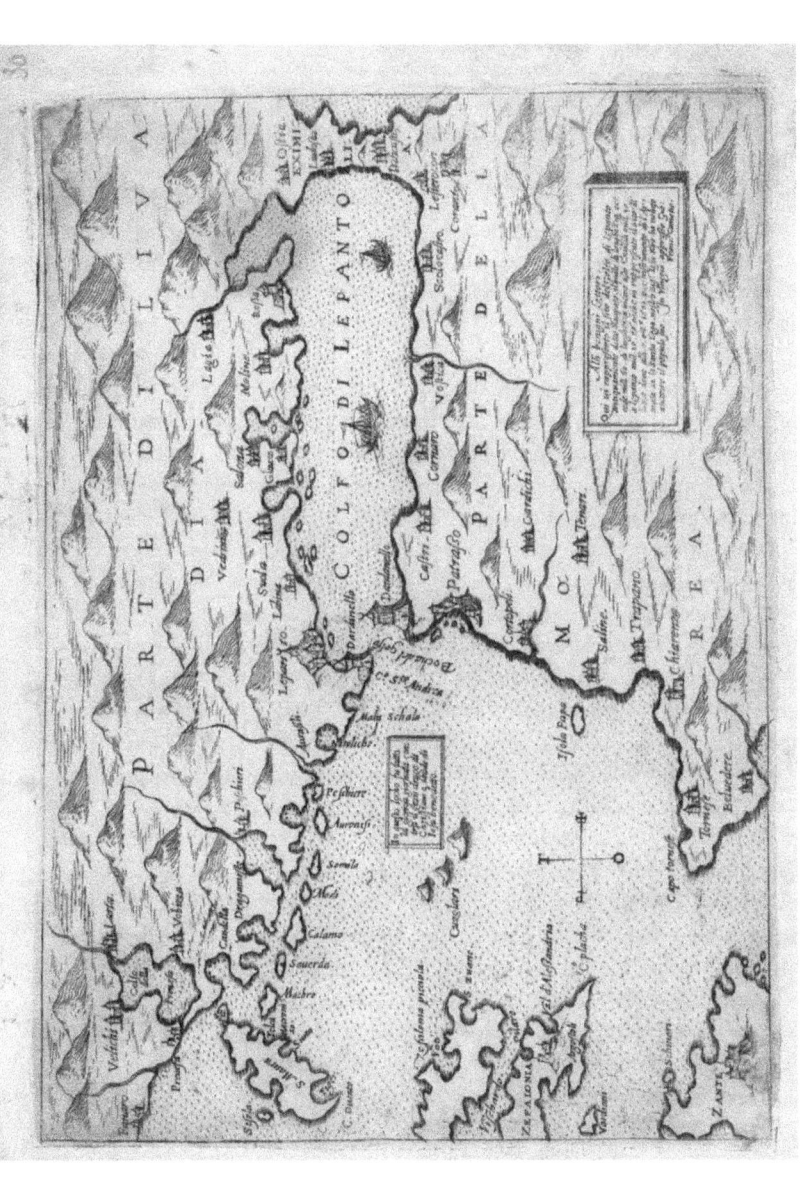

Figure 6.1 Map of the Gulf of Lepanto by Giovanni Francesco Camocio. Map 30 in *Isole che son da Venetia nella Dalmatia et per tutto l'arcipelago, fino a Costantinopoli* (Venice: Simon Pinargenti et compagni, 1573), from Biblioteca Histórica "Marqués de Valdecilla," call number FLL 9665. Reproduced by permission.

ends, transporting the reader to the battle site, just off the Isthmus of Naupactus at the point where the Achelous River (today Akheloos) flows into the sea. In these documentary aims, the *Austrias Carmen* resembles many poems Spence, Lemons, and I have edited, where poets use precise cartographic discourse to pinpoint the battle site. But Latino's poetic map of the glorious naval battle also shows traces of the more vexed local history that defines his epic. In particular, the "generous Maecenas" invoked in the middle of this documentary passage pulls the reader back from Lepanto to Granada.

The patron in question is Pedro de Deza y Guzmán, an inquisitor who served in dual roles, as president of Granada's royal Audiencia and Chancillería, the judiciary institutions that represented royal power in the region. An epilogue ("Peroratio") that follows the *Austrias Carmen* states that "Deza hoc opus componi iussit" (Deza bade this work be written).[12] Latino's relationship with this official requires sensitive contextualization on our part, given Deza's dubious distinction as a particularly unsympathetic hardliner in an era where they were all too plentiful. He had arrived in Granada to oversee the implementation of the *pragmáticas* to eradicate the region's Islamic heritage and, along the way, gain greater control of Morisco economic activities. His intransigence in implementing these measures had sparked the 1568 uprising. When the rebellion proved more durable than expected, Deza advocated for and then supervised the controversial expulsion of the realm's Moriscos, against the opposition of prominent nobles and some churchmen in the region. At the time where Latino prepared his Lepanto epic for publication, Deza was spearheading an ambitious campaign to repopulate confiscated Morisco lands in Granada with Old Christian settlers from Castile's northern realms.[13] The scholars who have worked to illuminate Latino's place within the literature of the African Diaspora do not examine the implications of the freedman's praise for the official most directly responsible for the persecution of Granada's Morisco communities.[14]

As we assess Latino's ties to him, we would do well to consider the bind of any ordinary citizen. Post-bellum Granada was devastated by war and wracked by the infighting of the city elite. One document that may help explain Deza's commission of Latino's poem is the lengthy and damning dossier that a royal *visitador* (auditor) compiled in the wake of the revolt. This audit and Deza's reactions to it show the extent to which the poisonous factional politics that stretched from the royal court to Granada had shaped official policy towards the Moriscos of Granada. They also would have cast a shadow on any city residents who lacked the safety of family wealth and influence.[15] The more than one hundred accusations run the gamut from bureaucratic arcana to salacious comedy and dispiriting tragedy. The *visitador* accused the churchman of wearing hunting capes in deep green and dazzling purple that were inappropriate for a priest. Witnesses alleged that Deza's servants routinely brought the wife of a man jailed in the Chancillería prison up to his quarters during siesta time. Others reported that he sold free *moriscas* to slave traders from Portugal and Ceuta. The inquisitor angrily rejected the charges as fabrications of his enemies. But even Don Juan de Austria – at a particularly frustrating point in the Crown's efforts to suppress the revolt – had concluded that Deza was the main obstacle to the surrender of rebels. He thus urged his main ally at court to show the king that "la manera de proceder que el presidente de Granada ha tenido y tiene con esta gente [Moriscos], que es cierto muy contraria a la que ha convenido y conviene llevar" (the course of action that the president of Granada has taken and is taking towards this people, which is truly contrary to what has been and is appropriate). Another letter validated the boundless hatred that Moriscos harboured towards Deza. Viewing this antipathy as the prime obstacle to rebel surrender, Don Juan advised Philip II to grant the controversial churchman a face-saving sinecure as a bishop to get him away from Granada.[16] Against this backdrop, Deza seems to have commissioned Juan Latino to insert him into an epic celebration of Lepanto, as part of an array of strategies to defend his actions and retain his lucrative position.

Barring further document discoveries in the archives of Granada's Audiencia and Chancillería, we have no evidence beyond Latino's Lepanto volume that would allow us to assess how much or little the freedman identified with the persecution of Granada's Moriscos. What we can reasonably infer is that, given the resilience of the hardline faction at court that had sponsored Deza, Latino would not have gained such fast publication approval had he not validated this circle's much-criticized policies. Books that directly recounted recent and controversial events often waited years to clear publication hurdles. For instance, the soldier Luis Mármol Carvajal sought to publish his account of the Morisco revolt soon after the events took place, yet his chronicle languished for over two decades.[17]

From another perspective, the patronage history of Juan Latino's Lepanto epic typifies a tension within Renaissance letters. Poets across Europe cultivated Vergilian literary genres, attracted, in large measure, by the idea that the Mantuan reached the pinnacle of patronage in Augustan Rome. Yet as these writers offered effusive praise to powerful leaders of their time, they contended with knowledge of their flaws and widespread contempt for flatterers. In this respect, Juan Latino offering his epic to Deza treads on the same delicate ground as Ariosto before Cardinal Ippolito d'Este.[18] Distinguished company notwithstanding, the intense temporal immediacy between the *Austrias Carmen* and the events it narrates carries particular dangers.

We see this peril at once as Latino's poem begins, not with a Homeric invocation of a muse or a Vergilian distillation of the subject matter, but with praise for Deza's controversial actions in Granada. Adapting the Latin hexameter to convey the Spanish monarchy's bureaucratic structure, the opening verses call to "Deza gravis meritis, pietate insignis avita, / cui dotes animi reddit natura benigne, / clarus ab officiis et regis munere praeses" (Deza, dignified by your service and marked by your ancestral piety, on whom nature generously bestowed all the gifts of mind and soul; renowned official and leader of the royal chancery; *Austrias Carmen*, 1–3, *princeps* fol. 2r). The introductory sequence (1–29) then praises the subsequent expulsion of Moriscos from Granada to other parts of Castile.

Yet this official's protagonism does fade when real-time narration of fighting at Lepanto begins. The poetic voice also sheds the formulaic rhetoric of holy war to paint a stark picture of human suffering. Note how the following verses depict the cannon fire from the Venetian galleasses as it rains on Ottoman fighters:

> Sulfura iamque globos spargebant picea fumo
> permixtos, crebris aether micat ignibus ingens.
> Tunc sonitu curva et resonabant litora late,
> fluctibus in mediis geminantia saepe fragorem.
> Non lapides iactos Turcae perferre valebant.
> Saxis nam crebris repetebat saepe procella;
> queis capita et dentes, oculos cerebrumque refringi,
> malas, mandibulas, resoluta et pectora cernas.
> Rupibus et nubes iam terque quaterque cadebat
> machina, nec colubri poterant, nec sulfura pelli.

(And now the pitch-black sulphur discharges clouds mixed with smoke, as the mighty ether flashes with repeated fire. Then the curved shoreline resounds far and wide, sometimes echoing the din in the middle of the waves. The Turks are unable to endure the volley of stones. The storm is relentless, dense with rocks: you could see heads, teeth, eyes, and brains shattered by them, cheeks, jaws, and torsos gone limp. Three and four times the war engine dropped clouds of rock. Neither culverins nor artillery fire could be repelled; *Austrias Carmen* 1016–25; *princeps* fol. 20v.)

This direct examination of the destructive power of cutting-edge weapons contrasts with a pattern Michael Murrin identified in the vernacular epic depictions of Lepanto by Alonso de Ercilla and Juan Rufo. Specifically, Murrin drew attention to how they avoided explicit discussion of the firearms at Lepanto and thus sidestepped the ethical dilemmas that followed from their growing tactical importance.[19] In contrast, Latino focuses on the mutilated bodies of anonymous fighters. Momentarily, the rhetoric of religious warfare attenuates. The pathos here of the mutilation and horrific deaths that unnamed common soldiers suffer registers a Lucanian sensibility, recalling the naval battle in *De bellum civile* 3.567–77. This subtle allusion to Lucan contrasts to the explicit emulation of Vergil's *Aeneid*.

As a counterpoint to the modern artillery that the Holy League vanguard deploys, the Ottoman admiral, Müezzin-zâde Ali Pasha, raises his composite recurved bow. This weapon, which demanded long years to master, epitomized the medieval military arts losing ground to new weapon technologies. The portrait of the adversary thus takes on a strong elegiac tone: "Nunc Bassan gladio pugnat nunc flectit et arcum, / brachiaque extendens nunc mittit ab aure sagittas" (Now the pasha wields the sword, now he bends the bow, and extending his arms he launches arrows from ear level; *Austrias Carmen*, 1050–1; *princeps* fol. 21r). Following the battle as it unfolds in the first reports and news bulletins that circulated, Latino captures the moment when Spanish forces board Ali Pasha's flagship. Soldiers engage in vicious hand-to-hand combat in the cramped confines of the galley deck. Turkish fighters tremble with fear of death. Men fall into the sea and flail like dolphins.

Suddenly, the action verbs of desperate fighting yield to an impersonal verb construction. Attention once again focuses on Ali Pasha: "Hic Bassan caesus fertur gladioque perisse, / atque humilis miles truncum liquisse superbum" (At this moment, Ali Pasha is said to have been struck and to have perished by the sword. Some lowly foot soldier is said to have left nothing but a proud torso; *Austrias Carmen* 1075–6; *princeps* fol. 21v). Tellingly, the impersonal verb *fertur* and the vague subject *humilis miles* combine to blur the executioner's agency.

Direct narration of combat resumes briefly, but stops again as the poetic voice catches sight of the Ottoman commander's severed head, which Spaniards have displayed on a pike: "Iam Bassan truncus summas volitare per undas, / atque caput magnum praefixum cuspide acuta, / praelongo in pilo, magno clamore videntum. / Terribiles oculos nequeas adversa tueri, / ora viri tristi nigroque fluentia tabo. (Now the mutilated Pasha drifts atop the waves and his great head is displayed up high on the sharp tip of a long pike, with a great cry from those watching. You could hardly look at the fighter's terrifying eyes, oozing with miserable black gore; *Austrias Carmen* 1194–8; *princeps* fol. 23v). Horrifying on its own terms, the tragic force magnifies when a margin gloss directs the reader to a relevant *exemplum*: "Euriali, et Nisi sic capita Vergil[ius] cecinit" (thus Vergil narrated in verse the [severed] heads of Euryalus and Nisus; *Austrias Carmen* 1204, margin; *princeps* fol. 23v). This annotation registers Juan Latino's own vocation as a Latin teacher. In effect, the marginal instruction highlights this episode as a "scene of instruction," to apply Jeff Dolven's characterization of how grammar school instruction informed Renaissance reading strategies.[20] What knowledge might this didactic gloss impart?

Intriguingly, the reference foregrounds a notoriously ambiguous story of empire-building.[21] In book 9 of the Aeneid, Nisus, the elder of two friends whose relationship is depicted with powerful homoerotic undertones, plans a daring night-time raid on the Rutulians' camp in order to break their blockade and get a message to Aeneas, taking advantage of the fact that the enemies are sleeping off a wine-soaked banquet. Euryalus, his young friend and lover, insists on accompanying him. The two young warriors set out in the middle of the night, blessed by the assembled Trojan leaders, who offer them a dazzling array of prizes once their mission is accomplished. But when they enter the enemy camp, the desire for loot delays them; they massacre sleeping Rutulians and strip them of their armour and weapons. When they finally continue their planned route at daylight, the reflection of a purloined helmet Euryalus has donned alerts Rutulian sentries. Weighed down by his spoils, the young Trojan warrior is trapped. Nisus tries in vain to offer himself as a hostage, but is also killed in revenge, whereupon both heads are displayed on pikes. Vergil inserts a rare apostrophe to culminate the episode: "Fortunati ambo! si quid mea carmina possunt, / nulla dies umquam memori vos eximet aevo / dum domus Aeneae Caitoli immobile saxum / accolet imperiumque pater Romanus habebit" (How fortunate, both at once! / If my songs have any power, the day will never dawn / that wipes you from the memory of the ages, not while / the house of Aeneas stands by the Capitol's rock unshaken, / not while the Roman Father rules the world; *Aeneid* 9.446–9.)[22] Speaking in the voice of a schoolmaster, the annotation draws Latin apprentices' attention to a rare Vergilian apostrophe through a transposition into indirect discourse ("Euriali, et Nisi sic capita Vergil[ius] cecinit"). In narrative terms, the reference to the story of Nisus and Euryalus marks a transition at Lepanto: Spaniards, taking stock of their triumph, turn to the business of gathering the war spoils that will be their compensation; the discipline that won the battle gives way to near mutiny.[23]

Lexical and metrical parallels add more layers to the engagement with the episode of Nisus and Euryalus. The cries prompted by Ali Pasha's severed head, "praelongo in pilo, magno clamore videntum" (high on the sharp tip of a long pike, with a great cry from those watching; 1196–7), draw on the scene of the severed heads of Nisus and Euryalus raised high amid enemy victory calls: "praefigunt capita et multo clamore sequuntur" (they even impale the heads ... baiting them with outcries; *Aeneid* 9.466; Fagles, 281). The "sad black gore" emanating from Ali Pasha's severed head ("nigroque fluentia tabo," 1198) likewise amplifies the natural revulsion through allusion to the same passage, with its "nota nimis miseris atroque fluentia tabo" (men stunned by the sight of the men they know too well ... dripping gore; *Aeneid* 9.472; Fagles, 282). When Ali Pasha's bereft sons plead with their Spanish captors for a swift mercy killing to avoid humiliating captivity, they beg them to "in nos ardenter mites convertite ferrum" (be kind, and turn your sword zealously against us; *Austrias Carmen* 1252). These words echo the plea of Nisus when he offers his life to save the trapped Euryalus, "in me convertite ferrum" (turn your blades on me; *Aeneid* 9.427; Fagles, 280).[24] The repeated citation, in effect, insists that Lepanto's aftermath be studied side-by-side with the passage in *Aeneid* 9.

From one perspective, the bravery and camaraderie of the two young Trojans model the martial values that Renaissance schoolmasters sought to inculcate through epic.[25] The episode, after all, promotes normative military values as it highlights a story of two youths who give their lives but gain immortality through poetry. Yet the positive message, like the fleeing warriors themselves, comes loaded with heavy baggage. Specifically, scholars have noted the ironic allusion to Dolon's disastrous raid in the *Iliad* 10: in both cases, the lure of abundant enemy spoils drives the ill-fated expedition.[26] Given this literary lineage, the repeated, even insistent citations of the Nisus and Euryalus episode in the *Austrias Carmen* warn, through allusion, how an economic motor of warfare can undermine its tactical and strategic motives. Such warnings cut close to home for the poet in Granada.

As officials in Latino's home city fought their frustrating and prolonged campaign to suppress the rebellion, they contended with a soldiery obsessed with looting as the only reliable means of timely compensation. Chronicler Diego Hurtado de Mendoza recounts a series of fiascos that resulted. For instance, in the first year of the revolt, two captains led a search party of 800 men to the mountain redoubt of Válor, in pursuit of Abén Humeya, the rebel leader. Their ostensible target had already fled to a hideaway. Nonetheless, the search party captured and killed the Morisco emissaries who arrived to negotiate, after which they slaughtered unarmed villagers and sacked their homes. At daybreak, they fled at the sight of a band of rebels led by the very leader they had intended to capture. Hurtado de Mendoza thus recounts their fate: "los nuestros al nacer del día partiendo la presa, en que había ochocientos cautivos y mucha ropa, las bestias y ellos cargados, tomaron el camino de Orgiba, ... mas los soldados por no desamparar la presa hicieron poca resistencia ... en fin del todo puestos en rota sin osar defenderse ni huir, muertos los capitanes y oficiales; rendidos los soldados y degollados: con la presa a cuestas o en los brazos" (at daybreak, our men were dividing the booty, in which there were 800 captives, much clothing, pack animals; laden, they made for the Orgiba road ... but the soldiers, not wishing to surrender the booty offered little resistance ... in the end all subject to destruction without daring to defend themselves or flee: captains and officers dead; soldiers captured or with throats slit while holding fast to the booty in their packs or arms).²⁷ As in the story of Nisus and Euryalus, the night-time raid and slaughter gives way to a morning retreat foiled by the weight of their loot. Only about forty of the original eight hundred royal troops returned to Granada. Far from its being exceptional, many observers conceded that frenetic looting was a recurring obstacle to the rebellion's pacification.²⁸

At the time when Juan Latino took on the task of writing his Lepanto epic, such memories of the Granada campaign were raw. The freedman was, after all, memorializing the actions in naval combat of the same *tercios* and commanders who had ravaged Granada's hinterlands like swarms of locusts. If he wrote from his home in the Santa Ana parish alongside the Darro River, he would have looked out onto the empty, looted houses of the lower Albaicín. Against this grim backdrop, the good news of a decisive and swift victory at Lepanto must have boosted spirits. The protagonists were familiar, but their destructive power played out far from home.

To close the *Austrias Carmen*, the poet bridges the two scenes of recent military action by taming Vergil's rumour-mongering *Fama*. Where her flight in *Aeneid* 4 (174–88) undoes Dido by spreading news of her affair with Aeneas, Latino's Christianized messenger bears the news bulletins of the naval victory from Italy to King Philip II's Escorial palace (*Austrias Carmen* 1576–1600; *princeps* fol. 30v). From court, she spreads word to Granada. *Fama* also bears news of the much-awaited birth of a royal heir, just two months after the triumph at sea (1712–14; *princeps* fol. 33r). Charged with renewed optimism, the closing verses foresee bountiful harvests from the pastures and golden fields ("mollibus hinc flavus gaudebit campus aristis," *Austrias Carmen* 1828; *princeps* fol. 35v). The two auspicious events, Lepanto and the royal birth, dispel the clouds over the war-torn Granada. The final verses prophesy that the might of King Philip and his newborn son Ferdinand will subject still more vanquished people to Christ's power.

Visions of a new, international order anchored by Spanish military power soon clouded. From many angles, the years after Lepanto would more closely resemble the darker shadings of the poem's real-time battle narration. Pius V, whose crusading zeal proved decisive in forming the Holy League, died the following spring. His alliance did not live much longer, as Venetians negotiated a separate peace with the Ottomans. Don Ferdinand, the crown prince whose birth Latino celebrates in the *Austrias Carmen*'s closing passage, died in early childhood, in the same year Don Juan de Austria succumbed to disease (1578). Posthumously, Philip II granted his illegitimate half-brother the royal title he had sought to no avail when leading Crown forces in Granada and Lepanto, a claim the *Austrias Carmen* airs repeatedly.²⁹

Ironically, the only clear winner in this story of Granada-in-Lepanto is the implacable Pedro de Deza. Crown officials ultimately followed Don Juan's advice for a face-saving promotion and transfer out of Granada. Not long after the Crown visitor completed his damning investigation, Deza was awarded a cardinal's hat for Seville and dispatched to Rome. There, historian Thomas Dandelet has recorded how he became a pillar of "Spanish Rome," amassing a princely fortune.[30]

Back in Spain, Juan Latino's landmark epic faded from view. The only known re-edition of the *Austrias Carmen* in the seventeenth century labels the epic *rarissima* (extremely rare).[31] The freedman, for his part, suffered a posthumous canonization through the filter of racial stereotype, as Baltasar Fra Molinero and John Beusterien have shown. Indeed, Juan Latino is best known to Hispanists as the comic hero of the eponymous play by Diego Ximénez de Enciso; this drama pivots on the racial stereotypes that Beusterien and Fra Molinero catalogue, straying far from the rare reliable sources on Latino's life.

Fittingly, a major step towards an adequate recontextualization of Latino has resulted from the efforts of scholars of literature of the African Diaspora. Of particular importance is the new attention that Henry Louis Gates and Maria Wolff drew to Latino by noting he is the first black African writer known to have published a book of poetry in a European language. Recently, J. Mira Seo has expanded these inquiries about Latino in the history of African Diaspora literature, while adding analysis of the freedman's intense engagement with the classical literary tradition.[32]

To complement this ongoing rediscovery of Juan Latino, Spence, Lemons, and I draw attention to the freedman's implication in the most significant news event of his time. By reflecting on Lepanto in Latin hexameter verse, Latino forged a bond with the dozens of other poets abroad who embraced Catholic Europe's international language. Reading the *Austrias Carmen* in the company of works by twenty-two other neo-Latin poets from across the Italian peninsula, readers can chart many lines of inquiry and points of contrast. For instance, Latino's deployment of Vergil's *Fama* to explain how news of the naval battle reached *Granadinos* with what seemed lightning speed correlates to a meta-literary dimension within some of the Latin poems from Italy. As such, *Fama* provides a focal point for meditations on the impact of the printing press.

This point of contact offers just one of many perspectives from which we envision a recovery of Juan Latino within the original publication context of the *Austrias Carmen*. A striking duality challenges the literary critic here. Responding to news bulletins and eye-witness testimony of Lepanto, Juan Latino – in parallel to his counterparts throughout the Italian peninsula – embraces the role of a neo-Latin poet as a privileged steward of Europe's literary tradition.

But along the way, he and his Italian counterparts claim a voice in mediating news of the day that we are more apt today to associate with pundits, bloggers, and journalists. So doing, they proffer poetry as a medium with the power to engender an informed and engaged citizenry. Part of this engagement draws on the anti-Muslim crusade that had powered the Holy League Alliance. But these Lepanto poets also highlight Mediterranean cultural reference points that undercut anti-Muslim rhetoric. A few writers even expose looting and excess cruelty of the Catholic victors, albeit through cautious and subtle allusions. In Latino's positioning as a poet and educator of Granada, the human drama that plays out far away in the eastern Mediterranean invites uncomfortable reflections on unspeakable suffering closer to home.

NOTES

1   See Aurelia Martín Casares, *Martín Casares, Aurelia. La esclavitud en la Granada del siglo XVI: género, raza y religión* (Granada: Universidad de Granada, 2000), esp. 204–7. I thank Sarah Spence and Andrew Lemons for insights they have shared with me about Juan Latino's literary practice in the course of our collaborative edition and translation, *The Battle of Lepanto*, ed. Elizabeth R. Wright, Sarah Spence, and Andrew Lemons, I Tatti Renaissance Library 61 (Cambridge: Harvard University Press, 2014). Support for this research has come from an NEH Scholarly Editions and Translations Grant, a residency at the Rockefeller Foundation's Bellagio Center, and a University of Georgia Willson Center Faculty Research Grant.
2   A useful point of departure for study of the Morisco revolt of 1568–70 remains the classic study by Antonio Domínguez Ortiz and Bernard Vincent, *Historia de los moriscos: Vida y tragedia de una minoría* (Madrid: Biblioteca de la Revista de Occidente, 1978), see esp. 17–33. See also David Coleman, *Creating Christian Granada: Society and Religious Culture in an Old-World Frontier City, 1492–1600* (Ithaca: Cornell University Press, 2003), 181–6; and James Amelang, *Historias paralelas: Judeoconversos y moriscos en la España moderna* (Madrid: Akal, 2011), 35–85.
3   The claim of birth in *Aethiopia* (sub-Saharan Africa) in a statement ("Haec, Ioannes Latinus …") prefaces Juan Latino, *De augusta et catholica regalium corporum translatione* (Granada: Hugo de Mena, ca 1576), fol. n.n. A history of the dukes of Sessa states he was born to black slaves in the family's estate in Baena and recounts how he secretly attended his master's lessons; see Francisco Fernández de Córdoba (abbot of Rute), *Casa de Córdoba, y origen de la fundación y Antiguedad de esta ciudad* (ca 1620), manuscript 3271, Biblioteca Nacional de España (Madrid), fol. 174r. I retrace Latino's career as an educator and Latin poet within the context of Granada in a monograph in progress, "The Epic of Juan Latino."

On Latino's life, see Antonio Marín Ocete, "El negro Juan Latino: ensayo de un estudio biográfico y crítico," published in two parts under the same title in *Revista del Centro de Estudios Históricos de Granada y su Reino* 13, nos 1–2 (1923): 97–120, and 14, nos 1–2 (1924): 25–82. Frederick Douglass's denunciation of the wilful destruction of black families opens his *Narrative of the Life of Frederick Douglass* (New York: Library of America, 1994), 15; he recounts his clandestine education on 37–48. James Amelang suggests how to link Juan Latino in particular and Mediterranean slave narratives more generally to Atlantic slave narratives in a lecture, "Writing Chains: Slave Autobiography from the Mediterranean to the Atlantic," Transcultural Perspectives on Late Medieval and Early Modern Slavery in the Mediterranean, University of Zurich, 15 September 2012, publication forthcoming. I thank Professor Amelang for sharing a typescript version.

4 On the positive assessment of Ethiopian converts in Christian tradition, see Jean Marie Courtès, "The Theme of 'Ethiopia' and 'Ethiopians' in Patristic Literature," in *The Image of the Black in Western Art: From the Early Christian Era to the "Age of Discovery*," ed. David Bindman and Henry Louis Gates, Jr, vol. 2 of 4, 199–214 (Cambridge: Belknap Press of Harvard University Press, 2010), esp. 207–8; Frank M. Snowden Jr, *Before Color Prejudice: The Ancient View of Blacks* (Cambridge: Harvard University Press, 1983), 100–1; and Baltasar Fra Molinero, *La imagen de los negros en el teatro del Siglo de Oro* (Madrid: Siglo XXI, 1995), 5–6. For the medieval associations of blacks with invading Almoravid armies, see Jean Devisse, "The Black and His Color: From Symbols to Realities," in Bindman and Gates, *Image of the Black in Western Art*, 73–137, esp. 77–80. Associations in Granada of newly transported blacks from Africa with an alleged Islamic conspiracy perpetrated by Moriscos are recorded by Luis del Mármol Carvajal, in his *Historia de la rebelión y castigo de los moriscos del Reino de Granada* (Málaga: Juan René, 1600), fol. 33v.

5 Slave population estimates are in Martín Casares, *La esclavitud en la Granada del siglo XVI*, 115, while the population decline from expulsion is recorded in Antonio Cortes Peña and Bernard Vincent, *Historia de Granada* (Granada: Don Quijote, 1986), 3:61.

6 On the *tercios* of Granada and Lepanto, see Geoffrey Parker and I.A.A. Thompson, "The Battle of Lepanto, 1571: The Costs of Victory," *Mariner's Mirror* 64, no. 1 (1978): 13–21, esp. 17. For histories of Lepanto, see John Francis Guilmartin's *Gunpowder and Galleys: Changing Technology and Mediterranean Warfare at Sea in the 16th Century*, rev. ed. (1974; London: Conway Maritime, 2003); and Niccolò Capponi, *Victory of the West: The Story of the Battle of Lepanto* (London: Macmillan, 2006). Tallies of slaves and other spoils appear in the first commanders' reports sent to the Spanish king, transcribed in *Colección de documentos inéditos para la historia de España (CODOIN)*, ed. Martín Fernández de Navarrete,

Miguel Salvá, and Pedro Sainz de Barranda (Madrid: Viuda de Calero, 1843), 3:227–36.
7   The approbation dated 30 October 1572 supports the inference that Latino toiled to finish by the battle's first anniversary. See Juan Latino (Joannes Latinus), *Ad catholicum, pariter et invictissimum Philippum Dei gratia hispaniarum regem ... epigrammatum liber ... Austrias Carmen* (hereafter *Austrias Carmen*) (Granada: Hugo Mena, 1573). The volume appeared in print shortly after April 1573.
8   See José López de Toro, *Los poetas de Lepanto* (Madrid: Instituto Histórico de Marina, 1950), 24–5; and Carlo Dionisotti, "La guerra d'Oriente nella letteratura veneziana del Cinquecento," in Dionisotti, *Geografia e storia della letteratura italiana* (1967; Turin: Einaudi, 1999), 201–26, esp. 221–3. On Lepanto's cultural impact in Venice, see Iain Fenlon, in *The Ceremonial City: History, Memory and Myth in Renaissance Venice* (New Haven, CT: Yale University Press, 2007).
9   Wright, Spence, and Lemons, *Battle of Lepanto*.
10 Jenny Jordan illuminates the post-Lepanto boom in map-books in "Galley Warfare in Renaissance Intellectual Layering: Lepanto through Actium," *Viator* 35 (2004): 563–79; as well as in "Imagined Lepanto: Turks, Mapbooks, Intrigue, and Spectacular [*sic*] in the Sixteenth-Century Construction of 1571" (PhD diss., University of California – Los Angeles, 2004). See also Georgia Tolias, "*Isolarii*, Fifteenth to Seventeenth Century," in *Cartography in the European Renaissance*, ed. David Woodward, vol. 3, bk 1 of *The History of Cartography*, 263–84 (Chicago: University of Chicago Press, 2007). On the literary connection between Actium and Lepanto, see David Quint, *Epic and Empire: Politics and Generic Form from Virgil to Milton* (Princeton: Princeton University Press, 1993), 21–49.
11 Parenthetical citations include line numbers that correspond to the edition of Juan Latino, *The Song of John of Austria (Austrias Carmen)*, in Wright, Spence, and Lemons, *Battle of Lepanto*; folio numbers correspond to the *princeps* (Juan Latino, *Ad catholicum, pariter et invictissimum Philippum Dei gratia hispaniarum regem ... epigrammatum liber ... Austrias Carmen*), which is now available on Google books. I thank Leah Whittington, our editor at the I Tatti Renaissance Library, for her many valuable suggestions.
12 The "Peroratio" appears at the end of Latino, *Austrias Carmen*, n.n. (second gathering F1r).
13 For Deza's life and career, see José Martínez Millán and Carlos J. de Carlos Morales, eds., *Felipe II (1527–1598): la configuración de la Monarquía Hispánica* (Salamanca: Junta de Castilla y León, 1998), 362–3. A concise statement of his negative impact in Granada appears in J.H. Elliott, *Imperial Spain: 1469–1716* (1963; London: Penguin Books, 1990), 238–9. On the campaign to resettle confiscated Morisco lands with settlers from northern Castile, see Manuel Barrios Aguilera, *Moriscos y repoblación en las postrimerías de la Granada islámica* (Granada: Diputación Provincial de Granada, 1993).

14 See Baltasar Fra Molinero, "Juan Latino and His Racial Difference," in *Black Africans in Renaissance Europe*, ed. T.F. Earle and K.J.P. Lowe, 326–44 (Cambridge: Cambridge University Press, 2005): "The composition opens with prayers in Granada both for the distant victory and for the continuing repression" (335). He does not mention that the passage praises Deza. See also J. Mira Seo, "Identifying Authority: Juan Latio, an African Ex-Slave, Professor, and Poet in Sixteenth-Century Granada," in *African Athena: New Agendas*, ed. Daniel Orrells, Gurminder K. Bhambra, and Tessa Roynon, 258–76 (New York: Oxford University Press, 2011), 271: "Apart from a brief, allusive mention of the Moriscos as a *gens iniqua* (line 31), however, Latino declines to pursue the topic further." On the continued dominance of the hard-line minister (Cardinal Diego de Espinosa) who sponsored Deza, see Geoffrey Parker, *Felipe II: La biografía definitiva*, trans. Victoria E. Gordo del Rey (Barcelona: Planeta, 2010), 531–69.

15 The dossier compiled by the *visitador* (auditor) is preserved in the Archivo General de Simancas, Cámara de Castilla, legajo 2737. Deza's own correspondence with his sponsors at court about this examination attests to treacherous faction politics (Instituto Valencia de Don Juan, Envío 8). On how faction politics shaped the policies in Granada, see the concise assessment in Elliott, *Imperial Spain*, 238–9.

16 Letters of Don Juan de Austria to Ruy Gómez de Silva (August 1570) are transcribed in *CODOIN*, 28:127–9.

17 Mármol Carvajal refers to his completed history of the revolt in his landmark *Primera parte de la descripción general de África* (Granada: Rene Rabut, 1573), fol. 278r, noting that his history of the revolt should appear in print soon; however, his *Historia de la rebelión y castigo de los moriscos del Reino de Granada* was delayed until 1600.

18 See Wilson-Okamura, *Virgil in the Renaissance* (Cambridge: Cambridge University Press, 2010), esp. 50–9.

19 See Michael Murrin, *History and Warfare in Renaissance Epic* (Chicago: University of Chicago Press, 1994), 138.

20 See Jeff Dolven, *Scenes of Instruction in Renaissance Romance* (Chicago: University of Chicago Press, 2007), 10–17; and Andrew Wallace, *Virgil's Schoolboys: The Poetics of Pedagogy in Renaissance England* (Oxford: Oxford University Press, 2010), esp. 178–227. See also José María Anguita and Elizabeth R. Wright, "Sombras de la *onorosa praeda*: un *exemplo* virgiliano para un aula granadina," *Criticón* 115 (2012): 105–23, which examines the Nisus and Euryalus episode with reference to the centrality of epic in the Latin classroom.

21 Useful surveys of differing interpretations appear in Elizabeth Block, "The Narrator Speaks: Apostrophes in Homer and Vergil," *Transactions of the American Philological Association* 112 (1982): 7–22, esp. 17–19; and Nicolas Horsfall, ed., *A Companion to the Study of Virgil* (Leiden: E.J. Brill, 1995), 170–8.

22 *The Aeneid*, trans. Robert Fagles (New York: Penguin Books, 2006), 281. To avoid confusion with the line numbers of the Latin text, subsequent citations appear in parenthesis with the translator's name and page number.
23 On the mutiny and the literary allusions that inform it, see Elizabeth R. Wright, "Scrutinizing Early Modern Warfare in Latin Hexameters: The *Austrias Carmen* of Joannes Latinus (Juan Latino)," in *Poiesis and Modernity in the Old and New Worlds*, ed. Anthony J. Cascardi and Leah Middlebrook, 139–58 (Nashville: Vanderbilt University Press, 2012).
24 For analysis of the cross-cultural dimensions of the lament by Ali Pasha's captive sons, see Elizabeth R. Wright, "Narrating the Ineffable Lepanto: The *Austrias Carmen* of Joannes Latinus (Juan Latino)," *Hispanic Review* 77, no. 1 (2009): 71–91.
25 Walter Ong, "Latin Language Study as a Renaissance Puberty Rite," *Studies in Philology* 66, no. 2 (1959): 103–24, notes how schoolmasters used epic to find "cases of courage" for classroom study (114). As Wilson-Okamura notes in *Virgil in the Renaissance* (206), schoolmasters and commentators often extracted such cases from their original textual context to highlight under general topics, such as *war* or *prudence*.
26 See Sergio Casali, "Nisus and Euryalus: Exploiting the Contradictions in Virgil's 'Doloneia.'" *Harvard Studies in Classical Philology* 102 (2004): 319–54, see esp. 332.
27 Diego Hurtado de Mendoza, *Guerra de Granada*, ed. B. Blanco-González (Madrid: Castalia, 1970), 190–5; translation mine. The chronicler recounts a chain of similar disasters (see 177–9, 244–9, and 259–60).
28 See, for example, the discussion of allotment of spoils in Mármol Carvajal, *Historia de la rebelión y castigo de los moriscos del Reino de Granada* (fol. 204v).
29 Bartolomé Bennassar offers an account of this issue in his delectable *Don Juan de Austria: Un héroe para un imperio* (Madrid: Temas de Hoy, 2000), 1–27.
30 Thomas J. Dandelet, *Spanish Rome, 1500–1700* (New Haven, CT: Yale University Press, 2001), 54, 70, 79.
31 Juan Tamayo Salazar's *A Anamnesis, sive Commemorationis Sanctorum Hispanorum, ad ordinem, et methodum Martyrologii Romani, quo utitur Ecclesiae Catolica*, vol. 5 of 6 (Lyon: Philippe Borde, Laurent Arnaud and Cl. Rigaud, 1658) features the *Austrias Carmen* for 7 October, in the context of a calendar of saint days honouring Catholic martyrs (440–78).
32 On Latino's marginalization in seventeenth-century Spanish literature, see Fra Molinero's *La imagen de los negros en el teatro del Siglo de Oro* (125–62), and his "Juan Latino and His Racial Difference"; as well as John Beusterien, *An Eye on Race: Perspectives from Theater in Imperial Spain* (Lewisburg: Bucknell University Press, 2006), 106–14. Latino's foundational importance in literature of the African Diaspora is attested in Henry Louis Gates and Maria Wolff's "An Overview of Sources on the Life and Work of Juan Latino, the 'Ethiopian Humanist,'" *Research in African Literatures: The African Diaspora and Its Origins* 29, no. 4 (1998): 14–51; and more recently, Seo's "Identifying Authority."

chapter seven

Imperial Anxiety, the Roman Mirror, and the Neapolitan Academy of the Duke of Medinaceli, 1696–1701

THOMAS DANDELET

An empire's an empire,
but Julius Caesar is different from Caligula.
      Pier Ferdinando Casini, head of Italy's Union of Christian Democrats party,
      on Silvio Berlusconi and his government (*New York Times*, 17 November 2010)

In March 1696, Luis della Cedra, the duke of Medinaceli, was appointed viceroy of the Kingdom of Naples by the bewitched king of Spain, Carlos II. He was the last of a string of Spanish viceroys who had ruled in the name and place of the Spanish monarchs for almost two centuries. The grandson of the former viceroy of Naples, the duke of Santo Stefano, Medinaceli seemed born to the task. Over the five years that he ruled, he successfully faced a series of difficult challenges, including plague, revolt, and war. In the midst of all this, he introduced a surprising measure of intellectual openness and inquiry in the Neapolitan court, including the cultivation of an academy that was inaugurated on 20 March 1698.[1]

Loosely modelled after the Academy of Science in Paris, the academy of Medinaceli was also known as the Royal or Palatine Academy. For a period of three years, it met twice a month in one of the main rooms of the palace presided over by a president who held that office for one year. Niccolò Carmine Caracciolo, the prince of Santobuono, Filippo Anastasio, and Paolo Mattia Doria each occupied the position during the short life of the group. All of them also wrote prominent essays, which were preserved in three volumes that were produced to collect the proceedings. Entitled *Raccolta di varie lezioni academiche sopra diverse materie recitate nell'accademia dell' Ecc.mo Signore Duca di Medinaceli et Vicere et Capitan Generale nel Regno di Napoli*, the three volumes fill over 1,300 folios.[2] On the surface they are concerned with the distant past, but as the product of an empire whose fate was anything but certain, they also constitute reflections on the present and future of Naples and the Spanish Empire.

The Palatine Academy was the heir of the earlier Academy of the Investiganti, and the primary subjects of the many lessons presented to the group were history and natural science. More specifically, the proceedings and writings of the members focused on the history of ancient empires as well as on topics relevant to the management of their own kingdom, including hydrology, the nautical sciences, rivers, and mathematics. At the same time, the Palatine Academy played the important role of bringing the new philosophical ideas and debates of northern Europe to Italy, including the debate over ancient versus modern learning.[3] Contemporary scholars have noted the prominence of moderns such as Nicolò Caravita, and Cartesians like Gregorio Calaprese in the group. Among its members was a young Giambattista Vico, who spoke once to the assembled academy and wrote an essay on the theme of the sumptuous dining of the Romans.[4]

But the members of the Neapolitan Academy differed greatly from their more radical French counterparts on the question of history, or more specifically what area of history was important to study. While Descartes claimed that there was no reason that "the history of the Empire should be known any more than that of the smallest state of Europe," the members of the duke's academy privileged the theme of empire above all others. In this regard they had much more in common with their Italian Renaissance predecessors than with the emerging French philosophes.[5]

This was not surprising, given the imminent political crisis facing Naples and the Spanish Empire. By the 1680s, if not earlier, it was clear to European court observers that the Spanish Habsburg dynasty that had ruled Naples for two centuries was coming to an end. The impotence of the last monarch of the line, Charles II, signalled the biological failure of the Spanish Habsburgs and called into question the future of the Spanish Empire itself. On the eastern edge of the empire, the Spanish viceroy of Naples responded to this moment of anxiety in a way that was natural to a Renaissance ruler: he sponsored a group of historians whose main preoccupation was to reflect on past empires and especially on ancient Rome with the hope of gaining political guidance for their own time.

This was a Renaissance political tradition that constituted a primary intellectual foundation for the members of the Palatine Academy. Like humanists dating back to Petrarch, who had written the first Renaissance biography of Julius Caesar, the Neapolitan authors clearly thought the history of empires, and that of the Roman Empire above all others, was the most important historical model and mirror for understanding the political realities of their own day. Thus, they gave imperial histories pride of place in their conversations and historical writings.

The Neapolitan essays produced by the Palatine Academy must thus be seen as part of this long Renaissance intellectual tradition that focused on the imperial theme. In short, they constitute a late synthesis of and addition to the imperial Renaissance, a Renaissance focused on the revival of the texts and memories of the Roman Empire. Emerging in the fourteenth century, the imperial Renaissance sought to regain the political knowledge, lessons, and examples of the Caesars and the texts of their most illustrious writers with an explicit eye on the future. The writings of Julius Caesar, Marcus Aurelius, Tacitus, Suetonius, Plutarch, and many others appeared in numerous new editions in both the original Latin or Greek and the vernacular. Moreover, new commentaries on their work were produced while still other humanists modelled their work on ancient examples. Petrarch's life of Caesar in his *Lives of Illustrious Men*, for example, is clearly indebted to the life of Caesar in Plutarch's *Lives*, and it set the stage for many imitators in the following centuries.[6] At the same time, late Renaissance scholars like those of the Neapolitan Academy produced their own histories and interpretations of ancient Rome and her emperors. Far from being idle intellectual exercises, both earlier and later authors sought wisdom from the past as they plotted their own political futures. History was still the intellectual discipline most closely tied to political guidance and reflection.[7]

Italy in the early modern period was not the political centre of empire, but it was a central location for the literary rebirth of the imperial ideal, the major source of imperial political dreams and aesthetic revivals, a vital part of the Spanish Habsburg empire in the sixteenth and seventeenth centuries, and finally, an important player in the Austrian and French Empires in the later part of the period.

Seen from the perspective of the long arc of four centuries, empire was the dominant political reality in early modern Italy. Florence and Venice may have launched the republican Renaissance, while Venice kept the idea alive until Napoleon's conquest of 1796, but this was the minority party. Being subjects, or at least clients, of empire was the political norm for the majority of Italians throughout the early modern period. The ruling class, in particular, benefited from and bolstered this political system as they served as viceroys, governors, administrators, churchmen, and soldiers for the empire of the moment. It became natural for this class to learn how to cultivate and profit from empire, even if it was not their own. It was hard for them to imagine many political alternatives.

Coming to grips with this imperial past is also an essential component of a revision underway in the general political history of early modern Italy.

Studying and acknowledging the *depth and range* of the imperial Renaissance has simply not been done in Italian scholarship or more general scholarship on the period up to this point.[8] Celebrating the heroic republican past, the great cultural and intellectual accomplishments, and the occasional revolutions and resistance have obviously been more attractive for Italian and foreign scholars of Italy alike. Studying the impact of and depth of imperial domination from the viewpoint of the conquered has never been a popular topic. But a more accurate rendering of Italy's early modern past depends, in large part, on acknowledging and studying the cold, hard facts of imperial domination and Italy's response to it.

This is certainly true for early modern Naples. Indeed, the deliberations of the members of the Palatine Academy are one of the most expansive examples of late Renaissance rhetorical production focused on the legacy, meaning, and continued political relevance of empire. More specifically, of the 127 lessons that are preserved from the academy's deliberations, roughly one-third were reflections on ancient empire, and particularly on Rome.

The first volume contains eighteen distinct sections or essays. The first, by Calaprese, is concerned with the origins of empires, and it sets the stage for the next twelve essays dedicated to ancient empires preceding Rome, including the Assyrians, Persians, and Greeks. A long anonymous essay on the Roman Empire follows, which then leads into essays on individual emperors by the leading members of the academy: Julius Cesar by Tomaso Donzelli, Augustus Cesar by Carmine Nicolò Caracciolo, Tiberius by Filippo Anastasio, Caligula by Nicolò Caravita, and Claudius by Paolo Doria. The second volume continues the biographical model with twenty-six essays dedicated to individual emperors.[9]

A palpable imperial angst animates the project as a whole, and there is a range of opinions and judgments on the origins and legitimacy of empire. As the product of a long intellectual tradition, the essays contain echoes of the earlier Renaissance divide over empire: while humanists like Poggio, Bruni, and Machiavelli condemned it, others like Guarino Guarini, Flavio Biondo, and Giovio praised it as the natural and highest evolution of political life.

It was Guarino, to name a primary example, who advanced Julius Caesar as the political role model for Leonello d'Este, one of the earliest promoters of the imperial Renaissance. In a number of letters to the prince, Guarino praised Caesar's many virtues and triumphs while also drawing parallels between the magnificence of the d'Este princes and that of Julius and Augustus Caesar.[10] The lessons were embraced by Leonello, who made good use of the edition of Caesar's *Commentaries* that Guarino dedicated to him. He was reputed to prefer Caesar over all other ancient authors.[11]

Guarino's praise of Caesar and Leonello's admiration of him struck at the heart of the debate between the champions of the republican Renaissance and the imperial Renaissance. Guarino was himself at the centre of the debate when he engaged with Poggio Bracciolini in an exchange of letters that specifically compared the respective virtues and faults of Scipione Africanus and Julius Caesar.[12]

Poggio had provoked the argument in 1435 when he wrote a letter to the Ferrara humanist Scipione Mainenti that compared the two Romans. In his analysis, Scipione was worthy of praise for retiring after his many military victories, a selfless act that preserved the republic. Caesar, however, succumbed to the temptations of power, murdering his opponents, and imposing a tyranny on Rome. The contrast between the two men was clear: Scipione was celebrated for "justice, temperance, dignity, moderation, continence, integrity," while Caesar was condemned for "plundering, deceit, internal opposition, civil struggle, immoderate lust for power," and numerous other personal faults.[13]

Guarino's response to Poggio was a thirty-three page treatise that praised both Scipione and Caesar, while making it quite clear that Caesar was the more successful and important of the two because of the combination of his military greatness, political virtues, and literary production.[14] In this sense, Guarino echoed Petrarch's view as he provided a condensed version of the comparison and contrast provided by the two Petrarchan biographies of Caesar and Scipione.[15]

In earlier scholarship on the debate between Guarino and Poggio, the central political issue has been presented as a contest between liberty and tyranny.[16] Poggio's perspective, in a view famously promoted by Hans Baron, was a central plank in the political platform of the civic humanists that won the day in fifteenth-century Florence.[17] By implication and neglect, Guarino's position, a major element of imperial humanism, has been largely left out of this picture, even though it clearly won the day in fifteenth-century Ferrara, Mantua, Milan, Rome, sixteenth-century Florence, and eventually in seventeenth-century Naples.[18]

The debate between Guarino and Poggio was, on one level, a scholarly argument between two humanist friends who disagreed on the interpretations of and historical contrast between the two men, Caesar and Scipione. But on a larger scale, this debate was also about the competing political models of Roman Republic and Roman Empire. Guarino's student and patron, Leonello, would obviously not have described himself or his ancestors as tyrants or despots. Nor would he have acknowledged following the example of a tyrant. Rather he modelled himself after the ruler of the ancient world's greatest empire. It was

Caesar as wise ruler, author, and compassionate leader of the Roman Empire that inspired imitation and admiration.

It was this positive appraisal of the Caesars that generally dominated the views of seventeenth-century Neapolitan intellectuals as well. Of the many essays on the Roman Empire produced by the Palatine Academy, four stand out for their substantial reflections on the reasons and consequences of the rise of the Roman Empire, and they will be the focus of the analysis that follows here. They include the longest essay in the volume at eighty-seven folios, "Del' Impero Romano"; an essay on the first Caesar, "Di Caio Giulio Cesare," by the "dottore et fisico" Tomaso Donzelli; an essay on Augustus Caesar by Carmine Nicolo Caracciolo; and an essay entitled "Dell'origine degli Imperii" by Gregorio Caloprese. Together, they provide a solid sampling of the range of views expressed by the larger collection of essays on Rome as well as demonstrating the dominance of the pro-empire faction in the group.

The first of these, "Dell'Impero Romano," is notable both for its reliance on Tacitus as its main ancient source and as one of the few anonymous chapters in the group. The strong republican sympathies of this author are the likely reason for the anonymity, and he clearly represents the minority position. After tracing the rise and virtues of the Roman Republic in the first thirty-five folios of the essay, the author comes to Rome under Julius Caesar with a lament: "Rome ... Queen of the world ... was then forced not only to subject herself to the imperious commands of one of her own citizens, but also by the hand and work of that same man to watch with eyes filled with hot and sorrowful tears, as the Tiber flowed fast and troubled, swollen with streams of her own blood tyrannically shed."[19] The author goes on to say that after reading so much of the history of empire in the course of his work, he found his spirit oppressed by the extraordinary cruelty, killing, and tragedy. In short, he concludes with the harsh judgment that "every new Empire, as Rome then was, is violent and hateful."[20]

In stark contrast to the essays on Julius Caesar and Augustus Caesar that follow, this essay presents the early empire and emperors in a dark light. Augustus is presented largely as a successful manipulator of the public and new nobles. If there was any *Pax Romana* or golden age under him, you will not find it here. Tiberius, too, is presented as a skilful manipulator of the public who made the magistrate do the dirty work while he presented himself as the guardian of the public. The author compares him to Duke Valentino, the Borgia prince, who made his minister Remiro de Orco take the fall for his harsh measures and then had him killed. While Machiavelli had admired the raw power of the son of Pope Alexander VI, the author of this essay obviously does not approve. Machiavellian associations are used only to criticize, as when he describes the emperor Germanicus as using the cloak of the lamb to cover the true skin of a fox and heart of a wolf.[21]

With this strong critique of the early emperors firmly in place, the author nonetheless acknowledges that the history of the Roman Empire provided a "large theatre" in which one found both what was worth imitating and what was to be avoided."[22] Three emperors, in particular, provided good examples: Trajan, Hadrian, and Marcus Aurelius. Of these, and among all emperors, Trajan ranked first, since his reign was good for the republic and increased the stability of the monarchy. It was marked by a singular strength of arms, great justice in the application of the law, rare prudence, and personal valour. For all of these virtues, the senate had him proclaimed Pater Patria.[23] The author also pointed out that he was the first foreign prince – from the "Nazione spagnuola" – to rule Rome, and he concluded as a result that sometimes a foreign prince was a better ruler.[24]

In fact, all of this author's top picks among emperors were of Spanish origins "from Hispania," and the essay as a whole is a clear Spanish reading of Roman imperial history. The anonymous author was possibly Spanish himself, and his interpretation of the Spanish emperors, at least, has much in common with the history of the Roman emperors written by the royal historians Pedro Mexia and Ambrosio Morales in the sixteenth century.[25] Both also depicted Trajan as among the best of the early emperors, and, like the anonymous author from the academy, they both saw Hadrian as continuing the good governance of Trajan.

For twenty-three years Hadrian gave Rome the "greatness, majesty, and peace" that every Republic desires, according to the anonymous author in the Neapolitan volume.[26] Similarly, another Spanish favourite, Marcus Aurelius, was praised as a true philosopher king, and his government was judged to have been the happiest (*felicissimo*) among those of all the emperors, although he is faulted for dividing the empire.[27] This treatment of Marcus Aurelius has strong parallels with the work of Antonio de Guevara, another Spanish royal historian, whose work was also very popular in Italy and certainly familiar to the members of the academy.[28] Although this positive treatment of the "Spanish" emperors could be interpreted as partially redeeming the imperial tyranny imposed by Julius Caesar, there is no mistaking the harsh judgment of the anonymous author on the empire generally and its founder specifically.

This is all the more apparent when it is contrasted with the essay dedicated to Julius Caesar by Tomaso Donzelli.[29] The broad interpretation of the rise of empire and fall of the republic is similar to the earlier essay. First tracing the early political history of Rome, Donzelli agreed with the first author in praising the Roman Republic. In this version the kings grew hateful to people and were replaced by a republic whose councils restored liberty. An aristocracy of the virtuous and good replaced the tyranny of kings. The republic remained in this state for a long time, but eventually the aristocracy came to be dominated by a small oligarchy that followed only its own interests. A dictator then emerged in the context of discord and the revolt of the Gracci, and it was Julius who became the first perpetual dictator and de facto emperor. Thus, the Romans, as much as they hated the kings, nonetheless subjected themselves again to a tyrant and then to others who took the name of emperor.[30]

This perspective, while seemingly sympathetic with the republican Renaissance reading of the fall of Roman liberty, unravels in the section that follows on Julius Caesar. The author first follows Plutarch, Pliny, and Petrarch in praising Caesar's many virtues as an intellectual, poet, and patron of mathematics, philosophy, and astronomy. The Julian calendar and his *Commentaries* are highlighted among his intellectual accomplishments, and in the realm of governing his ability to cultivate friends through generosity and good will was noted as legendary.

All of these attributes are contrasted with the many political problems caused by the civil wars and the discord brought on by the decline of the republic. The author concludes that it was almost the inevitable will of the people of Rome that they be subjected "al dominio di un solo." In short, it was "most necessary" that the Roman Empire came to be subjected to the rule of Caesar.[31] This apology for Caesar represented the political realist's approach to the rise of empire. It was a fairly common Renaissance approach that allowed for a continuing praise of republicanism as the higher form of political life while also acknowledging the practical necessity of empire for the maintenance of order.

A third political tradition shaped the historical interpretation of the next essay, on Caesar Augustus by Carmine Nicolo Caracciolo, the prince of Santo Buono. Unlike the first two authors, Caracciolo began his history by placing the age of Augustus in the context of the world history of empires, including the Babylonians, Assyrians, Egyptians, Medes, Persians, and Greeks. All of these empires were treated with admiration for their accomplishments, and Caracciolo had special praise for Alexander the Great, whose success is seen as limited only by his early death. But the culmination of this ancient imperial march came with the Roman Republic after the conquests made by Caesar. It was only then that Rome remained "the one and only lord of all the world."[32]

Still, for Caracciolo, the imperial meaning of Julius Caesar was ambiguous. On the one hand, he celebrated the fact that it was under Caesar that Rome became queen of the world. But, on the other, when he wrote about the assassination of Caesar, he acknowledged that the murder was not necessarily unjustified, since he had robbed Rome of its liberty. This was a nod to the highest virtue of the republic, liberty, but it was not an acknowledgment of the superiority of the republic over the empire as a form of government. On the contrary: those defenders of the assassination who saw in it a restoration of the republic were also deluded. Their error was that they did not understand that Divine Providence meant for the disorders and tragedies brought on by too much republican liberty to be remedied by the dominion of one. This more happy monarchy was the only remedy for the discord of the *patria*, as Tacitus had noted. Moreover, the political evolution towards empire was the natural development that is mirrored in nature. The merging of smaller principalities and monarchies into empire is like the merging of streams and rivers into the sea. Once in the sea of empire, the smaller political units became placid and calmed.[33]

During the age of Augustus, the Golden Age, the author claims, this divine plan for empire was most fully realized in the ancient world. Augustus united the full power of monarchy in himself under the name of empire, quieting all previous discord. Everything was reduced to a state of placid tranquillity that allowed the world to enjoy the most happy universal peace that it had seen from the beginning of time.[34] Coming from the pen of a Neapolitan nobleman like Caracciolo, whose family had been one of the central supporters and beneficiaries of the Spanish Empire, this essay was a pearl of imperial nostalgia. It also most clearly interprets the reign of a particular emperor using the dominant political theory of empire in the high and late Renaissance, a theory that could be called "the divine right of emperors."

The first essay in the collection illuminated and explicated this theory more clearly. Written by Gregorio Caloprese, it is entitled "Dell'origine degli Imperii," and it is the most theoretical of all the essays. The central purpose of Caloprese was to refute unnamed political writers who "sought to put in doubt Divine Providence." These authors wanted to make man a monster who was not motivated by love, faith, or any innate religious sensibility. The political world of such creatures was inevitably the cruel and evil empire lamented by the anonymous author of the first essay on the Roman Empire. Obviously, this is also the world of Machiavelli.[35]

Caloprese argued that this view of human nature was largely wrong. Great men and great empires emerged out of the innate virtues of man. Great emperors were humane, liberal, beneficent, and generous. Men like Cyrus of the Persians, Alexander the Great, Scipione and Marcello, Caesar, Charlemagne, the Great Captain, Gonsalo de Cordova, and Charles V knew how to love and make others love them. Similarly they were faithful and had many good friends who were loyal to them because they had cultivated this loyalty with skill and diligence. The emperors' political judgments and actions are made freely and candidly, since they had the wisdom to know the difference between honest caution and unjust suspicion. These virtues, in particular, could have come straight out of Guevara's treatment of Marcus Aurelius, where they were also given pride of place.[36]

What then of that negative critique of the Roman Empire and emperors that virtually all of the authors of the Neapolitan Academy seemed to agree upon, namely that they deprived republican Rome and her citizens of their liberty? In the view of Caloprese, this was the necessary result of the weaknesses of men, for although it is the natural inclination of humans to love and be loved and live in community, they also have a propensity to avarice, ambition, and to pleasure of the senses. They are thus inclined to harm themselves and others and to be continuously at war. It is this constant discord and the accompanying fear for their well-being that leads humans to impose an authority upon themselves. More specifically, "they are constrained to create a person above them, with authority to make laws and to impose penalties and prizes with the goal of obligating everyone to act within the boundaries of honesty and justice. It is this which constitutes the nature of empires."[37] Empire, in this view, is the divine remedy to human weakness.

Read in the context of the imminent end of the Spanish Habsburg Empire, of which the kingdom of Naples was an ancient and important part, the imperial lessons provided by Caloprese and Caracciolo, in particular, clearly laid out the argument for a continuation of imperial rule in some shape or form. Empire was the natural and highest evolution of political life that led to peace and stability. Empire imposed honesty and justice on society. Empire was divine.

This was clearly not the view of the anonymous author of the long essay on the Roman Empire who saw it as cruel and bloodthirsty. In his view, empire deprived the republic of her liberty and made her weep. Perhaps this writer was a fan of Masaniello, hoping for a republican revival after the death of Charles II. This would explain his anonymity. Or perhaps, given the fact that this author viewed the later Roman emperors from Spain as admirable leaders under whom Rome thrived, the lesson of his reflection was aimed at an audience surely aware that the main contenders for the Spanish succession were the king of France and Holy Roman emperor. Reading between the lines, the French choice was one for a new empire while the continuation of Habsburg rule was a continuation of the line of good Spanish emperors.

Eventually, of course, the kingdom of Naples in the eighteenth century would experience new monarchs and imperial masters. The sponsor of the academy, the duke of Medinaceli, managed to last for only a short while after the beginning of the War of Succession. He was recalled to Madrid by Philip V, the grandson of Louis XIV, in 1701. What he thought about the reflections of the men who made up his academy is not known. But it is not hard to imagine that witnessing the bloodshed of the War of the Spanish Succession and the rise of the new French Empire in the following decade he may have been tempted to agree with the views of the anonymous author of the essay on the Roman Empire: "Every new Empire, as Rome then was, is violent and hateful."

For the members of the academy who remained in Naples, however, their reflections on empire almost certainly helped them to adjust and react to the new succession of rulers who came to town in the following decades. Much more than an aloof academic seminar on ancient history, the academy constituted a late Renaissance political think tank whose conversations served a contemporary purpose. As a mature and thick chapter in the long development of imperial humanism, the deliberations and publications of the academy underlined that the comparative study of empires, and especially the interwoven histories of Mediterranean empires, were essential to the art of ruling and living in the new age of empire.

This was one of the most fundamental, influential, and persistent strains of intellectual life and production in the early modern period. As the work of the academy revealed, it was also one of the most sophisticated branches of Renaissance learning, with a chronological and thematic breadth that already embodied in its own way what the introduction to this work called the "plural history of the intersection among empires" (2). While this chapter has focused primarily on the essays of the academy that analysed the Roman Empire, many others covered the long genealogy of Mediterranean empires from Alexander the Great to the Ottomans. Like the studies of contemporary scholars gathered in this volume that seek to understand the relationships between empires, the Neapolitan scholars were thus also deeply engaged with the project of "interimperiality," albeit without the name.

NOTES

1 See G. Galasso, *Storia D'Italia: Il Regno Di Napoli, Il Mezzogiorno Spagnolo e Austriaco*, Storia D'Italia, 15:756–93. For the intellectual context of the academy, see Biagio di Giovanni, "La Vita Intelletuale a Naploi fra la metà del '600 e la restaurazione del Regno," in *Storia di Napoli*, ed. Giuseppe Galasso (Cava dei Tirreni: Arti Grafiche Emilio Di Mauro, 1970), 6, no. 1, 401–534 (published by Societá Editrice Storia di Napoli, distributed by Edizioni Scientifiche Italiane). In contrast to the earlier academy of the *investiganti* that operated somewhat in the shadows, the academy of Medinacoeli was inaugurated "with great solemnity" in the duke's presence on 20 March 1698.

2 Biblioteca Nacional Madrid (BNM), mss 9110, 9221, 9222. Entitled *Raccolta di varie lezioni academiche sopra diverse materie recitate nell'accademia dell' Ecc.mo Signore Duca di Medinaceli et Vicere et Capitan Generale nel Regno di Napoli*. The volumes are 587 ff; 410 ff. and 360 ff. respectively. An additional manuscript that completes the series is in the Biblioteca Nazionale di Napoli, mss. XIII B, under the title of *Lezioni accademiche de' diversi valentuomini de' nostril tempi recitate avanti l'ecc.mo sig. Duca di Medinacoelli*. All of these manuscripts have recently been edited and published by Michele Rak, *Lezioni dell'Accademia di Palazzo del duca di Medinaceli* (Naples: Istituto Italiano per gli Studi Filosofici, 2000–5), vols. 1–5. For this chapter, I consulted the original manuscripts in Madrid. The citations are from the first two volumes, which are devoted entirely to the theme of empire. Volume 5 of the recent edition includes lengthy "historical notes" by M. Rak, whose essays are particularly valuable for the elaboration they provide on the Neapolitan intellectual context. They do not, however, spend much time on the essays on empire or analyse this theme as part of the longer Renaissance tradition of imperial histories and especially those from Spain.

3 Joseph M. Levine, "Giambattista Vico and the Quarrel between the Ancients and the Moderns," *Journal of the History of Ideas* 52, no. 1 (1991): 55–79. On the Palatine Academy, see especially 61–3.

4 Fausto Nicolini, *La Goivinezza di Giambattista Vico* (Bari: Laterza, 1932), 185–6.

5 Quoted in Levine, "Giambattista Vico," 64.

6 Andrew Pettegree, *The Book in the Renaissance* (New Haven, CT: Yale University Press, 2011), 187. This author credits Petrarch with nothing less than the revival of history, thanks to his *Lives of Famous Men*, a compilation in which the life of Caesar alone was by far the most expansive.

7 Anthony Grafton, "Historia and Istoria: Alberit's Terminology in Context," in *I Tatti Studies*, 1999, 49. Grafton provides one of the most succinct descriptions of the political purpose of humanist history writing when he quotes the humanist Lapo da Castiglionchio from a letter to Flavio Biondo. He emphasized that history was a rich source of wisdom for "the method of ruling the state, the reasons for undertaking wars, how they should be waged, and how far they should be prosecuted."

8 I have made a more detailed case for the importance of the imperial Renaissance in my essay "The Imperial Renaissance," in *The Renaissance World*, ed. John Jeffries Martin, 307–25 (Oxford: Routledge / Taylor and Francis, 2007), and most especially in my book *The Renaissance of Empire in Early Modern Europe* (New York: Cambridge University Press, 2014).

9 The third and shortest of the three volumes, ms. 9222, is not primarily about the Roman Empire, but rather related to themes central to governing the present empire including essays on the art of war, on hydrology, on the nautical sciences, on rivers, on mathematics, and many other topics in the natural sciences.

10 Maria Grazia Pernis, "Fifteenth-Century Patrons and the Scipio-Caesar Controversy," *Tex* 6 (1994): 185.
11 See especially Remegio Sabbadini, *La Scuola di Guarino Guarini Veronese* (Catania: Francesco Galati, 1896), 146.
12 Ibid.
13 Pernis, 182.
14 *Epistolario di Guarino Veronese*, ed. Remegio Sabbadini (Venice: C. Ferrari, 1919), 221–54, vol. 2, lett. 670, 221–54. This is among Guarino's longest letters, which underlines the importance of the topic for him. This was part of a debate that stretched out over five years and also included lengthy letters against Poggio defending Caesar from Ciriaco d'Ancona and Pietro Del Monte. For the details, see Sabbadini, 3:325. It is also worth noting Sabbadini's opinion that both Leonello and Guarino saw in Caesar "everything beautiful, everything good, everything great." 3:323. "tutto bello, tutto buono, tutto grande."
15 Sabbadini, *La scuola*, 146.
16 Coluccio Salutati, "De Tyranno," trans. and ed., Francesco Ercole (Bologna: Nicola Zanichelli, 1942), 174. "Per cui concludo con questo capitolo che Cesare non fu un tiranno, avendo a buon diritto e non illegalmente tenuto ed esercitato il governo." Before responding to Poggio, Guarino had also written a letter to Leonello in which he cited both contemporary and ancient authors who had judged Caesar favourably. These included the humanist friend of Petrarch, Coluccio Salutati, chancellor of Florence from 1375 to 1406, who had largely absolved Caesar from the charges of tyranny in much the same way Petrarch had. In his *Treatise on Tyranny* (1400) Salutati cited Seneca's account of all of the honours and titles heaped upon Caesar by the Senate and people after his assassination and concluded that "Caesar was not a tyrant, having a good right to govern and not one that was illegally held."
17 For the most famous treatment of the debate over Caesar, see Hans Baron, *The Crisis of the Early Italian Renaissance* (Princeton: Princeton University Press, 1966), 123–8.
18 That Renaissance humanism included alternatives to Baron's civic humanism has long been recognized. Paul Oskar Kristellar, for example, noted that "the civic humanism of Florence was opposed by the despotic humanism of Milan, Ferrara, and other centers." While accurate insofar as it describes humanist production under the patronage of princes depicted by critics as despots, despotic humanism falls short of describing the expansive political program of imperial revival that was the larger agenda of imperial humanism. Paul Oskar Kristellar, "Studies in Renaissance Humanism in the Last Twenty Years," in *Studies in the Renaissance* 9 (1962: 7–30. Quotation, 14.
19 BNM mss. 9110, ff. 287–373: "Dell'Imperio Romano." The author is only given as N.N. The text reads in part, "Roma, donna, e Reina del Mondo ... costretta

non solamente a soggiacere agl'imperiosi comandamenti d'un suo Cittadino, ma ancora per mano et per opera di quello, a mirare con occhi colmi di calde e dolorose lagrime correr torbido et precipitoso il Tevere, da fiumi di proprio sangue tirannicamente accresciuto." Fol. 323r.

20 Ibid., fol. 326v, "E perche ogni Imperio nuovo quale era il Romano, e violento et odioso percio i Principi nuovi et non ben fermi in uno stato hanno necessita di molti figli."

21 Ibid., fol. 328v. Commenting on Germanicus, the author evokes Machiavellian imagery when he writes that "lascio la finta veste di Agnello con iscoprire la propria di volpe che serrava cuore di Lupo."

22 Ibid., fol. 342r–43r: Claiming the intellectual pedigree of early Renaissance humanists in their views towards the discipline of history, the author cites the views of the fathers of Latin eloquence who called history "maestra della humana vita, vita della memoria, testimonio de Tempi, luce della verita, e quasi viva rappresentatione della reverendissima antichita." More specifically, he cites the history of the Roman Empire as revealing both that which was worth imitating and that which was best avoided. "si vede quasi in ampio teatro ... cio che ... fu degno d'una lodevole imitatione, et cio che merita rimpovero et abborrimento e da doversi giusta et honestamente evitare."

23 Ibid., fol. 344r, "Fu dunque il governo di Traiano di tanta utilita alla Repubblica e di tanto stabilimento alla Monarchia." His reign was marked by a "fortezza nell'armi, soave puritan e costume, soma giustizia nel giudicare, virtu tutte con rara prudenza, e valore praticate a tal segno che dal senato dopo molte deliberazione in suo honore fatte, fu detto Padre della Padria."

24 Ibid., fol. 343v, "Traiano, di cui piu ottimo principe tra Romani Imperadori non fu riconosciuto." "Egli benche di Nazione spagnuola."

25 Pedro Mexia, *Historia imperial y Cesarea* (Seville, 1545) This particular text was almost certainly used by all of the authors since it was one of the most popular histories of the Roman emperors published in the sixteenth and seventeenth centuries. The Italian translation, alone, went to press seventeen times between 1558 and 1688. Trajan was also described by Mexia as being among the best of the emperors and his portrait has much in common with that of the anonymous author.

26 BNM mss. 9110, fol. 348r. Continuing the good governance of Trajan, under Hadrian the "Imperio di Roma stabilito in una tal grandezza, e maestada" and for twenty-three years there was general peace that every republic desires.

27 Ibid., fol. 349r. "Fu in vero felicissimo il governo di questo Imperadore."

28 *The Golden Book of Marcus Aurelius and the Mirror of Princes*, by Antonio de Guevara, was one of the most popular guides for princes of the early modern era. Originally dedicated to Charles V, for whom Guevara was a councillor, the book

had the specific purpose of providing advice for ordering the young emperor's states and life using the supposed letters of Marcus Aurelius. First published in Seville in 1527, various editions of the book were translated and published repeatedly during the sixteenth and seventeenth centuries. More specifically, there were fifty Spanish editions between 1527 and 1698 and thirty-three Italian editions between 1542 and 1663. From Antonio Palau y Dulcet, *Manual del Librero Hispanoamericano* (Barcelona: Libreria Palau, 1953), 6:441–55.

29 BNM mss. 9110, "Di Caio Giulio Cesare," fols. 374r–415v.
30 Ibid., fol. 374rv: "onde i Romani, quantunque il nome di Re abborrissero: nondimeno sotto nome di Dittatore vennero ad esser nuovamenti soggetti ad un tiranno e ad altri successivamente, ch'ebbero poscia nome d' Imperadori, de quali la piu parte il dominio adoperando per l'utile lor private e secondo che meglio in talento veniva loro imponendo pene e premi a gli altri che no i meritav: e da parte la giustizia delle legge lasciando ingiustamente la vita, e l'avere de soggetti cittadin spesse volte malmenarono."
31 Ibid., fol. 397r: "Cosi bisogno che infatti l'Imperio di Roma necessitosamente sotto l dominio di Cesare venisse a soggiacere."
32 Ibid., fol. 418r, "si rese l'unica e sola signora del Mondo tutto nel tempo di Giulio Cesare."
33 Ibid., fol. 417r, "altro segno non da che d'una maestosa placidezza."
34 Ibid., fol. 418v. "venne Augusto ad unir in se nuovamente e perpetuamente la Monarchia tutta sotto il nome d'Imperio dopo di che con tale unione tutte la discordie acquetando ed il tutto riducendo nello stato piu perfetto d'una placida quiete fe al mondo godeve quella universale felicissima pace, che mai in esso sin dal suo primo principio a quell tempo era si veduta."
35 Ibid., 5:65-67, 74–6. Rak interprets many of the essays on empire as being used primarily as locations to comment on the civic politics of Naples, and he treats the Machiavellian theme principally in this context.
36 Ibid., Gregorio Caloprese, "Dell' origine degli Imperii," fols. 1–48v. fol. 30rv: The virtues of great men are described: "che siano humani, generosi, liberali, fedeli, affabili, e benefici, che sappiano amare e farsi amare che habbiano molti e buoni amici all intorno che doppo haver usata tutta la diligenza ch'e' necessaria in iscioglieri, stiano sicuri della lor fede, che sappiano risolvere et operare con liberta e franchezza che intendano la differenza che e' tra una honesta cautela et ingiusto sospetto."
37 Ibid., fol. 48r, "sono stati costretti a constituire persona sopra di loro, con autorita di far leggi, e d impor pene e premi al fine di obbligare tutti a trattenersi tra limiti della giustizi e dell'onesta: ch'e' quello che constituisce la natura degl'Imperi."

PART TWO

**IMAGINING THE MEDITERRANEAN
IN EARLY MODERN ENGLAND**

chapter eight

The Meta-Theatrical Mediterranean: Theatrical Contrivance and Miraculous Reunion in *The Travels of the Three English Brothers*, *The Four Prentices of London*, and *Pericles*

JANE HWANG DEGENHARDT

This chapter discusses three plays performed on the English public stage around the turn of the seventeenth century that represent the dispersal and ultimate reunion of family members in the region of the eastern Mediterranean. To varying degrees each of these plays figures the culminating familial reunion as a miracle brought about through divine providence. Whereas the whims of fortune drive the characters along separate and unpredictable courses, the hand of providence reunites the far-flung travellers at the plays' conclusions. This sense of providential intervention is underscored by the explicit religious themes and conflicts running through these plays, which are directly informed by the richly layered religious associations of their Mediterranean settings. At the same time, these reunions are facilitated through a range of theatrical contrivances that call attention to the gaps between the plays' divinely infused settings and the artifice of the stage, including the use of dumbshow, choric narration, grossly improbable coincidences, magical props and stage mechanics, and the convention of the deus ex machina. What happens when the dramatic representation of miracle converges with theatrical devices that generate a meta-theatrical effect? While one might easily assume that meta-theatrical effects detract from the sincere representation of miracles by drawing attention to their staging and their artificiality, in the plays that I discuss the convergence of meta-theatricality and miracle is mutually enhancing.

The wondrous effect of miraculous reunion in these plays may be attributed to their particular Mediterranean settings (Jerusalem, Ephesus), yet these plays also produce wonder by transforming the Mediterranean into a self-consciously theatrical space. In doing so, they show us how the geographical setting of the Mediterranean is integrated into a larger theatrical semiotics that cultivated new forms of audience engagement, imagination, and pleasure, and that enabled the public theatre to simulate the authority of divine providence. By drawing attention to the disjuncture between a place such as Jerusalem and its theatrical representation, these plays engaged their audience's active imaginations and fostered a particular kind of faith – which I shall call *theatrical faith* – in the stage's own interventions.

Like the other chapters in this section, this chapter explores the English stage's projection of the Mediterranean as an imagined, conceptual space, though it also focuses on how this imagined, conceptual space is specifically mediated – and transformed – by the theatre's own conventions and physical mechanics. The popularity of Mediterranean settings on the London stage reflects the increased importance this region assumed for the English in the late sixteenth and early seventeenth centuries as the result of trade interests. With England's growing participation in Mediterranean commerce, English citizens became more acutely aware of the imperial and religious threats posed by the Ottoman Empire, as well as of the dangers of piracy and captivity – all of which provided rich fodder for the stage. Many plays also tapped into the layered classical and medieval histories of particular Mediterranean sites and the intense inter-religious and inter-imperial struggles associated with these histories. However, the task of depicting these foreign and faraway places – whether in the context of the past, the present, or some combination of both – prompted playwrights to indulge their imaginations and to experiment with different theatrical modes of representation. The plays that I discuss address the challenge of representing geographic distance and travel by employing meta-theatrical devices (such as choric narration) that draw attention to the stage's artifice. They also attribute the improbable reunions of families dispersed in the Mediterranean to *both* the miraculous potential associated with Ephesus and Jerusalem – often expressed through a discourse of fortune or providence – and the self-conscious interventions of the stage itself. The challenge of depicting Mediterranean settings on stage, I argue, prompted playwrights to experiment with new forms of representation, and to fuse in complex ways the forces of divine providence and theatrical intervention. In turn, the meta-theatrical staging of providential reunion offered an empowering way of confronting some of the religious and political challenges associated with early English incursions in the Mediterranean.

The Travels of the Three English Brothers: Theatrical Intervention and the Geography of the Stage

The epilogue to Day, Wilkins, and Rowley's *The Travels of the Three English Brothers* (perf. 1607) stages a spectacle that both simulates and defies geographical distance through a highly self-conscious use of theatrical space. Noting that the play's three protagonists (based on real-life English adventurers Thomas, Anthony, and Robert Sherley) are physically dispersed across vast stretches of geography, both within the play's fictionalized plot and in actual life, the Chorus requests the audience's indulgence to unite the brothers through the art of the stage. Dividing the stage into three parts (one representing England, one Spain, and one Persia), the Chorus sets up for a brief dumbshow, described in the following stage directions: "*Enter three several ways the three brothers: Robert with the state of Persia as before; Sir Anthony with the King of Spain and others, where he received the Order of Saint Iago, and other offices; Sir Thomas in England, with his father and others. Fame gives to each a prospective glass: they seem to see one another and offer to embrace, at which Fame parts them, and so exeunt all except Fame.*"[1]

Purporting to offer each Sherley access to a framed spectacle of his far-flung brothers, the prospective glasses represent the stage's ability to elide spatial distance through a negotiation of its own material and semiotic conventions. As Henry Turner has argued, these evolving stage conventions were partly informed by emerging scientific spatial arts, including early modern technology, applied mathematics, and pre-scientific thought.[2] As Turner points out, the theatre itself was a form of mechanical science (like carpentry and engineering), and its conventions for representing place ("topographesis") drew upon geometric concepts to transport viewers across vast distances.[3] The scene's spatial manipulations demonstrate Turner's claim that the early modern theatre was "a highly spatialized mode of representation" and one quite focused on cultivating the art of spatial representation.[4] The division of the stage into three distinct parts and the entrance of the brothers from three different directions imply their geographical separation, while the prospective glasses through which the brothers view one another propose a use of technology that foreshortens distance. Yet if the division of the stage, the separate entrances, and the handheld props are meant to suggest the vast distance across which the brothers see one another, the actors ultimately come to stand in relatively close physical proximity, confined as they are by the dimensions of the platform stage. Thus, in seeking to represent both distance and the foreshortening of distance, the scene highlights a common condition of early modern theatre, in that its representational conventions must work against the physical properties of the stage.

As Cyrus Mulready has demonstrated, the representational capacity of the stage was stretched in particular by attempts to represent geographical expanses – a challenge that increased as audiences demanded plays featuring multiple geographies and long-distance travel.[5] Focusing specifically on stage romance, Mulready draws attention to how theatrical attempts to represent travel offended neoclassicists like Philip Sidney because they violated classical representational boundaries. Nevertheless, Mulready argues, "Sidney's call for dramatic unity ... ultimately proved hopeless against the mounting demand for plays that gave audiences representations of an expanded world."[6] As I go on to discuss, representations of travel across distant geographies may have been popular with English audiences not just because of early modern interests in overseas expansion, but also because of the opportunities they provided for cultivating new kinds of meta-theatrical effects, dramaturgical practices, and audience engagement. Rather than attempt to represent geographical distance mimetically, the final scene of *The Three English Brothers* calls attention to the theatrical contrivances that make such representation (im)possible. In doing so, it comments meta-theatrically on the limitations of the stage as well as its potential to operate outside the bounds of classical mimetic conventions. Because the audience views not what is seen through the prospective glasses (i.e., the characters' perspectives), but rather the spectacle of the characters viewing one another, the physical unity of their bodies is emphasized. At the same time, that unity is understood to be mediated through a technology that intensely heightens or transcends the abilities of natural vision.

The "prospective glasses" might have referred to telescopes or another kind of scientific device, but they would have also suggested magical devices, which were employed by magicians and conjurors in other plays such as Robert Greene's *Friar Bacon and Friar Bungay* (ca 1590). The two meanings of "prospective glass" operative in the late sixteenth and early seventeenth centuries – "a magic glass, mirror, or crystal in which it is supposed that distant or future events can be seen" and "a telescope or pair of binoculars" – reflect how the ability to see across distance was ambiguously attributed to both supernatural and scientific explanations, as well as reflecting the overlapping cultural spheres of magic and science (or the occult and natural philosophy).[7] Barbara Fuchs's discussion of the use of a crystal ball in which an Indian sorcerer can see the whole world in Alonso de Ercilla's *La Araucana* demonstrates how such technology brings together advances in optics, expanded geographies, and problems of representation.[8] As Stuart Clark has argued, advances in optical technology created uncertainties about whether such technology afforded greater access to natural truths or was duplicitous and therefore potentially dangerous and immoral.[9] The use of the prospective glasses in *The Travels of the Three English Brothers* evokes a similar ambiguity by at once proposing a technology that enhances the abilities of human vision and facilitating an impossible and highly theatrical reunion.

The form of reunion afforded by the prospective glasses, as well as the spectacle of the actors viewing one another through these devices, allude meta-theatrically to the magic and technology of the early modern stage itself. As the scene insists, the physical union of the brothers is not possible in real life and is made uniquely possible in the space of the theatre. Indeed, if the scene begins with Robert in Persia, Anthony in Spain, and Thomas in England, it concludes with their ceasing to be in these places; instead, they are relocated to a kind of no-place that can be read only as the space of the stage – the *same* stage. Thus, the technology that places them within one another's sights, and collectively within the audience's sights, locates them within an overtly theatrical – indeed, meta-theatrical – space. Relying less on the audience's suspension of disbelief than on its willingness to authorize the creative agency of the stage, the spectacle directly links the thrill and wonder of an impossible reunion to a theatrical contrivance.

In addition to offering a spectacle of wonder, the concluding spectacle also brings a kind of generic closure to the play by providing comic resolution in the form of familial reunion. In doing so, it imposes a kind of coherence onto an episodic plot of potentially arbitrary travel and dispersal. Fame, as the Chorus, proposes this intervention specifically in answer to the brothers' discontent at being separated around the globe:

> Unhappy [are] they (and hapless in our scenes)
> That in the period of so many years
> Their destinies' mutable commandress
> Hath never suffered their regreting eyes
> To kiss each other at an interview. (Epilogue, lines 3–7)

Thus, the Chorus sets the brothers' meta-theatrically facilitated reunion against the force of fortune – described as "their destinies' mutable commandress" – that divides them in real life and throughout the scenes of the play. Fortune – or the force of chance, hap, or luck – was frequently associated with overseas travel and commerce in early modern England. As the plays I discuss here demonstrate, the term *fortune* constitutes a pervasive keyword in scenes representing the unpredictability of travel and commerce. The common risks of sea travel (shipwreck, piracy, captivity, mutiny, sickness, hunger, death), as well as the financial gains and losses associated with maritime trade, suggested that such events might be controlled by forces of chance that operated independent from, or even in competition with, divine providence. *The Travels of the Three English Brothers* attributes not only the separation of the three brothers to fortune but also such misfortunes as the mutiny aboard Thomas's ship and his capture by Turks near Kea. In also emphasizing fortune's role in depleting the Sherleys' economic fortunes and reputations, the play illustrates how an emerging economic understanding of fortune (earned, as opposed to inherited wealth) became intertwined with the concept of cosmic chance in a culture undergoing transformation by maritime trade and exploration.[10] Because fortune resisted meaning or moral good, it threatened a kind of nihilistic chaos. However, if *The Travels of the Three English Brothers* dramatizes fortune's power to do bad in the world, it also sets out to harness and redirect the forces of fortune through its theatrical interventions.

By facilitating an unlikely reunion among the geographically dispersed Sherley brothers, the theatre operates something like the hand of providence in staging an intervention into fortune's course. In short, in order to give travel a comic resolution, the stage facilitated a reunion that aligned theatrical agency with the work of providence. As Alexandra Walsham describes it, early modern English providentialism amounted to a way of seeing the world. It constituted "a set of ideological spectacles through which individuals from all positions on the confessional spectrum were apt to view their universe, an invisible prism which helped them to focus the refractory meanings of both petty and perplexing events."[11] In providing a way of seeing that might override the work of fortune, the stage too offered such a prism. And if the stage enacted interventions and "miracles" that took liberties with the "truth" and depended upon theatrical contrivances or the work of the imagination, the theatrical effects of these interventions were no less wondrous because of their artifice. In fact, I would argue that these meta-theatrical moments had a kind of religious effect that was conveyed not just through their simulation of divine intervention and the affective responses they drew from their audiences, but through their very artifice.[12]

The Power of Seeing and Knowing

I begin with the example of an explicitly meta-theatrical reunion to offer context for the broader consideration of the trope of familial reunion that occurs in two other plays that dramatize extensive travel: Thomas Heywood's *The Four Prentices of London, with the Conquest of Jerusalem* (perf. c. 1594) and Shakespeare's *Pericles* (perf. 1608). In these two plays, family members are separated and then serendipitously reunited in cities located in the vicinity of the eastern Mediterranean. While the culminating reunions of these plays are not overtly meta-theatrical in the way of *The Three Brothers*, they suggest a degree of improbability and divine intervention that implicitly evokes theatrical contrivance. In the cases of *The Four Prentices* and *Pericles*, the specific settings for these reunions – Jerusalem and Ephesus, respectively – powerfully inform the magic of improbable reunion, which is cast in a rhetoric of providential triumph over fortune's whims. Jerusalem is located east of the far eastern point of the Mediterranean Sea, about thirty-five miles inland. Ephesus is situated more specifically on the Aegean Sea, an embayment of the Mediterranean Sea between the mainlands of Greece and Turkey, though of course Europeans would have accessed it by crossing through the Mediterranean. As English audiences would have known, these places had multivalent religious significance as temporally layered sites of conquest and conversion involving pagan, Jewish, Muslim, and Christian cultures. Drawing upon the histories of Christian crusade in Jerusalem and St Paul's missions in Ephesus, *The Four Prentices* and *Pericles*, respectively, encourage audiences to interpret the concluding reunions as attributable, at least partly, to a triumph of Christian faith. Accordingly, these plays present reunion in a miraculous light – an outcome that underscores a sense of Christian divinity that inheres in these Mediterranean sites.

Without lessening the affective impact of miracle, these plays also attribute the source of miraculous reunion as much to theatrical contrivance and performance as to divinity. Critics such as Nova Myhill, Anthony Dawson, and Susannah Monta have discussed similar kinds of performance effects on the early modern stage.[13] In varying ways, they identify a tension between an audience's engrossment in performance and its awareness of theatrical artifice. Myhill emphasizes the audience's discernment in interpreting a performance as either "authentic" or "counterfeit";[14] Dawson describes audience engagement as a tension characterized by the "doubleness of knowing and seeing, of metatheater and theatre, suspension and belief;"[15] and Monta draws a parallel between audience engagement and religious faith, with its inevitable intermixture of "doubt" and "belief."[16] By contrast, rather than interpret "knowing" and "seeing," or "doubt and belief," as oppositional effects, I seek to identify the wondrous potential of meta-theatrical awareness. I argue for a power in the magic of the theatre that is at the same time distinct from complete or naive engrossment – wherein theatrical artifice is neither consonant with idolatry nor a force of disenchantment, but rather has the potential to be wondrous in its own way.

I bring theatricality to the fore in order to consider not just what the stage can teach us about early modern conceptions of the Mediterranean, but to consider what happens to the Mediterranean world when it is transposed onto the stage, transformed, as it were, through the lens of the prospective glass. In other words, how does the theatre not only elide the distance between London and the distant geography of the eastern Mediterranean, but also transform this particular geographical place into a theatrical space of wonder? Critics such as John Gillies and D.K. Smith have importantly examined how early modern playwrights integrated cultural knowledge from other fields such as cartography in order to represent Mediterranean geographies, and others have productively shown how a range of non-dramatic archives may be brought to bear on dramatic representations of these geographies.[17] By contrast, I consider how the plays themselves create their own cultural knowledge by transforming these places into theatrical spaces. More specifically, I focus on how Heywood and Shakespeare self-consciously brought the Mediterranean to London audiences with an understanding of the stage as a unique vehicle for making knowledge public. One of the chief ways that the stage accomplished this was by engaging the public audience itself in a shared experience of wonder garnered through theatrical devices.

The Four Prentices of London: Seeing Differently in Jerusalem

The Prologue to Heywood's *Four Prentices of London* (probably first performed sometime between 1592 and 1594)[18] specifically calls attention to the public role of the stage and to this specific play's interest in bringing an unfamiliar history to a broad theatrical audience. The Prologue opens with three actors entering the stage to defend the play's performance. Asked by Player #1 to justify the play's authority as a "History" for those who "will believe nothing that is not in the Chronicle," Player #2 explains, "Our authority is a Manuscript, a book writ in parchment; which not being publique, nor generall in the world, wee rather thought fit to exemplifie unto the publique censure, things concealed and obscur'd, such as are not common with every one."[19] Thus, the play is framed as a rare and unfamiliar history that is being performed with the explicit purpose of bringing this history to public attention. In setting such an agenda, the Prologue imbues the stage with a distinct role that involves not just entertaining but also educating the public, and, in particular, exposing what is "not common with every one" so that it may become "communal."

At the same time, the claim that this particular story is entirely unknown to English audiences is partly disingenuous. The historical content of the play involves the figure of Godfrey of Bouillon, the leader of the First Crusade and the first Latin ruler of Palestine after the capture of Jerusalem in 1099. As Annaliese F. Connolly has discussed, this legendary figure was likely well known to English audiences.[20] Heywood's play remakes the Godfrey story by imagining Godfrey and his brothers as London apprentices and interweaving their conquest of Jerusalem with the story of their family's fall and rise, its dispersal and unlikely reunion in Jerusalem. In a sense Heywood's play does not so much bring something new to English audiences as it reinterprets a familiar history in a new way. It may follow that part of the pleasure of seeing a play such as *The Four Prentices* lay in experiencing its familiarity, as well as in seeing what new twist this production might add to the story. In addition to its thematic adaptation, Heywood's play remakes a familiar story through its extensive and innovative use of theatrical devices. In particular, through its self-conscious manipulation of audience engagement, the play enables spectators to experience Jerusalem as a highly theatricalized space.

One of the likely draws of *The Four Prentices* for English audiences was the setting of Jerusalem, explicitly advertised in the play's title (*The Four Prentices of London, with the Conquest of Jerusalem*) as well as its Prologue. Player #2 in the Prologue touts, "Had not yee rather, for novelties sake, see Jerusalem yee never saw, then London that yee see howerly?" (lines 31–3). The novelty of seeing Jerusalem was of course a rare opportunity for London theatregoers, the vast majority of whom would never see the real Jerusalem. In effectively eliding the distance between London and Jerusalem, the play transported audiences across the globe without their ever having to leave home. Such transportation constituted a unique property of the stage, whose sensory and physical orientations offered an experience acutely different from that of reading. But the Jerusalem to which audiences were transported was not experienced as a kind of ethnographic immersion or realism, as is characteristic of the experience of watching a film.[21] The stage was relatively bare; the only set piece consisted of "walls" around the city, which served as a backdrop for much of the action as well as a structure mounted by the actors. Such walls were common stage props used in many plays with settings located in any number of geographical places. But even aside from such material conventions (often conceived of as limitations), the early modern stage was simply not oriented to providing audiences with a realistic sensory experience of Jerusalem, replete with local texture. Rather, it conjured the attributes of Jerusalem through its representation of the kinds of things that happen there, and, by extension, through the particular logic of cosmic or divine authority that appeared to govern these events.

In that the Jerusalem of *The Four Prentices* is a place of rare and improbable good fortune, we might compare the theatre's transportation of audiences there to a view through a prospective glass in which impossible things are seen to be possible. More specifically, the Jerusalem shown through the prospective of *The Four Prentices* is a place of unlikely reunion, reversal of fortune, and homecoming. If the play transports audiences away from London, it also offers a home away from home for its London protagonists – four brothers, their sister, and their father. Its representation of Jerusalem as a site of serendipitous reunion is explicitly set against the preceding geographical dispersal of the family members across Europe and the series of chance encounters and misrecognitions that ensue.

As in *The Travels of the Three English Brothers*, the circumstances that take this family to sea and result in their separation from one another are explicitly cast in a language of fortune. The patriarch of the family opens the play by explaining the family's fall from nobility as a function of fortune:

> Daughter, thou seest how Fortune turns her wheel
> We that but late were mounted up aloft
> Lulled in the skirt of that inconstant Dame
> Are now thrown head-long by her ruthless hand
> To kiss that earth whereon our feet should stand. (lines 1–5)

Described metaphorically through the turn of fortune's wheel, the old earl has lost his land to the French king after aiding William the Conqueror in the Norman Conquest of England. As a result his four sons are reduced to living in London as citizens and tradesmen, apprenticed to a mercer, a haberdasher, a grocer, and a goldsmith. In a sense, these trades offer a way of dodging the force of fortune; as Guy puts it, whereas one who is "borne a Prince" risks being "cast downe / By some sinister chance, or fortunes frowne" having a trade offers "a meanes to purchase wealth … that still stayes with mee in the extream'st of all," even through the loss of "[e]state" and "honors" (lines 84–9). The play thus sets the economics of the London guilds against that of an inheritance system based on land that is destabilized by the Norman imperial conquest. The brothers ultimately regain their nobility by virtue of another imperial conquest – that of Jerusalem – but they must first abandon their trades and re-enter the insecure world of fortune to have the chance of rising up again. When a captain comes to London with a proclamation recruiting soldiers for the Holy Wars in Jerusalem, the brothers jump at the chance to improve their circumstances by joining the Christian forces (entering the service of Robert Duke of Normandy, son of William the Conqueror). They take their leave of London and its trades, followed by their sister and preceded by their father, who has also set off for the Holy Land on a pilgrimage. Their subsequent journey is characterized by accidents and lost ways, conflicts and misrecognitions, thus setting up Jerusalem as a destination that will eventually impose order onto this chaos of fortune.

   A crucial way in which the play imparts this story of fortune turned provident – both narratively and visually – is through its representation of travel, an action represented by the stage in imperfect and unique ways. Described by the Presenter, the fateful sea journey that leads to the brothers' separation emphasizes the power of fortune in guiding travel and associates it with the dispersal of family members. And, as with Anthony and Robert Sherley's journey to Persia, the play calls upon the audience's active participation to imagine their journey and the shipwreck that throws the brothers fatefully off course:

> Thus have you seen these brothers shipped to sea
> Bound on their voyage to the Holy Land
> All bent to try their fortunes in one Bark. (lines 249–51)
>
> ...
>
> Their instant fortunes I will soon express
> And from the truth in no one point digress. (lines 259–60)
>
> ...
>
> Imagine now yee see the air made thick
> With stormy tempests that disturb the main
> And the four windes at war among themselves
> And the weak bark wherein the brothers sail
> Split on strange rocks, (lines 265–9)
>
> ...
>
> [and they] Dispersed to several corners of the world (line 271)
>
> ...
>
> from their fortune all our scene must grow (line 273)

The audience's active role in imagining the journey, tempest, and shipwreck aligns them with the very force of fortune that guides the brothers' paths, simultaneously making the audience aware of theatrical artifice through the theatre's inability to mimetically represent travel and its risks.[22] Imagination is aided by the well-known trope of shipwreck, familiarized through the genres of epic and romance. This trope automatically evokes the powerful role of fortune and the notion of a journey characterized by chance, luck, and risk. The word *fortune* (or *fortunes*) appears three different times in the Presenter's speech, encapsulating monetary fortune as well as more general luck. Directly associated with the sea and the weather, fortune separates the brothers by casting them into different geographical regions or "corners of the world," spanning France, Italy, and Ireland. It also drives the subsequent scenes and structure of the play by propelling the brothers onto separate episodic paths. Their misfortunes at sea temporarily bring them even lower than they were as apprentices in London. But the severing of the family and the individual paths of struggle, misrecognition, and conflict that unfold only emphasize the triumphant reversal of fortune that takes place in Jerusalem, where the brothers not only recoup their nobility through imperial conquest but also experience the joy of reunion. If fortune guides the brothers' paths individually and episodically through Europe, providence draws these episodic paths together in Jerusalem.

The fantasy of rising out of the apprentice system is enabled by religious crusade, a fantasy afforded by the play's temporal fusing of the first Crusade with present-day London guild culture. As Jean Howard puts it, in transposing the story of Godfrey of Bouillon to London, Heywood "invites ordinary London theatergoers to feel that the brothers' crusade is their own, that even middling-sort adventurers can aspire to do chivalric deeds and win glory for their country in foreign lands."[23] At the same time, the play draws a clear division between the world of Jerusalem and that of London, figuring Jerusalem as a place that rectifies the losses wrought by fortune and that recuperates underlying nobility through its providential power. With their conquest of Jerusalem the brothers are able to shed their trades, even as they physically mark their conquest of the Holy Land with their livery. In essence, they exchange the crests of their trades for imperial crowns, recovered from the heads of the Muslim leaders and representing the brothers' new rule over Jerusalem, Sicily, and Cyprus. If middling London apprentices have become kings, it is only in Jerusalem, and more specifically in the Jerusalem of the live theatre, that this can take place.

Notably, this triumphant resolution comes not as a surprise for the audience, for the play's subtitle ("with the conquest of Jerusalem") as well as the legendary historical victory of the eldest brother's namesake, Godfrey of Bouillon, in the First Crusade make the military victory known. In addition, the excessive misrecognitions of the brothers (as they repeatedly cross paths and fight each other for romantic access to the woman they don't recognize as their sister) establish the expectation that one day they will realize they all know one another. The certainty of this outcome contains fortune's power to do bad, demonstrating how fortune is subject to a generic arc that guarantees a providential resolution. Thus, the audience's affective experience is not simply conditioned by genre but also mirrors the discourse of fortune as providential certainty. Alluding to this outcome, the Presenter reflects upon the brothers' separation:

> Thus have you seene these foure, that were but now
> All in one Fleete, a many thousand leagues
> Seuere'd from one another: Guy in France
> Godfrey in Bulloigne, Charles in Italy
> Eustace in Ireland 'mongst the Irish kernes.
> Yet Gentlemen, the self same wind and fortune
> That parted them, may bring them altogether.
> Their sister follows them with zealous feet
> Be patient, yee will wonder when they meet (lines 321–9)
> ...
> Grant them your wonted patience to proceed
> And their keen swords shall make the pagans bleed. (lines 334–5)

As the Presenter suggests, fortune will be made providential in time and with the aid of the audience's patience. From this point early on in the play, the audience is promised an experience of "wonder" at the play's conclusion. The explicit promise of this reward suggests not that wonder will emanate from the suspense of *not knowing* what will happen, but rather that it accords with the audience's theatrical expectation, that the play's self-conscious theatricality does not detract from its ability to elicit wonder. As I have been suggesting, the very familiarity of the story, and the audience's authorization of the theatrical contrivance needed to deliver a happy ending, contribute to the pleasure and delight of watching the play. If the play attributes its wondrous resolution to the magic of Jerusalem (and by extension to the magic of the theatre), it achieves this effect through a careful engagement of its audience's expectations and appreciation for theatrical devices.

The brothers' excessive misrecognitions of one another across Europe emphasize the theatrical self-consciousness with which the familial reunion takes place in Jerusalem. The main difference between Europe and Jerusalem seems to be that the protagonists don't recognize each other in Europe, whereas they do in Jerusalem. Europe is thus made strange, and Jerusalem rendered a place of familiarity – a distinction that seems to highlight the play's awareness of the fact that both places occupy the same bare stage and are differentiated primarily by how the protagonists see the world, and in particular one another, in these spaces, rather than how the space itself is seen. The farcical nature of the protagonists' misrecognitions of one another is enhanced by their individual decisions to brandish the insignia of their London guilds on their flags and shields – a device that makes them each immediately recognizable to the audience. The gross improbability of their multiple chance meetings, compounded by the fact that they never recognize one another when they meet, exemplifies Heywood's special brand of dramaturgy – inverting the confusions of Shakespeare's closely contemporary *Comedy of Errors*, in which recognition is forestalled because the protagonists never seem to run into one another. If, as Jeremy Lopez has argued, "the drama and its audience were very much aware of the limitations of the early modern stage, and that the potential for dramatic representation to be ridiculous or inefficient or incompetent was a constant and vital part of audiences' experience of the plays," Heywood seems to flaunt this potential for its own sake.[24] In doing so, he shows how the play's ridiculous improbabilities, rendered in ways that are theatrically self-aware, might also enhance its wondrous effect.

If the moment of mutual recognition and reunion in Jerusalem is *potentially* laughable, the success of the play seems to depend on its being not *merely* laughable. Overtly signposted, the moment is verbally punctuated by shouts of

"Eustace!" "Godfrey!" "Guy!" "And Charles!"; and then all together: "Brothers!" (line 2118). Though the brothers have unknowingly crossed paths multiple times, they have not recognized one another until now. Conceivably, the ridiculousness of this possibility should mitigate the miracle of their ability to finally know one another in Jerusalem. Pulling visually against the wonder of their paths repeatedly crossing as they each traverse a vast geographical distance is the relatively small physical space of the stage that inevitably places their bodies in close proximity to one another. And yet, despite the layered spatial effect of their physical movements – presentation pulling against representation – their convergence at the same time in Jerusalem yields a wonder that is manufactured partly through its theatrical contrivance. Witnessing the unlikely reunion, Robert, duke of Normandy, exclaims, "This accident breeds wonders in my thoughts" (line 2119). For the performance to succeed, the members of the play's audience must share to some degree in this sense of wonder, rather than simply mock the contrived nature of the miracle.

Recognition and reunion in Jerusalem are also inflected by a religious force manifested through the Christian conquest of Jerusalem, thus fusing theatrical contrivance with providential Christian triumph. Upon claiming Christian victory, Robert, duke of Normandy, beseeches his men to laud God "with penitentiall praises" and to "ascribe all glory to the heavenly Powers" (lines 2382–3) that aided their victory, to which Tancred adds, "We do abhorre a heart puffed up with pride / That attributes these conquests to our strength / Twas God that strengthened us and weakened them / And gave us Syon and Jerusalem" (lines 2385–8). This interpretation of Christian victory as ordained by God displaces the many errors directed by fortune on the way to Jerusalem. Indeed, whereas the word *fortune* occurs more than twenty times in the play before the brothers reach Jerusalem (a little more than halfway through the play), it is used only five times after that point. In the final speech of the play, Robert instructs the brothers to hang their "trophies" (helmets) in the temple of Jerusalem "as a remembrance of [their] fortune's past" (lines 2563–4). Christian providence in turn inflects the distribution of imperial territories among the four brothers, who regain their nobility (and more) when they literally put on the crowns of Jerusalem, Cyprus, and Sicily. Connolly draws an apt contrast between Heywood's providentialism and the ironic treatment of providential monarchs in Shakespeare's *Henry V* and Marlowe's *Tamburlaine*, which "mocks the idea of a providential God."[25] In the Jerusalem of *The Four Prentices*, God's intervening hand is fully empowered and receives sincere treatment, even as it is expressed through overt theatrical contrivances.

Perhaps surprisingly, given its post-Reformation context, the play comes close to staging God's presence in a way reminiscent of the medieval mystery plays.

Godfrey, the eldest brother, relinquishes the crown of Jerusalem to the next eldest and chooses instead to wear a crown of thorns in imitation of Christ's suffering. The casting of a London apprentice in this role may resonate with the performance of the mystery plays by local craft guilds. The play also cites the historical Godfrey of Bouillon, who according to legend refused the title and vestments of royalty, declaring he would never wear a crown of gold in the city where Christ wore a crown of thorns. As Elizabeth Williamson has discussed, religious stage props evocative of Catholicism or the medieval mystery tradition operated as "affective technologies" that translated an emotional charge from the religious sphere to the secular theatre, though not necessarily in any straightforward way.[26] In this case, the spectacle of an actor donning a crown of thorns – and leading a procession to "CHRISTS Tombe" (line 2571) – dangerously invokes the embodied staging of Christ while at the same time achieving dramatic distance through its self-conscious citational effect. In this way, it projects a complex fusing of religious and self-consciously theatrical power.

In addition, Godfrey's donning of the crown of thorns underscores how the brothers' restored noble status is ordained through an imperial conquest driven by religion rather than by economics. While Fanella Macfarlane has argued that the victory of Heywood's prentices poses an economic challenge to the large company monopolists who controlled England's overseas business and with whom London's domestic tradesmen were in direct conflict, the play seems insistently to divorce imperial conquest from global commerce, associating it instead with religious crusade.[27] It represents Jerusalem not as a place of trade or economic interest but as a site of holy wonder. This Jerusalem seems not to critique London and its mercantile practices but to be its antithesis – a place divorced from early modern economics. Having shed the livery of their London apprenticeships, the brothers, along with the other Christians, exit the stage in a procession towards the Holy Sepulchre (located somewhere offstage), fulfilling the earl's intention at the start of the play to undertake a pilgrimage to the Holy Land. As I have argued elsewhere, the threat of Islam and its contemporary association with the Ottoman Empire helps to justify the stage's empowerment of otherwise reviled Catholic rituals, practices, and objects.[28] Positively portrayed in this play are the trappings of Catholic crusade and pilgrimage, the performance of a holy procession, and the use of a crown of thorns as a stage prop. At the same time that the temporally and geographically distant setting of Jerusalem mitigates the controversial effect of these representations, it also heightens their religious meaning. Similarly, the setting of Jerusalem in this play lends credence to the staging of a miracle, aligning comic resolution with a miraculous conquest, and theatrical contrivance with divine intervention.

And yet the fact that Jerusalem is conquered by London apprentices who prominently display their trades by hanging their shields on the very walls of Jerusalem juxtaposes London economics with Christian providence in a way that calls attention to theatrical fantasy. Describing *The Four Prentices* as a particularly "experimental" play within Heywood's corpus, Jean Howard emphasizes how it "rewrites the chivalric romance to accommodate the interests of London guild culture."[29] The lampooning of a grocer-turned-knight in Francis Beaumont's *Knight of the Burning Pestle* (1607) responds to the ridiculousness of this fantasy. But as I have argued, and as the apparent success of *The Four Prentices* may demonstrate, it is a fantasy no less wondrous because of its theatrical contrivance. If Heywood's thematic adaptation of the Godfrey story represents a new experiment, it also works hand-in-hand with his extensive and innovative exploitation of theatrical devices. The combined mechanisms of Christian miracle and theatrical intervention transform Jerusalem into a place where one's recognition of one's own brother can be as wondrous as the conquest of Jerusalem by London apprentices.

Pericles: Divine/Theatrical Intervention and Miraculous Reunion in Ephesus

Shakespeare's *Pericles* (1608), performed within a year following *The Travels of the Three Brothers* and sharing a co-author in George Wilkins, also produces wonder through self-consciously theatrical effects. Like *The Four Prentices*, it locates these effects in an eastern Mediterranean city, where three family members reunite after fourteen years and where the fortunes guiding their movements turn out to be providential. Set in the ancient Greek Mediterranean, the world of *Pericles* is ruled ostensibly by pagan gods and the cosmic force of fortune, yet the distinction between pagan and Christian divinity eventually breaks down, as the pagan divine forces are implicitly assimilated with a Christian providentialism. The significance of Ephesus as not only the site of Diana's temple, but also of Christian conversion and miracles, prominent in St Paul's journeys, reinforces the play's fusing of pagan and Christian divinity. As Elizabeth Hart and Randall Martin have shown, Diana's Graeco-Roman associations with chastity diverged from Artemis's Hellenistic associations with fertility and childbirth, creating a productive tension between the two cultural influences.[30] What I suggest is not simply that the Christian supplants the pagan, but that the two merge to effect a single providential resolution to the play that veers from the confusions of fortune. At the same time, the providential interventions that bring about Pericles's miraculous reunions with Marina and Thaisa draw attention to the use of stagecraft, either by foregrounding the stage's mechanical special effects or by eliciting the audience's imagination to compensate for the inadequacies of the stage. If fortune is eventually revealed to be provident in this play – coming into focus as though viewed through a prospective glass – this revelation is shown to be a function of both divine providence and theatrical artifice.

The divine intervention that directly facilitates the familial reunion in Ephesus conjoins miracle with theatricality in ways that likely drew attention to the mechanics of the stage. In the final act, the goddess Diana appears and directs Pericles to travel to Ephesus, where he and Marina will be reunited with Thaisa, long presumed to be dead. I agree with Suzanne Gossett (as well as a number of other editors and critics of the play), who argues for the likelihood of Diana's descent onto the stage, linking the play "to the increasingly elaborate Jacobean court masques" as well as to a broader tradition of godly descents on the public stage.[31] I draw attention to the great dramaturgical power of such a spectacle and to how it self-consciously evokes an awareness of the theatrical contrivance of the deus ex machina as well as of the literal physical mechanics of lowering an actor onto the stage from above. To the accompaniment of music, the goddess would descend, offer Pericles a set of explicit directions, and then ascend from the stage:

> *Diana* [*descends*]
> My temple stands in Ephesus. Hie thee thither
> And do upon mine altar sacrifice.
> There, when my maiden priests are met together,
> Before the people all,
> Reveal how thou at sea didst lose thy wife.
> To mourn thy crosses, with thy daughter's, call,
> And give them repetition to the life.
> Or perform my bidding, or thou livest in woe;
> Do't, and happy, by my silver bow.
> Awake, and tell thy dream. [*She ascends.*][32]

Quite possibly, the actor descended and ascended by being lowered from an upper platform via a pulley system. In this case, his entrance would have relied upon the relatively crude mechanics of the early modern stage. The number of similar instances in which actors descended from above, including Jupiter in *Cymbeline*, Cupid in *Love's Mistress*, and Fortune in *The Valiant Welshman*, suggests that this was a familiar device for early modern playgoers. Alan Dessen and Leslie Thompson's *Dictionary of Stage Directions* identifies *descend* as a stage direction "roughly ninety times in sixty plays" and certainly a number of other plays featured descents from above, despite the omission of explicit stage directions in their early quartos.[33] In evoking the machines used in Greek tragedy to lower gods onto the stage, Diana's descent would have also drawn attention to the plot device of the deus ex machina, which offers an easy way of solving a problem in a play without necessitating further explanation. Horace and Aristotle disparaged playwrights' use of the device because of its crude theatrical contrivance and its introduction of improbability into a plot. Such potential criticism clearly applies to Diana's role in *Pericles*, where the need to resolve the plot by reuniting Pericles and Marina with Thaisa is perhaps too conveniently answered by a divine intervention. Early modern audiences would have recognized the contrived and convenient resolution afforded by Diana, as well as of the stage mechanics that likely brought her onto the stage. And yet, both the moment of Diana's appearance and that of the familial reunion that follows must have engendered wonder for early modern audiences in order for the play to be so successful. As I have been suggesting, this sense of wonder fully assimilated – even celebrated – an awareness of theatrical contrivance, rather than ignoring it.

The efficacy of Diana's intervention, in which theatricality merges with miracle, is demonstrated through the familial reunion that immediately follows upon Pericles's heeding of Diana's directives. Quite unabashedly, Pericles refers to the reunion with Thaisa as a "great miracle" (5.3.59). Such a reading of Diana's intervention and the resolution that follows suggests that they were portrayed with absolute sincerity. Perhaps because of its Catholic associations, the word *miracle* is relatively rare in Shakespeare's plays, appearing only thirty-one times in his entire dramatic canon, and most often in humorous or ironic contexts (*fortune*, by contrast, appears 509 times). In *Pericles*, the word is spoken earnestly and with reverence, as Pericles wonders "who to thank, / Besides the gods, for this great miracle" (5.3.58–9). He refers here not just to his reunion with Thaisa, but also to her restoration from apparent death, which he learns to have been facilitated by Cerimon, as well as by the fortune that cast her ashore in Ephesus. This moment, too, is linked to Diana, as Thaisa first calls out her name upon being revived: "Oh dear Diana, / Where am I?" (3.3.102). Thaisa will later describe Cerimon as a man "through whom the gods have shown their power," suggesting that he is a vehicle for (pagan) divinity (5.3.61). In addition to its authorization of pagan divine power, Thaisa's revival evokes the Christian miracle of resurrection. And, at the same time, it produces a wondrous theatrical spectacle, enhanced by the audience's awareness that, in seventeenth-century London, revival from death is something that happens exclusively (and often) on the stage. Myhill's discussion of the simultaneity of miracle and theatrical artifice seems apt here, and once again I draw attention to how these two forces might work hand-in-hand, rather than against one another, to create a wondrous effect.

If the "miracle" of Pericles's reunion with his family is informed by the theatrical artifice of Diana's intervention, this miracle is also authorized by the particular setting of Ephesus, which held rich associations with pagan as well as Christian divinity. As Randall Martin has discussed, ancient Ephesus was "a place of competing loyalties to a long-standing female-centered religion versus a transplanted patriarchal one."[34] Though also known for its major commercial seaport – both in ancient times and in Shakespeare's time – the Ephesus of *Pericles* is distinguished most by the temple of Artemis, one of the seven wonders of the ancient world. In that the temple serves as a sanctuary for Thaisa to live as a chaste widow, it draws more on Diana's identity as the Graeco-Roman patron of chastity than on that of her Hellenistic identity, Artemis, the deity of fertility and childbirth. Martin describes how both the European tradition of Diana and the Asian and Hellenistic worship of Artemis were assimilated by Christianity, when Mary, "their avatar," became known as the virgin mother of god."[35] At the same time, local worship of Artemis persisted until the fourth century, and the temple itself was a site of fierce resistance to Christian conversion and Paul's evangelizing missions. *Pericles* translates this history of violent conflict and transition into a seamless fusing of paganism and Christianity, figured on some level as a merging of fortune with providence. Though outwardly pagan, Shakespeare and Wilkins's Ephesus is a site of "miracle" and provident resolution. The triumph of providence over fortune is expressed by Gower's final epilogue, which sums up the fate of all the characters in the play: "In Pericles, his queen, and daughter seen, / Although assailed with Fortune fierce and keen, / Virtue preserved from fell destruction's blast, / Led on by heaven and crowned with joy at last" (Epilogue, 3–6). If pagan and Christian merge in the play's provident resolution to fortune's whims, they accomplish their victory through an unexpected miraculous intervention, which is authorized by both the theatrical stage and the divinely enchanted setting of Ephesus.

Crucial to this miracle (and to rendering fortune provident) is Pericles's obedience to forces that may look like whims of fortune but are later revealed to be providential. Often disparaged as a passive or one-dimensional character, Pericles may alternatively be seen to model a lesson of Christian patience. In response to Diana's directions, Pericles unquestioningly vows obedience, answering, "Celestial Dian, Goddess argentine, / I will obey thee" (5.1.237–8). After heeding rather than questioning this directive, no matter how seemingly arbitrary or nonsensical the message, Pericles is ultimately rewarded through reconciliation with his wife. His reunion with his daughter is similarly facilitated through a kind of obedience to forces greater than himself. Caught in a tempest, Pericles is "driven before the winds" to the coast of Mytilene (5.0.14). Though facilitated by forces of nature, this reunion parallels Pericles's reunion with Thaisa in that his complete surrender to a power greater than himself leads to unanticipated reward. Exhibiting a logic of Christian providence, the play's resolution suggests that Pericles's triumph is neither arbitrary nor brought about through his own direct agency, but rather the result of a patient obedience that propels him to travel passively.

Though the final reunion in Ephesus overshadows the significance of Pericles and Marina's reunion in Mytilene, it seems important to recognize the importance of this earlier reunion and how it, too, is facilitated by an intervention that draws attention to the mechanics of the stage. In this case, it is not an embodied goddess who brings about reunion, but a storm-ridden journey that randomly lands Pericles on the coast of Mytilene, the same city where his daughter was sold by pirates into a brothel. Narrated by Gower in two non-consecutive scenes, rather than physically enacted on the stage, the storm constitutes a form of intervention that differs in interesting ways from the intervention made by Diana. Following Dionyza's attempted murder of Marina and a dumbshow in which Pericles is confronted with Marina's coffin, Gower describes how Pericles sets sail from Tarsus for Tyre when

> ... He bears
> A tempest which his mortal vessel tears,
> And yet he rides it out. (4.4.29–31)
> ...
> Let Pericles believe his daughter's dead
> And bear his course to be ordered
> By Lady Fortune, while our scene must play
> His daughter's woe and heavy well-a-day
> In her unholy service. Patience then,
> And think you now are in Mytilene. (4.4.46–51)

As in *The Three English Brothers* and *The Four Prentices of London*, the Chorus steps in to narrate an instance of travel that the stage cannot easily represent. In addition, Gower asks the audience's leave for Pericles "to believe" that Marina is dead, to let him "bear his course" that is "ordered by Lady Fortune," and to have "patience" while the scene transitions to Mytilene before returning to Pericles's travels. In a sense, it lays bare the clunky mechanics of scene transition and the difficulties of representing simultaneous events in different settings. Quite antithetical to the scene of Diana's intervention that soon follows, this scene lays the burden of Pericles's redirected course on the audience. In effect, the audience is asked to conjure the journey and the storm in their imaginations, and to patiently indulge Pericles's perspective on the events that befall him, while knowing that Marina is alive and living in Mytilene. This solicitation of audience participation aligns the spectators' imagination and consent with the force of fortune ("Lady Fortune") that drives Pericles's course. In doing so, it draws attention to the theatrical nature of Pericles's travels and associates both the theatre and travel with the unpredictable force of fortune.

Lady Fortune's role in directing Pericles's course is not unique to this particular journey or episode in the play, suggesting that the providential nature of the storm can be perceived only after the fact. Prior to this trip, Pericles has undertaken a number of journeys through the Mediterranean Sea and encountered two previous storms of significant consequence – one that leads to his marriage to Thaisa and one during which his daughter is born and his wife is presumed to die. In these previous episodes, fortune plays a similar, crucial role: "Fortune ... threw him ashore" in Pentapolis (2.0.37–8); Pericles and Thaisa are thrown off course by "Fortune's mood" when departing Pentapolis for Tyre (3.0.46); when Thaisa's coffin washes ashore on Ephesus, Cerimon comments, "Tis a good constraint of fortune / it belches upon us" (3.2.55–6); and Marina attributes her landing in a brothel to "most ungentle Fortune" (4.5.100) and her devaluation in social status to "wayward Fortune" (5.1.80) These repeated references to "fortune" (the word appears twenty-one times in all throughout the play) suggest that, unlike Diana's intervention, the storm that takes Pericles to Mytilene represents just one more episode of fortune in a play that abounds with such episodes. And yet, *this* storm leads to an improbable reunion between Pericles and Marina that serves as a partial comic resolution to the plot, soon followed by the reunion of the whole family in Ephesus. If this storm is revealed ultimately to be providential through its wondrous consequences, it relies on the audience to perceive it as such by retrospectively understanding this instance of fortune to be different from and more meaningful than the previous ones.

When Gower re-enters the stage after two intervening scenes set in Mytilene to complete his narration of Pericles's journey, he similarly elicits the active participation of the audience to bring about the providential reunion between father and daughter:

And to [Marina's] father turn our thoughts again,
Where we left him, on the sea. Where there him lost,
Whence, driven before the winds, he is arrived
Here where his daughter dwells, and on this coast

Suppose him now at anchor. (5.0.12–16)

...

In your supposing once more put your sight:
Of heavy Pericles, think this his bark,
Where what is done in action, more if might,
Shall be discovered, please you sit and hark. (5.0.21–4)

In beseeching the audience to "turn their thoughts" to Pericles at sea, to "suppose" that he is "now at anchor," and to "think" that the stage is his "bark," Gower emphasizes how much he relies upon the intervention of the audience (and not that of the storm) to carry out the redirection of Pericles's course. By offering an extreme instance in which the stage fails at mimetic representation, Gower's speech also calls attention the difficulty of theatrical faith. Describing how a similar moment of choric narration in *The Winter's Tale* elicits audience belief, Monta explains, "There is something 'willing here,' but it is not exactly or simply a suspension of disbelief – the audience is asked to engage imaginatively despite and because of [the Chorus's] insistence on the shortcomings of dramatic fiction."[36] Through its implicit acknowledgment of theatrical inadequacy, Gower's narration reminds us of how belief in the theatre is always beholden to an audience, and of how all theatrical representation relies on the imagination and faith of spectators.

Pericles's structural excesses and the difficulty of staging its extensive traversals of time and space contribute to its lesson of fortune made provident, as well as to the audience's pleasure in observing the work of the stage. The play's episodic structure reinforces this message by presenting an unrelated series of journeys to multiple, seemingly random destinations that turn out to have providential significance. Unlike in *The Four Prentices*, the audience experiences the recognition that fortune is in fact providential almost simultaneously with Pericles, at the end of the play. In addition, the episodic structure divorces travel from an explicit goal or ambition, depicting the traveller not as a subject but as an object tossed from place to place. Gower as choric narrator serves a key function in helping to knit together the disjointed episodic structure, as well as exposing its gaps and breeches. When Gower says to the audience, "I do beseech you / To learn of me, who stand [in the] gaps to teach you / The stages of our story," he draws attention to his role in shaping both what is seen and not seen: the "gaps" occupy the stage as surely as the "stages," or episodes, themselves (4.4.7–9). Often Gower's narration seeks to fill the gaps for what the stage cannot show. For example, in the fifth scene of the play, Gower describes Pericles's journey from Tarsus to Pentapolis:

> For now the wind begins to blow;
> Thunder above and deeps below
> Make such unquiet, that the ship
> Should house him safe is wreck'd and split,
> And he, good prince, having all lost,
> By waves from coast to coast is tossed.
> All perishen of man, of pelf,
> Ne aught escapend but himself;
> Till Fortune, tired with doing bad,
> Threw him ashore to give him glad. (2.0.29–38)

Here, Gower functions as a meta-theatrical device that compensates for the difficulty of staging sea travel. However, in narrating what cannot be shown, Gower also exploits the aspects of theatrical experience that are auditory, rather than visual, and that call upon the audience's imagination to envision the spectacle in their mind's eye. The anachronisms in Gower's language help to shape the imagined experience by invoking a world and a literary tradition from the past, and by thus rendering the narration less immediately transparent for early seventeenth-century audiences. If Pericles's toil is characterized by "letting go and letting God," the audience performs an opposite form of labour in actively transporting Pericles through the work of the imagination.[37]

Such transportation across vast expenses of geographic space and fourteen years of time requires compressions that make the play suitable for live theatrical performance. Rather than obscure these compressions, the play draws the audience's attention to them, and in doing so flaunts its awareness of the packaging of material for commercial consumption. For example, at the beginning of act 4 (scene 15),[38] Gower reflects on the process of compression as he tells of Dionyza's growing jealousy of Marina and her intention to have her murdered:

> ... The unborn event
> I do command to your content,
> Only I carry winged time
> Post on the lame feet of my rhyme,
> Which never could I so convey
> Unless your thoughts went on my way. (4.0.45–50)

Here Gower draws attention to his poetic "rhyme," which compresses and in effect stands in for events that the stage does not show. More efficient than theatrical enactment, Gower's poetic narration repackages a story that is too long for the stage so that it might be suitable for theatrical performance, but as Gower makes clear, such repackaging would not be possible without the "thoughts" of the audience. The absence of spectacle and mimetic representation on the stage solicit a distinct kind of audience interaction – an effect highlighted against the contemporary trend of staging elaborate spectacles in court masques.

I suggest that *Pericles*'s excesses – its expanses of time and space, and its loose, episodic structure – as well as its gaps, added something positive to the play in the form of theatrical pleasure and entertainment. Cyrus Mulready persuasively argues that early modern audiences' expanding geographic and cultural imaginings, satisfied by romance's depiction of faraway places, prompted playwrights to defy neoclassical standards for dramatic unity, despite the costs of doing so.[39] But could it also be that *Pericles*'s popularity with early modern audiences encourages a different understanding of how audiences interacted with and appreciated the theatre on a meta-theatrical level, taking pleasure in witnessing the gaps and limitations of the stage, and the exposure of its mechanics? In transporting audiences to the eastern Mediterranean, plays such as *The Four Prentices* and *Pericles* simultaneously made spectators aware of the disjuncture between verisimilitude and theatricality, the arbitrary chaos of fortune and the framed prospective of providence.

The three plays I have discussed are among many English plays of the same period that depict travel in the spaces of the eastern Mediterranean.[40] This geographical region was of heightened importance to the English in the late sixteenth and early seventeenth centuries, largely because of English interests in Mediterranean commerce, as well as because of the looming religious and imperial threat posed by the Ottoman Empire. Places such as Jerusalem and Ephesus were also sites of past Christian struggle that assumed new topical relevance as the English contemplated Christian vulnerabilities in these now Ottoman-controlled territories. And yet, as this chapter has attempted to demonstrate, eastern Mediterranean settings also provided a unique opportunity for the theatre to experiment with new forms of representation because of the very difficulty of depicting travel and geographical distance on the stage. While at times the stage construed its inability to represent travel mimetically as an inadequacy, it also used these moments to produce meta-theatrical effects that cultivated new and sophisticated forms of audience engagement and pleasure. In addition, the plays I have discussed drew upon Christian histories of conflict and triumph in Jerusalem and Ephesus to stage miracles of familial reunion, but they also effected these miracles in overtly theatrical ways that drew attention to the theatre's own evolving semiotic conventions, physical mechanics, and dramaturgical practices. In doing so, these plays mobilized theatrical artifice to create a sense of wonder that was entirely distinct from, but not necessarily less powerful than, miracles of a divine nature. In transforming the Mediterranean into an overtly theatrical space, the early modern English theatre operated something like the hand of providence and cultivated among audiences a faith in the theatre's own unique contrivances.

NOTES

1 *The Travels of the Three English Brothers*, ed. Anthony Parr (Manchester: Manchester University Press, 1995), Epilogue, stage direction following line 13. Subsequent quotations from the play will be cited parenthetically by scene and line number.
2 Henry Turner, *The English Renaissance Stage: Geometry, Poetics, and the Practical Spatial Arts 1580–1630* (Oxford: Oxford University Press, 2006).
3 Ibid., 30.
4 Ibid., 2.
5 Cyrus Mulready, "'Asia of the one side, Affric of the other': Sidney's Unities and the Staging of Romance," in *Staging Early Modern Romance: Prose Fiction, Dramatic Romance, and Shakespeare*, ed. Valerie Wayne and Mary Ellen Lamb, 47–71 (London: Routledge, 2008). See also, Mulready, *Romance on the Early Modern Stage: English Expansion before and after Shakespeare* (New York: Palgrave Macmillan, 2013).
6 Mulready, "'Asia of the one side,'" 49.
7 "prospective glass," OED online.
8 Barbara Fuchs, *Mimesis and Empire: The New World, Islam, and European Identities* (Cambridge: Cambridge University Press, 2001), 40.
9 Stuart Clark, *Vanities of the Eye: Vision in Early Modern European Culture* (Oxford: Oxford University Press, 2007); see especially "Prestiges," 78–122.
10 According to the *Oxford English Dictionary, fortune* assumed the meaning of a "position determined by wealth" or an "amount of wealth" in the late sixteenth century; the earliest example of this usage cited in the *OED* is from 1596. See *fortune, OED* online.
11 Alexandra Walsham, *Providence in Early Modern England* (Oxford: Oxford University Press, 1999), 3.
12 For a discussion that gestures in a similar direction, see Erika T. Lin, *Shakespeare and the Materiality of Performance* (New York: Palgrave Macmillan, 2012), esp. on "religious ecstasy" in chap. 3.
13 Nova Myhill, "Making Death a Miracle: Audience and the Genres of Martyrdom in Dekker and Massinger's *The Virgin Martyr*," *Early Theatre* 7, no. 2 (2004): 9–31; Anthony Dawson, with Paul Yachnin, *The Culture of Playgoing in Shakespeare's England* (Cambridge: Cambridge University Press, 2001); and Susannah Brietz Monta, "'It

is requir'd you do awake your faith': Belief in Shakespeare's Theater," in *Religion and Drama in Early Modern England*, ed. Jane Hwang Degenhardt and Elizabeth Williamson, 115–37 (Farnham: Ashgate, 2011).
14 Myhill, "Making Death a Miracle," 9.
15 Dawson, with Yachnin, *Culture of Playgoing*, 107.
16 Monta, "'It is requir'd,'" 124.
17 John Gillies, *Shakespeare and the Geography of Difference* (Cambridge: Cambridge University Press, 1994). D.K. Smith, *The Cartographic Imagination in Early Modern England: Rewriting the World in Marlowe, Spenser, Raleigh, and Marvell* (Aldershot: Ashgate, 2008). Many critics have relied on other archives such as pamphlet literature and travel narratives to illuminate dramatic representations of the Mediterranean. See, for example, Nabil Matar, *Islam in Britain, 1558–1685* (Cambridge: Cambridge University Press, 1998); and Daniel Vitkus, *Turning Turk: English Theater and the Multicultural Mediterranean, 1570–1630* (New York: Palgrave Macmillan, 2003).
18 For an overview of critical speculation regarding the dating of the play, see Mary Ann Weber Gasior, ed., *The Four Prentices of London* (New York: Garland, 1980), vii–xv.
19 *The Four Prentices of London*, ed. Mary Ann Weber Gasior (New York: Garland, 1980), Prologue, lines 25–30. Subsequent quotations from the play will be cited parenthetically by line number. This edition follows the 1615 quarto, which does not contain headings for act or scene divisions, other than for the Prologue and a single heading for "Actus primus, Scoena prima."
20 Annaliese F. Connolly, "Guy of Warwick, Godfrey of Bouillon, and Elizabethan Repertory," in *Early Modern England and Islamic Worlds*, ed. Bernadette Andrea and Linda McJannet (New York: Palgrave Macmillan, 2011), 150. Godfrey's story was disseminated in contemporary publications such as Richard Carew's 1594 translation of the first five cantos of Tasso's *Gerusalemme liberata*. It may have also inspired two other plays referenced in Henslowe's *Diary*, namely *Jerusalem*, performed in 1592 at the Rose by Lord Strange's Men, and *Godfrey of Bullen*, performed in 1594–5 by the Admiral's Men.
21 For a related discussion of the relationship between early film and the viewer, see Tom Gunning, "The Cinema of Attraction: Early Film, Its Spectator, and the Avant-Garde," in *Film and Theory: An Anthology*, ed. Robert Stam and Toby Miller, 229–35 (Malden, MA: Blackwell, 2000). Gunning argues that film prior to 1906 established a particular relationship with its viewing audience by presenting a visual travelogue of exotic places and drawing on the illusory power of these views.
22 Indeed, as Erika T. Lin has argued, what we now understand as mimetic representation (something akin to realism) differs from early modern mimesis,

which worked in conjunction with an allegorical mode of understanding; see Lin, *Shakespeare and the Materiality of Performance*, chap. 3.
23 Jean Howard, "Thomas Heywood: Dramatist of London and Playwright of the Passions," in *The Cambridge Companion to Shakespeare and Contemporary Dramatists*, ed. Ton Hoenselaars (Cambridge: Cambridge University Press, 2012), 121–2.
24 Jeremy Lopez, *Theatrical Convention and Audience Response in Early Modern Drama* (Cambridge: Cambridge University Press, 2007), 2.
25 Connolly, "Guy of Warwick," 148.
26 Elizabeth Williamson, *The Materiality of Religion in Early Modern English Drama* (Farnham: Ashgate, 2009), 27.
27 Fenella Macfarlane, "'To 'try what London apprentices can do': Merchant Chivalry as Representational Strategy in Thomas Heywood's *The Four Prentices of London*," *Medieval and Renaissance Drama in England* 13 (2000): 141.
28 Jane Hwang Degenhardt, *Islamic Conversion and Christian Resistance on the Early Modern Stage* (Edinburgh: Edinburgh University Press, 2010).
29 Howard, "Thomas Heywood," 121.
30 Elizabeth Hart, "'Great is Diana' of Shakespeare's Ephesus," *Studies in English Literature 1500–1900* 43, no. 2 (2003): 347–74; and Randall Martin, "Rediscovering Artemis in *The Comedy of Errors*," *Shakespeare and the Mediterranean: Selected Proceedings of the International Shakespeare Association World Congress, Valencia, 2001*, ed. Tom Clayton, Susan Brock, and Vicente Fores, 363–79 (Newark, DE: University of Delaware Press, 2004).
31 Suzanne Gossett, ed., *Pericles*, Arden edition, 3rd ser. (London: Thomson Learning, 2004), Introduction, 81.
32 Ibid., 5.1.227–36. Subsequent quotations from the play will be cited parenthetically by act, scene, and line number.
33 A portion of this number refers to descents through a trapdoor located in the stage and to descents "from a state." Alan Dessen and Leslie Thompson, *A Dictionary of Stage Directions in English Drama, 1580–1642* (Cambridge: Cambridge University Press, 1999), 67–68.
34 Martin, "Rediscovering Artemis," 369.
35 Ibid., 364.
36 Monta, "'It is requir'd,'" 116.
37 For a discussion of how *Pericles* effaces the labour of early modern travel, see Daniel Vitkus, "Labor and Travel on the Early Modern Stage: Representing the Travail of Travel in Dekker's *Old Fortunatus* and Shakespeare's *Pericles*," in *Working Subjects in Early Modern English Drama*, ed. Michelle Dowd and Natasha Korda, 225–42 (Farnham: Ashgate, 2010).
38 The 1609 quarto was divided into scenes and not acts, consistent with the episodic structure of the play. Many modern editions, including the one cited in this chapter, impose act divisions, a practice that began with the third folio.

39 Mulready, "'Asia of the one side.'"
40 For discussions of some of these plays, see, for example, Tom Clayton, Susan Brock, and Vicente Forés, eds., *Shakespeare and the Mediterranean* (Newark, DE: University of Delaware Press, 2004); and Goran Stanivukovic, ed., *Re-Mapping the Mediterranean World in Early Modern English Writings* (New York: Palgrave Macmillan, 2007).

chapter nine

Copying "the Anti-Spaniard": Post-Armada Hispanophobia and English Renaissance Drama

ERIC GRIFFIN

In breefe, such is this comparison that if some Rhetoritian would employ his eloquence in framing of a long and lively Antithesis, he could not in the world find a subject more sortable to his purpose then the comparing of our conditions with those of this mongrell generation.

A Comparison of the English and Spanish Nation (1589)[1]

In England, the period following the Armada crisis of 1588 saw a marked increase in the publishing of anti-Spanish propaganda. Contrary to the lessons of Whig historiography, contemporaries realized that the defeat of Philip II's Enterprise of England had settled nothing. Seeking to capitalize on the fear and fervour generated by a crisis that had not yet reached the mythic status accorded it by later generations,[2] the Elizabethan regime mobilized a network of printers, propagandists, translators, and hack writers coordinated by William Cecil.[3] Their publications elevated an inflammatory rhetoric of ethnicity to a volume not previously heard in England. This discourse — which to this point had been more characteristic of the Dutch nationalists, French anti-Leaguers, and Huguenots who had been demonizing Spain for more than a generation — extended the dichotomizing discourse characteristic of Reformation polemic in order to subvert virtually every "kind and quality" that could be associated with Spanish nationality.[4] Yet more deleterious was the way this discourse erased evidence of cultural complementarity, overwriting the field of Anglo-Hispanic relations with English national significance.[5]

Later decades confirm that the English propaganda effort of the 1590s may have been one of the most devastating ever launched. Certainly audiences were moved while reading of the legendary cruelty ascribed to his countrymen by

Bartolomé de Las Casas.⁶ But to have witnessed the excesses of Spanish blood embodied in the denser social context of the theatre would have moved passions yet more *affectively*.⁷ In other words, while pamphlets and polemics were important agencies for the dissemination of anti-Spanish sentiment, in terms of audience affect, the Hispanophobic attitudes they inculcated were in all likelihood more effectually delivered in the period's drama than by the clamorous invective rolling from Cecil's presses. What the propaganda proposed, the theatre realized.

Although recent work has partially dislodged the triumphalism of earlier scholarship, it often remains forgotten that prior to the 1580s the English had been more prone to Spanish alliances than to Spanish antagonisms. During the early days of Elizabeth Tudor's reign, when Philip II offered the wobbly regime protection, there had been little incentive for any but the most extreme Protestants to demonize Spain in the manner of their Continental co-religionists. After 1585, the threat of a Spanish invasion changed this picture. When we examine how the English began to imitate, or "coppie," the representational strategies of Continental propagandists, the role that Hispanophobia played in the conception of an English national community in opposition to the "fictive ethnicity"⁸ it had begun to imagine as essentially Spanish comes vividly into relief. By 1623–4, Protestant England's demonization of Spain became fixed in public memory. This chapter will chart this ethnicizing process, but before we hear Hispanophobia being given theatrical voice, it will be useful to note how the typologies common to Continental anti-Hispanism were disseminated in England within the public sphere of early modern print.⁹

I

In 1570, just prior to the great florescence of dramatic literature we associate with the English Renaissance, John Foxe asserted, "Preachers, printers, and players ... be set up of God as a triple bulwarke against the triple crown of the Pope."¹⁰ By the mid-1580s, William Cecil had begun to put such a three-pronged strategy into practice, employing a coterie drawn from each of these groups to serve the promotional needs of the Elizabethan state.

The publicity network Cecil drew together included men like the Francophile Edward Aggas, who translated some thirty works produced in the context of France's Wars of Religion; Anthony Munday, the highly regarded poet, playwright, and translator of Spanish romances, a long-time literary insider, sometime Roman Catholic, and intelligencer; Richard Field, a Stratford native and early publisher of Shakespeare's *Venus and Adonis* (1593) and *Rape of Lucrece* (1594), who also wrote works of Protestant religious instruction in Spanish for distribution in Spain; and Rodrigo Lopez, the Portuguese *converso*, physician, businessman, and Spanish language translator who would be famously executed for treason in 1594. At the centre of Cecil's clique was the controversial printer and stationer John Wolfe.[11]

Although his ruthless business practices would earn him a reputation as the "Machiavel" of the London publishing world,[12] Wolfe's industry eventually made him the owner of more presses than anyone in England, excepting the Queen's official printer.[13] In addition to dominating the foreign sector of the English book trade, to which end he appears to have frequented the Frankfurt book fair in search of titles, Wolfe was privy to information from abroad that placed him advantageously within England's emerging news industry.[14] Wolfe's resourcefulness in issuing indexed Italian books with false title page imprints brought him to the attention of Cecil, who began to employ the strategy for the publication of his own political propaganda in foreign languages.[15] During the peak years of 1589–90, with men like Aggas, Munday, Field, and Lopez working overtime, the Wolfe-Cecil network produced perhaps seventy translations from French and many more from Dutch, Spanish, and other languages, as well as numerous newsletters and dispatches of comparable propaganda value.[16]

Among the most potent of the French tracts published by Wolfe was *The Coppie of the Anti-Spaniard* (1590) (figure 9.1), a translation of *Coppie de L'Anti-Espagnol, faict à Paris* (1590), attributed to Antoine Arnauld (1560–1619) and Michel Hurault (d. 1592). Englished by Munday, *The Coppie* vigorously promoted Hispanophobic views in order to demonize by association the policies of the Catholic Guise party in support of Henri Bourbon, who at this point remained Protestant. Delivering its vitriol in the ad hominem mode favoured by so many propagandists of the time, the polemic demonized the Roman Catholic Spanish as "impious Atheists" (9), a nation of "naturall Marranos" (17), ruled by a "tyrant" (33), whose subjects it racialized as "these Negroes" (35). The rhetorical question begged at every turn was clear: what else could be expected from a miscegenated race of Jews, Arab Muslims, and African Moors? Or, as framed in Munday's translation, "Shall the Countrie of France become servile to the commandement of the Spaniard? ... Of this demie Moore, demie Jew, yea demie Saracine?" (9). With the threat of another Armada looming, and a comparable English succession crisis on the horizon, *The Coppie* delivered an obvious message: for France, read *England*.

Focused as they were on France's internal politics, Hispanophobic polemics such as the *Anti-Spaniard* could have been digested only by readers willing to wade through their laborious circumlocutions and recitations of dynastic infighting. Far more direct was another of Wolfe's titles, *A Pageant of Spanish Humours, Wherin are naturally described and liuely portrayed, the kinds and quallities of a*

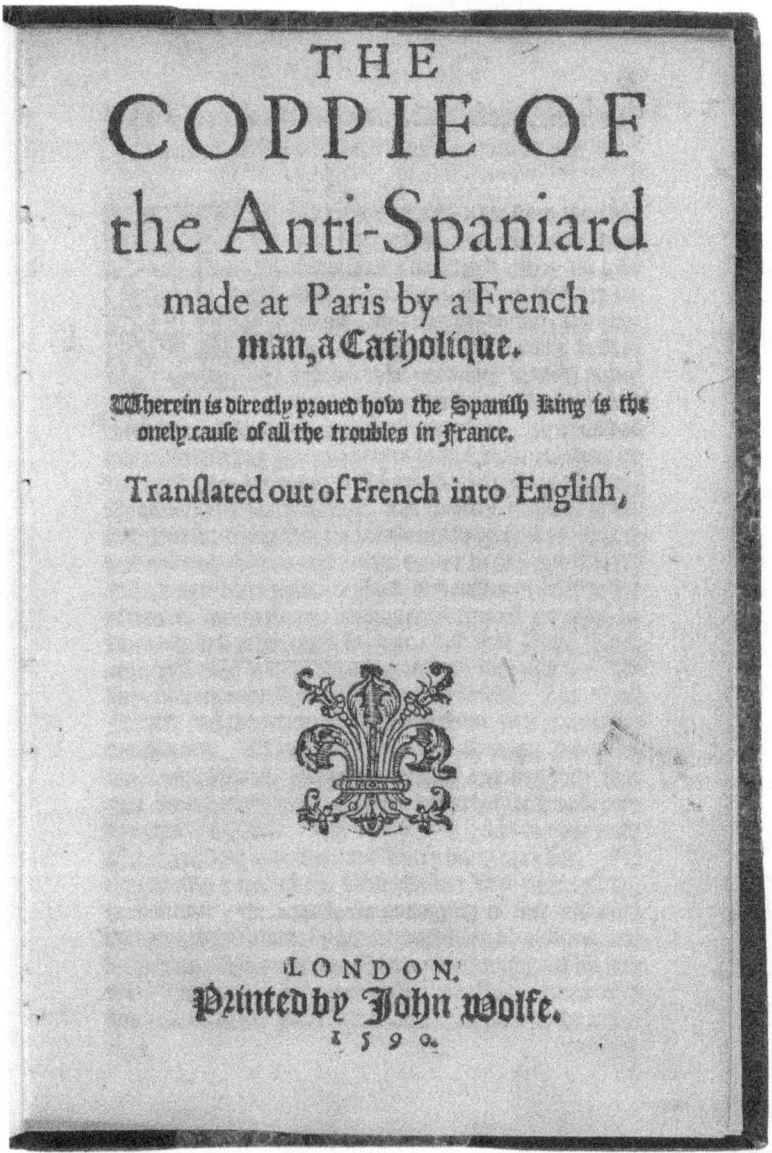

Figure 9.1 *The Coppie of the Anti-Spaniard* (1590), attributed to Antoine Arnauld and Michel Hurlault, translated by Anthony Munday and printed by the Elizabethan stationer John Wolfe, the vigorously Hispanophobic polemic was printed in both Paris and London. By permission of the Folger Shakespeare Library.

signior of Spaine, a pamphlet "Translated out of Dutche."[17] Offering a set of sixteen mnemonic emblems supported by didactic verses, image and text together defined the essential characteristics – or "kinds and qualities" – associated with "the Spaniard." Distributed widely across the Continent, these typologies were passed down with remarkable consistency through several generations.

Although not published in England until 1599, the *Pageant* had been circulating on the Continent in multiple languages for nearly thirty years. By 1571, the French *Emblesmes sus les actions, perfections, et Meurs du Segnor Espagnol* and the German *Emblemata: Welch das Leben, die thaten, sitten und wunderbare verwandlung dess Sigor Spangniolis* had appeared as elaborately illustrated broadsides, and both were printed again in 1581 (see figure 9.2), probably in response to Philip II's annexation of Portugal. Reputedly copied from a Spanish-language original – although probably falsely attributed to a "native" Spanish writer – the *Pageant* demonstrated "the life, deeds, customs, and marvelous metamorphosis of Signior Spagniol."[18] So widely distributed were the *Emblesmes* that Arnauld and Hurault apparently took for granted that readers of *L'Anti-Espagnol* would be well acquainted with these sixteen types, for within *The Coppie* they refer scornfully to "these sixteene Cavalieros and their adherents, which live but by the spoile of us, which glutte themselves with our blood" as "the ministers and officers of Spanish tiranny" (25), repeating the commonplaces portrayed in the *Pageant*.

The Cecil network also became adept at producing Hispanophobic publications of a distinctively English cast. Among the most important may be *A Fig for the Spaniard and Spanish Spirits*.[19] Published in 1591 and 1592, and featuring Elizabeth's authorizing counterfeit, the tauntingly jingoistic screed proved so notorious that Richard Verstegen answered its charges in the Antwerp-published *Declaration of the True Causes of the Great Troubles Presupposed to be Intended Against the Realm of England* (1592). Wondering how it was that "Cecill was now come to beare so great sway in the courte" (63), and arguing, "It his he, that hath bene the causer of al the inconveniences, troobles, and daungers, that the realme hathe alredy past, or dothe presently sustaine, or hereafter my suffer" (67), the Catholic exile Verstegen deemed it not amiss "to give some caveat of a vile and hatefull kynde of dealing, which the adversary of late hath used in divulging nu[m]bers of false and defamatorie libells" (74). Verstegen argued that the misrepresentations propagated in these printed slanders "custome hathe made so familiar to the libellers themselves, that ... they seme to have forgotten, there is any difference between lying and telling t[r]uth" (74). Referring to specific titles and calling out offenders by name – foremost among them *A Fig for the Spaniard* and its printer John Wolfe (76) – Verstegen claimed, "In these and other lyke lybells, it seemeth they have challenged unto themselves a kynde of privilage, to raile and rave at Princes, and to be[lie] and slaunder whome they list ...

Figure 9.2 Circulating on the Continent as early as 1571, and printed by John Wolfe as *A Pageant of Spanish Humours* (London, 1599), *Emblemata: Welch das Leben* and its French and English variants reduced "Signior Spagniol" to sixteen essential types. Germanisches Nationalmuseum, Nürnberg. By permission.

which equity & truthe have ever detested, and all honorable states and honest myndes, do utterly abhorr" (76). Lamenting the state of a Christendom in which Lutheran and Calvinist sectarians each worship their "misnamed," "supposed," or "peculier" Gospels, Verstegen bade "A fig to the figmonger" and asked his readers to "suspect the discordant English Gospell of heresy, and the Gospellers libells, of malitious lies" (77). Verstegen's attempt to discover Cecil's libels may have been welcomed by English Catholics, but the Elizabethan propaganda machine rolled on; for generations thereafter its "slanders" become a "truth" of English history, represented as gospel in print, from the pulpit, and onstage.

II

As anthropologist William Beeman observes, "Theater does more than engage participants in the immediate context of the theatrical event. It evokes and solidifies a network of social and cognitive [associations] existing in a triangular relationship between performer, spectator, and the world at large."[20] In sixteenth-century England, this social and cognitive network had been made and remade multiple times:[21] in the face of religious, dynastic, and other social instabilities, the nexus of English print and theatrical culture contributed a new form of participatory community, where variously invested "publics" could gather to witness multiple personal and collective social anxieties, aspirations, and resistances.[22] If there were a dozen public theatres in London, each capable of admitting as many as 1,500 audience members per show, in season up to 25,000 people per week may have attended performances.[23] These theatrical venues would have provided an experiential community surpassed only by required church attendance. In the wake of the Armada, among the things English audiences saw performed there were the rhetorical operations typical of Hispanophobia.

Three relatively minor playwrights, Robert Wilson, Robert Greene, and George Peele, appear to have been the first to realize the didactic and dramatic potential of the propaganda being published by the Cecil network.[24] I am not suggesting that Wilson, Greene, and Peele were the first English dramatists to have written in an anti-Spanish mode. In the run-up to the Armada, Thomas Kyd's *Spanish Tragedy* represented Spain and Portugal within a recently united Iberia as a decadent "Babylon" providentially bound to fall, while at virtually the same moment, John Lyly's well-known dramas, *Endymion* (ca 1588) and *Midas* (ca 1590), deployed classical precedents in order to critique Philip II's misguided support for Mary Queen of Scots and England's Catholic gentry or to allegorize the hubristic excesses of the Spanish Crown.[25] Nor am I suggesting that particular propaganda texts may in every case be identified as the "sources" for anti-Spanish references. Rather, the convergence of a similar set of Hispanophobic indices in multiple plays suggests the broad dissemination and popular appeal of the typologies that comprise the discursive formation scholars now recognize as the Black Legend. Although the attribution and dating of many Renaissance plays remains imprecise, among those still extant, works by Wilson, Greene, and Peele stand out as the earliest to have realized the potential *as drama* of the material circulating in the era's Hispanophobic propaganda.

A Puritan dramatist with ties to the earl of Leicester and a founding member of the Queen's Men, Robert Wilson is most often remembered for *The Three Ladies of London* (ca 1584) – a play that prefigures the multicultural Mediterranean of *The Merchant of Venice*.[26] Whereas Wilson's earlier play featured Italians, Turks, and a Jewish usurer named Gerontus (considered a precursor of Marlowe's Barabbas and Shakespeare's Shylock), his sequel, *The Three Lords and The Three Ladies of London* (1590), which had been produced by Queen Elizabeth's men as early as 1588, places in the city three avaricious "Lords of Spaine": "Ambition," "Pride" and, "Tyranny" (A2).[27] Each personated in a manner reminiscent of the Vice figures of earlier theatrical fashion, Wilson's Spanish villains are drawn by "pleasure, wealth and policy" to a London represented as a thriving "market towne." Soon they are joined by their equally contemptible pages – "Shame," "Treachery," and "Terror" – who arrive onstage intent on besting "Los Luteranos Angleses" (G3).

Although performed nearly a decade before they were published in England as *A Pageant of Spanish Humours* (ca 1599), the commonplaces attached to Wilson's three Spanish lords – those invoked by Arnauld and Hurault in *L'Anti-Espagnol* and its 1590 English translation – correlate directly with those published in 1571 and 1581 as the French *Emblesmes* and the German *Emblemata*.[28] In Wilson's play, as in the French and German broadsides, emblem eleven marks the Spaniard as "Ambitious"; emblem five, "A Peacocke," suggests his pride or vanity; and emblem twelve colours him "Bloodthirstie and tyrannous." But being typical (and typological) "Signiors of Spaine," Ambition, Pride, and Tyranny also wish to gull the "English Lutherans" of their wives. In exhibiting the hypersexuality attributed to the Spanish in much Black Legend propaganda, Wilson's lords and their pages thus embody "Naturall kinde" number six, "A Foxe to Deceive women." As the emblem warns, although the Spaniard's "pockey selfe ... is wholly infected," to deceive women is still his "continual studie" (B–B2v). Although the personal emblem of one of Wilson's Spanish lords is, probably not coincidentally, a "Peacocke," I do not mean to suggest that the transmission here is direct – at least not from any extant English text. It is sufficient to note that in the manner of the commonplaces represented in the Continental precursors of the Englished *Pageant*, Wilson's stick-figure Spaniards play upon typologies that have been widely distributed over the course of several decades in multiple languages.

In its efforts to cultivate English national identity, the most significant feature of Wilson's play may be the way it constructs England within the global imperial contest in which it had only recently begun to factor, for when Shame, Treachery, and Terror tumble onto the stage, they bear a shield emblazoned *Non sufficit orbis* (G2v) (see figure 9.3). Signifying "the world is not enough," the motto had been added to the Spanish Habsburgs' traditional arms, *Plus Ultra*, "yet still further," following Philip II's 1580 unification of Spain and Portugal.[29] Similarly ridiculed in *The Coppie of the Anti-Spaniard*, the ideal of "universal Monarchy" – the dream of a globally unified Christendom – had been advanced by such noted theorists of empire as St Augustine, Joachim of Fiore, and Dante Alighieri. Well into early modernity the dream of an *immensum imperii corpus* – with the Spanish monarchy at its head – would be promoted by such "Hispanized" figures as England's Cardinal William Allen and the Florentine Dominican Tomasso Campanella.[30]

With respect to the appearance of *Non sufficit orbis* in Wilson's play, it is possible to propose a fairly direct line of transmission, for the playwright cribs an episode from *Sir Francis Drake's 1585–86 West India Voyage*, published immediately upon Drake's return by the Stratfordian Richard Field, who may have been jailed for rushing its diplomatically sensitive content into print before it had cleared government censors. Soon to be published with official sanction by Richard Hakluyt, Wilson's adaptation recalls the response of several English seamen who had glimpsed the newly enhanced Habsburg arms painted on an interior wall while ransacking the Spanish governor's mansion in Santo Domingo.[31] As reported by Thomas Cates, "by some of our companie it was told [to the Spaniards that] if the Queene of England would resolutely prosecute the warres against the king of Spaine, he should be forced to lay aside that proude and unreasonable reaching of his, for he should finde more then inough to do, to keep that which he had alreadie, as by the present example of their lost towne."[32]

Much in the spirit of Cates's narrative, Wilson's rendering humorously recasts English plunder as an honourable response to Spain's "proude and unreasonable reaching." Performing England's role as a bulwark against Habsburg imperial aims, Wilson "coppies" Drake's 1585 privateering raid in such a way as to prefigure England's temporally more recent Armada victory. As the *Non sufficit orbis* emblem circulates from Europe to the New World, and from one discursive genre to another, the official significance of the "high" universal mission Cardinal Allen so admired is emptied out in order to be reconstituted as low satirical humour. It is, after all, English women whom Shame, Treachery, and Terror – being typical Spaniards – covet in *The Three Lords and The Three Ladies*, nearly as much as they desire English lucre.

Figure 9.3 *Non sufficit orbis*. The Spanish motto as described in Thomas Cates's narrative, *Sir Francis Drake's West India Voyage* (1589). Reproduced by publisher Richard Field, the emblem made its way to the stage in Robert Wilson's contemporary play, *The Three Lords and the Three Ladies of London* (1590). Courtesy of the John Carter Brown Library at Brown University.

Suggesting both the circular nature of the propaganda enterprise and the way translation and publication could be geared to local and temporal exigencies, we find the West India Voyage incident repeated in *A Pageant of Spanish Humours*. Occurring some twenty-eight years after the first verified publication of the German and French versions, and eleven after its incorporation in Wilson's play, the *Pageant* also describes the episode narrated by Cates. "As appears by the writing of their own Historiographers," he writes, "the avarice of the Late Romans, Turks and Heathens, were but toys to his [the Spaniard's], not only for money, but also to scrape to himself every thing else, and so tyrannize over all the world, which they also shewe in the Indies, where above the Spanish Armies at S. Domingo it is written, *To*[do] *es nuestro to*[do] *es mío*: As also thereon standeth a horse, with his hinder feete in the worlde, and seemeth with his fore feet, to leape out of the same, and of his mouth this motto. The world doth not suffice me, whereby they shewe their insatiable covetousnesse" (B3v).

A Pageant of Spanish Humours thus reveals several aspects of the process by which the Black Legend achieved and maintained its rhetorical force. First, "the writing of their own [Spanish] Historiographers" is scanned for episodes that may be turned, in rhetorician Thomas Wilson's formula, "cleane contrarie,"[33] in order to reveal the "true nature" of Spain's imperial mission. This "evidence" is then confirmed via the experience of Englishmen abroad, who verify the very qualities and kinds they are looking for: Spanish Ambition, Pride, and Tyranny. Upon publication, the account becomes canonical, entering a repertoire of Hispanophobic commonplaces that circulates within the public sphere until, "all telling veritie," as the Preface to *A Pageant* claims, "is landed on our English shore, wherein she is pleased to make a further progresse" (A3), and the "truth" of the Black Legend, having been emblazoned a generation and a half earlier in the Low Countries, has been translated to an English national context.

While the political cartooning of Wilson's city comedy sounds a number of the notes typical of Hispanophobia, *The Three Lords and Three Ladies of London* lacks the linkage of race and religion that soon makes the Black Legend an even more powerfully effective propaganda apparatus. Robert Greene's 1589 *Spanish Masquerado* makes this connection explicit. Dedicated to "the Right Worshipfull M. Hugh Ofley, Sherrife of the Citie of London," Greene's pageant clearly fuses religious and racialist elements for the edification of an English public still processing the meaning of their deliverance from Spain's Enterprise.

Declaring his own membership in this post-Armada public, Greene writes in the printed edition, "Hitherto ... I have writte of loves," but "now ... I have adventured to discover my conscience in Religion" (A3). The *Masquerado* then opens with a highly compressed staging of Reformation history, describing the faults of "this Monster ... Antechrist [sic] the Pope" (B2). After proclaiming the virtues of "Henrie the eight ... who seeing the abominatiõ of that proud Antechrist ... [had] pulled down [the Romanists'] sumptuous buildings ... [and] subverted their estate" (B2–B3), Greene's masque introduces none other than "Phillip king of Spaine," whom we find attired "like an Hermite ... riding towards the Church on his Mule, attended on onely with ... his slaves that are Moores" (B3). A figure reminiscent of Spenser's Archimago, the Philip of *The Spanish Masquerado* has been "housed from his infancie in the darke and obscure dungeon of Papistry." Taking "the Pope for Peter's successor," Philip is inspired to gather "a great Armado" of "Shippes huge and monstrous" (B3–B4).

When, "like brute beasts," his Spanish masquers cause "the Indians to be hunted with dogs, some to be torne with horses, some to have their hands cut off" (E2v–r), Greene copies the Las Casean cruelty topos. He also joins the spiritual darkness of Spain's Roman Catholic faith with the skin colour of Philip's "Moores." To adapt Kim Hall, who notes how "the trope of blackness" could be "applied not only to dark-skinned Africans but to Native Americans, Indians, Spanish, and even Irish and Welsh as groups that needed to be marked as other," *The Spanish Masquerado* demonstrates how the Black Legend "draws power from England's ongoing negotiations of African difference and from the implied color comparison therein."[34] Just as *The Anti-Spaniard* had incited "the fortunate and flourishing armies" of the French king "to go and abate the pride and insolencie of these [Spanish] Negroes" (35), Greene "colours" the Spanish in order to mark their ethnicity with an African taint. It is a strategy employed at virtually the same moment by his contemporary, Edward Daunce, in the *Brief Discourse of the Spanish State* (1590), published by Shakespeare's associate Richard Field. "The *Mores* in eight monthes conquered *Spaine*," Daunce wrote, "and ... the *Spaniards* were eight hundred years before they recovered that losse: during which time, we must not thinke that the *Negroes* sent for women out of *Aphrick*."[35] When Greene's pageant concludes by coupling the notion that a "mercifull God" had made England "like Eden, a second Paradise" (G4) with a view of Spain as England's religious and ethical opposite, Greene's *Pageant* ritually reforms the "Citie of London" by setting England's purified religion against the superstition of Spanish Catholicism and casting English nationality in opposition to a Spain ethnicized at its root by its Moorish (read: African) antecedents.

Turning finally to *The Famous Chronicle of King Edward the First* (published in 1593, but performed as early as 1590), we find George Peele emphasizing the reformation of the English capital city in yet more material terms.[36] In order to cleanse public memory of prior Anglo-Hispanic complementarity, Peele rewrites the significance of the marriage of Edward I (who reigned 1272–1307), and his Spanish wife Eleanor of Castile (ca 1244–90). How thoroughly Peele's play reforms public memory may be witnessed by juxtaposing it to Raphael Holinshed's assessment of the life of Eleanor of Castile, published just three years earlier. "In the nineteenth yeare of king Edward," Holinshed writes, "queen Elianor king Edwards wife died upon saint Andrews eeven ... neere to Lincolne ... [H]aving now lost the iewel which he most esteemed, he returned towards London to accompanie the corps unto Westminster, where it was buried ... She was a godlie and modest princesse, full of pitie, and one that shewed much favor to the English nation ... In everie towne and place, where the corps rested by the waie, the king caused a crosse of cunning workmanship to be erected in remembrance of hir, and in the same was a picture of hir ingraven. Two of the like crosses were set up at London, one at Charing and the other at Westcheape."[37] As Holinshed records, no fewer than three public memorials to Queen Eleanor's life were visible in London: her tomb in Westminster Abbey, and the city's two Eleanor Crosses, one at Charing and one at Westcheape.

Midway through Peele's *Famous Chronicle* we encounter in London Queen "Elinor" and Princess "Jone" (historically, Joan of Acre, 1272–1307) making their way across "Charing greene." Edward I's queen and daughter have been transported from the play's opening setting in Wales, where Elinor had arrived, much in the manner of Philip in Greene's pageant, in "in her litter bourne by Moores." While in Wales, Elinor had plotted the brutal murder of a third female character, "London Maris," the lord mayor's wife. Now, on London's Charing Commons, Princess Jone confronts her mother with her crime. In a hyperbolic denial of any connection with Maris's murder, Elinor blasphemes, "Gape earth and swallow me, and let my soule / Sincke down to Hell if I were Autor of / The womans Tragedy" (18.2197–8). "Sincke" Elinor does. As her astonished daughter Jone looks on, the earth opens to swallow her. Following Elinor's descent, the mould of Charing Green "is new closed up again" (18.2201).

It is not difficult to imagine how this symbolic act must have been staged – the boy actor playing Jone affecting disbelief while the one personating the queen drops beneath the boards. In the next scene, with Eleanor's rising again at Potters Heath, Peele's audience would have seen an amazed Elinor first "bewaile her sinfull life" (20.2289) and then be shriven by none other than her husband Longshankes. In a scene much like the one Shakespeare will devise for *Measure for Measure*, Edward disguises himself as Elinor's "ghostlie Father" (21.2353) in order to take his wife's confession that she had previously committed incest with Edward's brother, Edmund, "uppon [her] bridal couch and by [her own] concent" (23.2476), and that their daughter Jone had been a bastard "baslie borne, begotten of a Frier" (23.2494).

Peele's *Famous Chronicle* thus embodies several additional ways in which the Black Legend could be mobilized in order to reform once-Catholic England temporally and spatially. By resurrecting a widely known historical figure of Spanish ancestry, Peele recalls a long tradition of Anglo-Hispanic interrelation and alliance. By representing an "Elinor" whose typically "Spanish" sexual transgressions bring shame upon the English royal house, Peele calls into question the legitimacy of a reign three hundred years in the past. Casting Eleanor as a villainess capable of unspeakable treachery, cruelty, and depravity, the play rewrites English history in order to stage, and, as important, to make public, hand-in-hand with "typical" Roman Catholic corruption, the cruelty being promoted in anti-Hispanic polemic as an essential Hispanic "qualitie."

Peele's "sincking of Queene Elinor, who sunck at Charingcrosse, and rose again at Pottershith, now named Queenehith," thus lays claim to the Eleanor Crosses celebrated by Holinshed – which marked the twelve stops made by the Anglo-Castilian queen's funeral cortege between Lincoln and London. Three of the original gothic crosses may still be viewed today, at Geddington, Northampton, and Walton, while a reconstructed Eleanor Cross marks the entry to London's Charing Cross Station. Peele's play endows these spaces with new, reformed – that is, exclusionary, Protestant, and nationalist – meaning. By way of the original cultural landmark, which also delimited the geographical centre of the City of London and would have been known to virtually everyone attending *The Famous Chronicle*'s performance, Peele enacts England's religio-political reformation by rewriting the historical significance of a three-hundred-year-old sign of Anglo-Spanish cooperation as an early type of Spanish invasion.

Though little known today, Peele's vision of Eleanor's sinking appears to have achieved a measure of cultural influence. By 1600, a ballad version, to be sung to the tune of "Gentle and Courteous" – which must surely have been an ironic musical reference – had appeared as "The Lamentable fall of Queene Elnor, vvho for her pride and vvickednesse, by Gods iudgment, sunke into the ground at Charing crosse, and rose vp againe at Queene hiue." Confirming the ballad's popularity, reprints survive from 1628, 1629, 1658, and 1664 (see figure 9.4). These last two editions are of particular interest because Charing Cross, pictured clearly in the broadside, had been pulled down in 1643, when, during the English Civil War, Parliament's Committee for the Demolition of Monuments of Superstition and Idolatry undertook further reform of England's public spaces.[38]

By ridiculing Spanish policy, dichotomizing and ethnicizing Spanish nationality, and erasing any signs of prior Anglo-Spanish complementarity – whether commercial, religious, or dynastic – Robert Wilson, Robert Greene, and George Peele remap and reconfigure England's public spaces as a reformed, nationalist landscape. It is as if they had borrowed their rhetorical strategies directly from another tract purportedly brought over from France, *A Comparison of the English and Spanish Nation* (1589), from which this chapter takes its epigraph. As he "lively deciphered" the "nature of both Nations" (A3v–r, D3), translator Robert Ashley wrote, "In breefe, such is this comparison that if some Rhetoritian would employ his eloquence in framing of a long and lively Antithesis, he could not in the world find a subject more sortable to his purpose then the comparing of our conditions with those of this mongrell generation" (D3v). "I would say more," he continues, "were it not for displeasing of the delicate sort: and we have here set the Spaniardes on stage ... to furnish our selves with laughter at their charges. And I pray you what man is there so melancholy, that could forbeare laughter" (E1v).

Framing their own "long and lively" antitheses, Wilson, Greene, and Peele intervene theatrically in a complex, interwoven, and evolving historical relationship. The rhetorical strategies their dramas employ – the antithetical logic of which turns "cleane contrary" virtually every index of Spanish identity as the opposite of everything essentially English – run through the range of tropes and figures that comprise the Black Legend, even as they demonstrate how the raw material of Hispanophobia could circulate from nation to nation and from genre to genre within the sphere of early modern print. From print these Hispanophobic commonplaces moved to the London stage, and from the stage they soon found their way into popular culture via booksellers, ballad-hawkers, and apparently, even by street-singers. As they rehearse Spain's colonial atrocities and its mixed racial heritage, at once staging Iberia's culture as alien and performing the consequences of Spanish imperial domination, these dramatic productions and broadsides, like the Black Legend tracts from which they borrow, overwrite England's own participation in a common Catholic past, erase its own applications of exemplary violence, and mask its own mixed ethnic heritage.

I do not wish to imply that England's post-Armada theatre functioned as merely some sort of official state apparatus; London's multiple theatregoing publics would have interpreted the plays they saw performed in multiple ways. As the Office of Revels was well aware, and as postmodern critics have so often pointed out, the stage could be a site of resistance to government policy as readily as of support. But in the case of the Cecil network, some of the hands that penned pamphlets and polemics also wrote plays. By the end of Elizabeth

Figure 9.4 The "lamentable fall of Queen Elenor." Surviving in editions from 1628, 1629, 1658, and 1664, this adaptation of George Peele's history play, *The Famous Chronicle of Edward I* (ca 1590), associated the Eleanor Cross at Charing Green with Spanish villainy in opposition to the virtues it traditionally commemorated. By permission of the University of Glasgow Library, Special Collections.

Tudor's reign, the Hispanophobic typologies observable in these productions and many others like them would become part of the common vocabulary of English dramaturgy.[39]

III

"Plague of those pestilent pamphlets," declares the Black Knight in Thomas Middleton's *A Game at Chess* (1624), "those are they / That wound our cause to the heart" (2.2.97–8).[40] Recognized immediately by Globe playgoers as Don Diego Sarmiento de Gondomar, Spain's resident ambassador to England 1613–18 and 1620–2, Middleton's character vents a frustration echoing Richard Verstegen's *True Causes* complaint of 1592. In the context of the so-called Spanish Match – James I's attempt to engineer the third Anglo-Hispanic dynastic alliance in little more than a century – the lines ironically celebrate an English propaganda triumph. It is in relation to the astonishing diplomatic collapse of ca 1623–4, during which nearly two decades of patient Jacobean calculation would come to naught, that the effectiveness of the Elizabethan "printing, playing, and preaching" formula may be gauged.

With the ascension of James Stuart to the throne of England, the Anglo-Spanish ceasefire had been immediate. If adventurers like Walter Raleigh, Richard Hawkins, and others who stood to gain from a continuation of Elizabethan privateering practices objected loudly, "probably a majority of the political nation," as Kenneth Andrews observes, "welcomed the end of a burdensome war, looking forward to a resurgence of trade which very soon became a fact as the Iberian ports were opened to English ships."[41] The English had begun to weary of foreign involvements during the period of dearth and social unrest that came with Elizabeth's later reign, and in 1597–8 they had fallen just short of coming to terms with the French, Dutch, and Spanish at the conference that produced the Treaty of Vervins.[42] Confirming his interest in attaining the *status quo ante bellum*, almost immediately upon formalizing the *Pax Hispanica* with the 1604 Treaty of London, the Anglo-Scottish king began to weigh the possibilities for the Habsburg union he would covet throughout his reign.[43]

For seven years James would entertain the prospect of marrying his eldest son Henry, the Prince of Wales, with two Spanish Habsburg princesses: first to be suggested was the Infanta Ana, Philip III's eldest daughter; subsequently her younger sister, the Infanta María, was considered. In spite of the threat to Jacobean ecumenicalism posed by the Gunpowder Plot, strictures against Catholic worship had been gradually relaxed, and overt expressions of hostility towards Spain remained proscribed.[44] Following Henry Stuart's untimely death in November 1612, and the following year's celebration of the marriage of James's daughter Elizabeth to Frederick, the elector Palatine, the notion of a Spanish Match for his younger son Charles had been revived. By 1617 John Digby had carried a draft of the proposed marriage treaty to Madrid.[45] Unhappily, deliberations coincided with both the outbreak of the Bohemian War and the trial and execution of Sir Walter Raleigh, which followed hard upon his ill-advised Guiana incursion. The British king's un-English "appeasement" of Spain, ca 1618–24, precisely the period in which the Spanish Match was being negotiated, prompted an explosion of anti-Hispanic propaganda that may have surpassed the output of the 1590s.[46]

Perhaps not surprisingly, these years also saw a spate of new "Spanish plays."[47] The playwrights who were now the elder statesmen of Jacobean drama had themselves experienced the Hispanophobic flush of the Armada crisis. As their later work demonstrates, these dramatists were well acquainted with the rhetorical and representational strategies of the generation ahead of them. William Rowley's *All's Lost by Lust* (ca 1618–19), to take one example, staged the Spanish ethos after the manner of Edward Daunce, and Edmund Spenser, whose *A View of the State of Ireland* (ca 1597) also racialized "mingled" Spain,[48] locating Spanish decadence in the original mixing from which that nation had been born. Middleton and Rowley together produced *The Changeling* (1622), probably the most rabidly Hispanophobic play of the era excepting Middleton's anti-Spanish tour de force, *A Game at Chess*. The year 1623 also gave English readers new editions of Thomas Kyd's *Spanish Tragedy* (ca 1587–92) and Thomas Heywood's celebration of the Elizabethan years, *If You Know Not Me You Know Nobody* (ca 1605), which was published twice that year, as well as the first printed edition of Webster's *Duchess of Malfi* (ca 1613) and the revival of Thomas Dekker's *Match Mee in London* (ca 1611),[49] works that similarly grounded their arguments in the excesses of Spanish blood. While the appearance of this cluster of Spanish plays is historically significant, it is *A Game at Chess* that reveals both how well the anti-Hispanic rhetoric of the Elizabethan years had been mastered by England's Jacobean playwrights and how thoroughly anti-Hispanism had been absorbed by the theatregoing public.

In what will be his final dramatic production, Middleton raises the ghosts of the Elizabethan past in order to bring them into typological (and ideological) relation with the Jacobean present. Alluding repeatedly to the print wars, Middleton incorporates references to all that had transpired between England and Spain "since '88" – including the Armada, the Dutch Wars, the Lopez and Gunpowder Plots, the covert activities of Jesuit missionaries, Spain's New World conquests, English privateering successes, and Raleigh's unfortunate trial. Representing allegorically the concluding set of moves in a match translated from the bloody waters of the 1580s and 1590s to the diplomatic channels of the 1620s, Middleton "discovers" as black-and-white binaries a historically much "greyer" episode in which war had been carried on by other means. In the process, his play elevates the collapse of James's marriage negotiations into the apocalyptic register of the Armada crisis, thereby according to a failure of "British" policy the mythic status of England's signal event.

From our historical remove, the importance of *A Game at Chess* lies as much in the quality and quantity of extant contemporary response as it does in the play's dramaturgic innovation, for it is in the remarks of contemporaries – including English, Spanish, and Continental observers – that the long-term effectiveness of the concerted rhetorical effort to recast England's traditional ally as its traditional enemy may be judged.

How deeply Middleton's satire cut is revealed by Gondomar's successor, Ambassador Don Carlos Coloma, in the letter he posts to the Conde-Duque Olivares on 20 August 1624. Coloma reports, "The actors whom they call here 'the King's men' have recently acted, and are still acting, in London a play that so many people come to see, that there were more than 3000 persons there on the day that the audience was smallest."[50] He observes, "The subject of the play is a game of chess, with white houses and black houses, their kings and other pieces, acted by the players, and the king of the blacks has easily been taken for our lord the king, because of his youth, dress, and other details" (194). Alongside the play's "remarkable acts of sacrilege and ... other abominations," the ambassador describes how the actors "summoned St Ignatius from hell, and when he found himself again in the world, the first thing he did was to rape one of his female penitents" and "showed ... the cruelty of Spain and the treachery of Spaniards, and all of this was set forth so personally that they did not even exclude royal persons" (194–5). Quickly identifying the play's anti-Catholic posturing and mobilization of the Las Casean stereotypes with which his nation had been so often painted by Dutch, French, and English propagandists, Coloma marvels at both the play's astonishing popularity, wherein "during these last four days more then 12,000 persons have all heard the play ... including all the nobility still in London," and the way the play's audiences were being affected. "All these people come out of the theatre so inflamed against Spain," he writes, "that, as a few Catholics have told me who went secretly to see the play, my person would not be safe in the streets" (197). Concluding, Ambassador Coloma even remarks how he had been greeted by "some filthy songs that Buckingham makes his musicians sing" (197).

As England and Spain had been working towards accord for a generation – having walked right to the brink of a new dynastic union – we must ask how it was that, upon attending a performance of *A Game at Chess*, "all these people" had "come out of the theatre so inflamed." The major contributing factor must have been that their passions had been tutored (and Tudored) in particular ways of remembering, and especially, of forgetting the English past, even as they had been conditioned to see the Spanish as their now "traditional" ethnic opposites.[51] If the 1590s had been a time of scarcity, disease, and dissatisfaction, what was now remembered was Gloriana's militarism in the face of the Spanish threat – a threat the English had been persuaded was now repeating itself in the dynastic manoeuvring associated with the Spanish Match.[52]

Among the English reports on *A Game at Chess*, John Woolley's letter to William Trumbull of 6 August 1624, written just one day after the play had opened, may be most revealing of this phenomenon. "All the nues I have hearde since my comming to toune is of a nue Play acted by his Maiesties servants," Woolley writes. "It is called a game at Chess, but it may be a Vox popoly, for by reporte it is 6. tymes worse against the spanyard."[53] In describing the play as "a Vox popoly," Woolley, like Middleton's Black Knight, makes a direct connection between *A Game at Chess* and the period's Hispanophobic propaganda effort. Indeed, he interprets the play's enthusiastic reception in relation to the most infamous Hispanophobic publications of his day, the two parts of Thomas Scott's *Vox Populi*.

Among Scott's many anti-Spanish tracts, his *Vox Populi* satires – the publication of which had so offended James that a warrant had been issued for the pamphleteer's arrest – stand out as signposts marking an important shift within England's public sphere.[54] If Cecil's propaganda network had shaped opinion largely on behalf of monarchical policies, Scott's aim was to move public opinion and monarchical policy towards the parliamentary interests in which Middleton and a number of his playwriting associates were also invested.[55] In order to do so, they had to unseat the "Spanish faction," a coalition of native Catholic peers they believed to be exerting undue influence on their king.[56] It was to unsettle these "Hispaniolated" interests that these English "Puritans" turned to the Hispanophobic rhetorical strategies of the past.

If, in Elizabethan Hispanophobic discourse, proximity to Africa had begun to signify the miscegenated "blackness" of Spain, we find the propagandist Scott returning to precisely this note in *The Second Part of Vox Populi* (1624). In this satirical meeting of "a Spanish Parliament," one of Scott's fictionalized Spanish dukes proposes, "It may be they hate us for the same cause, that France, Germany, Italie, and the rest of the Countries of Europe, for that many of us are discended of the Moorish race" (13). While certainly the colour of the Spanish House could be generalized by viewers in terms of a moral "blackness," for a culture that had made *limpieza de sangre*, purity of blood, a defining virtue, this obvious racial association would have been both ironic and doubly insulting – all the more so because *limpieza* was not necessarily linked to skin colour in early modern Spain.[57]

A Game at Chess may have been seen by "one seventh of the total population of London,"[58] with attendance at the play cutting across social, economic, and confessional boundaries. If we can construe from audience affect, the reaction of England's various publics to the play's performance suggests that by 1624 opposition to Spain gave significant numbers of James Stuart's subjects their surest sense of *feeling* English.[59] Contributing to this structure of feeling was the black/white binary upon which Middleton's drama was built.[60] As Gary Taylor has observed, we see in *A Game at Chess*, "for the first time in English literature," a work embodying "an organized and unified whiteness."[61] If this whiteness is not positioned against African blackness per se, Middleton's Spaniards, like those of England's Hispanophobic propaganda, are blackened – as Hall suggests and as Spanish contemporaries appear to have recognized – by African proximity.

Ironies permeate the Anglo–Spanish relationship throughout the Jacobean years. A principal model for James's union of the "British" kingdoms had been the Hispano-Lusitanian linkage of 1580. Scorned as an example of Spanish "tyranny" in countless propaganda tracts, the dynastic joining had been identified by royal jurists as "the likest to ours."[62] And as Barbara Fuchs has shown us, the Maurophobic colouring of Spain as an "African" nation was often accomplished by "turning inside out" Spain's standard modes of self-representation.[63] As comprehensively as Middleton's dramatic vision condenses Protestant historical memory, what *A Game of Chess* wilfully forgets – its black-and-white binaries not withstanding – is that the Jacobean era was characterized nearly as much by Hispanophilic aesthetic tastes as it was by Hispanophobic resentments.[64] So fixed were they on Spain's perceived colonial successes that the English, as Brian Lockey's chapter in this volume demonstrates, even turned to Spain's management of their Morisco problem in dealing with the native population in Ireland.[65] In no sphere of English life was this period's Hispanophilia more prevalent than in English theatrical culture, where the documented influence of Spanish writers was substantial.[66] And yet, in spite of the positive modes of Anglo-Hispanic cultural exchange that also characterized the years of James's reign, the popularity of Middleton's final play suggests that if England's conflicted publics could not come to accord over what it meant to be "British" or "Christian," they could, during this singularly theatrical moment, agree that since they were not "black," they could no longer entertain, in the words attributed to the earl of Essex's ghost by Thomas Scott, "Treaties of Matches, or whatsoever else with the perfidious and daungerous Spanish Nation."[67]

NOTES

1 R[obert] Ashley, *A Comparison of the English and Spanish Nation* (1589), E1v.
2 See David Cressy, *Bonfires & Bells: National Memory and the Protestant Calendar in Elizabethan and Stuart England* (Phoenix Mill, Stroud: Sutton Publishing, 2004), 110–29.
3 See Denis B. Woodfield, *Surreptitious Printing in England* (New York: Bibliographical Society of America, 1971), 34–45.
4 The phrase is from H.W. trans., *A Pageant of Spanish Humours, Wherein are naturally described and liuely portrayed, the kinds and quallities of a signior of Spaine* (London, 1599).
5 Thomas Hylland Eriksen, *Ethnicity and Nationalism: Anthropological Perspectives* (London: Pluto, 1993), distinguishes processes of "complementarisation," which recognize difference as "an asset" in order to produce a "shared field" for "We–You" relationships, from the process of "dichotomisation," which "essentially expresses an Us–them kind of relationship" (26–8).
6 The roots of the Black Legend in Las Casas are well established. For recent work, see Margaret R. Greer, Walter D. Mignolo, and Maureen Quilligan, *Rereading the Black Legend: The Discourses of Religious and Racial Difference in the Renaissance Empires* (Chicago: University of Chicago Press, 2007), 5–9; Benjamin Schmidt, *Innocence Abroad: The Dutch Imagination and the New World, 1570–1670* (Cambridge: Cambridge University Press, 2001), 87–99; and my own *English Renaissance Drama and the Specter of Spain: Ethnopoetics and Empire* (Philadelphia: University of Pennsylvania Press, 2009), 44–8.
7 OED sense 1 a. Of or relating to the affections or emotions, esp. as contrasted with the intellect or rational faculty; emotional.
8 "Fictive Ethnicity" is Etienne Balibar's phrase. See Étienne Balibar and Immanuel Wallerstein. *Race, Nation, Class: Ambiguous Identities*, trans. Chris Turner (London: Verso, 1991), 96–7.
9 A.E.B. Coldiron, "Public Sphere/Contact Zone: Habermas, Early Print, and Verse Translation," *Criticism* 46, no. 2 (Spring 2004): 207–22.
10 Quoted in John N. King, *Foxe's Book of Martyrs and Early Modern Print Culture* (Cambridge: Cambridge University Press, 2006), 70.
11 See the relevant DNB entries.
12 H.R. Hoppe, "John Wolfe, Printer and Publisher," *Library* 4, no. 14 (1933), 241–74.
13 Lisa Ferraro Parmellee, *Good Newes from Fraunce: French Anti-league Propaganda in Late Elizabethan England* (Rochester: University of Rochester Press, 1996), 32.
14 Ibid., 50; Barbara Fuchs, "The Spanish Race," in Greer, Mignolo, and Quilligan, *Rereading*, 88–98.
15 Parmellee, *Good Newes*, 33.

16 Ibid., 31.
17 OED sense 1. Of or relating to the people of Germany.
18 See Wolfgang Harms, *Deutsche Illustrierte Flugblätter des 16. und 17. Jahrhunderts* (Munichen: Kraus International Publications, 1980) 2:72–7. Thanks to Bethany Wiggin for sharing this remarkable broadside at the Clark Library conference that inspired this volume. Philippe Erlanger, *The Age of Courts and Kings: Manners and Morals 1558–1715* (London: Weidenfeld & Nicolson, 1967), attributes the *Emblesmes* to Simon Mollard, finding them already circulating France, ca 1560. Fernand Braudel, *The Mediterranean and the Mediterranean World in the Age of Philip II*, trans. Siân Reynolds, 2 vols. (1949; New York: Harper and Row, 1973) 2:833, observed that Signior Espagnol was present in the south of France, ca 1605.
19 See Griffin, *English Renaissance Drama*, 103–6.
20 William O. Beeman, "The Anthropology of Theater and Spectacle," *Annual Review of Anthropology* 22 (1993): 386.
21 After Bruno Latour, *Reassembling the Social: An Introduction to Actor-Network Theory* (Oxford: Oxford University Press): "Relating to one group or another is an ongoing process of uncertain, fragile, controversial, and ever-shifting ties" (28).
22 If London theatres attracted a microcosm of English society, it is important to imagine these spaces as of "jostling interactivity" and "multiple kinds of expression." See Bronwen Wilson and Paul Yachnin, eds., *Making Publics in Early Modern Europe: People, Things, Forms of Knowledge* (New York: Routledge, 2010), 5–9.
23 Arthur F. Kinney and David W. Swain, eds., *Tudor England: An Encyclopedia* (New York: Garland, 2001), 693; Andrew Gurr, "The Shakespearean Stage," in *The Norton Shakespeare*, ed. Stephen Greenblatt et al. (New York: W.W. Norton, 1997), 1031.
24 For a fuller discussion of these plays, see Griffin, *English Renaissance Drama*, 49–66.
25 See David Bevington's introductions in *John Lyly, Endymion*, ed. David Bevington (Manchester: Manchester University Press, 1996) 27–35; and *John Lyly, Galatea/Midas*, ed. George K. Hunter and David Bevington, 132–38 (Manchester: Manchester University Press, 2000).
26 See Jonathan Burton, *Traffic and Turning: Islam and English Drama, 1579–1626* (Newark: University of Delaware Press, 2005), 219–21; Daniel J. Vitkus, *Turning Turk: English Theater and the Multicultural Mediterranean, 1570–1630* (New York: Palgrave Macmillan, 2003), 173–7; Lloyd Edward Kermode, *Aliens and Englishness in Elizabethan Drama* (Cambridge: Cambridge University Press, 2009), 59–78. See also, *DNB*, "Robert Wilson."
27 Database of Early Modern English Playbooks, http://deep.sas.upenn.edu/search.php.
28 This correlation suggests how thoroughly encoded these typologies had become by the late sixteenth century. The circulation of the German and French texts

suggests one means of dissemination, but equally relevant is the recognition that the English themselves were circulating through the contested Habsburg territories, bound as they were to Continental military, commercial, and religious relationships.

29 See David Harris Sacks, "'To Deduce a Colonie': Richard Hakluyt's Godly Mission in Its Contexts, c. 1580–1616," in *Richard Hakluyt and Travel Writing in Early Modern Europe*, ed. A. Daniel Karey and Claire Jowitt, 201–9, Hakluyt Society, extra ser. no. 47 (Aldershot: Ashgate, 2012).

30 See Anthony Pagden, *Lords of All the World: Ideologies of Empire in Spain, Britain and France, c. 1500–c. 1800* (New Haven, CT: Yale University Press, 1995), 13.

31 Thomas Cates, *A Summarie and True Discourse of Sir Frances Drakes West Indian Voyage. Wherein were taken, the Townes of Saint Iago, Sancto Domingo, Cartagena & Saint Augustine* (London: Richard Field, 1589), in *Sir Francis Drake's West Indian Voyage, 1585–86*, ed. Mary Frear Keeler (London: Hakluyt Society, 1981), 245.

32 Ibid., 245–6.

33 Originating in the mid-sixteenth century (as a term in rhetoric, denoting the turning of an argument against the person who put it forward), and derived from Latin *inversio*(n-), from the verb invertere, inversion was a favoured trope of the Reformation. *OED*, sense 1a: 1598, J. Florio, *Worlde of Wordes, Inuersione*, "an inuersion, a turning inside out, or upside downe, a misplacing sense. 2a: 1551, T. Wilson, *Rule of Reason* sig. Ij^v, "You maie confute the same by inuersion, that is to say, turning his taile cleane contrarie."

34 Kim F. Hall, *Things of Darkness: Economies of Race and Gender in Early Modern England* (Ithaca, NY: Cornell University Press, 1995), 7.

35 Edward Daunce, *A Brief Discourse of the Spanish State* (London, 1590), 31.

36 See George Peele, *The Famous Chronicle of King Edward the First*, in *The Life and Works of George Peele*, ed. Charles Prouty Tyler (New Haven, CT: Yale University Press, 1952–70), 2:69–170; E.K. Chambers, *The Elizabethan Stage*, 4 vols. (Oxford: Clarendon, 1923), 3:460.

37 Raphael Holinshed, *Chronicles of England, Scotland and Ireland* (repr., London: J. Johnson, 1807–8), 2:492.

38 William Cobbett and John Wright, eds. *Parliamentary History of England: 1066–1803*. (1808; New York: Johnson Reprint, 1966), 3:162.

39 See Griffin, *English Renaissance Drama*, 207–10.

40 *A Game at Chess* quotations are from Thomas Middleton, *A Game at Chess*, ed. T.H. Howard-Hill (Manchester: Manchester University Press, 1993).

41 See Kenneth R. Andrews, *Trade, Plunder and Settlement: Maritime Enterprise and the Genesis of the British Empire, 1480–1630* (Cambridge: Cambridge University Press, 1984), 253–4.

42 See R.B. Wernham, *The Return of the Armadas: The Last Years of the Elizabethan War against Spain, 1595–1603* (Oxford: Oxford University Press, 1994), 205–9, 214–31.

43 See Lynn Redworth, *The Prince and the Infanta: The Cultural Politics of the Spanish Match* (New Haven, CT: Yale University Press, 2003), 7–9; Alexander Samson, ed., *The Spanish Match: Prince Charles's Journey to Madrid, 1623* (Aldershot: Ashgate, 2006), 1.
44 Louis B. Wright, "Propaganda against James I's 'Appeasement' of Spain," *Huntington Library Quarterly* 6 (1942–3): 149–72.
45 Redworth, *Prince and the Infanta*, 10–18.
46 See Jerzy Limon, *Dangerous Matter: English Drama and Politics in 1623/4* (Cambridge: Cambridge University Press, 1986), 1–19; A.A. Bromham and Zara Bruzzi, *The Changeling and the Years of Crisis, 1619–1624: A Hieroglyph of Britain* (London: Pinter Publishers, 1990), 8–9.
47 Annabel Patterson, *Censorship and Interpretation* (Madison: University of Wisconsin Press, 1984), 85. Among the moment's many "Spanish plays" are Fletcher's *Rule a Wife and Have a Wife* (ca 1624), *The Chances* (ca 1617–25), *The Island Princess* (ca 1619–21), *The Pilgrim* (1621), Fletcher and Massinger's *The Spanish Curate* (ca 1622), Massinger's *The Duke of Milan* (ca 1621–3), *The Renegado* (1624), and *The Spanish Viceroy* (1624, unlicensed), Dekker's *The Noble Spanish Soldier* (ca 1622), and Middleton, Rowley, Ford, and Dekker's *The Spanish Gypsy* (1623).
48 Edmund Spenser, *A View of the State of Ireland*, ed. Andrew Hadfield and Willy Maley (Oxford: Blackwell, 1997), 49–50.
49 "An Old Playe," relicensed 21 August 1623. See Gerald Eades Bentley, *The Jacobean and Caroline Stage* (Oxford: Clarendon, 1941), 3:256.
50 Coloma's translated letter is reprinted in Howard-Hill, *Game at Chess*, 194–8.
51 Ernst Renan, "What Is a Nation?," trans. Martin Thom, in *Nation and Narration*, ed. Homi K. Bhaba (London: Routledge, 1990), 11.
52 This recurring theme is perhaps most vividly evoked in Thomas Scott's *Vox Coeli, or News from Heaven* (1624), in which the ghost of Elizabeth I instructs, "O but it is the Spanish Match which will give fire to England, and make her welter in her miseries, and flame in her calamities and afflictions" (52).
53 From Howard-Hill, *Game at Chess*, 192–3.
54 Gary Taylor, "Historicism, Presentism and Time: Middleton's *The Spanish Gypsy* and *A Game at Chess*," Sederi 18 (2008): 167, reads this moment in relation to "the transition between dynastic and ideological systems of governance."
55 On this "Parliamentary Puritan" interest, see Margot Heineman, *Puritanism and Theatre: Thomas Middleton and Opposition Drama under the Early Stuarts* (Cambridge: Cambridge University Press, 1980), 258–83.
56 See Limon, *Dangerous Matter*, 9; Heinemann, *Puritanism*.
57 See Barbara Fuchs, "Mirror across the Water," in *Writing Race across the Atlantic World: Medieval to Modern*, ed. Phillip Beidler and Gary Taylor (New York: Palgrave Macmillan, 2005), 8–11.

58 See Gary Taylor, "A Game at Chess: A Later Form," in *Thomas Middleton: The Collected Works*, ed. Gary Taylor and John Lavagnino (Oxford: Oxford University Press, 2007), 1825.
59 Cressy, *Bonfires & Bells*, writes, "Much of the festivity appears to be spontaneous, and some of it got out of hand, but other elements were carefully stage-managed ... Authenticity and manipulation are not, however, necessarily mutually exclusive" (101). "In October 1623," he continues, "the bells of churches were rung with enthusiasm, for hours on end, in a communal exorcism of the Spanish threat ... Citizens experienced an interlude of love, harmony, healing, togetherness, bonding, and joy, akin to the communitas described by [anthropologist] Victor Turner" (105).
60 Raymond Williams, *Marxism and Literature* (Oxford: Oxford University Press, 1977), 128–35; Peter Lake, "Anti-popery: The Structure of a Prejudice," in *Conflict in Early Stuart England: Studies in Religion and Politics, 1603–1642* (London: Longmans, 1989), 72–4, is historically relevant.
61 Gary Taylor, *Buying Whiteness: Race, Culture, and Identity from Columbus to Hip-Hop* (New York: Palgrave Macmillan, 2005), 134. Taylor also observes, "The English sense of their own whiteness, epidermal and moral, developed alongside their sense of the darkness of a southern European [Spanish] enemy" (239).
62 Henry Savile, *Historicall Collections*, in *The Jacobean Union: Six Tracts of 1604*, ed. Bruce R. Galloway and Brian P. Levack (Edinburgh: Scottish Historical Society, 1982), 229.
63 Barbara Fuchs, *Exotic Nation: Maurophilia and the Construction of Early Modern Spain* (Philadelphia: University of Pennsylvania Press, 2008), 120.
64 See Stephen Wittek, "Middleton's *A Game at Chess* and the Making of a Theatrical Public," *Studies in English Literature 1500–1900* (forthcoming), on the multi-vocal appeal of the play.
65 See also Barbara Fuchs, "Spanish Lessons: Spenser and the Irish Moriscos," *Studies in English Literature 1500–1900* 42, no. 1 (2002): 43–62.
66 See, especially, Dale B.J. Randall and Jackson C. Boswell, *Cervantes in Seventeenth-Century England: The Tapestry Turned* (Oxford: Oxford University Press, 2009), 1–56; Bentley, *Jacobean and Caroline Stage*.
67 Thomas Scott, *Robert Earle of Essex his ghost, Sent from Elizian* (1624), 14.

chapter ten

Spain and the Rhetoric of Imperial Rivalry in Webster's *The Duchess of Malfi*

EMILY WEISSBOURD

Antonio, the luckless steward in John Webster's *The Duchess of Malfi* (1613–14; published 1623), casts a horoscope upon the birth of his first child: "The duchess was delivered of a son 'tween the hours twelve and one in the night, anno domini 1504 – that's this year – decimo nonno decembris – that's this night – taken according to the meridian of Malfi."[1] While the lines seem innocuous enough, their specificity is striking. Why might Webster take the unconventional step of informing the audience exactly when the play takes place? The language of the line itself emphasizes the date, as the character who reads the horoscope aloud repeats "that's this year" and "that's this night." Barring other circumstances, it is already atypical for Webster to so deliberately state the year in which his story takes place. In addition, the use of this date has spawned a series of lengthy footnotes on Webster's anachronism; several scenes later, when only a few years have passed within the world of the play, another character evokes the Battle of Pavia of 1525, a historical event that took place over twenty years later. Here again the play gestures to a very specific historical moment, and one that does not align chronologically with the date emphasized in the horoscope.[2]

Despite these references, which anchor *The Duchess of Malfi* in a particular time (or rather times) and place, the specifics of the play's setting have received little critical attention. Instead, the play has been most often referred to in passing as a quintessential example of the early modern English taste for "Italianate" drama; G.K. Hunter dubbed it one of "the two greatest plays in the tradition" (the other being Webster's *The White Devil*).[3] There are a number of interpretations of Italianate drama: as evoking, in the words of Jack D'Amico, everything from "the promise of the new Humanism and the dangers of the old Catholicism, [to] the intrigues of court and the glories of art"; as a site of the frequent cross-cultural interaction that a presumably more homogeneous London would not have offered; and as a conventional locus for veiled critique of Jacobean decadence within England itself.[4] Variations on all of these interpretations appear in critical studies of *The Duchess of Malfi*, yet in all of these instances critics have treated the play's setting as evoking a singular (if complex and contradictory) imagined Italy.[5]

I propose that we read the play in the context that is at once broader, taking into account the multiple national and imperial histories of the early modern Mediterranean, and also more specific in its analysis of the history that the play evokes. Reading *The Duchess of Malfi* as "Italianate" in general terms obscures the fact that both in the time in which the events of the play take place and the time in which it was written, Amalfi – as part of the Kingdom of Naples – was under the control of the Spanish Empire. Webster's play engages with a transnational early modern Mediterranean, taking into account shifting boundaries and imperial struggles within the region. Placing the play in this broader context allows us to see that a pointed critique of the Spanish Empire is central to *The Duchess of Malfi*.

Webster and Spanish Naples

When the duchess of Malfi – who is never given a name – marries her steward in secret, she rightly fears the anger of her brothers, a cardinal (also unnamed), and Ferdinand, duke of Calabria. Her marriage is kept hidden for enough time to allow the duchess and Antonio to produce three children. Eventually, through the agent Bosola, a spy in the duchess's household, the brothers discover her transgression and the identity of her secret husband. Murder, madness, plotting, and poison ensue; by the end of the play, the duchess, Antonio, two of their three children, and the evil brothers have all been killed.

Antonio's horoscope informs us that this mayhem unfolds against the backdrop of Spain's struggles to control Naples. The rulership of Naples had a long and contentious history in the medieval and early modern periods; the kingdom was alternately claimed – and fought over – by France, Aragon, and (following the unification of Castile and Aragon) Spain. From 1499 to 1504, Louis XII of France and Ferdinand of Aragon fought over the kingdom; control was ceded to Spain in 1504. By the time *The Duchess of Malfi* was written, Naples was part of the Spanish Empire and appeared in English texts as a warning against the perils of Spanish rule. A 1590 English translation of Antoine Arnauld's French propaganda tract *The Coppie of the Anti-Spaniard* presents Naples as an example of what France should strive to avoid: "Our gentlemen of France will never be brought everie New yéeres daie to purchase a license from a Castillian, whereby they may be authorized, (if they so please) to weare a weapon by theyr side, as it is notoriously knowen, that those fewe which remain of the Nobilitie of Naples, are inforced to do to this daie."[6] In 1592, Francis Bacon wrote in "Observation upon a libel" that Philip II of Spain was determined to reduce the Netherlands to "a martial government like unto that which he had established in Naples and Milan, upon which suppression of their liberties ensued the defection of these provinces."[7] In both of these texts, Naples exemplifies a European kingdom that suffers the indignity of Spanish occupation.

The status of Naples as an imperial holding of Spain may help us to interpret the specific dates to which Webster alludes. France officially surrendered Naples (including Amalfi) to Spanish control on 31 January 1504. This means that, by announcing the birth of the duchess's first child in December 1504, Webster sets the play at the moment when Naples has just been incorporated into the Spanish Empire. Webster also refers to the battle of Pavia of 1525, which was a decisive victory for the Spanish against French forces in the Italian war of 1521–6. In the third act, a minor character, Malateste, informs the cardinal that the latter must turn soldier: "The Emperor / Hearing your worth that way ... joins you in commission / With the right fortunate soldier, the Marquis of Pescara, / And the famous Lannoy" (3.3.1, 3–5). The cardinal replies with a question: "He that had the honour / Of taking the French King prisoner?" (3.3.5–6). Malateste, Charles de Lannoy, and the marquis de Pescara are all historical figures; they fought on the side of Spain in the battle of Pavia, winning a decisive battle for the emperor, Charles V; Lannoy did, in fact, take King Francis I of France prisoner. Thus both references serve as a reminder of the might of the Spanish Empire. In fact, *The Duchess of Malfi* repeatedly evokes moments at which Naples might have fallen into French rather than Spanish hands, but did not do so. This repetition serves as a reminder of Spanish might; it also begins to suggest that the troubles in Malfi are the product of Spanish misrule.

Webster's primary source for this story – which is based on historical events – also sets the play in a particular time period. It is not, however, either of the years to which Webster gestures. William Painter's *Palace of Pleasure*, a translation, through Belleforest's French, of Bandello's Italian *Novelle*,[8] opens its story by setting the scene: "a right pitifull Historie done almost in our time, when the French under the leading of that notable Gaston de Foix, vanquished the force of Spaine and Naples at the journey of Ravenna in the time of ye French king called Levves the twelfth."[9] In other words, Painter sets the play in 1512 and provides a backdrop of French ascendance over Spain. Webster chose not to follow Painter's precedent, but instead explicitly underscores a Spanish victory over the French.

These dates are not the only way that *The Duchess* evokes the calamity of Spanish occupation. The play begins with an otherwise anomalous reference to the French court, from where Antonio has just returned (and in this, Webster follows Painter). When a courtier asks Antonio how he liked France, he responds,

> To a fixed order, their judicious king
> Begins at home: quits first his royal palace
> Of flattering sycophants, of dissolute
> And infamous persons, which he sweetly terms
> His master's masterpiece, the work of heaven,
> Considering duly that a prince's court
> Is like a common fountain, whence should flow
> Pure silver drops in general; but if't chance
> Some cursed example poison't near the head,
> Death, and disease, through the whole land spread
>
> (1.1.5–15)

This monologue has been a source of debate for critics, some of whom have argued that it postdates the play's first performance in 1613 or 1614.[10] Specifically, they suggest that it refers to the 1617 assassination of the Maréchal d'Ancre, a powerful advocate of Spanish interests in the French court. This assassination caused a stir in England as well; in fact, no less a personage than King James affirmed that *not* to applaud D'Ancre's death was "to brand oneself as 'more than half Spanish.'"[11] However, as R.W. Dent's meticulously researched *John Webster's Borrowing* shows, the passage also draws quite closely on Elyot's sixteenth-century *Image of Governance*.[12] Thus it may simply assert a commonplace and completely predate the incident at the French court. In either case, whether the passage's praise of France is specific to a single event or a more general encomium, if we situate the monologue in the context of the French and Iberian struggle over Italy, its relevance becomes more apparent. The French court appears as an imagined alternative to a corrupt Spanish Empire, in implicit contrast to the vice and scheming of the Aragonese nobles presented in the play.

While the image of a prince's court as a fountain is an early modern commonplace, it is also particularly resonant in the context of anti-Spanish propaganda. It is typical of anti-Spanish rhetoric to present the Spaniard as miscegenated, his blood mixed with that of Moors and Jews. For example, the tract *A Comparison of the English and Spanish Nations*, translated from French into English in 1589, informs us, "For even as waters which run out of sulphur springs, have alwayes a taste of brimstone, so men have alwaies imprinted in their manners the vertuous or vitious qualitie of their ancestors." The tract goes on to describe Spaniards as a "mongrell generation."[13] Similarly, Edward Daunce's 1590 "A Briefe Discourse of the Spanish State" characterizes Spaniards as a "spring of all filthinesse."[14] The "pure silver drops" of the fountain of the French king's court offer a marked contrast to the tainted waters used so often as a metaphor for the Spaniard's natural temperament

Scholars such as Edmund Campos, Barbara Fuchs, Eric Griffin, and Gary Taylor, among others, have extensively documented the flourishing of the "Black Legend" of Spanish cruelty in this period: English, French, and Dutch anti-Spanish propaganda that branded Spaniards as rapacious imperialists eager to establish universal monarchy, and as simultaneously excessively proud of their lineages and themselves of impure blood, the miscegenated offspring of Moors and Jews.[15] As Eric Griffin discusses in this volume, in England the early seventeenth century saw a resurgence of popular anti-Spanish sentiment as a response to discussions of a marriage alliance between the royal houses of England and Spain. The *Duchess of Malfi* was first performed in late 1613 or early 1614, not long after the arrival in England of the Spanish Ambassador Gondomar. While a Spanish match between Charles I and the Infanta of Spain was not officially proposed until 1617, such an alliance had been discussed for years (first between Prince Henry and the Infanta) and Gondomar's 1613 arrival intensified negotiations. More significantly, the play was first published in 1623, the year when Prince Charles made his disastrous incognito trip to Spain to woo the Infanta. The fact that the play was first printed in 1623, when anxiety about the Spanish Match was running high, suggests that the printer may have hoped that the text's engagement with Spanish rule in Naples would provide compelling topical reading matter to potential buyers.

Although I am anchoring *The Duchess* in contemporary discussions of Spanish Empire, I do not want to suggest that the play is only – or even primarily – an allegory of the contemporary political situation, merely a cautionary tale about the dangers of Spanish rule. When focusing on the implications of specific names and dates, as I have done here, it is easy to fall into the trap of attempting to decode a text, to suggest that these references are a way of sneaking a particular message past the censors to a politically attuned audience. And that is one part of my argument: that these references to dates and historical events, as well as the Neapolitan setting, would have triggered associations with the Spanish Empire in early modern English theatregoers. But *The Duchess of Malfi* is far too rich and complex a play to reduce to a cautionary tale or political allegory. Attending to the play's evocation of Spain, however, also clarifies the text's persistent rhetoric of purity (or, alternately, corruption) of the duchess's body and blood, for *The Duchess of Malfi* represents its villains' fixation on the "purity" of their sister's blood and body as a particularly Spanish vice.

Antonio and "The Royal Blood of Aragon and Castile"

It is no great stretch to characterize the duchess's brothers as given to Spanish vices, as the two characters are given a Spanish pedigree.[16] When the cardinal and Ferdinand first discover that the duchess has had a child, the cardinal proclaims, "Shall our blood, / The royal blood of Aragon and Castile, / Be thus attainted?" (2.5.21–3). These lines explicitly signal the brothers' Spanish descent, since the unification of the Crowns of Aragon and Castile in 1469 was a foundational moment for the establishment of Spain as a nation. The cardinal and Ferdinand are also repeatedly referred to as the "Aragonian brethren," which may again serve as a reference to Spain.[17] This reference, however, is more ambiguous; historically, the duchess of Malfi and her family were descendants of the House of Aragon, offshoots of which ruled for hundreds of years in both Sicily and Naples. Thus, referring to the cardinal and Ferdinand as "the Aragonian brethren" may not mark them as particularly Spanish. Indeed, the term is lifted directly from Painter, who repeatedly refers to "the Aragon brethren."

But the Aragonian name carries connotations in the play that are different from those in its source text. Painter's novella emphasizes the nobility rather than the nationality of the siblings' bloodline. For example, when the duchess contemplates courting Antonio she chastises herself: "It appertaineth vnto me to shew my self, as issued forth of the Noble house of Aragon. To me it doeth belong to take héede how I erre or degenerate from the royall bloud wherof I came."[18] The duchess does refer to the House of Aragon, but she does so to underline the family's nobility and the unsuitability of her infatuation with Antonio. This and other references in the novella label the duchess and her siblings as descendants of a royal bloodline, but do not primarily associate that bloodline with specific national or cultural affiliations.

In Webster's *The Duchess of Malfi*, as we have seen, references to historical events link the "Aragonian brethren" to the Spanish Empire as Painter does not. Webster also deviates from his source in applying the descriptor "Aragonian brethren" to the duchess's villainous brothers, but never to the virtuous duchess herself. Similarly, Webster draws attention to the Spanishness of the House of Aragon in his choice of a name for one of the play's principal villains – a name that does not appear in any of his sources. Webster calls the duchess's brother Ferdinand; this is, of course, the name of Ferdinand of Aragon, ruler with his wife Isabella of Castile of the united Crowns of Castile and Aragon, and the king who took control of Naples following Spain's victory over the French in 1504. Famously, these are also the monarchs responsible for the *reconquista* of Spain from the Moors and the expulsion of Spain's Jews in 1492. Thus Ferdinand's name evokes the expulsion of Jews and Moors, as well as a presumed Spanish obsession with purity of blood.[19]

Ferdinand's intense, even incestuous preoccupation with the purity of his sister's "blood" (in the context specifically of sexual transgression) has been central to any number of critical studies of the play.[20] When Ferdinand's accomplice and hireling Bosola suggests that instead of tormenting the duchess Ferdinand ought to provide "beads and prayer-books" (4.1.118), Ferdinand replies, "Damn her! That body of hers, / While that my blood ran pure in't, was more worth / Than that which thou wouldst comfort, called a soul" (4.1.118–20). In marrying Antonio, the duchess has stained her bloodline; by polluting her bloodline, she has also tainted Ferdinand's. This line serves in part as an anti-Catholic critique of idolatry, with Ferdinand mistakenly valuing the duchess's body over her soul. Yet it also resonates more specifically with a presumed Spanish obsession with bloodlines.

This connection to Spain is reinforced by the way that, on multiple occasions, the play associates Antonio with Jews. In order to conceal her secret and allow Antonio to escape from her brothers, the duchess pretends to accuse him of badly managing her finances. Her excuse for sending him away is "My brother stood engaged with me for money / Ta'en up of certain Neapolitan Jews, / And Antonio lets the bonds be forfeit" (3.2.169–71). She asks one of the guards who has come to drive him away what he thinks of Antonio. The guard replies, "He could not abide to see a pig's head gaping; I thought your grace would find him a Jew" (3.2.215–16). Near the play's end, the cardinal sends the villain Bosola to find Antonio, instructing him to look for him by discovering "what fellows haunt the Jews for the taking up / Great sums of money" (5.2.135–6).

Even if Webster does not intend to mark Antonio explicitly as Jewish, associating him with Jews – and especially with money-lending – highlights the steward's social mobility, not to mention the chaos that such mobility provokes. As Peter Berek has astutely observed about a slightly earlier period,

> The theater of the 1590s was obsessed by the possibilities that identity might be willed or chosen and social position achieved by deeds, not birth ... Marranos, or Iberian Jews claiming to be converted to Christianity, are plausible representations of the idea that identity is not stable and can be created by individuals themselves. Moreover, emerging ideas about the fluidity of personal identity are closely associated with new entrepreneurship and social mobility. The traditional association of Jews with money-lending and other forms of commercial enterprise makes Jews in Elizabethan England, as they have been since, suitable representations of ambivalent feelings about economic innovation and social change.[21]

In this light, it does not seem at all surprising that the play would link Antonio to Jews, especially since, as the duchess's steward, he is responsible for managing her finances, and since his marriage to her precisely emphasizes the possibility – not to mention peril – of achieving a social position on the merit of deeds rather than of birth. Thus on one level the play's evocation of Jews has to do more generally with the symbolic function of the Jew in early modern English drama. But it also conjures up the specific history of presumed Spanish obsessions with purity of blood, especially when read in conjunction with Ferdinand's preoccupation with the duchess's "tainted" bloodline.

A similar tension between a more general symbolic function and a specific reference to Spanish vices emerges in reading the play's references to "impure blood" in the contexts both of Jewish descent and sexual transgression; after all, it is conventional in the period to represent many forms of illicit sex – and particularly rape and adultery – as a stain on a family's bloodline.[22] Thus Ferdinand's assertion that his sister's blood is no longer "pure" certainly refers to the stain of what he considers to be an illicit sexual relationship on her part. But here, too – as is true for the reference to Jews discussed above – *both* the general and the more specifically anti-Spanish implications of a reference to "pure blood" operate simultaneously. While the primary form of "impurity" that stains the duchess's blood may be her sexual transgression, the language used also invokes a presumed Spanish obsession with bloodlines. Representations of Spaniards as obsessed with blood purity and a critique of the corrupt Spanish empire are intertwined in *The Duchess of Malfi*.

The View from Spain: Lope de Vega's
El mayordomo de la duquesa de Amalfi

Focusing exclusively on English texts about Spanish vices can unwittingly perpetuate stereotypes about Spain that are themselves the long-standing legacy of the Black Legend, especially if we regard an English play such as *The Duchess of Malfi* as reflecting actual early modern Spanish prejudices and practices. In fact, such English representations of Spain often flatten the complicated and often-ambivalent depictions of purity of blood found in early modern Spanish texts. Fortuitously, the *Duchess of Malfi* provides an unusually rich context in which to analyse the difference between early modern English and Spanish representations of purity of blood, for Lope de Vega wrote a play, *El mayordomo de la duquesa de Amalfi*, which is based on the same Bandello novella that Webster used (in Painter's translation) as his primary source text. The two plays were apparently written in isolation, with neither author aware of the other's work; although Lope's play was written before Webster's, some time between 1599 and 1606, it was not printed until 1618, after Webster's *Duchess* was written.[23] Despite treating the same subject matter, Lope's *Mayordomo* and Webster's *Duchess* each use the Neapolitan setting as well as notions of blood and familial honour to very different ends.

The Spanish text does not mark Naples as a Spanish imperial holding, as the English text does. While the duchess's brother is referred to as Julio of Aragon, their name – and blood – are not linked to Castile as they are in Webster's play; similarly, while Webster's *Duchess* makes several references to "the emperor," presumably Charles V of Spain, no such authority appears in Lope's *Mayordomo*. Instead, the setting appears not so much an imperial holding as a separate state. The final lines of Lope's play emphasize that it is set in Italy: "Aquí dio fin la trajedia, / senado, del *Mayordomo*, / que como pasó en Italia, / hoy la han visto vuestros ojos" (Here ends the tragedy, oh spectators, of the *Steward*, which you have witnessed today, just as it took place in Italy).[24] One of the villains of Lope's play, who has no equivalent in either Bandello – the shared source text – or Webster, is Ottavio de Medici, a suitor to the duchess who makes much of his Medici name and ancestry. Neither does *El mayordomo* share the English *Duchess*'s anti-Catholic bias. While the Spanish duchess has a brother who is a cardinal, he does not appear onstage, and he is not involved in the plot to end her life – it is her brother Julio who alone orchestrates the death of the duchess, the steward, and their children.

What may be more surprising is that imagery of pure as opposed to tainted blood is much more prominent in Webster's play than it is in Lope's. The terms *honor* and *sangre* (or blood) do appear in Lope's play, but the rhetoric of infected blood that pervades Webster's *Duchess* is not nearly as central to *El mayordomo*. Moreover, Antonio is not connected with Jewishness in the Spanish play as he is in the English. Instead, his marriage to the duchess is consistently linked to a community of virtuous peasants, who live in "the mountains." When they marry, they dress as peasants and abscond to this mountain village to keep away from prying eyes. And when they have children, they secret them away to that same village, where they are brought up by a peasant couple. The children appear onstage dressed (as the stage directions specify) *a lo villano* or in the peasant style.[25]

By representing the duchess and Antonio's relationship and their children in the context of simple but virtuous mountain peasants, Lope's play draws on a tradition in the Spanish *comedia* – found in plays like *Fuenteovejuna*, *La villana de Getafe*, and *El alcalde de Zalamea*, among many others – in which peasants lay claim to honour, because although they are not noble they are "*limpios*," or pure-blooded. The fiction of the pure-blooded peasant dictates that those who live in the country (and particularly in mountainous places) have been sufficiently isolated to avoid intermarriage with Moors and Jews.[26] And while *El mayordomo* is explicitly set in Italy, its lower-class characters speak in a rustic dialect associated with rural Spanish peasants. Thus it is these moments that evoke questions of "purity of blood" in the Spanish play. However, unlike in Webster's play, such moments, far from emphasizing an unbridgeable difference in blood between the duchess and her steward, suggest that they are in fact compatible. In part because Antonio is linked to "peasant honour," his marriage to the duchess becomes less transgressive.

Indeed, overall, Lope's play is more sympathetic to the duchess and Antonio than is Webster's. In *El mayordomo* the duchess has a grown son from her first marriage who is capable of ruling her first husband's estate; thus her marriage does nothing to disturb patrilineal succession. Further, this first son supports her marriage when he learns of it, telling Antonio, "Fía de mi voluntad, / que te estimo como a padre / que a mí me dio ser mi madre / y a ti te dio calidad" (Trust in my goodwill, since I consider you like a father; my mother gave life to me, and to you she gave gentility) (798). The duchess's son models an appropriate response to her marriage; this contrast renders her murderous brother's actions completely unjustifiable. Indeed, the duchess's son vows revenge on his uncle in the play's final scene. The Spanish play makes clear that the source of the tragedy lies in the duchess's brother's unwillingness to accept her marriage, rather than the inherent unsuitability of an alliance between a duchess and a steward.

The hysteria surrounding the mingling of the duchess's "pure" blood with Antonio's in Webster's play also bears comparison with another Lope de Vega play with a Neapolitan setting: *El perro del hortelano* (The dog in the manger). This play, too, depicts the romance between a high-ranking noblewoman and a member of her household. Its protagonist, the Countess Diana, falls in love with her scribe and makes her affections known; the scribe, Teodoro, despite initial anxieties about their difference in station, reciprocates her affections. But there the resemblance between the two plays ends, for *El perro del hortelano* is not a revenge tragedy but rather a festive comedy. Thus in the end the low-ranking Teodoro is reclaimed as the long-lost son of a nobleman whose child was abducted in infancy by pirates. This narrative is the familiar stuff of romance, of course, but the Spanish play offers an unexpected twist: the "discovery" of the scribe's noble origins is in fact an elaborate ruse engineered by Teodoro's clever sidekick; Teodoro is not in fact the long-lost child, but simply happens to be the right age and to share his name. By the end of the play, Teodoro's true humble origins are something of an open secret; he tells his lover Diana, who emphatically declares that she is not bothered in the least, and in the final lines of the play enjoins the audience, "que a nadie digais, se os ruega, / el secreto de Teodoro" (I entreat of you, do not tell anyone Teodoro's secret).[27] While Diana and Teodoro's marriage is certainly problematic (hence the need for an elaborate deception), the play treats that problem as a violation of social codes rather than an existential crisis about the value of noble blood. The Spanish play treats the difference in "blood" between countess and scribe as a social convention that can be circumvented with a little ingenuity, a suitable subject for comedy as well as tragedy.

It is important to keep such satiric Spanish representations of the value of "blood" in mind when tracing the ways that Webster's *The Duchess of Malfi* draws on Spain. Doing so allows a distinction between English representations of Spain, coloured by the Black Legend, and early modern Spanish literary and cultural production. This distinction becomes more important in the context of plays that, unlike *The Duchess of Malfi*, explicitly address questions of Jewish and Moorish difference. Often, when we discuss plays that evoke both questions of purity of blood and Spain – plays like *Othello, The Merchant of Venice*, and *Lust's Dominion* – we describe these English texts as somehow absorbing an obsession with purity of blood that originates in Spain. Marc Shell, Janet Adelman, and Mary Janell Metzger have discussed this issue in *The Merchant of Venice*, a play that is of course very engaged with Jewish "blood" and also features a prince of Aragon.[28] These critics argue that *Merchant*, in evoking Spain, draws on and duplicates a Spanish protoracialist logic about blood difference. My reading of *The Duchess of Malfi* demonstrates that moments in English literature that evoke a Spanish obsession with pure blood – whether in the context of sexual transgression, Jewish descent, or some hybrid of the two – do so in part to articulate a critique of the Spanish Empire and so should not be understood as simply representing a racializing discourse of "impure blood" that originates in Spain. Indeed, *El mayordomo de la duquesa de Amalfi* and *El perro del hortelano* are only two Spanish texts among many that show how complex Spanish representations of transgressions against a "pure" bloodline can be. Comparing these texts, and registering how they are informed by contemporary events, can help us to understand how a play like *The Duchess of Malfi* uses a presumed Spanish obsession with purity of blood to highlight *English* concerns about bloodlines. Specifically, the "corruption" of noble blood through intermarriage in the English play is not in fact analogous to early modern Spanish representations of "blood" difference.

Most importantly, such comparisons can help us to disentangle early modern English representations of Spain – which are, after all, hardly unbiased – from actual Spanish texts and cultural practices. Plays like *The Duchess of Malfi*, *The Changeling*, *Lust's Dominion*, and *Othello*, among others, depict the tragic consequences of alliances that transgress social boundaries, evoking Spain when they do so. *The Duchess of Malfi*, as well as other early modern English plays, constructs its own version of Spanish prejudices; however, comparing Webster's *Duchess* to its Spanish counterpart reveals that the English text essentializes "blood" difference far more than the Spanish play, even as it displaces such prejudices onto Spain. A comparative reading of English and Spanish texts – one that takes into account the multiple imperial histories in which they are imbricated – allows us to see that part of what is at stake in English representations of Spanish fixations on "purity of blood" is particularly English anxieties about blood, identity, and social mobility.

NOTES

1 John Webster, *The Duchess of Malfi*, ed. Leah Marcus (London: Arden Shakespeare, 2009), 2.3.56–9. All further citations are from this edition and will be cited parenthetically in the body of the text.
2 I should clarify that what sparked my curiosity was not the anachronism of setting a play simultaneously in 1504 and 1525: after all, it was common practice for

early modern playwrights to play fast and loose with chronology, as any number of examples attest. Rather, what interested me about these moments is their specificity. Why does Webster make a point of evoking these particular time periods?

3 G.K. Hunter, "English Folly and Italian Vice," in *Dramatic Identities and Cultural Tradition : Studies in Shakespeare and His Contemporaries; Critical Essays* (New York: Barnes & Noble Books, 1978), 123.

4 Jack D'Amico, *Shakespeare and Italy* (Florida: University Press of Florida, 2001), 9. For Italy as a site of cross-cultural interaction, see Lara Bovilsky, *Barbarous Play: Race on the English Renaissance Stage* (Minneapolis: University of Minnesota Press, 2008), esp. 103–34. The most famous articulation of the Italy-as-England theory of Italianate drama remains G.K. Hunter's: "Italy became important to the English dramatists only when 'Italy' was revealed as an aspect of England." Hunter, "English Folly and Italian Vice," 113.

5 Examples of this generalized reading of Webster's Italy include Michele Marrapodi, who writes, "In John Webster's Italianate tragedies the scorn of the victims is so ingeniously carried on as to produce bizarre, almost laughable, effects. Revenge and counterrevenge appear thematically linked with the Italianate coloring of the stage court, naturally flowing from it and presented as a common practice of Renaissance Italy"; and Rolan Wymer, "Once more we find ourselves in a sixteenth-century Italian court where the ruthlessness of great men and the corrupt authority of the Catholic church – a linkage vividly dramatized by the Cardinal's exchange of his ecclesiastical robes for armour – combine to crush any possibilities of a healthy or honest existence." Michele Marrapodi, "Retaliation as an Italian Vice in the Renaissance Drama," in *Shakespeare's Italy: Functions of Italian Locations in Renaissance Drama*, ed. Michele Marrapodi, A.J. Oenselaars, Marcello Cappuzzo, and L. Falzon Santucci (Manchester: Manchester University Press, 1997), 200; Rolan Wymer, *Webster and Ford* (New York: Palgrave Macmillan, 1995), 52.

6 Antoine Arnauld, *The Coppie of the Anti-Spaniard made at Paris by a French man, a Catholique. Wherein is directly proued how the Spanish King is the onely cause of all the troubles in France. Translated out of French into English* (London, 1590). Early English Books Online.

7 Francis Bacon and Basil Montagu, *The Works of Francis Bacon, Lord Chancellor of England* (Carey, 1841), 2:256.

8 For a detailed analysis of the sources of *The Duchess of Malfi*, see Gunnar Boklund, *The Duchess of Malfi: Sources, Themes, Characters* (Boston: Harvard University Press, 1962), 1–24.

9 William Painter, *The second tome of the Palace of pleasure conteyning store of goodly histories, tragicall matters, and other morall argument, very requisite for delighte and profit. Chosen and selected out of diuers good and commendable authors* (London, 1567), 186. Early English Books Online.
10 Leah Marcus, introduction to *The Duchess of Malfi*, by John Webster (London: Arden Shakespeare, 2009), 95.
11 Cited in ibid.
12 Robert William Dent, *John Webster's Borrowing* (Berkeley: University of California Press, 1960), 175–6. Dent notes, "Despite the similarity of Webster to Elyot, Webster's source may well lie elsewhere. The basic idea and image may be found in countless Renaissance works" (176).
13 *A comparison of the English and Spanish nation: composed by a French gentleman against those of the League in Fraunce, which went about to perswade the king to breake his alliance with England, and to confirme it with Spaine. By occasion whereof, the nature of both nations is liuely decyphered. Faithfully translated, out of French by R.A.* (London, 1589), 19–20. Early English Books Online.
14 Edward Daunce, *A briefe discourse of the Spanish state vvith a dialogue annexed intituled Philobasilis* (London, 1590), 36. Early English Books Online.
15 See, among others, Edmund Valentine Campos, "Jews, Spaniards, and Portingales: Ambiguous Identities of Portuguese Marranos in Elizabethan England," *English Literary History* 69, no. 3 (2002): 599–616; Barbara Fuchs, "Sketches of Spain: Early Modern England's 'Orientalizing' of Iberia," in *Material and Symbolic Circulation between Spain and England, 1554–1604*, Transculturalisms, 1400–1700 (Aldershot, UK: Ashgate, 2008), 63–70; Eric J. Griffin, *English Renaissance Drama and the Specter of Spain: Ethnopoetics and Empire* (Philadelphia: University of Pennsylvania Press, 2009); Gary Taylor, "Historicism, Presentism and Time: Middleton's *The Spanish Gypsy* and *A Game at Chess*," *SEDERI: Yearbook of the Spanish and Portuguese Society for English Renaissance* 18 (2008): 147–70.
16 I am far from the first to have considered this. As M.C. Bradbrook observes, "The Spanish rulers of the kingdom of Naples could be interpreted in the light of contemporary Spanish honour and Spanish pride." She then explains Ferdinand's descent into madness: "For a Jacobean, the madness of the Spanish royal house and the Spanish code of honor would have sufficed to explain all this." Muriel Clara Bradbrook, *John Webster, Citizen and Dramatist* (London: Weidenfeld and Nicolson, 1980), 145, 157.
17 They would be comparable in this context with Portia's suitor Arragon in *Merchant of Venice*; Shakespeare's foolish honour-obsessed prince has been frequently read as satirizing Spanish foibles.

18 William Painter, *The second tome of the Palace of pleasure conteyning store of goodly histories, tragicall matters, and other morall argument, very requisite for delighte and profit. Chosen and selected out of diuers good and commendable authors* (London, 1567), 173. Early English Books Online.

19 As Leah Marcus observes, "The name Ferdinand instead evokes another member of the house of Aragon, Ferdinand d'Aragona of Spain; he and his queen were the Ferdinand and Isabella who sponsored Christopher Columbus' voyage to the New World in 1492 ... This was, in other words, the Ferdinand who expelled the Jews and Muslims from Spain and set in motion an elaborate system of rules by which his countrymen eventually had to demonstrate *limpieza de sangre* – purity of blood from Moorish or Jewish admixtures – in order to assume any type of government post (Sweet). The historical Ferdinand's emphasis on the purification of Spanish blood resonates strongly with Webster's Aragonese brothers and their obsession with the purity (and corruptibility) of their own and their sister's blood." Marcus, "Introduction," 26.

20 For a "review [of] the critical history of Ferdinand's incestuous desires," see Frank Whigham, *Seizures of the Will in Early Modern English Drama* (Cambridge: Cambridge University Press, 1996), 190–1.

21 Peter Berek, "The Jew as Renaissance Man," *Renaissance Quarterly* 51, no. 1 (1998): 130.

22 Shakespeare's poem *The Rape of Lucrece* and Middleton and Rowley's *The Changeling* (also set in Spain) are two examples among many of texts that describe illegitimate sexual congress as a "stain" on the blood.

23 Luciano Garcia, "*The Duchess of Malfi* and *El mayordomo de la duquesa de Amalfi* revisited: some differences in literary convention and cultural horizon," in *Spanish Studies in Shakespeare and His Contemporaries*, ed. José Manuel González Fernández de Sevilla (Newark, DE: University of Delaware Press, 2006), 299–300; Boklund, *Duchess of Malfi*, 22–4.

24 Lope de Vega, *Comedias*, ed. Jesús Gómez and Paloma Cuenca (Madrid: Fundación Jose Antonio de Castro, 1993), 13:799. All further citations are from this edition and will be cited parenthetically in the body of the text.

25 In the third act, for example, one stage direction reads, "Sale Antonio con Doristo, y Alejandro, niño, vestido de villano, y Leonora, niña, de villanita" (enter Antonio with Doristo, and with Alejandro, the boy, dressed as a peasant, and Leonora, the girl, as a little peasantess) (771).

26 Noël Salomon, *Lo Villano en el Teatro Del Siglo de Oro* (Madrid: Editorial Castalia, 1985), 109–20, 684–702.

27 Lope de Vega, *El perro del hortelano y el arenal de Sevilla* (Madrid: Espasa-Calpe, 1983), 94.

28 Janet Adelman, *Blood Relations: Christian and Jew in* The Merchant of Venice (Chicago: University of Chicago Press, 2008); Mary Janell Metzger, "'Now by My Hood, a Gentle and No Jew': Jessica, The Merchant of Venice, and the Discourse of Early Modern English Identity," *PMLA: Publications of the Modern Language Association of America* 113, no. 1 (1998): 52–63; Marc Shell, "Marranos (Pigs), or from Coexistence to Toleration," *Critical Inquiry* 17, no. 2 (1991): 306–35.

chapter eleven

Catholics and Cosmopolitans Writing the Nation: The Pope's Scholars and the 1579 Student Rebellion at the English Roman College

BRIAN C. LOCKEY

Cosmopolitans and the Christian Commonwealth

Rome was both the centre of the ancient world and, with respect to the threat posed by the Ottoman Turks, the centre of the Christian world, but for English Protestants and their allies on the Continent, it was also the centre of the despised Roman Church. Educated English Protestants therefore perceived in Rome a complex locus of attraction and repulsion. The example of the young Philip Sidney, who had travelled throughout Europe extensively from 1572 to 1575, is instructive. From November 1573 to August 1574, Sidney was based in Venice and Padua, where he met and consorted with numerous Catholic and Protestant luminaries from the Continent and England.[1] While in Italy, he made a month-long excursion to Genoa and Florence, and his correspondence with his French tutor, Hubert Languet, shows that he sought to visit Rome as well, despite Languet's warnings that travelling to Rome would be more dangerous for Sidney's body and soul than travelling to Constantinople.[2] Sidney's Latin letters show that Sidney frequently referred to the "Christian commonwealth [*respublica Christiana*]," a term traditionally employed by Roman Catholics to acknowledge that for them Europe comprised a transnational Christian polity governed by a spiritual sovereign. (Sidney's Protestant interlocutors such as Languet and Wolfgang Zundelin, in contrast, seemed to prefer the term "Christian world [*orbis Christianus*]," to describe collectively the temporal realms of secular Christian princes, riven as they were by sectarian division and civil war).[3] But even as he sojourned in Italy itself, Sidney could nevertheless express a fervent desire that an Ottoman invasion would destroy Italy and extirpate Rome and everything it stood for from the Christian body politic: "What could be more devoutly wished than that [a Turkish invasion of Italy]? In the first place it would remove that putrid limb which for so long has corrupted the whole Body of the Christian Commonwealth [*totum Corpus reipublicae Christianae*], and destroy the factory in which, as you write, the causes of so many ills are forged."[4] How do we explain such contradictory English attitudes towards Rome and the "Christian commonwealth" over which it claimed to preside? Most importantly for my purposes, what was the relationship between the traditional notion of the Christian commonwealth and English national identity, as it was developing during the latter half of the sixteenth century?

Disputes between confessional identities during the early modern period often conceal significant similarities between Catholics and Protestants on the question of England's national identity and its relations with Europe. As I show in this chapter, the global perspective of the English Jesuits, particularly their desire to view England as part of Christendom or an encompassing Christian commonwealth, was shared to a certain extent by conformist English writers such as Sir John Harington and even one of their avowed enemies, Anthony Munday, who served the Crown as a "pursuivant" of renegade Jesuit priests and Catholic recusants.[5] Moreover, this shared perspective, which I characterize as "cosmopolitan," was actually opposed to an insular belief, shared by both the old Marian Catholic establishment and some English Protestants, in the purity of Welsh or British or English identity.[6] My larger purpose here is to use the Mediterranean context to show that perspectives on English national identity and myths of national origin often cut across confessional boundaries in ways that complicate the common view of the distinction between English Catholics and Protestants.

In March 1581, during the first Jesuit mission to England, the Jesuit priest Edmund Campion, while on the run from pursuivants and spies, completed his famous tract *Rationes decem*. Published secretly by Father Robert Persons, SJ, at Stonor Park, Henley, later that month, the *Rationes decem* contained Campion's criticisms of the Anglican settlement, addressing diverse theological questions such as what authority should be given to scripture versus the church fathers, the paradoxes and sophisms of Lutheran and Calvinist doctrine, and the nature and government of the Catholic Church.[7] The climax of the tract occurs in the last few pages, where I would argue its true purpose is revealed. Here Campion addresses himself directly to Elizabeth and takes her to task for her claim of royal supremacy over the ecclesiastical realm. The passage is worth quoting in full:

> I call to witness ... Princes, Kings, Emperors, and their Commonwealths, whose own piety and the people of their realms, and their established discipline in war

and peace, were altogether founded on this our Catholic doctrine. What Theodosiuses here might I summon from the East, what Charleses from the West, what Edwards from England, what Louises from France, what Hermenegilds from Spain, Henries from Saxony, Wenceslauses from Bohemia, Leopolds from Austria, Stephens from Hungary, Josaphats from India, Dukes and Counts from all the world over who by example, by arms, by laws, by loving care, by outlay of money, have nourished our Church [*nostram Ecclesiam nutrierunt*]! For so Isaias foretold: Kings shall be thy foster-fathers, and queens thy nurses (Isaias xlix, 23) [*Sic enim praecinuit Isaias* (xlix. 23): *Erunt reges nutricii tui, et reginae nutrices tuae*].

Listen, Elizabeth, most powerful Queen, for thee this great prophet utters this prophecy, and therein teaches thee thy part. I tell thee: one and the same heaven cannot hold Calvin and the Princes whom I have named. With these Princes then associate thyself, ... I call to witness all the coasts and regions of the world, to which the Gospel trumpet has sounded since the birth of Christ.[8]

In this passage, Campion presents himself as speaking from the perspective of a vast array of like-minded monarchs from the Continent and beyond. Campion was of course personally familiar with some of these kingdoms, and it is consistent with this border-crossing, cosmopolitan perspective that a few pages later, Campion ends the tract with the note, "Valete. Cosmopoli 1581 [Farewell. From the City of the World 1581]."[9]

Two aspects of this passage immediately stand out with regard to the issues of cosmopolitanism and the relationship between England and the transnational Christian realm, which the Roman curia claimed as its spiritual dominion. First, Campion's self-presentation is remarkably similar to the first use of the term *cosmopolitan* or *cosmopolitical* in the English language by John Dee in his *General and Rare Memorials pertayning to the Perfect Arte of Navigation* (1577), a tract whose ostensible purpose was to provide a plan for the establishment of a permanent English naval force. Dee claims to have "looked into the State of Earthly Kingdoms, Generally, the whole World ouer" and now to have found "hym self, *Cosmopolites*: A Citizen, and member, of the whole and only one Mysticall City Vniversall: And so, consequently, to meditate of the Cosmopolitical Gouernment therof, vnder the King Almighty [God]."[10] As a universal citizen, Dee views his identity as not limited to the kingdom or country of his birth – he is therefore uniquely suited to theorizing transnational values that could simultaneously (and paradoxically) defend and justify an increased centralization of English state power. Dee's ability to speak from the cosmopolis or "the city of the world" qualifies him to pronounce authoritatively on the peoples and nations of the world and especially to offer advice and counsel to Christian sovereigns. Campion's confessional purpose in his tract is quite different from Dee's attempts to counsel Elizabeth on defence policy in the *Memorials,* but the two stances are also similar in that each presents himself as a worldly well-travelled figure whose cosmopolitan knowledge qualifies him to advise the Queen.

Second, Campion's use of the passage from Isaiah 49:23, "Kings shall be thy foster-fathers [*nutricii*], and queens thy nurses [*nutrices*]," is intended to characterize how temporal magistrates should ideally serve the Roman Catholic Church within the transnational Christian commonwealth. It is therefore central to his appeal to Elizabeth that she realign her kingdom with the church and those sovereigns who serve it. Indeed, despite Campion's assurance in the other document he published while in England, the "Challenge to the Privy Council," that he would refrain from dealing "in any respect with matter of state or policy of this realm," Campion's more educated readers would have understood his use of the verse from Isaiah as an overt political gesture, which endorses the papal claim that the spiritual realm, presided over by the Holy See, had primacy over the temporal realm of individual Christian sovereigns.[11] In this respect, the pope was the ultimate cosmopolitan figure, theoretically capable of offering advice and correction to each sovereign within his vast Christian commonwealth.

Campion's use of this verse places the entire tract within the context of contemporary writings, which utilize such claims for papal supremacy over the spiritual realm to justify the pope's right to correct or even depose a sinful, tyrannical, or heretical sovereign. In 1571, for example, the exiled Catholic priest Nicholas Sander used the verse from Isaiah in the second book of his influential tome, *De Visibili Monarchia Ecclesiae,* in order to make a case for papal primacy over the temporal realm of individual sovereigns and to justify the pope's excommunication and deposition of Elizabeth in 1570. He explains,

> Since thus it was said to the Apostles, *Go, teach all the peoples,* and when in the name of the people kings also are understood: and bishops and priests will have succeeded the apostles in the service of teaching: actually in the post of teaching the bishop is greater than his own king: ... Isaiah predicted *Kings will be foster fathers to the Church of Christ, and they will bow down before you with their faces to the ground; they will lick the dust at your feet. And you will know, that I am Lord?* [Isaias praedixit, *Reges fore nutricios Ecclesiae Christi, & vultu in terram demisso adoraturos illam, & mox subiungit: Scies, quia ego Dominus (Isai 49)?*] This [verse] is truly a sign that the Lord reigns in us, if we embody so much of the church itself, such that it appears obvious that the ministers of Christ are greater than king and queen are [*ministros Christi maiores quo libet Rege ac Regina esse*].[12]

Sander's larger purpose in claiming that bishops were greater than kings and queens was to justify the bishop of Rome's deposition of Elizabeth I, a legitimate sovereign who had nevertheless introduced dangerous heresies into her realm. Likewise, in the *Defence of English Catholics* (1584), Cardinal William Allen employs Isaiah 49:23 to justify his argument that "the spiritual hath right to correct the temporal" when the temporal realm is corrupted by heretical or tyrannical magistrates. And finally, in his *Motives*, Richard Bristow asked his readers to consider "what Church it is which conformably to these Prophecies [in Isaiah 49:23] hath brought the mighty Princes of the world, Kingdoms of the earth, and States of Common-wealthes to submit their Septers vnder Christ our Lord & Governement of his Church."[13]

It is a curious aspect of the translators Anthony Munday and Sir John Harington that each was in his own way affected by the life and death of Edmund Campion, Munday as a witness at Campion's trial and execution and Harington as a transcriber of some of his writings.[14] I suggest that these writers of fiction were not necessarily drawn to Campion out of disguised Catholic sympathies, as has been suggested by Donna Hamilton and Gerard Kilroy from different perspectives; rather, both Harington's and Munday's writings share cosmopolitan elements that could be found in the Catholic account of papal supremacy, which Campion and other Jesuits and Catholic exiles championed.[15] Harington's and Munday's different engagements with these issues has the effect of reconfiguring in secular terms an issue that, for the Jesuits, was a matter of church and state with political implications concerning the papal right of deposition. As we shall see, some of Harington's and Munday's writings can be interpreted as championing a secular version of the papal or episcopal overseer, responsible for correcting an errant or tyrannical sovereign. Finally, parallel to those Catholic exiles who sought to reintegrate the English realm into the transnational Roman Catholic commonwealth, Harington's and Munday's translations and other writings can be read as analogously bringing the English polity closer to Continental Europe.

In 1602, in his *Tract on the Succession to the Crown*, Harington gave his own reading of Isaiah 49:23. Writing from the perspective of an outsider to religious controversy, Harington confesses that he needed to consult the Queen's chaplains on the question of supremacy. Harington infuses his judgment with his signature satirical wit:

> If Peter being confirmed himself must confirme and conforme his fellowes, doth it followe he must place and displace kings? The prophet saith "Kings shal be thy nutricii *et reginae nutrices*," queens thy nurses: and sure where they be nurses, the

milkes they give commonly is rentes and revenewes; and such milke hath that Church of Rome suckt frome their nurses of England a long tyme. But since that Churche did *luxuriari in Christo*, as St Paul saith of the wanton widdowes, since they did like ungratefull babies suck blood for milke, and byte their nurses nipples, who can blame her if for milke she give them *Pap with a Hatchet*, as is the proverbe.[16]

Harington composed this manuscript for the archbishop of York, Tobias Matthew, in order to champion the cause of James VI of Scotland for succession to the English throne. In this passage, Harington shows a familiarity with the reading of the verse from Isaiah that was prevalent among English Catholic exiles, but he also refutes that reading, claiming that a tyrannical church had no claim over a long-suffering and abused state. And yet, in spite of what seems to be an unequivocal view against papal supremacy, Harington does grant that some Catholic grievances concerning the Tudor Crown are justified. For example, he criticizes the fact that Henry VIII "made Cromwell his vicegerent in Causes Ecclesiasticall, setting him, a layman, and as he writes an unlearned man, over all bishops and clergie," and more importantly, he attacks Elizabeth herself because "contrarie to the use of all Christian countries, [during] a great part of her Majesties reigne no bishopp was of the Counsell."[17] If Catholic exiles like Sander and Allen imagined the relationship between the pope and the sovereign as one in which "the spiritual hath right to correct the temporal," then so too did Harington imagine a bishop as privy councillor playing a role analogous to the pope, correcting the sovereign from within the council when her conduct merited such correction.

We encounter a related set of themes in Harington's most famous original tract, *A New Discourse of a Stale Subject, Called the Metamorphosis of Ajax*, published anonymously in 1596.[18] The *New Discourse* is putatively about Harington's servant Thomas Combe's invention of the first primitive flushable privy, or the "device" as it is referred to throughout the tract.[19] It has long been noted that the *New Discourse* is substantially more complex than simply constituting a space within which to introduce the invention of the "device." For example, it is clear from certain passages in the tract that Harington empathized with the English Catholic community, especially their suit for religious tolerance. However, I would argue that what attracts Harington to that community as well as to Wardour Castle, the seat of the recusant Arundells and the place where the first such flushable device was installed, is the perceived cosmopolitan character of some members of that community.[20] Harington compares the Arundells' Wardour Castle with China, the West Indies, and finally Eldorado in Guiana. In contrast, the rest of England is presented in the *New Discourse* negatively, as a realm that "in few places affoords more pleasures" than those that can be found at Wardour. In other words, the singularity of Wardour is that it provides a link to the outside world, to the non-English, to travel, and to the exotic.[21]

Furthermore, one of the most memorable parts of the *New Discourse* has a bearing on the pope's correction of temporal magistrates. Towards the end of the *New Discourse*, Harington compares himself to a Roman magistrate, Plinius Secundus from the city of Amestris in Asia Minor, who successfully convinced the Roman Emperor Traianus to cover the open sewer running through the city of Amestris. Harington imagines a similar contemporary scenario involving his home town of Bath. Figuring himself as a local magistrate of the town, he composes his own letter to Emperor Traianus, in which he asks the emperor to "authorise me, or some wiser than me" to install covered sewers in Bath that will improve the promising but decaying infrastructure of his town.[22] A number of aspects of this analogy are significant in terms of the supremacy issue. First, note that Harington does not draw a direct analogy between Emperor Traianus and Queen Elizabeth, as one would expect. Rather than doing so, he addresses a Traianus, whose contemporary equivalent, he implies, is Robert Devereux, earl of Essex. The passage in question reads,

> And I have thought sometime with my selfe, that if I were but halfe so great an officer under our most gracious Emperesse, who is indeed worthy, and only worthie to be Trajans Mistresse, as Plinius secundus was under that Trajan; I would write for the mending of such a lothsome fault in my neighbour town of Bath (where many noble persons are oft annoyed with it) as Plinie did for Amestris. Yet whie may I not by *Poetica licentia*, and by an honest & necessarie figure (in this age) called *Reprehensio*, imagine my selfe for halfe an houre to be *Secundus*, and suppose some other, that perhaps at this houre is not farre from Trajans countrey, to be that worthiest Trajan?[23]

The last sentence in which he imagines "some other" being "at this hour ... not farre from Trajans countrey" as Traianus is a notable reference to the earl of Essex being a commander of the expedition to Cadiz, which set sail on 1 June 1596 (*A New Discourse* appeared in print later that year).[24]

The response to Harington's tract was, to say the least, not positive. Almost immediately after its publication, Harington was threatened with a suit in the Star Chamber, ostensibly due to very direct criticisms of the earl of Leicester found in the tract. However, Jason Scott-Warren has suggested that passages such as this one, which figures Essex as Emperor Traianus and seems to discuss the prohibited subject of the Queen's marriage (he calls her "our most gracious Emperesse, who is indeed worthy, and only worthie to be Trajans Mistresse"), were the real cause of Harington's troubles.[25] I suggest further that the entire episode can be understood as a secular reconfiguration of the supremacy issue. The actual letter to Traianus, which follows this passage, is conflicted about the relationship between the emperor and the Queen – Harington addresses Traianus as "your Lordship," suggesting that the letter is meant throughout to be understood as referencing Essex, the courtier and member of the Privy Council who was the Queen's favourite subordinate. And yet, within the imaginary universe of the Roman Empire, Harington's analogy with Plinius's original letter suggests that England is one province within the Roman Empire and that, by writing this letter to Emperor Traianus rather than Queen Elizabeth, Harington is appealing to a "higher" imperial authority that supervises the Queen's power.[26] It is also not hard to imagine that the entire episode is intended to be critical of Elizabeth's authority – Harington's expression of astonishment that the original Emperor Traianus responded to Plinius's request suggests perhaps that Harington's contemporary local magistrates could expect much less attention from Queen Elizabeth. In this respect, the passage seems motivated by the same reasons that later motivated Harington to complain that Elizabeth had declined to appoint a bishop to the Privy Council for so long a period of time during her reign. In effect, Harington conjures up an ancient Roman emperor who would play a moderating role analogous to the role of Sander's pope, a figure who could oversee the English sovereign and who could be appealed to, when she herself proved to be delinquent in her duties.

In addition, of course, the passage seems to suggest Essex as a potential husband and overseer of Elizabeth, something Harington had obliquely suggested earlier in his lengthy commentary on the fifth book of his translation of *Orlando Furioso* (1591), in which he had written about Genevra's marriage to a social inferior: "It is no disparagement for the greatest Emperesse in the world to marrie one that is a gentleman by birth."[27] Indeed, like his fictional letter to Traianus in the *New Discourse*, Harington's commentaries on his translation of *Orlando Furioso* reveal anxious ruminations about the exercise of temporal sovereignty without some form of papal or imperial oversight. Thus, Harington's opening commentary on the first canto recounts the story of Pope Leo III's deposition of the tyrannical Empress Irene, and the pope's subsequent appointment of Charlemagne as Holy Roman emperor, which incidentally Robert Persons included as an example in his argument in favour of the papal deposition of tyrannical monarchs in the *Conference on the Next Succession* (1594). But unlike Persons, who upholds the primacy of the spiritual realm over the temporal, the events of Ariosto's poem occur under the auspices of a code of transnational justice that is more chivalric than Christian.[28]

Rebellion and Papal Supremacy

The catholic conception of papal supremacy, which saw the pope wielding authority over the conduct of temporal sovereigns, seems to have influenced even zealously anti-Catholic writers such as Anthony Munday. Two accounts of the 1579 student rebellion at the English College at Rome make this clear: the *English Romayne Life* (1582), Anthony Munday's printed account of his travels to Rome and his sojourn at the English College, and "A Storie of Domesticall Difficulties in the English Catholike cause" (1600), Robert Persons's manuscript account of the rebellion.[29] Munday's and Persons's seemingly opposed perspectives on the revolt reveal a common view of papal intervention, which in turn yields insights into English perceptions of papal supremacy and the marginal yet significant forms of cosmopolitan English identity that I am investigating here.

Persons's relation is the more complete and less well known of the two accounts. He begins by summarizing the dispute, which erupted in 1579, immediately after the foundation of the college, that had, until then, been a hospital for English pilgrims. In that year, Morys Clynnog, the Welsh secular priest who had been warden of the original hospice, was able to procure a breve from the pope that made him perpetual rector of the college, and quickly thereafter, an administrative dispute broke out into a "nationall quarrell ... between the Englishe and the Welche."[30] At the time, Persons reports that there were thirty English scholars and seven or eight Welsh scholars living at the college. Persons, like Munday, reports that the English students complained that the entire missionary purpose of the college was forfeit if they "should continewe in that sorte under Mr Morrice [Clynnog's] his government, whome theye avouched to have no care of making men for England, nor sending them thither, but only to entertayne them in Rome, and that such was the resolution and purpose of his Contreymen [i.e., the Welsh] in the Colledge."[31]

While it is likely that the protesting English students were also biased against the Welsh, their public concern was for the larger goal of the mission to England and Wales, and they viewed Jesuit leadership over the college as necessary precisely because the Jesuits were perceived to be impartial on questions of national bias.[32] In a petition to Cardinal Giovanni Morone, the students list three reasons for their appeal for Jesuit leadership at the college, one of which is the necessity of impartially adjudicating and therefore mitigating tensions between the Welsh and English within the exile community. Their petition reads, "When among the two populations of England, the English and the Welsh, some natural root of discord exists, it seems necessary that such men preside over us, who are alien from affection for whichever part [*ut tales nobis viri praesint, qui sint alieni ab utriusque partis affectu*]; in other respects now it is proved by experience, that these two peoples are unable to live together."[33]

Likewise, rather than overt expressions of ethnic interest, Persons's letters to his colleagues put forward the seemingly impartial argument that English dominance over the Welsh was part of the customary geopolitical order, confirmed through analogies with the current balance of power between the actual kingdoms of England and Wales. In a letter to his fellow Jesuit William Goode, Persons recounts the conversation between an unnamed individual – probably a priest, perhaps even Persons himself – sympathetic to and familiar with the English students, and Tolomeo Galli, the cardinal of Como, who seems initially to have been more sympathetic to Clynnog. After Como explains that he himself would have simply encouraged the English students to leave the college if they were not prepared to submit to Clynnog, Persons goes on to explain the transformation that the anonymous interlocutor has caused in the cardinal of Como's thinking:

> Whereto the Cardinall answered that he understood the diversity betwixt Englishmen and Welchmen was nothing more than might be betwixt two divers provinces [as] Tuscan[y] and Romagnia. Whereto replyed this man that he understood the matter farre otherwise, and thought that his Grace was not informed in the matter, for that the Welchmen and Englishmen were (putting aside Religion) as might be Mores and Spaniards. For as the Spaniards got Spayne from the Mores and after held them under, so Englishmen had done in tymes past the ould Britans, which were now called Welchmen, albeit in successe of tyme they have now imparted to them their privileges and freedomes and do account of them as of Englishmen naturall, excepting only that they use great moderation in promoting them to honours at home; and therefore naturally it is as much repugned to Englishmens harts to be subiect to the government of Welchmen as Spaniards to Mores or Frenchmen to Spaniards. These words seemed not a little to move the Cardinall whereupon after a little pause he brake out and said, I knew not of this so fully before.[34]

In the light of such geopolitical analogies, Persons himself sees rebellion against the colleges' magistrates under the aegis of church authority as a model that could be exported to England. In his letter to Goode, he explains in some detail how the students' audacious petition to Morone would serve them well in their confrontation with the English Crown:

> This act of thers [the English seminarians] before the Cardinall [Morone] was straightway knowne and talked of all over Rome, for there were at it all the family of the Cardinall and did wonder to se such liberty of speech, before so great

a personage. And albeit I thinke there must needes passe many excesses amongst so much as was spoken in that place, of so many Youthes; yet many men did imagine to see a certayne company of *Lawrences, Sebastians* and the like intractable fellowes, who brought Emperours and princes to desperation to deal with them, for that they could neyther with giving or taking away, neyther with faire wordes nor with foule bring them to condesent to any one little poynt that they misliked. Many also strangers made this consequent; if these fellowes stand thus immovable before such Princes in Rome, what will they do in England before the Heretiques? And many said that they doubted before of things reported of English Priests in England, and of their bould answers, reported by Letters, but now they could beleeve anything of them.[35]

According to Persons, the courage of the English seminarians in standing up to Cardinal Morone, Archdeacon Owen Lewes, and Father Clynnog would serve them well in their confrontation with English magistrates. The seminarians are compared to the early saints, St Lawrence and St Sebastian, who confronted and were martyred by pagan Roman emperors. Ultimately, of course, it is papal intervention into the affairs of the English college that authorizes and legitimizes their rebellion. In effect, the student rebellion ends with the pope's deposition of Clynnog and his ally Lewes, which by analogy justifies the power of papal deposition within the geopolitical sphere of relations between Rome and the English Crown. In other words, what makes their rebellion exemplary is precisely the fact that it was not a rebellion at all — rather, it was a request for intervention by a supreme authority into the decisions of a lesser magistrate. By analogy, Persons and his allies sought to restore the same kind of papal oversight to the English Crown. Indeed, the pope's use of prerogative powers to resolve the conflict within the English college replicates the geopolitical result that Sander, Persons, and other English Jesuits sought in their analogous support for Pope Pius V's public deposition of Queen Elizabeth in 1570.[36]

Munday's account of the student revolt follows, in abbreviated form, the events found in Persons's version, although from the perspective of someone who sought primarily to expose the den of iniquity and treachery that, for English officials, constituted the Collegium Anglorum. Munday concludes his brief account of the troubles in Rome by remarking, "Thus was the strife ended, and myself and my fellow [Thomas Nowell] admitted by the Pope's own consent to be scholars there."[37] The pope therefore provides a special imprimatur for Munday's place at the college, offering his own consent for Munday's continuing studies. And given that Clynnog seems to have had a special antipathy towards Munday himself, attempting at one point to expel him from the college, the pope's resolution of the ethnic infighting between the Welsh and English populations of the English College redounds especially favourably to Munday's situation.[38]

Munday's account of this resolution ultimately influenced his fictional and non-fictional writings in two ways. First, a common strategy throughout all three of Munday's pamphlets on the trial of Edmund Campion and his associates is to refer repeatedly to his travels to the Continent and to his former identity as the "pope's scholar," as a way of granting his voice authority. In his account of Edmund Campion's execution, for example, he recounts, "When I came to Roome, I was allowed the Popes Scholler, and liued there in the Seminarie among them."[39] This last claim, that he was "allowed the Popes Scholler" is a recapitulation of the title page of the pamphlet where he notes that he was "sometime the Popes scholler, allowed in the seminarie at Roome amongst them." The title reminds the reader of the exceptional nature of Munday's biographical narrative: like Campion and his confederates, Munday was once a student at the English college in Rome, in danger of being on the wrong end of "how they [English authorities] deal with such secret seducers." Yet rather than getting him executed as a traitor, his former role as the "pope's scholar" is integral to his role as public champion of the English Crown's strategy for dealing with the Jesuit missionaries.[40] In other respects, it is central to his self-portrayal as a well-travelled authority on the Catholic enemy. Second, anxiety over the ability or inability to correct a sinful, oppressive, or wayward magistrate is a constant theme in Munday's subsequent fictional works, especially his dramatic works, the chivalric romances that he chose to translate, and even some of the London pageants. His dramatic works, for example, feature laypersons such as the magician John A Kent, the Catholic martyr Sir Thomas More, the Protestant martyr John Oldcastle, and the medieval hero Robin Hood, who all assume the role of corrector or protector of a sovereign in need or who has fallen into sin.[41] Essentially, all of these roles translate the papal right of correction and deposition, which Catholic exiles like Persons and Sander defended in Pope Pius V's deposition of Elizabeth, into secular fictional works. In effect, these works portray figures such as Robin Hood correcting and punishing bad sovereigns, thereby translating a secular version of papal supremacy into the English public sphere. Once again, I am not arguing that Munday was a crypto-Catholic – only that he adopted a secularized version of the cosmopolitan perspective of his enemies in his own fictional works.

In order to show how closely related Persons's and Munday's perspectives on individual and national identity were, I would like to conclude by placing this cosmopolitan view of national identity in the context of other competing Catholic and Protestant views of the nation. During the years leading up to the

English students' revolt of 1579, a fault line was emerging within the English exile community in Rome between a reforming Jesuit faction led by Persons and Allen, and a Marian Catholic faction.[42] Persons notes as early as 1575 that while all English Catholic exiles residing in Rome desired the "conversion of there countrey," they "agreed not well in the meanes or the manner of consultation: Sir Francis Inglefield, D. Saunders and D. Allen were commonly of one minde, but Sir Thomas Stukeley, D. Lewes and D. Morrice [Clynnog] of another."[43] The conflict between these two factions was based on two earlier perspectives on the function of the English colleges on the Continent, the first that saw the colleges working primarily to supply the English mission with new priests, and the second that saw the colleges as preserving the basic structure and composition of the church for the time when Catholicism would (most thought inevitably) return to England.[44] Although Persons tried to present himself as impartial in this controversy, it is fair to say that Persons was central to the former perspective (that of Englefield, Saunders, and Allen), while Morys Clynnog was the central figure within the Catholic exile community sharing the latter perspective (that of Stukeley, Lewes, and Clynnog).

Most significant for my purposes, the distinction between the ideological perspectives of the Persons faction and the Clynnog faction figure as two different conceptions of nationhood, which can be seen by comparing two different Catholic plans for the invasion of England. Morys Clynnog's plan, sent to Pope Gregory XIII in 1575, was to have the invasion force proceed through Wales since, as he notes, "in Wales above all … hardly one in a thousand to-day can be found who is a heretic [i.e. Protestant]."[45] This was in contrast to Allen and Englefield's subsequent plans in which the invading force was to enter England through Liverpool.[46] Clynnog's perspective was driven by a historical narrative of immemorial Welsh Catholicism similar to the Galfridian pseudo-history that appeared in the writings of contemporary common law jurists such as Sir Edward Coke.[47] As Clynnog describes Wales, "This region is nearly one-third of the kingdom of England: where scarcely a single man in a thousand will be found to be a heretic. The British people indeed is the original stock of that island, which to this day retains the ancient British language (which the English do not understand since they are of Saxon descent) and the ancient, the ancestral Catholic faith [Britannicus enim populus illius insulae indigena est, qui adhuc retinet, et priscam Britannorum linguam (quam Angli, ut ex Saxonia oriundi non intelligent) et antiquam atque avitam quoque fidem catholicam]."[48]

Here Clynnog presents Wales's retention of its ancient Catholic identity as tied to its immemorial British character. What is implicit in this passage is that subsequent conquests of the British Isles by the Saxon and Norman invaders introduced the seeds of heresy from which the English now suffer. In contrast to these outsiders, the original inhabitants of the island remain steadfast in their original pristine state.

Clynnog's position bears some resemblance to the account of Christianity's introduction into England favoured by John Foxe and Richard Hooker, which Persons criticized at length in his massive *Treatise of Three Conversions of England*.[49] Similar to Clynnog's presentation of a pure British Catholicism that preceded the heretical corruptions introduced by the Saxons and Normans, for example, Foxe sees the pagan Saxon invaders as having managed almost to eradicate both native Christianity and the original Britons from the country, with the exception of those Britons who fled to Wales.[50] But Foxe takes the argument further, suggesting that Christianity in Britain preceded any ecclesiastical allegiance to Rome. Foxe claims that, according to an ancient letter sent by Pope Eleutherius to the early British king, Lucius, Britain was already a Christian polity when Lucius asked Pope Eleutherius to assist him in setting up an ecclesiastical legal structure.[51] If this conception of Christianity's origins in ancient Britain were proved to be correct, an English sovereign, as holder of the supreme office that had originally initiated obedience to Rome, was now free to reclaim that ancient freedom from Rome. Thus, according to Persons, Foxe wants to maintain that "*Eleutherius* conuerted not *King Lucius* at all: but onlie holp perhaps to conuert him, or to instruct him better in religion (being a Christian before)."[52] In doing so, Foxe wants to maintain that, from the very beginning, the King had prerogative over the form that the ecclesiastical polity would assume.

But Persons maintains that Foxe's account of Pope Eleutherius's missive to King Lucius is flawed because of Foxe's tendentious presentation and reading of the letter. If he had translated the Latin title of the original epistle, his reader would have never doubted that, even during the early period, the pope exercised supremacy over kings and temporal magistrates: "And so he plaieth the Fox in every thing. But, to returne again to this latin title of the epistle, there is another cause, why Iohn Fox would not translate it into English. And this is, for that it is said therein that it was written by the Pope *ad correctionem Regis & Procerum regni &c.* to correct the King, and nobility of the realme. Which proueth that the Pope tooke himself to be their Superiour also in those daies, and they to be subject to his correction. For which causes Fox his schollers, *Holinshed*, *Hooker*, and *Harrison* do leaue out this title altogeather in their chronicles."[53]

What emerges in the contrast between Persons and both his Protestant and Catholic opponents are two conceptions of the nation. Clynnog imagines a Catholic purity that has existed in Wales from the beginning of the Christian era or at least beyond any recorded memory. In the case of Foxe and his Protestant allies, a similar historical account of early Britain is used in order to make the case that claims for papal supremacy over England have no basis in ecclesiastical history.[54] In contrast, Persons champions the legacy of the ancient imperial Rome, which, by conquering Britain, was understood to have introduced Christianity into the region. As a result, like Campion, Persons imagines a broadly transnational Christian commonwealth, with the English realm as one province in it and the English sovereign as subordinate to papal oversight.[55] From Persons's perspective, having the status of both conqueror and conquered is central to England's participation in the larger Catholic identity of the Christian commonwealth over which the pope and the Roman curia preside.

Legal historians have generally associated the notion of an unbroken legacy of British national and religious identity that we find here in Clynnog and Foxe with seventeenth-century common lawyers and puritans, who were attempting to define the limits of the English sovereign's power on the basis of immemorial custom, which had supposedly preceded the prince's sovereignty.[56] As Clynnog's invasion plan shows, traditional Marian Catholics, who were trying to preserve their own customary outlook in the face of Jesuit reform and Protestant hegemony, believed similar myths about Britain's origins. So while the conceptions of English sovereignty and nationhood in Persons, Harington, and Munday were similarly cosmopolitan, Foxe's and Clynnog's conceptions of nationhood were both based on an ideal of immemorial national purity, untrammelled by corrupting foreign invaders or institutions. Thus the widely accepted scholarly account of the early modern ideological production of English nationhood, according to which two opposing religious conceptions of the nation existed – one Protestant and the other Catholic – is erroneous.[57] Conceptions of nationhood crossed confessional lines, and what emerges is an opposition between Catholic and Protestant cosmopolitans who saw England as an integral part of Christendom, or secular Europe, or Continental affairs, and Catholic and Protestant adherents to the myth of English or British national purity.

NOTES

1 See James M. Osborne, *Young Philip Sidney 1572–1577* (New Haven, CT: Yale University Press, 1972), 109–219.
2 "Hubert Languet to Sidney, Vienna, 11 June 1574," in *Correspondence of Sir Philip Sidney*, ed. Roger Kuin (New York: Oxford University Press, 2012), 1:251–6.
3 See Sidney's references to the transnational *"respublica Christiana"* in ibid., 1:159 [162 (Kuin's English trans.)], 230 [231]; 2:736 [737]. In contrast, see Languet's and Wolfgang Zundelin's use of the phrase *orbis Christianus* (1:137 [139], 268 [270], 289 [291], 330 [336]; 2:823 [826], 928 [931]). For discussion of the typical

Catholic use of the phrase *respublica Christiana*, see Stefania Tutino, *Empire of Souls: Robert Bellarmine and the Christian Commonwealth* (Oxford: Oxford University Press, 2010), esp. 14. In a letter to Languet on 10 March 1578, Sidney refers to the French Huguenots as constituting a *"respublica Christiana,"* thus using it in a way that was more typical of his fellow Protestants, who often described a nation-state such as England as a Christian commonwealth (2:820 [821]). See the introduction to my *Early Modern Catholics, Royalists, and Cosmopolitans: English Transnationalism and the Christian Commonwealth* (Burlington, VT: Ashgate, 2015), for a brief discussion of how Protestants and Catholics used the term *Christian commonwealth* differently.

4 "Sidney to Hubert Languet, Venice, 15 April 1574," in Kuin, ed., *Correspondence* 1, 158–64.

5 For the global character of the Jesuit order, see Luke Clossey, *Salvation and Globalization in the Early Jesuit Missions* (New York: Cambridge University Press, 2008); and Markus Friedrich, "Communication and Bureaucracy in the Early Modern Society," *Schweizerische Zeitschrift für Religions- und Kulturgeschichte* 101 (2007): 49–75. For a sense of how this global character was inscribed into the constitutional documents of the order, see the *Regulae Societatis Iesu ad usum nostrorum tantum* (Rome: Apud Curiam Praepositi Generalis, 1935), 34–5; and the 1550 version of the *Formula* (*The Formula of the Institute*, Notes for a Commentary by Antonio M. de Aldama, SJ, trans. Ignacio Echaniz, SJ [St Louis: Institute of Jesuit Sources, 1990], 9). For background on Munday's interactions with Catholics, see Donna Hamilton, *Anthony Munday and the Catholics 1560–1633* (Burlington, VT: Ashgate, 2005), 7–40.

6 For historical and intellectual accounts of cosmopolitanism during this period, see Margaret C. Jacob, *Strangers Nowhere in the World: The Rise of Cosmopolitanism in Early Modern Europe* (Philadelphia: University of Pennsylvania Press, 2006), chap. 3; and Derek Heater, *World Citizenship and Government: Cosmopolitan Ideas in the History of Western Political Thought* (New York: St Martin's, 1996), chap. 3.

7 Edmund Campion, *Rationes decem quibus fretus B. Edmundus Campianus certamen adversariis obtulit in causa fidei, redditae academicis angliae* (Ten reasons proposed to his adversaries for disputation in the name of the faith and presented to the illustrious members of our universities), ed. and trans. John Hungerford Pollen, SJ (St Louis: B. Herder, 1914). For context, see Richard Simpson, *Edmund Campion: A Biography* (London: Williams and Norgate, 1867), 212–17; and Evelyn Waugh, *Edmund Campion: A Life* (London: Longmans, Green, 1935), 141–73.

8 Campion, *Rationes decem*, 84–5, 142–3.

9 Ibid., 87, 145.

10 John Dee, *The Perfect Arte of Navigation* [London, 1577] (repr.: New York: Da Capo Press Reprint, 1968), sig. G3v. For context, see William H. Sherman, *John Dee: The Politics of Reading and Writing in the English Renaissance* (Amherst: University of

Massachusetts Press, 1995), 115–200; Frances A. Yates, *The Occult Philosophy in the Elizabethan Age* (Boston: Harvard University Press, 1979), 75–95; Peter J. French, *John Dee: The World of an Elizabethan Magus* (London: Routledge & Kegan Paul, 1972), 182–90; and Richard Deacon, *John Dee: Scientist Geographer, Astrologer, and Secret Agent to Elizabeth I* (London: Muller, 1968).

11 Campion, "Challenge to the Privy Council," in *Rationes decem*, 7–11, esp. 8.

12 "Cum igitur Apostolis dictum sit, *Ite, docete omnes gente (Matth. 28)*, cumque; gentium nomine reges etiam earum comprehendantur: & Episcopi ac Presbyteri Apostolis in officio docendi successerint: profecto in docendi munere maior est Episcopus Rege suo: tantum abest, vt Rex Episcopi caput in omibus rebus & causis esse queat. Qui tamen titulus non Regi modo, sed etiam Reginae ab istis hominibus, in Anglia nuper decreto publico tributus est. Isaias praedixit, *Reges fore nutricios Ecclesiae Christi, & vultu in terram demisso adoraturos illam*, & mox subiungit: *Scies, quia ego Dominus (Isaie 49)*? Hoc enim vere signum est, Dominum regnare in nobis, si tantum deferamus Ecclesiae ipsius, ut palam appareat, ministros Christi maiores quo libet Rege ac Regina esse." Nicholas Sander, *De visibili monarchia ecclesiae, libri VIII: in quibus diligens instituitur disputatio de certa & perpetua Ecclesiae Dei tum successione tum gubernatione monarchica, ab ipso mundi initio vsque ad finem: deinde etiam ciuitas diaboli persaepè interrupta progressio proponitur, sectaeque omnes & haereses confutantur, quae vnquam contra veram fidem emerserunt : denique de Antichristo ipso & membris eius, deque vera Dei & adulterina diaboli ecclesia, copiosè tractatur ... cum indice rerum & personarum locuplete* (Antuerpiae: Apud Ioannem Foulerum, MDLXXVIII [1578]), sig. E4v; my trans. For context, see Thomas McNevin Veech, *Dr Nicholas Sanders and the English Reformation 1530–1581* (Louvain: Bureaux du Recueil, 1935).

13 Cardinal William Allen, *A true sincere and modest defence of English Catholiques that suffer for their faith both at home and abrode: against a false, seditious and slaunderous libel intituled; The execution of iustice in England. VVherein is declared, hovv vniustlie the Protestants doe charge Catholiques vvith* (St Louis: B. Herder, 1914), 2:9, 13; Richard Bristow, *A Brief Treatise of Divers Plaine and sure waies to finde out the truth in this doubtfull and dangerous time of Heresie [Bristow's Motives]* (Antwerp, 1599), sigs X7v–X8.

14 For Munday's encounter with Campion, see Hamilton, *Anthony Munday and the Catholics*, 31–72; and Celeste Turner, *Anthony Mundy: An Elizabethan Man of Letters* (Berkeley: University of California Press, 1928), 51–62. Munday's own account of his encounters with Campion and the English Catholics can be found in Anthony Munday, *A breefe discourse of the taking of Edmund Campion* (London: J. Charlewood for W. Wright, 1582); Munday, *A discoverie of Edmund Campion and his confederates* (London: J. Charlewood for E. White, 1582); Munday, *A breefe answer made unto two seditious pamphlets, the one printed in French, and the other in English* (London: J. Charlewood, 1582); and Munday, *The English Roman Life*, ed. Philip J. Ayres (Oxford: Clarendon, 1980), 67. For Harington's perspective on Campion, see

Gerard Kilroy, *Edmund Campion: Memory and Transcription* (Burlington, VT: Ashgate, 2005), 66–71, 89–120; and Kilroy, "Introduction," in *The Epigrams of Sir John Harington*, ed. Gerard Kilroy (Burlington, VT: Ashgate, 2009), 5–22, 72–3. For the possible Catholic context of Harington's writings, see Jason Scott-Warren, *Sir John Harington and the Book as Gift* (New York: Oxford University Press, 2001), 86–98.

15 For the crux of Hamilton's argument that Munday was essentially a Catholic loyalist, see Hamilton, *Anthony Munday and the Catholics*, xvi–xvii. For the crux of Kilroy's argument that Harington employed his "Rabelaisian mask" to argue for the toleration of Catholics, see Kilroy, *Edmund Campion, Memory and Transcription*, 69–94. Kilroy's argument is the more subtle, claiming as he does that Harington had been indelibly influenced by Campion's life and death and suggesting that, at the very least, he had Catholic sympathies (Kilroy, *Edmund Campion*, 70). However, as Michael Questier has shown, English Catholic identity during this period was based upon existing within "a series of entourages and networks," and neither Munday nor Harington ever really participated in any such network (Michael C. Questier, *Catholicism and Community in Early Modern England: Politics, Aristocratic Patronage and Religion, c. 1550–1640* [New York: Cambridge, 2006], 9). In fact, the only network in which Munday did participate until at least 1612 was intelligencer Richard Topcliffe's network, whose purpose was to hunt down Catholic recusants and seminarians.

16 Sir John Harington, *A Tract on the Succession to the Crown*, ed. Clements R. Markham, CB (London: J.B. Nichols and Sons, 1880), 116. The reference to the proverb "Pap with a Hatchet," meaning to punish someone by giving them a benefit, seems to be an ironical reference to John Lyly's anti-Martinist tract, *Pap with a Hatchet: Being a Reply to Martin Mar-Prelate* (1589), *Re-printed from the Original Quarto Edition with An Introduction and Notes* (London, 1844). Whereas in this passage, Harington is justifying Queen Elizabeth's rejection of papal supremacy (giving them "Pap with a Hatchet"), Lyly's tract was written in defence of the Episcopal hierarchy against Martin Marprelate's attack on the English bishops and the established church. In this respect, Harington seems to be stressing his own conformity: he supported Elizabeth taking the "Hatchet" to Rome, while at the same time making reference, through his allusion to Lyly's tract, to his support for English bishops.

17 *Tract on the Succession*, 117.

18 Sir John Harington's *A New Discourse of a Stale Subject, Called the Metamorphosis of Ajax*, ed. Elizabeth Story Donno (New York: Columbia University Press, 1962).

19 As a number of commentators have pointed out, the second section of the *New Discourse* that describes the invention was probably written by Combe, not Harington. See Scott-Warren, *Sir John Harington*, 57.

20 See Donno's commentary in Harington, *New Discourse*, 232n149; Kilroy, *Edmund Campion*, 90–6; and Scott-Warren, *Sir John Harington*, 86–98.

21 Harington, *New Discourse*, 174–5.
22 Ibid., 143.
23 Ibid., 141.
24 For context, see Scott-Warren, *Sir John Harington*, 75–80.
25 Referencing Elizabeth with the title "Mistresse" has a double-edged meaning here in the late sixteenth century. On the one hand, this title references Queen Elizabeth's sovereignty over her subjects, including Essex. On the other hand, "Mistresse" could also have a more suggestive meaning: "a woman loved and courted by a man; a female sweetheart" (*OED*). Scott-Warren, *Sir John Harington*, 79–80.
26 Harington, *New Discourse*, 142–3. Note that Harington ascribes his nomination to the position of Steward of Bath to the members of the Privy Council, rather than the Queen: "This I do write, because your Lordship, and the rest of her Majesties most honorable counsel, thought me once worthy to be Steward of that towne" (143). In so doing, his letter reflects, by way of analogy with imperial Rome, the notion that the Privy Council had a quasi-imperial supervisory role with regard to Elizabeth's sovereignty.
27 Sir John Harington (trans.), *Ludovico Ariosto's Orlando Furioso*, ed. Robert McNulty (Oxford: Clarendon, 1972), 68.
28 Ibid., 28. See also R. Doleman [Robert Persons], *A Conference about the Next Succession to the Crown of Ingland* (Antwerp: Arnout Conincx, 1594 [vere 1595]), sigs E5–E5v.
29 Munday, *English Roman Life*; Robert Persons, "A Storie of Domesticall Difficulties in the English Catholike cause," in *Miscellanea II, Publications of the Catholic Record Society*, ed. J.H. Pollen, SJ, no. 2 (London: Arden, 1906), 48–185.
30 Persons, "Storie," 86.
31 Ibid., 87.
32 See the "Memorialles given up by the Schollers against Mr Morrisse," prepared by the English students for Cardinal Morone, in Persons, "Storie," 102–17. For background, see Thomas McCoog, SJ, *The Society of Jesus in Ireland, Scotland, and England 1541–1588: "Our Way of Proceeding?"* (New York: E.J. Brill, 1996), 105–8.
33 "Cum inter duos Angliae populos, Anglos et Wallos, sit aliqua naturalis radix discordiae, videtur necessarium, ut tales nobis viri praesint, qui sint alieni ab utriusque partis affectu, alioquin experientia jam probatum est, hos populos simul non posse vivere: imo quod infinito cum dolore nostro dicimus, hoc tempore probamus." "Memorialles" in Person, "A Storie," 103, my trans.
34 Persons, "The copy of a larg Letter and relation wrytten by F. Persons unto F. William Goode ...," in Persons, "Storie," 156–7. For an exploration of British archipelagic analogies to the relationship between the Spaniards and the Moors,

see Barbara Fuchs, "Spanish Lessons: Spenser and the Irish Moriscos," *Studies in English Literature 1500–1900* 42, no. 1 (2002): 43–62.
35 Persons, "Storie," 146–7.
36 See for example, Persons, *Conference*, sigs D6–G6.
37 Munday, *English Roman Life*, 94.
38 Ibid., 80–7.
39 Anthony Munday, *A breefe discourse of the taking of Edmund Campion*, sig. D1v.
40 Ibid., title page. For other references to Munday as the "pope's scholar" or as a recognized scholar at the seminary, see *A breefe and true reporte, of the execution of certaine traytours at Tiborne* (London: J. Charlewood for W. Wright, 1582), sig. C1; and *A breefe aunswer made vnto two seditious pamphlets* (London: J. Charlewood, 1582), sigs D4–D4v.
41 See Anthony Munday, *John A Kent and John A Cumber; A Comedy, Printed from the Original Manuscript*, ed. J. Payne Collier (London: Printed for the Shakespeare Society, 1851); Anthony Munday and others, *Sir Thomas More*, ed. Vittorio Gabrieli and Giorgio Mechiori (New York: Manchester University Press, 1990); Munday, *The Huntington Plays: A Critical Edition of the Downfall and the Death of Robert, Earl of Huntington*, ed. John Carney Meagher, 2 vols. (New York: Garland Publishing, 1980); Michael Drayton, Richard Hathway, Anthony Munday, and Robert Wilson, *The First Part of the true and honorable historie, of the life of Sir John Old-Castle, the good Lord Cobham* in *The Oldcastle Controversy: Sir John Oldcastle, Part I and The Famous Victories of Henry V*, ed. Peter Corbin and Douglas Sedge (New York: Manchester University Press, 1991), 36–144. See, for example, *The Downfall of the Earl of Huntington*, in which Robin Hood punishes and corrects Prince John's immoral and tyrannical actions during King Richard's absence. At the end of the play, Robin presents King Richard with a chastened and reformed Prince John: "Here is Prince John, your brother, whose revolt / And folly in your absence, let me crave, / With his submission may be buried. / For he is now no more the man he was, / But duetifull in all respects to you" (2757–61).
42 See John Bossy, *The English Catholic Community 1570–1850* (London: Darton, Longman & Todd, 1975), 25–34.
43 Persons, "Storie," 64.
44 McCoog, *Society of Jesus*, 104–8, esp. 107. For discussion of the tensions and the disagreements between the English Jesuits led by Persons and the Marian Catholic exiles led by Clynnog and Owen Lewis, see Bernard Basset, SJ, with a preface by Terance Corrigan, SJ, *The English Jesuits: From Campion to Martindale* (New York: Herder and Herder, 1967), 27–96; Bossy, *English Catholic Community*, 35–48; Questier, *Catholicism and Community*, 157–68, 288–314; and T.G. Law, ed., *The Archpriest Controversy: Documents relating to the Dissensions of the Roman Catholic Clergy*

1597–1602, 2 vols. (New York: Camden Society, 1896–8), 1:ix–xxvii. See also Morys Clynnog's conception of Welsh purity in J.M. Cleary, "Dr Morys Clynnog's Invasion Projects of 1575–76," *Recusant History* 8, no. 5 (1966): 300–21.
45 Cleary, "Dr Morys Clynnog's Invasion Projects," 307; trans. Cleary.
46 Ibid., 311.
47 This is a reference to the fact that Coke based his account of legal history in dubious sources such as Geoffrey of Monmouth's *Historia Regum Britanniae* in order to make his claim for the existence of an unbroken legacy of English legal customs going back to the ancient Britons. Brian Lockey, *Law and Empire in English Renaissance Literature* (New York: Cambridge University Press, 2006), 80–5.
48 Cleary, "Dr. Morys Clynnog's Invasion Projects," 306; trans. M. Cleary.
49 Persons, *A Treatise of Three Conversions of England from Paganisme to Christian Religion*, 3 vols. (St Omer: Fracois Bellet, 1603–4).
50 John Foxe, *The Acts and Monuments of John Foxe: A New and Complete Edition*, 8 vols., with preliminary dissertation by Rev. George Townsend, ed. Stephen Reed Catley (London: R.B. Seeley and W. Burnside, 1841), 1:327–8.
51 Foxe, *Acts and Monuments*, 1:307–10; Persons, *Treatise of Three Conversions*, 1:F4; 1:F5v. For background, see Victor Houliston, *Catholic Resistance in Elizabethan England: Robert Persons's Jesuit Polemic, 1580–1610* (Burlington, VT: Ashgate, 2007), 101.
52 Persons, *Treatise of Three Conversions*, 1:E8.
53 Ibid., 1:F5v.
54 For the legal and political context here, see Glen Burgess, *The Politics of the Ancient Constitution: An Introduction to English Political Thought 1603–1642* (University Park, PA: Penn. State University, 1992), 121–30; Brian Levack, *The Civil Lawyers in England, 1603–1641* (New York: Oxford University Press, 1973), 131–50; and Lockey, *Law and Empire*, 148–9, 163, 174–5.
55 Persons' notion of Britain's history is similar to that of the civil lawyers and supporters of Chancery during the early seventeenth century, who saw the English inheritance of the Roman *ius commune* as having been introduced by the Roman empire. It is therefore no surprise to find Persons siding with the civil lawyers and attacking their bête noire, Sir Edward Coke, along similar lines in *An Answer to the Fifth Part of Reportes Lately set forth by Syr Edward Cooke*, which refuted Coke's argument that the jurisdiction of the ecclesiastical courts was subordinate to the English common law. Robert Persons, *An Answere to The Fifth Part of Reportes Lately set forth by Syr Edward Cooke, Knight, the Kinges Attorney generall* (Antwerp, 1606), sig. B3v. See Sir Edward Coke, *The Selected Writings of Sir Edward Coke*, 3 vols., ed. Steve Sheppard (Indianapolis, IN: Liberty Fund, INC, 2003), 1:125.
56 John Dykstra Eusden, *Puritans, Lawyers, and Politics in Early Seventeenth-Century England*, 2nd ed. (New York: Archon Books, 1968), 131–41.

57 See, for example, Richard Helgerson, *Forms of Nationhood: The Elizabethan Writing of England* (Chicago: The University of Chicago, 1992), 249–94, which uses Foxe's *Acts and Monuments* as well as Richard Hooker's *Laws of the Ecclesiastical Polity*, along with numerous secular works from the period, in order to illustrate the Elizabethan writing of the English nation. Helgerson claims that the most important event in such a writing was "the separation of the English church from the church of Rome" (251), a statement with which I would not necessarily disagree. My intention here is to show that an English conception of nationhood characterized as defined by a Protestant notion of the nation divorced from Catholicism and Catholic notions of nationhood is inaccurate. See Christopher Highley, *Catholics Writing the Nation in Early Modern Britain and Ireland* (New York: Cambridge University Press, 2008), for some perspective.

chapter twelve

Viewing Spain through Darkened Eyes: Anti-Spanish Rhetoric and Charles Cornwallis's Mission to Spain, 1605–1609*

WILLIAM S. GOLDMAN

As rain poured down from a darkening afternoon sky on 16 May 1605, an Englishman newly arrived in Spain met the greatest lords and nobles of the Spanish court just outside Valladolid, the Spanish capital. What was supposed to have been a grand entrance into the city was instead – as the result, according to the Englishman's account, of the tardiness of several Spanish grandees – a complete disaster of rain, wind, galloping horses, and splashing mud as an afternoon storm soaked the assembled hosts. Nobles dove into carriages, turned their horses, and fled, and all the order and ceremony that normally accompanied official business of the Spanish court dissolved into the morass of the road from Simancas. The Englishman observed with considerable understatement that the entire experience "proved not Answerable to Expectation."[1]

So began Sir Charles Cornwallis's four-year tenure as England's first resident ambassador at the court of Spain in almost forty years, since Philip II demanded the recall of English ambassador John Man in 1568 as England and Spain began a long preamble to war. Cornwallis's diplomatic correspondence with his superiors in London – particularly Secretary of State Robert Cecil, Lord Salisbury – is a fascinating testament to the power of experience to overcome the prejudices brought about by alien and disparate cultures, and constitutes a record of his thoughts and observations on the land, people, and government of what was then the greatest state in Europe. The gulfs of distance, language, religion, and temperament separated Northern Europe from the Mediterranean, and England from Spain, mortal enemies until James I expressed his peaceful intentions in 1603. Even after the conclusion of a formal treaty of peace in 1604, Philip III's Catholic kingdom remained a bitter moral foe of Protestant England.[2] Cornwallis's letters demonstrate his complicated relationship with Spain and its people, alternately excoriating the Spanish for perceived mismanagement of their country and praising the individuals with whom he had personal dealings for their kindness and attention. A close reading of his rhetoric demonstrates his convenient reliance, as he began his tenure in Spain, on the familiar tropes of the anti-Spanish Black Legend to comprehend the alien land and customs of the Mediterranean. Yet by the date of his departure he no longer resorts to anti-Spanish rhetoric; instead, he displays a nuanced appreciation for Spanish customs and people, and an acceptance of Spanish values and customs far removed from his initial reactions. Cornwallis's mission bridged a gap between the Protestant mores of the Atlantic and the Catholic traditions of the Mediterranean, a gap that at times seemed unbridgeable to contemporaries steeped in anti-Spanish propaganda. Yet shared goals, including the resumption of normal trading relations and the safeguarding of nationals in foreign lands, proved an antidote to claims of an inherent irreconcilability between these two erstwhile enemies. The example of Cornwallis's transition from reflexively anti-Spanish sentiment to an equitable evaluation of his hosts illuminates the impermanent effect of anti-Spanish propaganda on an Englishman of the age, and demonstrates that, at least at the elite level, the two kingdoms – and the two great seas they embraced – were not quite as distinct as the rhetoric of the age would suggest.

Charles Cornwallis was a fairly representative example of the English gentry in the early Stuart period. Son of a Catholic servant to Mary Tudor, he was knighted in 1603 and made a member of Parliament in 1604, unlike his father, a fully convinced Anglican, for evidence of which we need look no farther than to note that he was sent to the court of Spain, the most devoutly Catholic land outside of Rome itself.[3] In the following year, he was dispatched with Charles Lord Howard, the earl of Nottingham, who represented England at the official ratification of the Treaty of London that ended the long Armada War. As evidenced by his initial displeasure with all things Spanish, Cornwallis's views of Spain were heavily influenced by what would later be termed the Black Legend. This should not come as a surprise: the overall sentiment towards Spain in the late Elizabethan era was decidedly anti-Catholic and anti-Spanish; much of the information readily available in England about Spain consisted of anti-Spanish treatises, pamphlets, and translations.[4] Several historians have put forward theories about the origins of the Black Legend, including Sverker Arnoldsson, who, in his seminal work on the topic, located the phenomenon in Italy during the fifteenth century.[5] Arnoldsson defines the concept as follows: Spaniards – as a "race" and individually – were guilty of "cruelty, despotism, pride, falsehood, close relations with the hated Catholic Church and the Inquisition, and of [being] a racial mixture of Moors, Jews and *marranos*."[6] Regardless of its origins, by the early seventeenth century, the English stereotype of Spanish cruelty and avarice was universal.[7]

While it cannot be known exactly which texts informed Cornwallis's views on his new station, it is likely that an educated Englishman of his age would have been familiar with Haklyut's *Principal Navigations* and *Discourse on Western Planting*, Foxe's *Book of Martyrs*, Holinshed's *Chronicles*, and many other similar works that included a strong dose of anti-Hispanism. Las Casas's *Brevissima relación* was translated into English in 1583, and a veritable tide of anti-Spanish propaganda attended the murder of William of Orange in 1584, and the dispatch of the Invincible Armada four years later. Elizabeth herself castigated the Spanish character in her *Declaration of the Causes Moving the Queen of England to give aid to the Defence of the People ... of the Lowe Countries*, which was reprinted in the 1587 version of Holinshed's *Chronicles*.[8] Antonio Perez's *Relations*, translated immediately on their publication in 1594, created a major stir in England, where the exiled counsellor of Philip II spent several years. Spenser's *The Fairie Queene* was widely read, and *Othello*, with its Moorish general and anti-Spanish flavour, was first performed in 1604. Anonymous plays including the sensational and wildly popular *A Larum for London* took the graphic brutality of Spanish villains, including the duke of Alba, to new heights, and the list of plays, pamphlets, and books goes on and on.[9] In addition, the broad anti-Catholic literature of the period was a dominant theme of English texts and would have certainly been a part of Cornwallis's education as a gentleman and an Englishman.[10]

As Cornwallis made his way to Spain, then, we can comfortably conjecture that he was familiar with the anti-Spanish bent of English political and popular culture and saw the Spanish through darkened eyes. His early reports to England back up that supposition. But what is interesting here is not that Cornwallis was a creature of his age and harboured anti-Spanish sentiment coloured by the litany of supposed Spanish calumnies popularized in England and the Low Countries. Instead, it is that Cornwallis's views changed markedly during his tenure as ambassador. By the time he left Spain in September 1609, he was no longer vehemently anti-Spanish and in fact exhibited significant friendship with individual Spaniards, as well as a far more nuanced view of the court and the country. More importantly, as he became more comfortable with the culture of the Spanish court and the realities of the Spanish judicial system, much of his criticism of Spain and Spaniards fell away, revealing a grudging admiration for various aspects of the land. This chapter will demonstrate that the more contact Cornwallis had with Spain and Spaniards, the less salience the Black Legend held for him, strongly suggesting that while anti-Spanish and anti-Catholic writings dominated English rhetoric about Spain and Catholicism, those views were not immutable. For the general English population, Spain was a land of pride, poverty, and popery; for Cornwallis – who, after all, had lived within Spain itself – it was something much more, a land and a people worthy of admiration and respect, a land not so different from England. The Black Legend may have been effective at ginning up anti-Spanish fervour in Northern Europe, but it was not all-powerful. Cornwallis's letters shed a very different light on English-Spanish relations, colouring them much brighter than their customary darkened shades.

Without a doubt, Cornwallis thinks the worst of Spain before he even arrives, and utilizes the rhetoric of the Black Legend almost casually in his reports to London. Early on, he writes to Salisbury about the great feasts and kind treatment Nottingham's party received in Spain, and then changes course dramatically, stating, "I hold this Estate to be one of the most confused and disordered in Christendome." In the same letter, he laments that England has been taken in by Spanish bravado and military propaganda, and has made peace with such a weak state: "If this Peace had not been concluded, in mine owne Understandinge I see not how it had been possible for him [Philip III] longe to have borne out the infinite Waight of Chardges and Business laud upon him. His debts are greate; out of his Dominions he draweth littell, the Profitts not surmounting his yearly Charge." Continuing, Cornwallis ties the plight of Spain's fisc to its heretical religion: "But I suppose the Account of their many Ducketts is not unlike the Tally they use to make by their Rosaries of their Prayers, for as the one serves them to make themselves greate in Opinion without the Effects, so doe the other give an Appearance of Pietie and Devotion, without the workinge Power of either."[11] The gruelling journey over the mountains from La Coruña to Valladolid leads Cornwallis to grumble about travel within Spain, with its poor roads, uncertain provisions, and dreadful inns.[12]

Yet his descriptions of the official reception for Nottingham – a series of huge court affairs including the procession and feast of Corpus Christi, the baptism of the future Philip IV, and the ceremony of ratification itself – are far more revealing of his mindset at the beginning of his mission. In them, he demonstrates the core tension of his tenure in Spain: between his preconceived notions of Spain and its people and his personal experiences living and working with Spaniards. When describing the last of the many great ceremonies of Nottingham's visit, a bullfight in the Plaza Mayor in Valladolid, he takes great pains to express his admiration for how the English were treated in matters of precedence, as well as personally.[13] Several pages of flowery descriptions of the festivities are festooned with comments describing Spanish hospitality: "We were very royally entertained and feasted" at the duke of Lerma's table with the king in attendance, he writes.[14] He has many fine words about Spanish officials themselves, giving possibly the kindest description of Philip III ever recorded by an impartial observer: "I assure your Lordshipps that the King's Presence ... promiseth and performeth more than we expected ... I take him to be of an exceeding good Nature, and of a plaine Heart."[15] Yet Cornwallis does manifest some doubts about the Spaniards with whom he deals, writing to Sir Henry Wotton, the famous English ambassador at Venice, of his lack of faith in the trustworthiness of the Spanish: "If Words, Countenances, and Actions of Complement and Curtesie may deserve belief, so many we have received and such to my self I daily find amongst them [the Spanish], as in Charitie I hold my self bound to believe their Intentions bee sincere and faithfull. Tyme the unmasker of all Feignings will discover the Truth." Cornwallis has experienced no breach of faith with the Spaniards – quite the opposite in fact, as he mentions numerous times – yet he still expects to be dealt with falsely. And in a letter to the lords of the Privy Council, Cornwallis laments the Spanish trait of keeping official secrets: "Their greatest Vertue is Secrecy in their Councells, and what is delivered or committed unto them, which I perceive to be exceeding hard here, by any means possible to draw from any of them."[16] It was not meant as a compliment. At the same time, the seemingly laudable trait of keeping official secrets is cast in a negative light, an example of the perceived baseness of the Spanish character. Cornwallis was torn between his preconceived notions of Spain and his actual experiences. The Black Legend warned him of the falseness of Spaniards; his letter to Wotton shows that he was still waiting to find it after several months in-country.

At the beginning of his time in Spain, Cornwallis spends considerable effort describing the state of Spain to his superiors. Passing through the mountains and valleys on the way from the seacoast to inland Valladolid, he remarks on "the exceedinge Barrenness of Place, and Povertye of that whole Countrey, [which] inforce us to many Sufferances."[17] He repeatedly returns to the theme of extreme want and need among the populace, and ruling classes' lack of care about what we today might term extremes of income inequality. With almost audible sighs, he details his realization that Spain was economically destitute after so many years of war, and sums up Spain's fiscal challenges brilliantly. "The King and Kingdome were reduced to such Estate," he writes to Salisbury in a personal letter, "as they could not in all liklihood have endured the Space of two Years more; [Philip's] owne Treasurie was exhausted, his Rents and Customes consigned for the most parte for the Payment of Money borrowed, his Nobilitie poor and much indebted, his Merchants wasted, his People of the Countrye in all Extreamitie of Necessitie, his Devices of gaining by the Increse of Valuation of Money, and other such of that Nature, all plaid over."[18] He paints a picture of a land crushed by want and suffering, of a population struggling to feed itself while an aloof aristocracy contents itself with sport, hunting, and lavish feasts. Spaniards themselves recognized the dangers of inequality and poverty, and produced a robust literature of *arbitrios* arguing for reforms.[19] In truth, Valladolid and especially Madrid – made the capital again in early 1606 – were cesspits compared with the (somewhat) more ordered streets of London and other English cities, and according to his correspondence, almost all of Cornwallis's experience of Spain occurred in those two places. Madrid lay on a high plateau with little water, and required thousands of mules to supply it with food; simply procuring enough to eat was a constant battle requiring Cornwallis to send members of his entourage to forage in the countryside. None of this endeared Spain to the English ambassador, a point he made repeatedly to Salisbury during the early stages of his tenure. By mid-1607, frustrated by the slow pace of business in the Spanish capital and the difficulties of living in the country, Cornwallis rhetorically throws up his hands: "God Almighty deliver me from amongst them," he laments to Salisbury.[20]

Cornwallis's activities consisted of more than feasts and official gatherings. His official brief was to ensure that Spain carried out the provisions of the newly signed peace treaty and to protect and expand English trade with Spain, and this he did as assiduously as he could.[21] At first, he finds himself repeatedly stymied by difficulties put in his path when trying to aid English sailors caught by customs officials in Spain's major port towns, or, more problematically, taken by the Inquisition for offences against the Catholic Church. Over and over during the first years of his tenure, he rails against the delays of high Spanish officials. The Spanish conciliar administrative system that to Cornwallis seemed designed to centralize authority but devolve responsibility was nothing but a cause of hardship and frustration: "When things consulted and determined here by the Counsels are sent to the Duke of Lerma (through whose Hands all Generations of Papers of what worth soever must have the Passage) if there be a Bird to be shot at in the Wood, an Hare in the Field, or Rabbet in the Burrough, the Papers lie dead tho' they concearne the Life or Soule of the Poore, or the greatest Good whatsoever of the Commonwealth."[22] Spaniards, according to Cornwallis, are both lazy and corrupt. Later, he finds himself oppressed by the intricate Burgundian court ceremony that Charles V instituted in Spain and that was based on the concept of the king keeping a proscribed distance from those around him in order to ceremonially separate the royal person from the rest of the world. His meetings with the king were staged events in which Cornwallis spoke at length and the king simply stood with a hand on a table and said little or nothing. The upshot was an endless series of delays for the cases of Englishmen who were languishing in jail in Cadiz and Seville and Barcelona while the duke of Lerma, the constable of

Castile, and even Philip III himself explained that there was simply nothing they could do.

Cornwallis was appalled at what he saw as a callous disregard for the well-being of individuals: "Injuries complained of there [in England] by the Spaniards, as they are instantly looked unto, so with the like Brevitie is there Care had that they be redressed. Here some end their Lives and all their Means, before they can bring any thing that toucheth upon Justice or Restitution."[23] In England, unlike Spain, these sorts of problems would never happen; only Spaniards could be so cruel. At the same time, he takes it for granted that cruelty is par for the course in Spain. For Cornwallis, it is an article of faith that James would be instantly available to see the Spanish ambassador to redress grievances, while in Spain, the court is always travelling or officials are otherwise unable to see him, demonstrating a complete disregard for their people and for the cares of office. In fact, the Spanish ambassador to the Court of St James, Pedro de Zúñiga, complained bitterly to his superiors on the Spanish Council of State about his difficulty obtaining an audience with James, who then was less than forthcoming with satisfactory answers.[24] London, it seemed, was no more amenable to the Spanish than Valladolid was to the English, but for Cornwallis, who of course had no direct experience of being a foreign ambassador in London, preconceptions combined with ingrained distrust and contempt for the Spanish led to a dubious comparison.

Yet despite Cornwallis's frustrations with the agonizing pace of the Spanish judicial and administrative system, his experience living in Spain slowly begins to influence his thoughts on the people and culture of this alien land. While complaining about his lack of access to the king, he admits, "For myne own private Parte [I] confess that I have no Cause to complaine, either of mine own Fortune or their Favours," an admission that all was not so bad as that. And though he struggles with Spanish formality and his expectation that Spaniards are prickly about their honour, he comes to the conclusion that, in dealing with court officials, "the best Course therefore ... is to deale with them in their own Fashion," an admission that there was, at least, some value in their behaviour.[25] Over the course of his first two years in Spain, one can discern an embryonic, rarely conscious realization that Spain is not quite as Cornwallis had envisaged it. He would never have admitted as much, but his letters betray this subtle shift as it occurs.

While Cornwallis was growing accustomed to life in Spain and becoming aware that the place did not generally live up to its evil reputation, in one area he remained unchanged in his views: the matter of religion. Throughout his time in Spain, he reports constantly on the movements, efforts, and perfidies of English Catholics in Spain. He rails against Father Joseph Creswell, the highest-ranking English Jesuit in Spain during his stay, although the ambassador tried to learn much from the priest before falling out with him in 1608 over a series of pamphlets.[26] In one particularly representative passage that combines the rhetorical tools of the Black Legend with humour, Cornwallis notes that the Spanish are sending a maid to convert James's wife, Anne of Denmark, to Catholicism. "This People superstitious and credulous in all things," Cornwallis sniggers, "hath given themselves some large measure of Hope that she shall effect it: for she is (they say) very witty and a good Speaker."[27] However, Anne had indeed converted at Holyroodhouse Palace in 1600 under the direction of Robert Abercromby, a Scottish Jesuit, and this fact was known by Philip III and Lerma as early as 1605. It is unclear how widespread the knowledge of Anne's Catholicism was, but it is plausible that Cornwallis would not have known the truth of the matter. Certainly, the Spanish, who saw in Anne a source of intelligence and influence at the English court, had little reason to publicize her secret religious beliefs.[28] Later, Cornwallis writes to Salisbury that Spanish medicine was so rudimentary that it consisted of "letting blood" and "sending for the Priest and Sacraments."[29] At other times, he takes Spaniards to task for letting "The Cleargy ... soe absolutely rule them" that they would stain their own honour if a priest ordered it.[30] And in 1607, for one of the last times, he combines several of the tropes of the Black Legend into one attack on Spain. He notes that he has sent his nephew, Thomas Cornwallis, to the English embassy in France, taking him out of the house of the constable of Castile for fear that the Spanish would corrupt him with both religion and money, two of the central pillars of the anti-Spanish libel: "The Jesuits ... finding him out of the fold, and his Weakness apt enough to receive another Print, so laboured with him, as had I not prevented it, they had not only fastined him to their superstitious Faith, but had made him a Pensioner to this State, and given him a first taste of their Spanish Coyne."[31] Catholicism and the gold of the Indies: with these foul tools did the Spanish devil bestride the Earth.

More telling perhaps is the subject of Cornwallis's ire in matters of religion. Early on, it is the Catholic religion itself, its priests and pious supplicants, whom Cornwallis attacks; later, as we can see above, it is the Jesuits and especially English Jesuits who come to the fore in his letters. Creswell becomes persona non grata at the English embassy, and his movements and meetings are tracked and reported on extensively. And Cornwallis goes to great lengths to distinguish between the constable of Castile and his promise not to convert the aforementioned Thomas Cornwallis, and the Jesuits who are eager to do so. This is an important distinction: after about mid-1607, Cornwallis no longer excoriates Catholicism or the Spanish themselves, but only the Jesuits and others who laboured to convert the English Protestants. He even stops his condemnation of the hated Inquisition, and in 1608 he manages to relate a Catholic religious ceremony – the swearing of fealty to the future Philip IV – with a decided level of equanimity. Although he himself was not in the church proper, he saw the entire proceedings through a window and related it in some detail.[32] He does so with no overt attacks on the Spanish religion, and he is evidently impressed with the pomp and power of the event. Over time, Cornwallis ceases his use of the rhetoric of the Black Legend to describe Spanish Catholicism, saving it instead for those who are actively trying to do his country and religion harm. While he never personally succumbs to the evident temptations of Catholicism as many of his household do (and despite his Catholic parentage), his first-hand experience with the Spanish softens his views on religion, even if his hatred of Jesuits becomes even more palpable.

Despite their religious persuasion, Cornwallis maintains a positive view of many individual Spaniards at court, especially in the later years of his posting. Early in his tenure, he makes several references to the "deceit" of Spaniards in general, a common theme of the Black Legend. And at Nottingham's departure in 1605, he would not take evident Spanish acts of good faith at face value, calling them nothing more than words and actions of courtesy and flowery language.[33] He attacks the Spanish for wilful stupidity: "Noble Lord, so variable they are here in the Humours, as I protest to God I know not what to think of them [Spaniards]. They daily distaste all manner of People that have to do with them, and not the least those of their own nation, so willfull and stupid they are."[34] Some of this sentiment could arise from a healthy scepticism of a diplomat in a new land, but it also echoes the English belief that the Spanish were both flowery and false.

Yet by the end of his term in Spain, Cornwallis has only kind words for individual Spaniards, the duke of Lerma being the only exception. In 1608, Cornwallis praises the constable of Castile in the highest possible terms, writing to the Privy Council that he is unparalleled as a person "from the Eminencye of his Place, the rare Understanding in Affaires of Estate, hardly to be equalled by any other of his Rancke either in this Counsayle or Kingdome, his Privity in the Intentions whereupon the Peace between our Kings (wherein his Excellency had so great a Hand) was founded; his settled good Opinion of my Sovereigne's Sinceritye; the good Inclinations which in all Occasions he had shewed to conserve the Amety; and lastly the much Demonstration he had made of Particular affection to my self."[35] And when Salisbury asks Cornwallis to see if he could purchase information from Secretary of State Andrés de Prada, Cornwallis responds in the negative, noting that Prada was a man of great virtue who was a good servant of his king and therefore would be unwilling to sell out his country.[36] Even more telling than his praise of individual Spaniards is Cornwallis's increasing use of Spanish words in his correspondence. Terms such as *ayo* for tutor, *consejo* for the Spanish councils, and *consulta* for the documents those councils produced become common, even as Latin equivalents drop from his lexicon.[37] Cornwallis's descriptions of what he has previously referred to as Spanish dithering in legal cases eventually take on a resigned, more knowing air. He laments the slowness of proceedings but does so with greater understanding of how the Spanish administrative system led to such delays and admits that it is not the fault of officials but of the system itself, a system he does not like, but one he learns to work with and within, aided by generous and conscientious officials and a country he understands far better than he did upon his arrival. Without a doubt, Cornwallis ends his time in Spain harbouring both admiration for the Spanish and respect for their institutions, a far cry from his beliefs upon landing in La Coruña. The first-hand knowledge of a traveller has trumped the ingrained power of the Black Legend and brought closer the lands and people of the Atlantic and Mediterranean.

So what can we conclude from the example of Charles Cornwallis's experiences in Spain? Cornwallis was a man of his time and of his class: he was comfortable with diplomacy and court politics, he was able to learn from his and others' mistakes, and he was, in general, quite good at his job. When he first arrived in Spain, he was convinced of many of the anti-Spanish tropes that pervaded England during these years. He saw Spain as a blighted land, poorly governed, and ready to rebel against its oppressive overlords. He thought of Spaniards in general as false, cruel, and overly religious. He regarded Spain not as a friend to England but as a once and future enemy. And he failed to understand many of the nuances and cultural norms that caused the Spanish to act in the ways that they did, especially concerning judicial suits and administrative practice. There was nothing abnormal about any of this, and in many ways, he was responding to the literature, drama, and a general climate in England that represented Spain as a foreign and enemy land in a region of Europe that held both peril and promise for the English.

Yet, over time, much of his opinion changed. He was always far more positive about individual Spaniards than he was about Spaniards as a whole. Interestingly, he almost never mentioned race as a distinguishing characteristic – or cause – of Spanish perfidy. The Moorish and Jewish roots of Spain and its people did not enter into his letters, despite the popularity in England of the racial makeup of Spaniards as the sine qua non of the country's Otherness. He praised the king and his high counsellors, preened when grandees paid him calls, and enjoyed the marks of precedence and ceremony the Spanish lavished upon him. One of the most likely causes of his change of tone was class affiliation: he understood men of his own class, was flattered by the attention paid him by his social betters at court, and had dealings with few who were not members of the nobility. They spoke his language, so to speak, acted in a courtly manner he could understand, were full of blandishments and assurances – whatever their real intentions – and Cornwallis was predisposed to see the best in men whom he wished to emulate. In short, he wanted to belong to the great noble culture of the Mediterranean, and in the end that was a more important motivation than his original distrust of Spaniards. The vast wealth and conspicuous consumption of the Spanish court and high nobility also must have done its work to impress the debt-ridden Englishman and convince him of the value of at least a working relationship with these men. The concept of a permanent ambassador was relatively new in the early seventeenth century, and to some extent, Cornwallis and the Spanish were making it up as they went along; it was therefore not surprising that Cornwallis would have developed a new admiration for his hosts in a more fluid diplomatic milieu. And James's policy towards Spain was one of friendship, an important marker for Cornwallis's attitude in Spain.

But Cornwallis also toned down his attacks on Spanish character as the years went by, until he was even gently chiding Salisbury for his harsh views of individual Spaniards.[38] Cornwallis became more culturally aware of the differences between Spain and England, and mostly stopped using England as a foil for traits he did not like about Spain. Though the judicial proceedings that were his main area of diplomatic effort did not proceed any faster, he became more adept at putting pressure on places that were most likely to bear fruit and stopped complaining so bitterly to London about delays. It helped that many of the suits went his way – a fact that argued well for the probity of the Spanish judicial system – and English sailors were, in general, not allowed to languish in Inquisition or customs jails for overly long periods. And even his views on religion moderated, at least to some extent, allowing him to relate to Catholic ceremonies with equanimity and with a minimum of opprobrium. His hatred of Jesuits – English ones especially – did not disappear, but he had a far gentler view of Spanish Catholicism after several years in the country. Overall, his time in Spain did not make him a Hispanophile – far from it – but the rhetoric he used to describe Spain had less and less in common with the calumnies of the Black Legend. They were criticisms grounded in experience and reality, not in the propaganda of an anti-Spanish literature, and it was that experience that, in the end, determined Cornwallis's attitude towards Spaniards and the Mediterranean world they inhabited. The Black Legend of the early seventeenth century relied for its efficacy on the Northern European population having almost no personal experience with Spain or the Mediterranean; that in itself is a clue to how even its purveyors felt about its veracity. Cornwallis found, somewhat to his surprise, that the Spanish were not as evil as he had been led to believe, and he lived a more comfortable life in the country than he originally thought possible. Cornwallis's example shows that English views of Spain were nuanced and complicated in the Stuart period, particularly for those who saw the country with their own eyes.

NOTES

* The author wishes to thank the William Andrews Clark Memorial Library and the UCLA Center for Seventeenth- and Eighteenth-Century Studies for making the research for this chapter possible. A version of this chapter was presented at a conference entitled "Rivalry and Rhetoric in the Early Modern Mediterranean" organized by Barbara Fuchs at the William Andrews Clark Memorial Library, UCLA, in 2012.

1 Sir Charles Cornwallis to Lords of the Privy Council, 18 May 1605, Valladolid. Cited in Edmund Sawyer, *Memorials of Affairs of State in the Reigns of Queen Elizabeth and King James I. Collected, Chiefly from the Original Papers of Ralph Winwood* ... 3 vols. (London, 1725), 2:68. Hereafter known as *Winwood Memorials*. All dates are Old Style.
2 There was, of course, a sizeable Spanish faction at the English court throughout the Tudor/Stuart period, one that would become quite powerful under the influence of the Count of Gondomar in the second decade of the seventeenth century. See Juan Dúran-Loriga, *El embajador y el Rey: el conde de Gondomar y Jacobo I de Inglaterra* (Madrid: Ministerio de Asuntos Exteriores, 2006); Linda Levy Peck, ed., *The Mental World of the Jacobean Court* (Cambridge: Cambridge University Press, 1991).
3 Throughout his correspondence, Cornwallis expresses a profound fear of Catholic infiltration into his household and works assiduously to prevent what he sees as contamination. He begs Salisbury repeatedly for new English servants to replace the ones who keep dying in the fetid Madrid climate and to avoid having to employ Catholics in his household. See, for instance, Cornwallis to Sir George Carew, English ambassador in France, n.d. (early 1607), Madrid, *Winwood Memorials*, 2:295–6.
4 For the influence of anti-Catholic propaganda in England, see Anthony Milton, "A Qualified Intolerance: The Limits and Ambiguities of Early Stuart Anti-Catholicism," in *Catholicism and Anti-Catholicism in Early Modern English Texts*, ed. Arthur Marotti (London: Macmillan, 1999) esp. 109–10.

5 Sverker Arnoldsson, "La leyenda negra: estudios sobre sus orígenes," *Goteborgs Universitets Arsskrift* 66, no. 3 (1960): chaps 1 and 2.
6 Ibid., 9. Translation is the author's.
7 See Margaret R. Greer, Walter D. Mignolo, and Maureen Quilligan, eds., *Rereading the Black Legend: The Discourses of Religious and Racial Difference in the Renaissance Empires* (Chicago: University of Chicago Press, 2007), esp. chaps by Barbara Fuchs, Edmund Valentine Campos, and the afterword by Walter Mignolo; Sandra Clark, "Spanish Characters and English Nationalism in English Drama of the Early Seventeenth Century," *Bulletin of Hispanic Studies* 84, no. 2 (2007): 131–44.
8 Raphael Holinshed, *Chronicles of England, Scotlande, and Irelande* (London, 1587), 2:1187–90.
9 Clark, "Spanish Characters," 132. Also see Alexander Samson's excellent online bibliography of early modern Spanish publications translated into English: http://www.ems.kcl.ac.uk/apps/index.html.
10 See Arthur Mariotti, *Religious Ideology and Cultural Fantasy: Catholic and Anti-Catholic Discourses in Early Modern England* (South Bend, IN: University of Notre Dame Press, 2005).
11 Cornwallis to Lords of the Council, 18 May 1605, Valladolid, *Winwood Memorials*, 2:74.
12 For more about the terrible traveling conditions in Spain during the period, see John Stoye, *English Travellers Abroad, 1604–1667: Their Influence in English Society and Politics*, rev. ed. (New Haven: Yale University Press, 1989), chap. 4.
13 Cornwallis's description of the bullfight is likely the earliest English account of such a spectacle. He is not impressed: he laments the cruelty to the horses, which were not armoured as they are today and therefore were killed at an alarming rate. He is shocked at the waste of good horseflesh; he makes no mention of the waste of good beef.
14 Cornwallis to Cranbourne, 31 May 1605, Valladolid, *Winwood Memorials*, 2:71.
15 Ibid.
16 Cornwallis to Lords of the Council, 9 July 1605, Valladolid, *Winwood Memorials*, 2:87–8.
17 Cornwallis to Cranbourne, 31 May 1605, Valladolid, *Winwood Memorials*, 2:71.
18 Cornwallis to Cranbourne, 2 June 1605, Valladolid, *Winwood Memorials*, 2:75–6.
19 An excellent example of the genre available in a modern edited edition is Cristóbal Pérez de Herrera, *Amparo de pobres* (1598; Madrid: Espasa-Calpe, 1975).
20 Cornwallis to Salisbury, 30 May 1607, Madrid, *Winwood Memorials*, 2:307–8.
21 James's official instructions for Cornwallis can be found at *Winwood Memorials*, 2:64.
22 Cornwallis to Salisbury, n.d. (1605), Valladolid, *Winwood Memorials*, 2:150.
23 Cornwallis to Northampton, n.d. (1605), Valladolid, *Winwood Memorials*, 2:151–2.

24 See, for example, Pedro de Zúñiga to Philip III, Archivo General de Simancas, sección de Estado, legajo 2586, fol. 68, 8 October 1607, London, deciphered.
25 Cornwallis to Northampton, n.d. (1605), Valladolid, *Winwood Memorials*, 2:151–2.
26 For more on this interesting kerfuffle, see Albert J. Loomie, *English Polemics at the Spanish Court* (New York: Fordham University Press, 1993).
27 Cornwallis to Salisbury, n.d. (1605), Valladolid, *Winwood Memorials*, 2:96–7.
28 J.D. Hanlon, *Catholic Encyclopedia*, 2nd ed. (London: Gage, 2006), 1:467–8.
29 Cornwallis to Salisbury, n.d. (mid-1606), Madrid, *Winwood Memorials*, 2:236–7.
30 Cornwallis to Salisbury, 28 June 1606, Madrid, *Winwood Memorials*, 2:261–2.
31 Cornwallis to Sir George Carew, n.d. (early 1607), Madrid, *Winwood Memorials*, 2:295–6.
32 Cornwallis to the Lords of the Council, 9 January 1608, Madrid, *Winwood Memorials*, 2:365–7.
33 Cornwallis to Lords of the Council, 9 July 1605, Valladolid, *Winwood Memorials*, 2:87–8.
34 Cornwallis to Salisbury, n.d. (mid-1606), Madrid, *Winwood Memorials*, 2:236–7.
35 Cornwallis to Lords of the Council, 6 August 1608, Madrid, *Winwood Memorials*, 2:424–6.
36 Cornwallis to Salisbury, 16 October 1607, Madrid, *Winwood Memorials*, 2:348–9.
37 The most interesting aspect of Cornwallis's increasing use of Spanish is his assumption that Salisbury and others in London would understand him. However, given the importance of Spain to the affairs of Europe in the early seventeenth century, it should not be such a surprise that many in London at least understood the language, especially since French was not yet the European lingua franca. See Stoye, *English Travellers Abroad*.
38 For a good example of this, see Cornwallis to Salisbury, 14 October 1607, Madrid, *Winwood Memorials*, 2:348–9, in which Cornwallis gently rebukes Salisbury for asking him to ferret information from Andrés de Prada, explaining that no gentleman could ask that of another gentleman. Also see Cornwallis to Salisbury, 10 December 1608, *Winwood Memorials*, 2:460–2.

Contributors

Palmira Brummett is visiting professor of history at Brown University.

Thomas Dandelet is associate professor of history at the University of California – Berkeley.

Jane Hwang Degenhardt is associate professor of English at the University of Massachusetts Amherst.

Andrew W. Devereux is assistant professor of history at Loyola Marymount University.

Barbara Fuchs is professor of Spanish and English at the University of California Los Angeles, and director of the Center for Seventeenth- and Eighteenth-Century Studies and the William Andrews Clark Memorial Library.

William S. Goldman is assistant professor of international studies at the University of San Francisco.

Eric Griffin is professor and chair of English at Millsaps College, and director of the Millsaps Latin American Studies Program.

Carina L. Johnson is professor of history at Pitzer College.

Brian C. Lockey is associate professor of English at St John's University in New York.

Ania Loomba is Catherine Bryson Professor of English at the University of Pennsylvania.

Larry Silver is Farquhar Professor of art history at the University of Pennsylvania.

Emily Weissbourd is visiting assistant professor of English at Bryn Mawr College.

Elizabeth R. Wright is associate professor of Spanish at the University of Georgia.

Index

Aachen, Hans von, *Allegory of the Turkish War, The Battle of Sissek*, 71–2, 78nn40–2
Adelman, Janet, 227, 232n28
Aelst, Pieter Coecke van, 65, 76n23
Africa: African Diaspora, 127, 132, 139, 144n32; in anti-Spanish discourse, 193, 202, 210–11; Black Africans, 31n39, 31n44, 126–8, 139, 143n14; Black Atlantic, 13, 27, 32n57; and "blackness" as difference, 22, 26–7, 193, 202, 211; eastern, southern Africa, 21, 26, 127, 140n3; and Islam, 20, 22, 28, 108, 115, 117n4, 120n30, 141n4, 193; and the Mediterranean, 19–28, 30n21, 65, 95–6n6, 102, 141n3; and New World slavery, 23–5, 28, 32n48; North Africa, 15, 19–23, 28, 76n24, 110; in pro-Spanish discourse, 108, 115, 120n30; and Spain, 6, 21, 24, 31n30, 110, 127–8, 139, 140n3, 141n4, 143n14. *See also* slavery
Africanus, Leo, *A Geographical History of Africa*, 19, 22, 30n21, 31n31
Africanus, Scipione, 149, 153
Aggas, Edward, 192–3

Aksan, Virginia, 37, 54n11, 56n26, 95n4
Alexander VI, Pope, 109, 112, 114, 123n42, 150
Alexander the Great, 34, 152–3, 155
Alighieri, Dante, 102, 199
Ali Pasha, Müezzin-zâde, 135–7, 144n24
allegory: in theatre, 188–9n22, 197, 208, 221–2; in visual art, 53, 58, 69–73, 77n36, 78nn36–7
Allen, William, *Defence of English Catholics*, 199, 245, 237–8, 249n13
alliances: 7, 69, 72, 79n44, 113, 129; "impious," 46, 63, 65, 75n15, 106, 109, 115, 206; marriage, 19–20, 23, 26, 207, 221, 226–8; shifting, 28, 138, 192, 204, 207, 230n13; transgressive, 20–1, 228. *See also* Holy League
Alpujarras. *See* moriscos
alterity, 4–6, 30n27, 31n29, 33–5, 54n4, 81, 95n3
Americas. *See* New World
D'Amico, Jack, 217
Amin, Samir, *Eurocentrism*, 13
Anastasio, Filippo, 145, 148
Appleman Williams, William, 18, 30n15
Arabs, 62, 64, 66, 193; Arabic, 15, 68

Aragon, Crown of, 101, 222–3. *See also* Ferdinand of Aragon
Ariosto, Ludovico, *Orlando Furioso*, 133, 240, 251n27
aristocracy, 24, 151–2, 260
Aristotle, 180, 186
Arnauld, Antoine, *Coppie de L'Anti-Espagnol, faict à Paris*, 193–5, 198, 218–19, 229n6
Arnoldsson, Sverker, 256, 267n5
Arrighi, Giovanni, 16–17, 29nn5–6, 29n9
Ascham, Roger, 84–5, 97nn14–16, 97nn18–20
Ashley, Robert, *A Comparison of the English and Spanish Nation*, 205, 212n1
assimilation, 20–1, 62, 128, 178, 180–1
Aurelius, Marcus, 147, 151, 154, 158–9n28
Austria, Don Juan de, 70, 128–9, 133, 138, 143n16, 144n29
Austria, Margaret of, 65
d'Avalos, Alfonso, 65

Baghdad, 36, 46, 56–7nn28–9
Balkans, 33–4, 37, 55n21, 63, 68, 104, 110
Bandello, *Novelle*, 219, 225
barbarity, 5, 21–2, 26, 86, 92, 99n44
Barbarossa, Hayrettin (Kheir-ed-Din), 45, 65–6, 76n24
Baron, Hans, 149, 157nn17–18
Beaumont, Francis, *Knight of the Burning Pestle*, 178
Beeman, William, 197, 213n20
Belgrade, 40, 46–7, 63
Bellini, Gentile, 60, 73–4n5, 74n11
Benzoni, Girolamo, *History of the New World*, 22, 31n33
Berbers, 65–6
Berek, Peter, 224, 231n21

Berlusconi, Silvio, 145
Beusterien, John, 139, 144n32
Bey, Ibrahim, 89–90
Bin Wong, L., 15, 29n4
Black Legend, 110, 212n6, 221, 267n5, 267n7; and England, 25, 198, 201–2, 204–5, 225, 227, 256–9, 262–5; and the Netherlands, 94, 100n49. *See also* blood purity; Elizabeth I; France
Blaeu, Willem and Joan, *Danubius Fluvius*, 58–9
blood purity, 7–8, 231n22; alleged Spanish obsession with, 222–4; in Black Legend, 25, 221–2, 227; in *The Duchess of Malfi*, 223–7, 231n19; English anxieties about, 222, 228; in Lope de Vega, 225–8; and miscegenation, 210–11, 220–1
Bouillon, Godfrey of, 170, 174, 176–8, 188n20
Bourbon, Henri, 193
Bracciolini, Poggio, 148–9, 157n14, 157n16
Brant, Sebastian, *Ship of Fools*, 60, 73n2
Braudel, Fernand, *Civilization and Capitalism, Mediterranean and the Mediterranean World in the Age of Philip II*, 3, 5, 13–16, 18, 20, 29n2, 29nn6–7, 213n18
Breydenbach, Bernhard von, 68
Brotton, Jerry, 19–20, 30nn19–20, 30n23, 76n23
Brown, Paul, 25, 32n47
Brummet, Palmira, 5, 56nn24–5, 116, 125n51
Bruyn, Abraham de, 67
Buda, 41, 43, 46, 56n26, 63
Burton, Jonathan, 6, 95n3, 213n26
Busbecq, Ogier de, 66, 89, 91, 98nn30–1, 99n38

Cabo Aseguinolaza, Fernando, 15
Caesar, Augustus, 148, 150, 152–3
Caesar, Julius, 145–52
Caligula, 145, 148
Caloprese, Gregorio, "Dell'origine degli Imperii," 150, 153–4, 159n36
Camocio, Giovanni Francesco, 129–31
Campion, Edmund, *Rationes decem*, 234–7, 244, 247, 248nn7–8, 249n11, 249–50n14, 250n15, 250n20, 252n39, 252n44
Campos, Edmund, 221, 230n15, 267n7
captivity: captives of Ottoman Turks, 48, 53, 64, 76n24, 85, 167; Christian captives, 21, 48, 53, 64; morisco captives, 126, 128, 137; and travel, commerce, 164, 167; Turkish captives, 69, 134–7, 144n24
Caracciolo, Carmine Nicolò, 145, 148, 150, 152–4
Carducho, Vicente, 69
Caribbean, 19, 25–7, 32n52
cartography: of Christian kings, 40–1; English, 48, 169, 188n17; French, 37–8, 46, 54n13; Habsburg, 5, 129–30, 132, 142n10; Ottoman, 5, 38, 43, 45–6, 56n27, 56n29; Venetian, 5, 39, 55n22. *See also* maps
Casale, Giancarlo, 116, 125n51
Casares, Aurelia Martín, 126, 128, 140n1, 141n5
Casas, Bartolomé de las, *Brevísima relación*, 192, 212n6, 257
Casini, Pier Ferdinando, 145
Cates, Thomas, 199–201, 214n31
"Catholic monarchs," 102–3, 106, 109–11, 114, 223. *See also* Ferdinand of Aragon; Isabella of Castile
Cecil, Robert (Lord Salisbury), 8, 255, 258–60, 262–3, 265, 266n3, 267n20, 267n22, 268n27, 268nn29–30, 268n34, 268nn36–8
Cecil, William, 8, 191–2, 197
Cedra, Luis della (duke of Medinaceli), 6, 145, 154, 156n2
Charlemagne, 61, 153, 240
Charles I of England, 208, 215n43, 221
Charles II of Spain, 145–6, 154
Charles V, Spanish king and Holy Roman emperor: 5, 41, 46, 153, 158–9n28, 235, 260; and conquest, 65–6, 69–71, 76n24, 77n33; and succession struggles, 80–5, 87–8, 92, 94, 97n12, 97n14, 98n28, 102, 219, 225
Charles VIII, French king, 101–2, 105–10, 114, 119n19, 119n23, 120n28–9, 121n35
Chaucer, Geoffrey, *Man of Law's Tale*, 20
Choiseul-Gouffier, Marie Gabriel Florent Auguste de, *A Picturesque Voyage to Greece*, 37, 40, 53, 54nn11–13
Christendom: Catholic threat to, 64; and England, 8, 234, 247, 258; French threat to, 101–16; geography of, 8, 38–41, 48, 53, 60, 68, 104, 112, 115, 234, 247, 258; Islamic threat to, 34, 43, 47–8, 61, 64, 69–70, 104, 110, 112; Latin, 80, 83–4; Protestant threat to, 69–70, 196–7; universal, 107, 199
Christianity: Calvinists, 196, 234, 235; Catholic-Protestant conflicts, 8, 69, 85, 192–3, 204, 233–4, 244–7, 247–8n3, 249nn13–14, 254n57, 256, 262; Christian identity, 40, 133, 235, 245, 247, 250n15; English Catholics, 197, 209, 234, 237, 239nn13–14, 250n15, 254n57; and Islam, 14, 21, 59, 128; Lutherans, 87, 196, 198, 234; New Christians, 127–8; Protestants,

69–70, 83–5, 97n12, 262. *See also* Christendom; conversion
Clark, Stuart, 166, 187n9
Claudius, 148
Clynnog, Morys, 241–7, 252–3nn44–6, 253n48
Cohen, Walter, 15, 29n3
Connolly, Annaliese F., 170, 176, 188n20, 189n25
conquest, 16, 53, 102, 124n47, 152, 208, 245; in English theatre, 168–74, 176–8; of Naples, 106–9, 123n42; of Granada, 110–11, 121n33, 223; Habsburg, 5–6, 69, 73, 76n24, 110, 115, 127, 147; Ottoman, 41, 45, 48, 55n16, 64–5, 67, 82–3, 96n11, 102, 104–5, 109, 116, 118n14
Conrad, Joseph, *Heart of Darkness*, 24
Constantinople (Istanbul), 34, 37; in Christian narrative, 40, 46, 125n48, 233; and diplomacy, 55n14, 60, 66, 73, 89, 91, 94, 125n48; in European visual culture, 46, 54n10, 61, 66, 76–7n27; Ottoman conquest of, 55n16, 82, 96n11, 102, 104, 106, 114
conversion, 169, 245, 262; to Christianity, 128, 141n4, 178, 181, 224, 246, 253n49; to Islam, "turning Turk," 47, 53n3, 58, 95n3, 188n17, 189n28, 213n26
Cornwallis, Charles: as English ambassador to Spain, 8, 255–68, 266n3, 267n13, 268n37; and English sailors, 260, 265; and Inquisition, 260, 263, 265; and Jesuits, 261–3, 265; and London, 256, 258, 260–1, 265, 268; on Spanish economy, 258–64; on Spanish leaders, 258, 260, 262–4; on Spanish traits, race, 263–5
Croatia, 39, 58, 72, 99n36

Crusade: First, 169–70, 173; rhetoric of, 3, 38, 65, 73n1, 106–7, 138, 140, 173–4, 177
Cyprus, 40, 95–6n6, 129, 174–6

Dandelet, Thomas, 6, 139, 144n30
Danube, 40–1, 46–9, 58–60, 63–4, 78n41
Daunce, Edward, "A Brief Discourse of the Spanish State," 202, 208, 214n35, 221, 230n14
Davenant, Charles, 15, 29n5
Davis, Robert, 24, 32n46
Dawson, Anthony, 169, 187n13, 188n15
Dee, John, 235, 248–9n10
Degenhardt, Jane, 7, 188n13, 189n28
Deleuze, Gilles, *Thousand Plateaus*, 14
Dent, Robert William, 220, 230n12
Derrida, Jacques, *Of Grammatology*, 14
Descartes, René, 146
Dessen, Alan, 179, 189n33
devil: and Christendom, 64, 69; in theatre, 21–2, 92–3, 100n46
Deza y Guzmán, Pedro de, 130, 132–4, 139, 142n13, 143nn14–15
Diest, Gillis Coppens van, 67–8
Diocletian, 62
Dionisotti, Carlo, 129, 142n8
Dolven, Jeff, 136, 143n20
Donzelli, Tomaso, "Di Cajo Giulio Cesare," 148, 150–1
Doria, Andrea, 65
Doria, Paolo Mattia, 145, 148
Doyle, Laura, 4, 9n1
Drake, Sir Francis, 199, 200, 214n30
dramaturgy, 166, 175, 179, 186, 207, 209
Dürer, Albrecht, *Frederick the Wise*, *The Martyrdom of the Ten Thousand*, 60–3, 68, 73–4nn3–6, 74n9, 74n11, 75nn12–13, 77n31

Elizabeth I, queen of England: and
anti-Spanish literature, 7, 191–2,
194–5, 197–8, 205, 207–8, 210,
256–7, 213n26, 214n42, 215n52;
and Protestantism, 97n16, 192n2,
234, 244, 249n13, 254n57, 256; and
supremacy, 234–40, 243–4, 250n16,
251nn25–6
Elyot, Thomas, *Image of Governance*, 220,
230n12
emblems, 39, 41, 43, 48, 58, 61, 68–9,
71–2, 78n41
England: Elizabethan, 7, 191–2,
197, 207–8, 212n2, 212n13, 224,
230n15, 253n51, 254n57; English
identity, 6–8, 199, 224, 228, 232n28,
234–5, 241, 244, 247, 250n15. *See also*
Elizabeth I; theatre, English
Epstein, Steven, 24, 31n40
Ercilla, Alonso de, *La Araucana*, 134, 166
Escorial Palace, 69–70, 78n36

Ferdinand I, Holy Roman emperor, 43,
81–2, 87–91
Ferdinand of Aragon, 102–14, 116,
188n13, 188nn17–18, 121n33,
122–3nn41–4, 218–19, 223, 231n19;
and son, Don Ferdinand, 69, 138
Fernández de Córdoba, Francisco, 127,
140n3
Ferrante I, king of Naples, 105–6, 199n19
Field, Richard, 192, 199–200, 202,
214n31
fortune, 108, 139, 261; in English
theatre, 22, 163–4, 167–8, 171–87,
187n10
Foucault, Michel, *Madness and Civilization*,
Order of Things, 14
Foxe, John, *Book of Martyrs*, 192, 212n10,
246–7, 257, 253nn50–1, 254n57

Fra Molinero, Baltasar, 139, 141n4,
143n14
France: and anti-Spanish discourse, 193,
195, 198, 201–2, 209, 213–14n28,
218, 220–1, 229n6; as enemy to
Christendom, 101–2, 105–16,
122n40; in English theatre, 173–4. *See
also* Francis I
Francis I, king of France, 219, 122n39;
and "impious alliance" with Süleiman
I, 46, 63, 65, 75n15, 106, 109, 115
Fuchs, Barbara, 4, 6–7, 19–21, 30n19,
32n51, 95n3, 166, 187n8, 211,
212n14, 215n57, 216n63, 216n65,
221, 230n15, 251–2n34, 266, 267n7

Gates, Henry Louis, 139, 141n4,
144n32
Germanicus, 151, 158n21
Gil Harris, Jonathan, 23, 31n34
Gillies, John, 169, 188n17
Gossett, Suzanne, 179, 189n31
Granada: Hispano-Muslim origins,
126–8; and Lepanto, 6, 129, 137,
139; New Christians in, 127–8; and
Nasrids, 109, 112; and slavery, 126–8,
133, 140–1nn1–6; War of, in Spanish
propaganda, 109–12. *See also* moriscos
Greco, El, *Adoration of the Holy Name of
Jesus*, 70, 78n37
Greece: as contested Christian space, 37,
40, 48, 52–3, 128, 169; as imagined
in English theatre, 163–4, 168–9,
178–83, 186, 189n30
Greene, Robert, 166, 197–8, 205;
Spanish Masquerado, 201–3
Griffin, Eric, 6–7, 213n19, 214n39, 221,
230n15
Guarini, Guarino, 148–9, 157n11
Guattari, Felix, *Thousand Plateaus*, 14

Guevara, Antonio de, 151, 154, 158n28
Guldenmundt, Hans, 63–4
Gunder-Frank, Andre, 15, 29n4

Hadrian, Roman emperor, 151, 158n26
Habsburgs. *See* Holy Roman Empire; Philip II; Spain
Harington, Sir John, *Tract on the Succession to the Crown*, 237–40, 247, 249–51nn14–28
Hart, Elizabeth, 178, 189n30
Hasan, Mulay, king of Tunis, 65–6, 76n24
Hawkins, John, 24
Hawkins, Richard, 207
He, Zheng, 16–18, 30n14
Hess, Andrew, 21, 31n30
Heywood, Thomas, *The Four Prentices of London, with the Conquest of Jerusalem*, 163, 168–78, 182, 184, 186, 188nn18–19, 189n23, 189n27
Holinshed, Raphael, *Chronicles of England, Scotlande and Irelande*, 203–4, 214n37, 246, 257, 267n8
Holy League, 70, 78n37, 135, 140
Holy Roman Empire, confessional divisions, 80; competing claims to, 80–2, 93; and Ottoman Empire, 58, 60–1, 63, 66, 68, 73, 75n15, 84, 89–90; and Persia, 72, 78n39, 79n44; Schmalkaldic War, 84–5. *See also* succession
Homer, 133, 137, 143n21
Horace, 180
Horden, Peregrine, 13–14, 28, 29n1, 32n59
Howard, Charles (earl of Nottingham), 256, 258, 263
Howard, Jean, 174, 178, 189n23, 189n29
Hulme, Peter, 18–19, 25–6, 30n16, 32n52

humanism: and competing ideologies, 17; and Spanish court, 111, 117; and Palatine Academy, 146–9, 144n32, 155, 156n7, 157nn16–18, 158n22
Humeya, Abén, 137
Hungary: as contested space between Christendom and Islam, 40, 45–6, 58, 71, 78n41, 80–1, 84–5, 89; Mary of, 72
Hunter, G.K., 213n25, 217, 229nn3–4
Hurault, Michel, *Coppie de L'Anti-Espagnol, faict à Paris*, 193
Hurrem, Ottoman sultana, 83, 86, 88
Hurtado de Mendoza, Diego, 137, 144n27

idolatry, 92, 169, 204, 223
Indian Ocean, 13, 23, 26–8, 32n57, 38
Inquisition, 256, 260, 263, 265
Ireland, 19, 202; and Catholicism, 251n32, 254n57; and colonization, 25–6, 28, 211; and English theatre, 19, 25, 173–4; and Holinshed, 214n37, 267n8; and Spenser, 208, 215n48, 216n65
Isabella (Isabel) of Castile: and French invasion of Italy, 106–11, 114; and Granada, 109–12, 122n38; and holy war, 102–3, 106–9, 111–14, 223; and Konstantine II, 38, 40, 43
Islam, 14, 21, 116; and Africa, 20, 22, 28, 108, 115, 117n4, 120n30, 141n4, 193; and Christianity, 14, 21, 34, 43, 47–8, 59, 61, 64, 69–70, 104, 110, 112, 128; conversion to, 47, 53n3, 58, 95n3, 188n17, 189n28, 213n26; and England, 169, 174, 177, 187n8, 188n17, 189n28; and Spain, 126–8, 231n19, 141n4. *See also* Moors; Ottoman Empire

Index

Italy: Battle of Pavia, 65, 217, 219; Council of Pisa, 111, 114; Italian Wars, 101–16. *See also* Naples; Rome; Sicily; Venice

James I, king of England, 209–11, 215n44, 220, 255, 261–2, 265, 266n1, 267n21; and Spanish Match, 7, 207–8, 210, 215n43, 221
janissaries, 48, 66, 83
Jerusalem: as centre of world, 101; and Christendom, 7, 40, 46, 107; in English theatre, 163–4, 168–78, 186, 188n20; Knights of St John of, 103, 111; and Ottoman Empire, 38, 88, 116; in travel narrative, 40
Jesuits, 70, 208, 234, 237, 241–5, 247, 248n5, 252n44, 253n51, 262–3, 265
Jews, 55n15, 88, 231n21; in English theatre, 169, 198, 223–4, 226–8, 232n28; and Spain, 7, 111, 193, 220–1, 223–4, 230n15, 256, 264
Johnson, Carina, 5, 98n32, 99n44

Kastan, David Scott, 19, 21, 30n17
Konstantine II, king of Georgia, 38–40, 43, 53, 55n15
Kyd, Thomas, *Spanish Tragedy*, 197, 208

Lamming, George, 23–4, 31n36
Languet, Hubert, 233, 247–8nn2–4
Latino, Juan (Joannes Latinus): *Austrias Carmen*, 126–44; background 126–7, 139; and Latin, 126, 129; on Lepanto, 129–35; on Ottoman suffering and captivity, 134–7. *See also* Granada
Lawrence, Jeremy, 24, 31n44
Lemons, Andrew, 129, 132, 139, 140n1, 142n9, 142n11
Lepanto: cultural productions and consumption of, 69–70, 129–30, 140; mapping of, 129–32, 142n10; weapons technologies, 134–5
Lerma, duke of, 258, 260, 262–3
Lewes, Owen, 243, 245
Ligon, Richard, 25, 32n50
Lockey, Brian, 8, 211, 253n47, 253n54
Lokman, Seyyid, 43, 45, 56n25
London: guilds and trades, 170, 172–5, 177, 178, 188nn18–19, 189n27, 193; and English theatre, 7, 163–4, 168–71, 174, 180, 182, 189n23, 197–8, 201–5, 208–9, 211, 213n22, 218, 244, 257
Loomba, Ania, 3–4, 30n19, 30nn26–7
Lope de Vega: *El mayordomo de la duquesa de Amalfi*, 8, 225–8, 231nn23–5; *El perro del hortelano*, 227–8, 231n27
Lopez, Jeremy, 175, 189n24
Lopez, Rodrigo, 193
López de Toro, José, 129, 142n8
Lorichs, Melchior, 66–8, 73, 76n27, 77n30
Louis XII, king of France, 111, 114, 218–19, 123n42, 235
Louis XIV, king of France, 54n10, 115, 154, 235
Low Countries (the Netherlands), 24, 64, 68, 81–2, 88, 93, 201, 219, 257
Lucan, *De bellum civile*, 135
Luther, Martin, 64, 76n22
Lyly, John, *Endymion*, 197, 213n25, 250n16

Machiavelli, Niccolò, 34, 148, 150, 153, 158n21, 159n35, 193
Mamluk caliphate, 83, 116, 125n49
Man, John, 255
maps: cartouches on, 40–1, 46–9, 51–2, 57n32, 129; emblems and mascots on, 39–41, 48; frames and borders

on, 34–5, 39; and map-making, 39, 41, 54n13, 55nn19–22, 56n24, 56n26; and narratives, 33, 35, 39–40, 43, 45–8, 64n9; portrait medallions on, 40–1, 43, 46–8, 55n20; rivalry and rhetoric in, 3, 33–53, 54n10, 57n32, 65; on tapestries, 65–6. *See also* cartography; Lepanto
Marlowe, Christopher, *Tamburlaine*, 176, 188n17
Mármol de Carvajal, Luis, 133, 141n4, 143n17, 144n28
Martin, Randall, 178, 181, 189n30, 189n34
Martyr, Peter, 111, 122n40
martyrdom, 61–2, 144n31, 187n13, 212n10, 243–4, 257
Marxism, 15–16, 29n8, 30n12, 31nn41–3, 32n53, 216n60
Matar, Nabil, 6, 188n17
Maximilian I, Holy Roman emperor, 58, 60, 62, 73n1, 77n33, 82, 87, 89–90, 94, 102, 109, 113
Maximilian II, Holy Roman emperor, 46, 78n36, 93, 96n7, 98nn33–4
Mediterranean: eastern, 20, 163, 168–9, 178, 186; as model for transnational analysis, 13–14; role of borders and frontiers within, 3, 5, 20–1, 23, 31n30, 33–5, 38–9, 41, 43, 46, 48, 53n1, 54n9, 56n24, 58–9, 71–3, 80, 89–90, 113, 140n2, 166, 218; as trans-imperial space, 33, 35, 37–8, 53n1
Mehmed I, 83
Mehmed II (Mehmet II), 74n11, 96n11, 102–4, 118n14
Mehmed III, 93, 99
Metzger, Mary Janell, 227, 232n28
Mexía, Pedro, 151, 158n25

Middleton, Thomas, *A Game at Chess*, 207–8, 209–11, 214n40, 215n47, 215nn54–5, 216n58, 216n64, 230n15, 231n22
mimesis, 4, 69, 95n3, 166, 173, 184, 186, 187n8, 188–9n22
Mira Seo, J., 139, 143n14, 144n32
Moffan, Nicholas de, 85–8, 97nn21–5, 98n29
Mohammed, the Prophet, 60, 64
Monta, Susannah, 169, 184, 187–8n13, 188n16, 189n36
Moors, 20, 257; and Africa, 19, 66, 193, 220–1, 223; Saracens, 38, 64, 95n6; and Spain, 7, 38, 128, 193, 202–3, 210, 226–7, 231n19, 251–2n34, 256, 264. *See also* Africa; Black Legend
Morales, Ambrosio, 151
Moretti, Franco, 14–15
moriscos, 6, 143n14; as captives, 126, 128, 137; expulsion of, 126, 128, 132, 134, 142n13; "Irish Moriscos," 32n51, 211, 216n65, 251–2n34; and Islam, 128, 141n4; persecution of, 126–7, 133; and rebellion, 126–7, 137–8, 140n2, 143n17, 144n28; as slaves, 126, 128, 132–3, 137, 141n5, 202
Morone, Giovanni, 241–3, 251n32
Mulready, Cyrus, 165–6, 186, 187nn5–6, 190n39
Munday, Anthony, *The Coppie of the Anti-Spaniard*, 192–4; in Rome, 234, 237, 241, 243–4, 247, 248n5, 249n14, 250n15, 251n29, 252nn37–41
Murad I, 83
Murad III, 40–1, 71, 91, 93
Murad IV, 35–6, 40
Murrin, Michael, 134, 143n19
Myhill, Nova, 169, 180, 187–8nn13–14

Naples, Kingdom of: as contested imperial space, 101–16; and Renaissance humanism, 145–55; in theatre, 217–28
Nasuh, Matrakçi, *Tarih-I Feth-i* Siklos, 45–7
New World, 38, 92, 187n8; and the Black Legend, 191–2, 201, 212n6, 257, 262; and slavery, 23–5, 28, 32n48; and Spain, 88, 115, 199, 208, 231n19; and *The Tempest*, 19–20, 22–5, 28, 31nn33–4

Orco, Remiro de, 150
Orientalism: and costume, 36, 58–62, 64–70, 72, 74n11; and inversion, 81; and Ottoman Empire, 60–1, 64, 72–3, 73n3, 73–4n5, 81, 90, 94–5; and representational mirroring, 80. *See also* Said, Edward
Orley, Bernart van, 65
Ortelius, Abraham: *Theatrum orbis terrarium*, 67; *Thesaurus Geographicus*, 39
Otranto, 103–5, 107–8, 110, 188n14
Ottoman Empire: and cartography, 5, 38, 43, 45–6, 56n27, 56n29; in English theatre, 167, 169, 188n17; as heir to ancient Rome, 33, 102; and Holy Roman Empire, 58, 60–1, 63, 66, 68, 73, 75n15, 84, 89–90; Ottoman identity, 34, 40; and the "impious alliance," 46, 63, 65, 75n15, 106, 109, 115, 206; and succession struggles, 5, 81–7, 89, 93–4, 96nn8–9, 96n11, 99n37, 100n48; and Venice, 33, 39, 54n4, 60–1, 68, 73nn3–5, 81, 95n4, 103, 105. *See also* captivity; conquest; Constantinople; Orientalism

paganism, 34, 61, 169, 174, 178, 180–1, 243, 246, 253n49

Painter, William, *Palace of Pleasure*, 219, 230n9, 230n12, 231n18
Palatine Academy, 145–59, 156n3; Guarino-Poggio debate, 149; imperial Renaissance, 146–9, 153–4; on liberty, 152–4; republican Renaissance, 147–50
Pannemaker, Willem de, 65
Panofsky, Erwin, 69–70, 75n14, 77–8nn35–6, 78n38
Peele, George, 197–8, 205; *Famous Chronicle*, 202–4, 206, 214n33, 214n36
Persia, 15, 62, 72, 78n39, 79n44, 86, 88, 148, 152–3, 165–7, 172
Persons, Robert, 234, 240–7, 251nn28–34, 252nn35–6, 252nn43–4, 253n49, 253nn51–3, 253n55
Petrarch, 102, 146–7, 149, 152, 156n6, 157n16
Philip II, king of Spain, 69–70, 78n37, 82, 84, 88, 93–4, 128, 138, 255, 257–8, 264
Philip III, 207, 255, 258, 261–2, 264, 268n24
Philip IV, 258, 263
pilgrimage, 68, 112–14, 172, 177, 241
piracy, 13, 21, 164, 167; corsair, 182
Piterberg, Gabriel, 3, 29n2
Pius V, pope, 70, 138, 243–4
Plinius, 239–40
Pliny, 152
Plutarch, 147, 152
Pomeranz, Kenneth, 15, 29n4
portraiture, 18, 61, 63, 72; engravings, 61, 68, 74n6; medals, 61, 74n10; medallions, 40–1, 43, 46–7; paintings, 62, 69–70, 74n11, 75n12, 79n44; self, 62, 66–7; woodcut, 63–4, 67–8, 74n10
Portugal, 16–17, 20, 24, 26, 31n43, 38, 133, 193, 195, 197, 230n15
Prada, Andrés de, 263, 268n38

Privy Council, 236, 240, 249n11, 251n26, 259, 263, 266n1
providentialism: in government, 152–3; in English theatre, 163–4, 167–8, 173, 176, 178–9, 181–2, 186–7, 187n11
Purcell, Nicholas, *The Corrupting Sea*, 13–14, 28, 29n1, 32n59

race, 18, 25, 27, 30n26, 210, 212n8, 212n14, 215n57, 216n61; and England, 31n43, 214n34, 229n4; and religion, 128, 201; Spanish, 144n32, 193, 210, 256, 264
Raleigh, Walter, 207–8, 188n17
rape: and bloodline, 224; of Christian women, 20–1, 26, 209; Shakespeare's *Rape of Lucrece*, 192, 231n22
Reformation, 75n16, 176, 191, 202, 204, 214n33, 249n12
renegades, 36, 88–9; *The Renegado*, 20, 215n47
Reuwich, Erhard, 68
Rhodes, 105, 111
Robert, duke of Normandy, 172, 176
Rome: legacy of ancient, 3–6, 20, 61–2, 133, 146; Ottomans as heirs to ancient, 33, 102; and the papacy, 53n2, 105–6, 109–10, 112–14, 241, 243–4, 247, 236–8, 240, 250n16; and Papal States, 104, 124n46, 188n14; Roman Church, 233–47; "Spanish Rome," 139, 144n30; study of ancient, 145–55
Rossi, Matteo, 41, 43–4, 46
Rothman, Natalie, 35, 54n6
Rowley, William, *The Travels of the Three English Brothers*, 164, 208, 215n47, 231n22

Rudolf II, Holy Roman emperor, 40, 71–2, 78n39, 78n43, 79n44, 93, 99n36
Ruiz, Teófilo, 3, 29n2

Sachs, Hans, *The Three Besiegers of Vienna*, 63–4
Sadeler, Aegidius, 72
Said, Edward, 81, 95n3, 95n5
Sander, Nicholas, *De Visibili Monarchia Ecclesiae*, 236–8, 240, 243–4, 249n12
Sanson, Nicolas, *Le Course du Danube*, 46, 49, 57n31
Santesteban, Cristóbal, 101–2, 110–11, 116n3, 121nn36–7
Santos, Francisco de los, 70, 77n36
Saxony, 235; Christian II, elector, 72; Duke Maurice, 84–5; John Frederick, elector, 62, 84
Scott-Warren, Jason, 239, 250n14, 251nn24–5
Senex, John, *Map of Greece*, 48, 52–3, 57n33
Serbia, 46, 58
Sessa, duke of, 127, 140n3
Selim I, 68, 77n33, 82–3, 86, 116, 125n49
Selim II, 83, 88, 90–1, 93–4
Shakespeare, William, 19, 187n12, 188–9n22, 213n23; and his contemporaries, 189n23, 192, 198, 202–3; and the Mediterranean, 170, 175–6, 188n17, 190n40, 229nn3–5, 230n17, 231n22; *Pericles*, 7, 168–70, 178–86, 187–8n13, 189nn30–1, 189n37; *The Tempest*, 3, 13–14, 18–29, 30n19, 31n35, 32n47
Shell, Marc, 227, 232n28
shipwreck, 19, 167, 172–3

Sicily, 88, 101–2, 109, 222; in English theatre, 174, 176
Sidney, Philip, 165–6, 187n5, 233–4, 247nn1–3, 248nn3–4
Silver, Larry, 5, 73n1, 74n10, 75n13, 77n29
slavery, 14, 18, 24, 27–8, 31n38, 141n5; Black African slaves on Iberian Peninsula, 24, 126–8, 140n3, 143n14; and children, 24, 128; Christian slaves, 48–9, 64, 83; and the English, 23, 24, 32n48; and Lepanto, 141; morisco slaves, 126, 128, 132–3, 137, 141n5, 202; and the New World, 23–4, 28; in *The Tempest*, 21, 23, 25, 27
Smith, D.K., 169, 188n17
Spain: and Africa, 6, 21, 24, 31n30, 110, 127–8, 139, 140n3, 141n4, 143n14; and anti-Spanish discourse, 7, 94, 191–5, 197–8, 201–2, 205, 207–11, 213n26, 213–14n28, 214n42, 215n52, 218–21, 225, 229n6, 256–7; Habsburg, 146, 199, 207; and Islam, 126–8, 231n19, 141n4. *See also* Black Legend; Granada
Spence, Sarah, 129, 132, 139, 140n1, 142n9
Spenser, Edmund, *The Fairie Queene*, 257; *A View of the State of Ireland*, 208, 215n48
succession, 155; and England, 193, 237, 240, 250nn16–17, 251n28; and filicide, 86, 88, 91, 96n11; and fratricide, 82, 91, 94; Habsburg, 81–2, 90, 94, 154, 226; Holy Roman Empire, 82, 84–5, 87, 90, 92–3; Ottoman, 5, 81–7, 89, 93–4, 96nn8–9, 96n11, 99n37, 100n48; War of the Spanish Succession, 154–5

Süleiman I, 43–5, 63, 66, 74n7, 77n33; and alliance with France, 46, 63, 65, 75n15, 106, 109, 115; portraits of, 61–2, 67–8, 77n33
Symcox, Geoffrey, 3, 29n2

Tacitus, 147, 150, 153
tapestry, 65–6, 68, 71–2, 76nn23–4, 216n66
taxes, 35, 89–90
Taylor, Gary, 211, 221, 215n54, 215n57, 216n58, 216n61, 230n15
theatre, English, 163–90; actors, 165–6, 170–1, 177, 179; audience engagement, 164–76, 179–80, 182–7, 187n13, 188n21, 189n24; chorus, 163–5, 167, 182; dumbshow, 163, 165, 182; mechanics, 163–5, 179–80, 182, 186; on Ottomans, 167, 169, 188n17; props, 163, 165, 177. *See also* conquest; fortune; London; providentialism; travel
Thompson, Leslie, 179, 189n33
Tiberius, 148, 50
Titian, 62, 69–70, 77–8nn35–6, 78n38
Tomlinson, Gary, 14, 27–8, 29n2, 32n58
Topsell, Edward, *The History of Four-Footed Beasts*, 26–7, 32n54
Traianus, 239–40
Trajan (Pater Patria), 151, 158nn25–6, 239
translation, 14–15; of anti-Spanish propaganda, 94, 193, 198, 201, 218–19, 221, 225, 256; and competing political claims, 83, 86–7, 237, 240; in diplomacy, 35–7; of the "other," 53
travel: narratives, 18, 21, 35, 37–8, 40, 91, 188n17; on the English stage, 163–8, 171–3, 178–9, 182–6, 187n1, 188n17, 189n37

treaties, 31n43; Habsburg-English, 207–8, 211, 255–6, 260; Habsburg-Ottoman, 80, 85, 89–90; Venetian-Ottoman, 39, 60. *See also* alliances

Tunis: Habsburg capture of, 65–6, 69, 80, 76nn23–4; as site of trade, diplomacy, war, 19–20, 65; in *The Tempest*, 19, 21, 23, 26, 30nn19–20; in visual art, 65–6, 71, 73, 76nn23–4

Turner, Henry, 165, 187n2

Tyson, Edward, *Anatomy of a Pygmie*, 26–7, 32n56

Ungerer, Gustav, 24, 31n39

Valladolid, 82, 255, 257–61, 266n1, 267n11, 267nn14–18, 267nn22–3, 268nn25–6, 268n33

Van der Aa, Pieter, *Turquie en Europe*, 48, 50–1

Vaughan, Alden and Virginia, 23, 31n36

Vecellio, Cesare, 67

Venice, 40, 55nn18–19, 147, 233, 248n3, 259; and Lepanto, 69–70, 131, 142n8; and Ottoman Empire, 33, 39, 54n4, 60–1, 68, 73nn3–5, 81, 95n4, 103, 105; *The Merchant of Venice*, 17, 198, 227, 232n28

Vermeyen, Jan, *The Sack of Tunis*, 65–6, 71, 73, 76n23–5

Verstegen, Richard, *Declaration of the True Causes of the Great Troubles Presupposed to Be Intended against the Realm of England*, 195–7, 207

Vienna, 41, 46–7, 80, 83–5, 89; siege of, 41, 63–5, 68, 80–1, 83–4

Virgil, *Aeneid*, 20, 129–30, 133, 135–9, 142n10, 143n18, 143nn20–1, 144n22, 144n25–6

virtues: and leaders, 88, 110–11, 148–54, 159n36, 202, 210, 263; in art and literature, 21, 69, 181, 206

Vries, Adriaen de, 71–2, 78n41

Wales, 179, 202–3, 207, 234, 241–3, 245–6, 252–3n44

Wallerstein, Immanuel, 17, 29n10, 30n13, 212n8

Walsham, Alexandra, 168, 187n11

Webster, John: *The Duchess of Malfi*, 8, 217–28, 229n8, 230n10, 231n23; and blood purity, 223–7; Spanish Naples, 218–23; and Jews, 223–4; and Lope Vega, 225–8; and sexual transgression, 223–4; and Spanish might and misrule, 219–20

Wild Man, 25–7

Wilkins, George, *Pericles*, 178, 181

William of Orange, 94, 100nn49–50, 257

William the Conqueror, 172

Williamson, Elizabeth, 177, 187–8n13, 189n26

Wilson, Robert, 197, 198, 205, 252n41; *The Three Lords and the Three Ladies of London*, 198–201, 213n26

Wolfe, John, *A Pageant of Spanish Humours*, 193–6, 198, 201, 212n4, 212n12

Wolff, Maria, 139, 144n32

Woolley, John, 210

world-systems theory, 5, 14–16, 18, 23, 28

Wright, Elizabeth, 6, 140n1, 142n9, 142n11, 143n20, 144nn23–4

Ximénez de Enciso, Diego, 139

Zundelin, Wolfgang, 234, 247n3

Zündt, Matthias, 40, 42, 43, 48, 55n20

Zúñiga, Pedro de, 261, 268n24

THE UCLA CLARK MEMORIAL LIBRARY SERIES

1. *Wilde Writings: Contextual Conditions*, edited by Joseph Bristow
2. *Enchanted Ground: Reimagining John Dryden*, edited by Jayne Lewis and Maximillian E. Novak
3. *Culture and Authority in the Baroque*, edited by Massimo Ciavolella and Patrick Coleman
4. *Ritual, Routine, and Regime: Repetition in Early Modern British and European Cultures*, edited by Lorna Clymer
5. *Momigliano and Antiquarianism: Foundations of the Modern Cultural Sciences*, edited by Peter N. Miller
6. *Monarchisms in the Age of Enlightenment: Liberty, Patriotism, and the Common Good*, edited by Hans Blom, John Christian Laursen, and Luisa Simonetti
7. *Thinking Impossibilities: The Intellectual Legacy of Amos Funkenstein*, edited by Robert S. Westman and David Biale
8. *Discourses of Tolerance and Intolerance in the European Enlightenment*, edited by Hans Erich Bödeker, Clorinda Donato, and Peter Hanns Reill
9. *The Age of Projects*, edited by Maximillian E. Novak
10. *Acculturation and Its Discontents: The Italian Jewish Experience between Exclusion and Inclusion*, edited by David N. Myers, Massimo Ciavolella, Peter H. Reill, and Geoffrey Symcox
11. *Defoe's Footprints: Essays in Honour of Maximillian E. Novak*, edited by Robert M. Maniquis and Carl Fisher
12. *Women, Religion, and the Atlantic World (1600–1800)*, edited by Daniella Kostroun and Lisa Vollendorf
13. *Braudel Revisited: The Mediterranean World, 1600–1800*, edited by Gabriel Piterberg, Teofilo F. Ruiz, and Geoffrey Symcox
14. *Structures of Feeling in Seventeenth-Century Cultural Expression*, edited by Susan McClary
15. *Godwinian Moments*, edited by Robert M. Maniquis and Victoria Myers
16. *Vital Matters: Eighteenth-Century Views of Conception, Life, and Death*, edited by Helen Deutsch and Mary Terrall
17. *Redrawing the Map of Early Modern English Catholicism*, edited by Lowell Gallagher
18. *Space and Self in Early Modern European Cultures*, edited by David Warren Sabean and Malina Stefanovska
19. *Wilde Discoveries: Traditions, Histories, Archives*, edited by Joseph Bristow

20. *Jesuit Accounts of the Colonial Americas: Intercultural Transfers, Intellectual Disputes, and Textualities*, edited by Marc André Bernier, Clorinda Donato, and Hans-Jürgen Lüsebrink
21. *Skepticism and Political Thought in the Seventeenth and Eighteenth Centuries*, edited by John Christian Laursen and Gianni Paganini
22. *Representing Imperial Rivalry in the Early Modern Mediterranean*, edited by Barbara Fuchs and Emily Weissbourd
23. *Imagining the British Atlantic after the American Revolution*, edited by Michael Meranze and Saree Makdisi
24. *Life Forms in the Thinking of the Long Eighteenth Century*, edited by Keith Michael Baker and Jenna M. Gibbs
25. *Cultures of Communication: Theologies of Media in Early Modern Europe and Beyond*, edited by Helmut Puff, Ulrike Strasser, and Christopher Wild
26. *Curious Encounters: Voyaging, Collecting, and Making Knowledge in the Long Eighteenth Century*, edited by Adriana Craciun and Mary Terrall
27. *Clandestine Philosophy: New Studies on Subversive Manuscripts in Early Modern Europe, 1620–1823*, edited by Gianni Paganini, Margaret C. Jacob, and John Christian Laursen
28. *The Quest for Certainty in Early Modern Europe: From Inquisition to Inquiry, 1550–1700*, edited by Barbara Fuchs and Mercedes García Arenal
29. *Entertaining the Idea: Shakespeare, Philosophy, and Performance*, edited by Lowell Gallagher, James Kearney, and Julia Reinhard Lupton
30. *Casanova in the Enlightenment: From the Margins to the Centre*, edited by Malina Stefanovska

www.ingramcontent.com/pod-product-compliance
Lightning Source LLC
Chambersburg PA
CBHW020634190326
41513CB00034B/686